Duty, Honor, Country

A HISTORY OF WEST POINT

In this beautiful place, the fairest among the fair and lovely Highlands of the North River, shut in by deep green heights and ruined forts, and looking down upon the distant town of Newburgh, along a glittering path of sunlit water, with here and there a skiff, whose white sail often bends on some new tack as sudden flaws of wind come down upon her from the gullies in the hills, hemmed in, besides, all round with memories of Washington, and events of the revolutionary war, is the Military School of America.

It could not stand on more appropriate ground, and any ground more beautiful can hardly be.

Charles Dickens, *American Notes*

Duty, Honor, Country

A History of West Point

STEPHEN E. AMBROSE

THE JOHNS HOPKINS UNIVERSITY PRESS
BALTIMORE AND LONDON

© 1966, 1999 The Johns Hopkins University Press
All rights reserved
Johns Hopkins Paperbacks edition, 1999
Printed in the United States of America on acid-free paper
9 8 7 6 5 4 3

The Johns Hopkins University Press
2715 North Charles Street
Baltimore, Maryland 21218-4363
www.press.jhu.edu

Library of Congress Cataloging-in-Publication Data will be found at the end
of this book.

A catalog record for this book is available from the British Library.

ISBN 0-8018-6293-0 (pbk.)

For Judy

Contents

Foreword

Nothing is more enjoyable to a West Point alumnus than spending an occasional evening with his reminiscences. I did that recently while reading *Duty, Honor, Country* and was amazed at how little some things change. The pleasures of cadet life were the same in my day as they were in Grant's and probably are today—the forbidden food tidbits smuggled in from the outside and enjoyed in barracks after taps, the long winter evenings spent in unauthorized meetings discussing graduation prospects, the practical jokes on each other or on the lowly plebe.

But beyond reminiscences there is always, when one thinks of West Point, an awareness of its grandeur and of its enduring contributions to the nation—on the field of battle, in civilian life, in industrial management, in education and science. West Point is best known for the consistently high quality of its graduates; anyone who has made it through four years at the Point is assumed, rightly, to possess attributes that will normally make him a good officer. Less well known is that through the generations the qualities West Point gives its graduates have proved to be easily transferable to most areas of civilian life, and West Pointers have made many significant contributions in non-military fields.

The reasons for this record of success are many, but one which I deem to be important is that the honor code has always been a pervasive part of the system. Despite one failure of the system, which Professor Ambrose discusses, it is the Corps' most treasured possession. In 1946, when I was beginning my duties as Chief of Staff and Maxwell Taylor his as Superintendent, we had an opportunity to discuss some of the Academy's post-World War II problems. Later I wrote him, elaborating on a few points: ". . . everyone familiar with West Point would instantly agree that the one thing that has set it definitely apart from every other school in the world is the fact that for a great number of years it has not only had an 'honor' system, but that the system has actually worked."

This achievement, I continued, was possible because the authorities refused to take advantage of the code to detect and punish minor violations of the regulations and because the continuity of the Corps led to the instilling in the new cadet "a respect amounting to veneration for the honor system. The honor system, as a feature of West Point, seems to grow in importance with the graduate as the years recede. . . ." Today I profoundly feel that in its perpetuation is one of the best assurances of our nation's future security.

The honor system has an obvious purpose at a school training young men who may someday be leading American soldiers on the battlefield or handling billions of dollars of public money or directing the affairs of a great corporation; still, it is only one part of the whole program. The Academy has always maintained high technical proficiency on the drill field and a sound educational program in the section room, but West Point gives its graduates something that far transcends the techniques and knowledge involved in developing, training, and leading an army. It helps them build character, integrity. This quality is more easily sensed than described, more readily felt than discussed, but at West Point it is as real as the honor code. Character is the Academy's overriding concern, a concern to which it has always given single-minded, almost fanatical devotion. It is because of this that West Point is hailed by military institutions throughout the world.

I concluded my letter to Superintendent Taylor by saying that by "efforts to graduate succeeding classes in which each individual will have a very definite feeling of responsibility toward the country, a very lively and continuing concern for his personal honor and for the honor system . . . West Point will continue to occupy its present place in the national consciousness and will be worth any sum that we must necessarily expend for its maintenance."

Professor Ambrose has rightly quoted a number of criticisms that have been directed toward West Point, but he places these in

Foreword

a perspective that clearly demonstrates their insignificance when compared to West Point's record of achievement.

In this scholarly and definitive history of a great American institution he tells us that early in the nineteenth century West Point used to refer to cadets who had been found deficient and were dismissed as "Uncle Sam's bad bargains." *Duty, Honor, Country* shows conclusively that the United States Military Academy has been one of Uncle Sam's best bargains.

Gettysburg
January, 1966

Introduction

William Faulkner used to speak of a sense of timelessness in the American South. The same sense prevails at the United States Military Academy. West Point regards its own past with veneration but—and this is more important—also as a living thing. It likes to think of itself as a changeless institution. The past is everywhere: in the museum, with its trophies from all American wars, in the architecture, in the cadet uniforms, in the old forts and antique cannon scattered about the post, in the names that haunt the barracks, names like Thayer, Mahan, Lee, Jackson, Grant, Sherman, Pershing, Eisenhower, and MacArthur. These things are a part of the substance of the Academy, as important as the curriculum, the section room, and the tactical training, all of which in any case also have century-old roots.

The long gray line goes by constantly. The cadet sees the veterans who have gone before him and the new plebes who will follow. He realizes that the whole is greater than its parts, that it embodies both past traditions and new wars, and he sees what it takes to be a soldier. Academy graduates continually renew their contact with the school; they often marry in the chapel, serve on the faculty as instructors or tactical officers, attend class reunions, and finally are buried in the cemetery. The constant funerals of the old graduates, with the flag over Trophy Point at half-mast, help the cadet visualize the long gray line. When a graduate of 1925 meets a graduate of 1955 in some Far Eastern outpost, the discussion can center around the same curriculum, subject matter, traditions, and often teachers. The two graduates probably share the same feelings about their alma mater, and even some of the slang they use may be identical.

Yet West Point has changed. In its first decade and a half it was mismanaged and at the end of the War of 1812 could only be considered a failure. Then in 1817 Sylvanus Thayer became Superintendent. He brought order out of chaos, making the Academy one of the great scientific institutions in the New World, a model for civilian schools to copy. It was vibrant and imaginative, proud of its series of brilliant Superintendents and its famous and creative faculty.

After the Civil War, however, and until the third decade of the twentieth century, the Academy stagnated. It became a small, forgotten, narrowly professional college tucked away in a corner of New York state, paying no attention to the outside world and receiving none in return. But in 1919, when Douglas MacArthur became Superintendent, once again the character of a man produced a radical change in the institution. He reformed and modernized the Academy, holding to those practices which had meaning while throwing out those that did not. MacArthur and his successors returned the Academy to the mainstream of American life, creating the well-esteemed institution of military education that now exists.

It is this story of timelessness and of change that I attempt to tell.

I have received uncommonly generous co-operation and aid in the preparation of this work. The officials in the Library, in the Museum, and at the Archives of the United States Military Academy have been exceedingly helpful. Colonel John Elting of the USMA Department of Military Art and Engineering has shared with me his vast knowledge of military history in general and of the Academy in particular. It is no exaggeration to say that his aid has been invaluable. Professor Russell Weigley of Temple University and Professor Alfred D. Chandler, Jr., of the Johns Hopkins University read parts of the manuscript and made useful suggestions. Professor Frederick Rudolph of Williams College and Miss Elizabeth Studley of the Johns Hopkins University read the entire manuscript; I am indebted to both for their aid.

Professor David Donald of the Johns Hopkins University first suggested this study, and he read a number of chapters. His perception has been both welcome and helpful. Mr. David Segal of New York City gave me intelligent direction and has been a patient and understanding confidant. Mrs. Elizabeth F. Smith, my typist, did a notably good job. I want to thank my wife for suggesting the title and Mr. Howard Webber for his perceptive and creative editing.

Librarians at the following institutions have gone out of their way to provide assistance: the Louisiana State University Library and Archives, the United States Military Academy Library and Archives, the Library of Congress, the Bowdoin College Library, the Milton S. Eisenhower Library at Johns Hopkins, the New York Public Library, the Eleutherian Mills Historical Library, and the National Archives.

I would finally like to express my deep appreciation for the constant encouragement I received from Professor William B. Hesseltine. He died shortly after I began this study, but whatever is of value in this history is due in large part to him. He was a great teacher with a deep dedication to history, whose mere presence was an inspiration.

The dedication is to the one who makes it all worthwhile.

STEPHEN E. AMBROSE

Baltimore
August, 1965

Duty, Honor, Country

A HISTORY OF WEST POINT

Chapter 1

The Beginning

The United States Military Academy came into being because of America's eighteenth-century military experience. West Point's founders also drew on the European past for guidance and inspiration; more to the point, the founders looked to the Europeans for examples of what should be avoided. Through a selective and typically American process, they extracted what was usable from the Europeans and added to it from their own experience, thereby creating a unique institution designed to serve and protect the unique republic.

At the opening of the eighteenth century in Europe, professional soldiers dominated warfare and enjoyed a secure position in Western society. Supposedly the guardians, and thus the servants, of the states, the standing armies of the Continent frequently ended by dominating and exploiting the societies they were supposed to defend. They became microcosmic societies in themselves, existing in fact to serve the interests only of their monarchs and sometimes only of their own officers. Prussia, the army with a state, is the classic example.

In such armies the officer corps was almost exclusively the property of the nobility, most of whose members were too ignorant or apathetic to earn a living in any other way. This gravitation towards the officer corps was especially felt by the minor nobility, whose members were so desperately poor they could not afford to secure the education of their children and perforce had to deliver up their sons "for the King's service." The mass of the soldiery came from the froth and scum of society, and men fought more from fear of their own officers than from hatred of the enemy. The rulers accepted this arrangement because it was the simplest way to buy aristocratic support and maintain their own positions, and except in Holland and England the combination of royal and aristocratic military power either prevented the growth of or destroyed representative and constitutional government. In short, the armies of continental Europe existed at the expense of all to maintain a system favorable to the few.

But in the eighteenth century change swept across Europe. Old, established customs gave way before the rationalism of the Enlightenment, which spared no institution in its constant questioning. The men of the Enlightenment were appalled by much of what their close examination of society revealed, but nothing upset them more than the standing armies. These armies, consisting of automatons and supporting ignorant aristocrats and absolutist monarchies, were a flagrant contradiction of the three pillars of Enlightenment thought, the Rights of Man, Nature, and Reason. The state would be better and more cheaply defended by armies that were "natural" and rational, armies composed of citizens from every class who would retain their rights while in the army and who would return to their civilian occupations at the conclusion of a war.[1]

While the thinkers of the Enlightenment were destroying the intellectual justification for the standing armies, the technological advances of the age were making it increasingly difficult for

[1] Alfred Vagts, *A History of Militarism: Civilian and Military* (New York, 1959), has an excellent discussion on the Enlightenment attack on the standing armies. He points out that Voltaire, despite his friendship with Frederick the Great, called soldiers hired murderers and maintained that since Sulla the armies had taken their pay from civilians in order to subjugate them. There is a thorough discussion of eighteenth-century armies in Richard A. Preston, Sydney F. Wise, and Herman O. Werner, *Men in Arms* (New York, 1956), 129–46; and in Theodore Ropp, *War in the Modern World* (New York, 1962), 53–59.

untrained noblemen to justify their possession of the officer corps. Exact scientific knowledge was becoming the *sine qua non* of a qualified artillery or engineering officer, and many aristocrats did not have, and sometimes refused to master, that knowledge. Those who did were usually the sons of the poorer nobility, or minor gentry, like Napoleon Bonaparte. But there were not enough of them, and the walls of class in military structure began to fall. There were promotions from the ranks for valor, and occasionally a valued non-commissioned officer's son would be put on the road to a commission. The sons of successful bourgeois, who as an article of faith placed great emphasis on education, received commissions in the scientific corps. The titled officers of higher rank, however, made certain that their bourgeois subordinates could aspire to nothing higher than the post of chief engineer, and they kept the infantry and cavalry regiments pure.

Artillery and engineering officers thought in the same terms as manufacturers, artisans, and businessmen, for like them they worked with machines that required exact knowledge. Like the bourgeois, officers in the scientific corps demanded results, a decent return on their investment. Unsatisfied with honor, they wanted a tangible profit. After the disaster at Jena, Prussian infantry and cavalry officers pretended to believe that the defeat had been an accident and saw no reason to change the composition of the army; the bourgeois joined with reformers in the army to demand otherwise.

But it was France which first seriously attempted to educate its officers. Under Louis XIV France had formed some cadet companies, and these were re-established between 1726 and 1733; in both cases the cadet companies were dissolved because of the total lack of discipline among the young nobles. The next move towards officer education was the École Militaire. Like the first Austrian academy, founded in the seventeenth century by a private capitalist named Baron de Chaos, the École Militaire was suggested by one of the brothers Paris, an eighteenth-century financier who made his fortune in war supplies. La Pompadour won Louis XV to the idea; a lottery, which financed the school, won the nobles, who only had to contribute their sons. The cadets would be five hundred impecunious noblemen, aged nine to eleven, "born without fortune," sons and orphans of families of the "old race." The founding decree of 1751 declared, "It is necessary that the ancient prejudice which has instilled the belief that bravery alone makes the man of war should give place imperceptibly to a taste for the military studies which we have introduced." The École Militaire was an excellent institution; its graduates gave France the best mathematicians, engineers, and artillery officers in Europe. After 1776, the school took on the added mission of serving as a higher institution of military education for the outstanding graduates of the military colleges founded in that year in the provinces. Among the early students was a graduate of the Collège Militaire of Brienne, Napoleon Bonaparte.

Five decades after the founding of the École Militaire the bourgeois revolution in France brought re-organization to the French army. Among other changes, the Jacobins created the École de Mars, a military academy designed to serve the purposes of the state, and abolished the aristocratic École Militaire. Wearing half-Greek, half-Roman costumes designed by Jacques Louis David, the sons of the middle class (as it turned out, the sons of the Jacobins) learned the science of war in a camp of tents. The school was more interested in politics than military affairs and became something of a bad joke. After the Thermidor, it gave way to the École Polytechnique, designed for the education of artillery and engineering officers and destined to surpass even the École Militaire.[2]

On the continent the French Revolution led to the first clash in centuries, on a large scale, between civilian and professional armies. The civilians won, thanks to their greater numbers, enthusiasm, and better officers—officers who were usually professionals from the minor gentry who had accepted the Revolution. Prussia, ignoring the extreme Junkers, adjusted to the new situation. Under the leadership of Scharnhorst the old military schools of the aristocracy were tossed aside, and in Berlin, Königsberg, and Breslau new academies of war created. Outstanding graduates went on to the post-graduate course in Berlin, where for three

[2] Vagts, *Militarism*, 54–55, 109.

years they studied mathematics, tactics, strategy, artillery, French, military geography, physics, and chemistry. The *Selekta* of this academy became the chief recruiting ground for the General Staff.[3]

England also responded to the rise of science. In 1741 King George II had agreed to found the Royal Military Academy at Woolwich. Designed to prepare "Gentlemen Cadets" for service in the engineers and artillery, Woolwich emphasized algebra, geometry, fortification, mining, gunnery, and bridge building. Graduates did not have to purchase a commission (the device used by the British to make certain officers were of the proper sort); they alone in the British army received one free. Most important, there was no legal restriction on the class origins of the cadets.[4]

In this age of scientific and social advance, the United States was born. It came into being, in part, because the American colonists objected to the military policy of King George III, for he "has kept among us, in time of peace, standing armies" and rendered "the military independent of, and superior to, the civil power." And after the successful completion of their Revolution, the leaders of the United States agreed that the greatest danger facing the world's first democratic nation was the growth of an aristocracy. They were also convinced, from their reading of Greek and Roman history, that aristocracies in a democracy arose from a military elite, which was produced by a standing army.[5] Further, they knew enough recent history to realize that the chief support of royal and aristocratic privilege was the army. They felt, therefore, that armies per se were dangerous.

But the new nation, or so its leaders thought, was surrounded by a hostile world. To the east, the powers of Europe were unwilling to accept one of the chief results of the Revolution, the creation of a democratic state. To the west the Indians, to the north

---

[3] Gordon A. Craig, *The Politics of the Prussian Army, 1640–1945* (New York, 1956), 45.

[4] Sir John Smyth, *Sandhurst* (London, 1961), 5–34.

[5] Charles F. Mullett, "Classical Influences on the American Revolution," *The Classical Journal*, XXXV (October, 1939), 97, points out that many American Revolutionary writers "declared that the threat of the sword to . . . liberty had been constantly revealed by Roman history."

the British, and to the south the Spanish were unwilling to accept one of the chief aims of the new nation, expansion.

Americans needed a defense policy. They insisted that it be both revolutionary and rational, that it eliminate the worst and incorporate the best features of the two basic forms of organization of an army: the standing army and the citizen army, or, as the English called it, the militia. They would break with the European example by relying on citizen-soldiers, who would pose no threat to society because they *were* society, for the bulk of the army's manpower, gaining at the same time a force whose ultimate possible size was enormous. But their contacts with European armies during the war, both French and British, convinced them of the necessity for trained officers. During the war America had relied upon Europe as the source of many officers in the specialized fields of artillery and engineering, but the United States could not continue to call upon foreigners and hope to retain its national independence, pride, or revolutionary purity. In any case, Americans had an opportunity to go far beyond the halting steps the Europeans had taken in educating their officers and opening positions in the army for men whose only claim was ability. America was free to create, free to educate all those with ability and to establish a trained body of professional soldiers whose sole qualification was merit.

The key to a rational, revolutionary defense policy, one that would defend the state at the least possible cost and the smallest conceivable risk, was the officer corps. Members must come from society as a whole, not a segment of it, must be available and able to train and lead citizen-soldiers in time of war, and must be either unwilling or unable to use their monopoly of knowledge for their own ends.

The genius of the United States Military Academy lay in these requirements. Thomas Jefferson, George Washington, John Adams, and the others who contributed to the formation of an academy hoped to satisfy the requirements by building an institution controlled by, and with students appointed by, civilians. The academy would impart to the students the knowledge that had to be kept alive in America if the country were to retain its independence. Graduates would diffuse this knowledge to the militia. The Regular Army played no part in the program; its function would be limited to Indian fighting. Graduates of the academy would not even be expected to remain in the army, where there probably would be no room for them in any case, but they were expected upon their return to civil life to join the local militia company and direct its training and, in war, its fighting. Under the circumstances, even if they had the inclination to use their knowledge to overthrow the state, their chances of success would be slim, since they would have no veteran professional troops under them. Instead of leading men who unquestioningly followed orders and accepted the most severe discipline, they would be leading their fellow citizens. Through the device of a civilian-controlled academy, Americans would enjoy an adequate defense while avoiding the dangers of a standing army.

Americans early recognized the need for an academy. The Revolutionary War had hardly begun when they became aware of their deficiency in military training and knowledge and began proposing the creation of a military academy. The first to do so was Colonel Henry Knox of the artillery.

Before the war Knox had owned "The London Book Store" in Boston, a resort for British officers stationed in the city. Knox frequently talked over military affairs with them. He was also a member of a local militia company, the crack Boston Grenadier Corps. On his own he had studied military science and engineering, and when war came Knox enlisted in the patriot cause, joining the army on the heights around Boston. On November 17, 1775, Washington made the self-trained, twenty-six-year-old Knox his chief of artillery. Taller even than his commander, Washington, Knox was a beefy man—he weighed nearly 300 pounds—with a large, bulbous nose. Contemporaries found him socially inept, perhaps because of his "Bacchanalian figure," his pompous walk, and his forceful, often profane, expression of strong opinions. He was energetic and ambitious. The first winter of the war, at his own suggestion, he undertook a hazardous expedition to Fort

Ticonderoga in order to bring back to Boston the British ordnance Ethan Allen had captured there. Late in January, 1776, Knox returned, dragging over the snow "a noble train of artillery." He continued to show the same energy and ability throughout the war, enough so to become one of Washington's closest friends and advisers. He fought in all the battles around New York City, directed Washington's artillery during the crossing of the Delaware River on Christmas night, 1776, before the attack on Trenton, and at Brandywine, Germantown, Monmouth, and Yorktown.

Knox was as able an organizer as he was a fighting man. After the end of hostilities, he conceived and organized the Society of the Cincinnati, composed of Revolutionary War officers, served as Indian commissioner, and as secretary at war under the Confederation. A "furious Federalist," he denounced the doctrine of states' rights and the Articles of Confederation and was a supporter of the Constitution. Under the new government, he once again served Washington, as his first Secretary of War.[6]

Even during the Revolutionary War Knox did not limit himself to fighting. The conflict had hardly begun when he was proposing a military academy, the graduates of which, he hoped, would provide the foundation for a "respectable army." He realized, however, that "the genius of the Republic seems adverse to the permanency of an Army, and every plan which may be proposed to render troops radically good would probably be regarded by many well intentioned citizens as the seeds of a standing army designed to overturn the liberties of the country."[7] Still, America needed an academy, for "as the army now stands, it is merely a receptacle for ragamuffins."[8] Knox pressed his views on John Adams, congressman from Massachusetts. In June of 1776 Adams guided through Congress an act creating the Corps of Invalids, an

[6] Dumas Malone (ed.), *Dictionary of American Biography* (New York, 1960), V, 475–77. Hereafter cited as *DAB*. Also Fairfax Downey, *Sound of the Guns: The Story of American Artillery* (New York, 1955), 28.

[7] James R. Jacobs, *The Beginning of the United States Army, 1783–1812* (Princeton, 1947), 288.

[8] *Centennial of the United States Military Academy at West Point* (Washington, 1904), I, 202. Hereafter cited as *CWP*. Jacobs, *Beginning U. S. Army*, 285.

organization that would give service to disabled officers by stationing them at inactive posts. One of their chief duties would be to impart military knowledge to "young gentlemen," ensigns assigned to the Corps. In July, 1777, a Frenchman, Colonel Louis Nicola, organized the Corps in Philadelphia. In 1781 it moved to West Point, New York, but few ensigns came to it and those who did found themselves laughed at by the veterans, who regarded their own positions as sinecures. The Corps was disbanded at the conclusion of the war.

Knox had been thinking more of a permanent academy, organized along the lines of Woolwich in England. During the winter of 1778 he opened his own academy at Pluckemin, New Jersey, where he gave lectures on tactics and gunnery, but active service soon brought a temporary end to his efforts. His idea, however, was not unnoticed. A key factor was the French alliance. American officers, untrained to a man, began to respect military education after coming into contact with French and European professionals. The intellectual ferment in the French army following the Seven Years War produced men like Napoleon, Berthier, Marmont, Carnot, and dozens of others; their immediate predecessors, and in some cases their contemporaries, were among the French officers serving in America during the war. The Prussian von Steuben and the Pole Kosciusko also enhanced the reputation of trained European officers. Their abilities tremendously impressed the Americans, especially Washington, and through their example helped prepare the ground for Knox's idea.

In 1783 Washington added his voice to that of Knox, calling for "academies, one or more, for the instruction of the art military." Washington declared, "I cannot conclude without repeating the necessity of the proposed Institution, unless we intend to let the Science [of war] become extinct, and to depend entirely upon the Foreigners for their friendly aid." Still nothing was done. As soon as the war ended, Congress indicated its feelings by declaring that "standing armies in time of peace are inconsistent with the principles of republican government, dangerous to the liberties of a free people, and generally converted into destructive engines for establishing despotism" and immediately reduced the army.[9] By 1785 there were fewer than 100 officers and men in the United States Army. Most were members of Colonel Alexander Hamilton's old artillery company, stationed at West Point, on the Hudson River in lower New York State.[10]

West Point was America's largest fort and the scene of a great deal of activity during the war. Washington considered it the most important military position in America. Now, however, the few men stationed there guarded stores and the spoils of the Saratoga, Stony Point, and Yorktown campaigns, when they were not shoveling snow or cutting grass. Meanwhile, the continued occupation of the Plain caused its owner, Stephen Moore of North Carolina, who had inherited the land, to petition Congress to provide for purchase of the land from him. Secretary of the Treasury Alexander Hamilton recommended the purchase, and on September 10, 1790, for $11,085, West Point and the surrounding land passed into the hands of the United States government.[11]

A year earlier the French Revolution had begun, and soon France was at war with England and Spain. The United States was an ally of France, and the European nation expected aid in what it considered a common cause. But Washington and his chief advisers, Hamilton and Jefferson, wanted to remain neutral. It was clear, however, that it would be nearly as difficult to maintain neutrality during a world war as it would be to participate. Even as Washington was issuing his neutrality proclamation, the government took steps to provide for the national defense.

On November 13, 1793, Washington turned a cabinet discussion to the question of the best manner of fortifying the principal

[9] *CWP,* I, 193–207; R. Ernest Dupuy, *Where They Have Trod: The West Point Tradition in American Life* (New York, 1940), 34–35; Downey, *Sound of the Guns,* 63–64.

[10] Alexander Hamilton's organization is still in the army, as the First Battalion, Fifth Artillery; it is the army's only direct link with Washington's Continentals.

[11] Herman Beukema, *The United States Military Academy and its Foreign Contemporaries* (West Point, 1939), 1–3; Edward O. Boynton, *History of West Point* (New York, 1863), 9–11. Through the years other purchases of land were made, eventually bringing the post to its present size.

harbors. Jefferson arose and announced that he was opposed to the federal government's undertaking the responsibility, because the states were competent to provide for their own defense. Hamilton prepared to disagree, but Knox spoke first. The Secretary of War observed that Jefferson was obviously wrong but that the discussion was academic in any case because no one in America knew how to build a fort. What was needed was a military academy, where young officers could learn the science of war. Jefferson broke in to declare his opposition to this proposal, saying that "none of the specified powers given by the Constitution would authorize" the creation of a national academy. Knox hotly defended his proposition; Jefferson continued to attack it. The argument ended when the President declared that although he thought an academy would be advantageous he "did not wish to bring on anything which might generate heat and ill humor" and ordered them to drop the subject.[12]

Washington could afford to end the cabinet discussion because Congress was ready to take action. On May 7, 1794, it provided for an increase in the Corps of Artillerists and Engineers—actually, the handful of men stationed at West Point—and created the rank of cadet. In France, the word meant the youngest brother of a family; in Spain, a young volunteer officer; in England, a young son who volunteered for service in India. In America, cadets were junior officers assigned to the Corps at West Point. They had the right to command, to sit as members of court-martial boards, and to employ servants. They were supposed to attend classes taught by older officers and learn their art—one provision of the congressional act was for the purchase of books and apparatus for military instruction—but the cadets found themselves spending more of their time doing irksome tasks senior officers wished to avoid, such as drill, paper work, and policing the grounds. No books were purchased, no classes were held.[13] At least in part this inaction proceeded

[12] Albert E. Bergh (ed.), *The Writings of Thomas Jefferson* (Washington, 1907), I, 409.
[13] Jacobs, *Beginning U. S. Army*, 297; Henry Barnard, *Military Schools and Courses of Instruction* (New York, 1872), 722; *CWP*, I, 213.

from the feeling, inherited from Europe and still present in the American army, that honor, courage, and loyalty were the important elements in a soldier's character, while knowledge was at best secondary.

In February, 1796, Lieutenant Colonel Stephen Rochefontaine took command at West Point with orders from the War Department to initiate a course of instruction. His general orders to the post on March 28 began, "To-morrow at 10 o'clock in the morning the officers are invited to meet at the instruction room to copy the several plans of fortification drawn after the directions of Muller." Rochefontaine's idea of imparting knowledge to officers as well as cadets proved disastrous. The officers, incensed at the insult to their position contained in the concept that they had anything to learn about their profession, promptly burned down the "Old Provost," the building that housed the instruction room. No classes were held.

The war in Europe, meanwhile, had grown in intensity and scope. In 1798 the United States began a quasi-war with France, the most advanced military nation in the world. In the École Polytechnique France was turning out the best officers in the world; entry and graduation alike depended upon hard work. The American army, on the other hand, could not even defeat savages—in 1791, the Indians dealt General St. Clair's army a disastrous blow—nor could its engineers build proper fortifications. The intricate operations and precise mathematics of European engineers were unknown in the New World.

On July 16, 1798, in an act to increase the size of the Corps a frightened Congress gave President John Adams power to appoint four teachers of the "Arts and Sciences" for the instruction of the cadets and young officers in the Corps of Artillerists and Engineers. Immediate defense was uppermost in the minds of the congressmen, but long-range needs were not forgotten. Charles Pinckney of South Carolina thought that the militia could handle most of the fighting, but not the engineering and artillery work. "A degree of education and study was necessary in that corps, which was not

[12]

required in any other," he said, while a Massachusetts congressman reminded the House of the absence of scientific officers at the beginning of the last war.[14]

Under the terms of the law the War Department gathered together at West Point a number of prospective students and made an attempt to organize a school, but again nothing came of it, as teachers could not be found. No one in America was capable of giving instruction in military engineering, and Adams had, in his words "an invincible aversion to the appointment of foreigners," because "it mortifies the honest pride of our officers, and damps their ardor and ambition."[15] Pressure to get some kind of establishment under way mounted. Hamilton, himself a former army officer, told the new Secretary of War, James McHenry, that the Army's greatest need was a military academy. "No sentiment is more just than this," Hamilton said, "that in proportion as the circumstances and policy of a country forbid a large military establishment, it is important that as much perfection as possible should be given to that which may at any time exist." Just as a farmer, if he "would secure his flocks . . . must go to the expense of shepherds," America had to have trained military men who could teach civilians the art of war.

Hamilton proposed a complete system of military education, with a "fundamental school" at West Point, a school for engineers and artillerists, another for cavalry and infantry, and a fourth for the navy. All cadets would spend two years at the fundamental

[14] *The Debates and Proceedings in the Congress of the United States, Fifth Congress, May 15, 1797, to March 3, 1799* (Washington, 1851), 1419–21.

[15] Charles F. Adams (ed.), *Works of John Adams* (Boston, 1856), IX, 65–66. Adams did offer a post to a Tory *émigré* from New England, Benjamin Thompson, by then Count Rumford. Thompson had held a commission in the British army during the Revolution and later won renown as a major general, minister of war, and privy councilor of Bavaria. He founded the Royal Institution of London, was a fellow of the Royal Societies of London, Berlin, and Munich, and had been made a count of the Holy Roman Empire. It took great effort for as fiercely loyal a patriot as Adams to offer the post to a Tory, but he evidently felt that Thompson was as close as he could come to getting an American teacher. Thompson declined.

school, then two more at the specialized institutions.[16] Hamilton showed his plan to Washington, and three days before his death the old general, in his last letter save one, replied. "The Establishment of an Institution of this kind," he said, "upon a respectable and extensive basis, has ever been considered by me as an Object of primary importance to this Country." Washington had no formal military education himself and therefore declined to comment on the details of Hamilton's plan, but he did urge Congress to establish at least one academy.[17]

Secretary McHenry, meanwhile, had received a plan for an academy from another source. During the expansion of the army in the mid-nineties, Louis de Tousard, who had fought in the Revolutionary War under General Lafayette, accepted a commission as major in the First Regiment of Artillerists and Engineers. In 1798 Major Tousard, who had attended the military academy at Strasbourg in his youth, prepared a memoir for McHenry on the "formation of a School of Artillerists and Engineers," in which he emphasized the importance of a complete course in the basic sciences, practical field instruction, the best possible faculty, and rigid discipline.[18]

McHenry combined the two recommendations and, on January 14, 1800, presented President Adams with a plan for a military academy. He proposed that the government follow Hamilton's suggestion and establish four schools, each organized in accordance with Tousard's plan. McHenry argued that the need for academies

[16] Henry Cabot Lodge (ed.), *The Works of Alexander Hamilton* (New York, 1904), VII, 179–86; Leonard D. White, *The Jeffersonians* (New York, 1951), 252. The idea of specialized schools was later taken up by the British, when they formed Sandhurst—an academy for infantry, cavalry, and staff officers— to complement Woolwich. As will be seen, the idea always had a certain support in the American army. Another revolutionary of another time, whose party also feared the standing army, put it this way: "As industry needs engineers, as farming needs qualified agronomists, so military specialists are indispensable to defence." The speaker was Leon Trotsky. Quoted in Isaac Deutscher, *The Prophet Armed: Trotsky: 1879–1921* (London, 1954), 408.

[17] John C. Fitzpatrick (ed.), *The Writings of George Washington* (Washington, 1940), XXXVII, 473.

[18] Norman B. Wilkinson, "The Forgotten 'Founder' of West Point," *Military Affairs*, XXIV (March, 1960), 177–80.

was immediate and great, for in a world at war the United States, no matter how pacific its intentions, must be prepared to defend itself. The people would not allow a standing army, so the country was forced to rely upon the skill of its officers and upon the strength of its fortifications for protection. Engineers were needed to build fortifications, and gunners to man them; academies were needed to train the officers.[19]

Adams sent McHenry's recommendations on to Congress and, while that body deliberated, he tried to execute the existing laws for the instruction of artillerists and engineers. Few cadets and no teachers had yet been assigned to the Corps. Adams told McHenry that if he could find the right men, he would appoint as many as sixty-four cadets, four teachers, and two engineers. The ambitious program fell short of the mark. When he left office in 1801, Adams had been able to find only twelve cadets and one teacher, George Baron, an Englishman who had been a mathematics instructor at Woolwich.[20]

Congress, meanwhile, did nothing. The chief reason was an unspoken but nevertheless real fear of a trained body of officers. Like most Americans, congressmen were torn between their knowledge of the need for engineers and artillerists and their knowledge that the French Revolution had been betrayed by just such officers. As things stood, the need was not great enough to overcome the fear, or rather, the threat of foreign domination did not seem as great as the possibility of an American Second Brumaire. A further impetus was needed before Congress would agree to a military academy. It came from the desire for an American institution concentrating on the sciences.

The colleges the United States had inherited from colonial America were patterned on Oxford and Cambridge. Ancient languages taught through the traditional scholastic methods were the core of the curriculum. Harvard, William and Mary, Yale, and the others were primarily designed to turn out lawyers and ministers, and religious texts were common to all. Newtonian science had made little impact, although six colleges did have courses in

[19] *American State Papers: Military Affairs*, I, 133–43.
[20] Adams, *Works*, IX, 65–66.

mathematics and natural philosophy (the Aristotelian term for physics), while an occasional faculty member argued for experiment and experience rather than revealed religion as sources of knowledge.[21] The Revolution had also started a new trend; as one result of its democratic tendencies state legislatures had begun to found colleges characterized by their openness as well as by their empiricism. In the twenty years following the end of the war nineteen new colleges sprang up. Their students were not interested in learning Greek and Latin, nor were the states that created the schools interested in teaching those languages. The students and the legislators agreed that the new colleges should teach courses of value here in this world, not in the next, and should aim to turn out responsible and useful citizens.[22] In a sense, the institutions represented an investment by the state in future public servants.

The new trend did not mean that utilitarian empiricism suddenly began to dominate American education. Whatever the founders of the new institutions wanted, teachers had to be found for the colleges, and most men qualified for the positions were oriented towards the classics. As late as 1824 Lafayette College felt it was taking a daring step when it introduced modern languages into the curriculum and attacked the classics as adding "no more to scientific knowledge than the croaking of frogs."[23] But the new ideas were in the air, and they did have support.

In the new nation there were four distinct, though not exclusive, ideas of the purpose of higher education. From the Renaissance there remained the ideal of education as a means of producing scholar-gentlemen; from the Reformation, the belief that education was a means of moral, ethical, and religious development; from the American Enlightenment, the notion that education was the business of the state, to be used to produce civic leaders; from the scientific revolution, the utilitarian idea of using education to

[21] Frederick Rudolph, *The American College and University* (New York, 1962), 29–30. My understanding of the development of higher education in America is greatly dependent on this excellent work. See also Samuel Eliot Morison, *Three Centuries of Harvard: 1636–1936* (Cambridge, 1936).

[22] Rudolph, *American College*, 35–36.

[23] Quoted in *ibid.*, 113.

master the physical world for man's progress therein. The trend seemed to be away from the first two sets of ideas and towards a combination of the second pair, but a valiant and persistent attempt to include the older notions led to the conglomerate curriculum that was common to most American colleges until after the Civil War.[24]

Thomas Jefferson was in the forefront of the battle between the old and the new. During the war, in 1779, he had tried to turn out the professors of divinity and oriental languages at William and Mary and substitute for them professors of law, chemistry, modern languages, and natural history. He was unsuccessful, but he did not stop trying. One of the ideas he began to advocate was a national university. An outgrowth of the Revolution, the idea of a national university which could help create a national sentiment and provide a practical education for future public servants was championed by Washington, Adams, Jefferson, and indeed every President before Andrew Jackson. Washington thought a national university would foster able public servants by freeing its students from the prejudices of sectionalism.[25]

In 1779 the American Philosophical Society offered a prize for the best plan of an American system of education. While the subject was under discussion, Dr. Benjamin Rush wrote an essay that was an able summary of the ideas of those who wanted to change the American system of education. Rush was an enemy of the classics and their major prop, the ancient languages. "While Greek and Latin are the only avenues to science," he said, "education will always be confined to a few people." He wanted to make knowledge universal, so that a republican form of government could be preserved, and argued that the classics were standing in the way of this achievement. Rush concluded, "To spend four or five years in learning two dead languages, is to turn our back upon a gold mine, in order to amuse ourselves catching butterflies."[26]

[24] Russel B. Nye, *The Cultural Life of the New Nation* (New York, 1960), 150.

[25] *Ibid.*, 42; Merle Curti and Vernon Carstensen, *The University of Wisconsin* (Madison, 1949), I, 13–25.

[26] Quoted in Allen Oscar Hansen, *Liberalism and American Education in the Eighteenth Century* (New York, 1926), 52–61.

[17]

The enemies of the classics wanted an education to be a useful thing both to the graduates and the society. President Joseph McKeen noted at Bowdoin College in 1802:

> It ought always to be remembered, that . . . institutions are founded and endowed for the common good, and not for the private advantage of those who resort to them for education. It is not that they may be able to pass through life in an easy or reputable manner, but that their mental powers may be cultivated and improved for the benefit of society. . . . Every man who has been aided by a public institution to acquire an education and to qualify himself for usefulness, is under peculiar obligations to exert his talents for the public good.[27]

What the empiricists were asking was how a knowledge of Greek and Latin could ever serve the public good.

When Jefferson assumed the Presidency in 1801, he was eager to found a national institution that would eliminate the classics, add the sciences, and produce graduates who would use their knowledge for the benefit of society. Within this framework, Jefferson realized that a military academy had the best chance of success. Those sectionalists opposed to a national university might be persuaded to support a national military academy, while the scholastics would be more willing to accept an empiricist academy than they would an empiricist university. Most politicians agreed that, aside from themselves—they could be said to need no specific formal training—the first servants of the nation would be military men, who clearly did. During a 1798 debate over a bill to create an academy, one congressman declared that he very much favored having trained officers, as "these are the most valuable set of men which a nation can possess, except it be wise legislators."[28] Others who would also serve, doctors, veterinarians, postmen, could be trained in already existing colleges, both private and state-supported, as could most infantry and cavalry officers. But no institution, either existing or planned, was supplying men trained in the skills of artillery and engineering. Therefore the only

[27] Quoted in Louis C. Hatch, *The History of Bowdoin College* (Portland, 1927), 19.
[28] *The Debates and Proceedings in the Congress,* Fifth Congress, 1421.

agency which needed specialists in these fields, the federal government, would have to supply the training. Finally, a properly organized academy, one in which civilian control was assured, would satisfy American ideas on the best way to organize for the national defense.

As President, Jefferson abandoned the constitutional objections he had once raised against a national academy and urged his Secretary of War, Henry Dearborn, to continue and even speed up the work McHenry and Adams had begun. Less than a month after the new administration took office, Dearborn ordered Tousard, now a lieutenant colonel, to West Point to take command of the garrison there. When not engaged in other duties, Tousard was to "give all the assistance in your power in the instruction of such officers and cadets as may be at West Point."

Tousard arrived in September, 1801. His faculty consisted of one teacher, Baron, and his student body consisted of twelve cadets. On September 21 Baron held his first class. He illustrated his lecture by making marks upon a standing slate with a white chalk, thereby introducing the blackboard to America. Baron held his classes in the mornings. Mathematics was the only subject, and the cadets devoted their afternoons to brief military exercises or field sports.

During Tousard's tenure of command the cadets appeared for the first time in public as a military unit. The occasion was the funeral of Captain John Lillie, who upon hearing Lieutenant Robert W. Osborn accuse him of stealing public property had died of an apoplectic fit. In 1802 Jefferson gave the captain's son, also John Lillie, an appointment as a cadet. At the time John was ten years and seven months old—he remained at West Point until 1805 without graduating.

The cadets ranged in age from 10 to 34. Some were married with several children, some were college graduates, one was an ex-British officer, another had practiced law before the Supreme Court of New York.[29] One was Joseph G. Swift, whose parents

[29] *CWP,* I, 218; Wilkinson, " 'Founder,' " *Military Affairs,* 180–87; Jacobs, *Beginning U. S. Army,* 198. Conditions at West Point were such that the Secretary of War wrote to an officer at the post, "By a letter from Mr. Baron

knew an officer who knew a neighbor of President Adams and was thus able to secure for the sixteen-year-old Swift, one day to become the most important man in the Academy's existence, a cadet appointment from the President. Swift's first assignment was to report for duty under Colonel Tousard, then in charge of the harbor at Newport, Rhode Island. Swift arrived in June, 1800. Tousard, grizzled soldier of fortune, received the boy with all the courtesy due an officer, invited him to dinner that evening, and introduced him to his wife. The next day Tousard gave Swift a case of Paris drawing instruments and sent him off on an inspection tour.

In 1801 Swift received orders to go to West Point. His experience succinctly illustrated the condition of the Academy. He set out from New York City, traveling up the Hudson. During the trip past the Revolutionary forts and batteries, his imagination wandered over the historic scenes connected with the river. He recalled the treason of Arnold, the fate of André. But he expected to find something extraordinary at West Point and was disappointed. The captain of the sailing vessel did not deign to put in at the small dock; Swift had to board a rowboat and be put ashore. "It was a calm October evening," he later remembered. "The only sound was that of the cow bell."

Lieutenants William Wilson and Lewis Howard, of the local garrison, made Swift a member of their mess, and Professor Baron gave him a copy of Hutton's *Mathematics* to study. He attended classes for four hours each morning. Mr. Baron, Swift thought, was "an able teacher," but he "was of rude manner." For his part, Baron thought Swift too friendly with the officers of the garrison and told him he ought to mess with the other cadets. When Swift

---

I have the unexpected and unpleasant intelligence that some subalterns, who were ordered to West Point for the purpose of instruction, refuse to attend and receive the instruction offered them by the wisdom of the Gov't. Those officers who refuse to receive instruction 'must be considered unfit for service.'" Dearborn to Major T. H. Cushing, October 19, 1801, Edward S. Holden Archives, USMA. Hereafter cited as E. S. H. Archives. The Secretary also had to caution the engineering officers of the post not to interfere with the students by giving them orders to do police duty, etc. Dearborn to Cushing, December 2, 1801, *ibid.*

refused, Baron sent his servant with a verbal order on the subject. Swift declined to receive an order from a servant. An hour later, Baron marched over to the artillery quarters, where he found Swift talking with Lieutenant Wilson.

"Do you refuse to obey my orders?" Baron demanded.

"No, sir, but I refuse to receive a verbal order by any servant," Swift replied.

"You are a mutinous young rascal," Baron declared. Swift thereupon leaped over a small fence separating them in order to attack his teacher. Baron fled towards his quarters, Swift following. Baron got there first, bolted the door, raced upstairs, threw open the window, and began hurling "coarse epithets" at Swift. The cadet replied in kind.

That evening Baron sent Swift a written order to consider himself under arrest. Swift sent a report of the incident to Secretary Dearborn, who advised him to make an apology to Baron. After consulting with his friends among the garrison, Swift declined to do so, contending that Baron's conduct was ungentlemanly and no apology could be made. Baron meanwhile was court-martialed, found guilty of various improprieties, and dismissed. The Board found Swift guilty "of using disrespectful words to a superior officer" but restored him to duty.[30] One cadet later remembered of this period, "All order and regulation, either moral or religious, gave way to idleness, dissipation and irreligion. No control over the conduct of the officers and cadets was exercised."[31]

Meanwhile, Jefferson was searching for a permanent Superintendent—Tousard was commander of the garrison, but had no official status with regard to the school. Like Adams, Jefferson felt the Academy should have a native American at its head. In May, 1801, he found his man.

Jonathan Williams was an outstanding figure of the Enlightenment. Son of a prosperous merchant and relative of Benjamin Franklin, Williams had spent most of his life in Europe, where

[30] Joseph Gardner Swift, *Memoirs* (privately printed, 1890), 19–31. Dearborn did order Swift to mess with the other cadets. Dearborn to Swift, December 5, 1801, E. S. H. Archives.

[31] Dupuy, *Where They Have Trod*, 41.

he conducted a mercantile business and worked for Franklin. In 1785 Williams returned to America, continuing there both activities. In 1799 he published the results of some experiments he had undertaken with Franklin in a treatise entitled *Thermometrical Navigation*. He also contributed to the *Transactions* of the American Philosophical Society, of which he was secretary and vice-president. These and other activities brought him to Jefferson's attention. To the President, Williams seemed an ideal man for the post of inspector of fortifications and Superintendent of the Academy at West Point because, although Williams had no military experience, engineering and artillery were really scientific subjects. The school itself still had no legal status, but Jefferson had introduced legislation to provide it in Congress.[32]

Williams accepted Jefferson's appointment, and on December 14, 1801, arrived at West Point. One of his first decisions was that the Corps of Artillerists and Engineers should be split into two distinct organizations, each with its own special tasks. Jefferson incorporated the recommendation into the proposed legislation he had before Congress.

On March 16, 1802, Congress authorized the President to organize a Corps of Engineers, which "shall be stationed at West Point . . . and shall constitute a military academy." The commander of the Corps, the Chief Engineer, would also be Superintendent of the Academy. The Secretary of War would purchase books, implements, and apparatus "for the use and benefit of the said institution."[33] Jefferson appointed Williams Chief Engineer and Superintendent.

The law, with all its vagueness (the Corps of Engineers, like its head, had a double function—to serve the engineering function and "to constitute a military academy") did not meet the recommendations or hopes of Knox, Washington, Tousard, Hamilton, or Jefferson. Still, it did recognize the need for a national academy, controlled by civilians, that would emphasize science and produce

[32] *DAB,* X, 280–82.
[33] *The Debates and Proceedings in the Congress of the United States,* Seventh Congress, First Session (Washington, 1834), 1312.

trained officers. The government had recognized, however feebly, that military service was a career and that the military art required training; it accepted responsibility for training its own servants and laid the foundation for the first organized professional body in the public service.[34] The Superintendent was an outstanding scientist. Perhaps he could turn West Point into the institution that the engineers, the militia, the army, and the nation so badly needed.

[34] White, *Jeffersonians,* 259.

Chapter II

The Foundling

The United States Military Academy had a difficult childhood. Public indifference, official hostility, and undue burden on an army too small to bear it combined to defeat the ambitious educational and military purpose of the Academy. It was run indifferently, its graduates were neither professional soldiers nor trained scientists, and there were few of them.

Physically, the Academy was unimpressive. Towering over it was old Fort Putnam, a stone, casemented fort built in the early days of the Revolution and containing a couple of twenty-four-pound guns. Down on the Plain, a small plateau of some forty acres jutting into the Hudson, there were a few houses for the officers. Superintendent Williams made his residence in Rochefontaine's old quarters and his headquarters in a small building known as the Salt Box. To the northwest, down by the river, there were two long, yellow buildings that were always locked. They contained the trophies and artillery captured at Saratoga, and cadets needed special permission to inspect them. To the east of the museums were a wooden armory and then a hospital. Up on the northeast angle of the Plain stood another Revolutionary fort, Clinton, already dilapidated. On the face of the cliff, between the southeast angle of Clinton and the river, was a rock garden which Tadeusz Kosciusko, who in 1778 had planned West Point's defenses, had constructed in his idle moments. Cadet Swift and one of the officers restored it, planting flowers and vines and building seats for reading.[1]

Organization was haphazard. The law provided for ten cadets attached to the Corps of Engineers and forty to the Artillery, but fewer than that were actually in attendance. Cadets received $16.00 a month plus two rations a day. The entire Corps of Engineers, which "constituted" the Academy, contained only one major, two captains, four lieutenants, and ten cadets. The major was the Superintendent, and the captains were the instructors. Like the officers, the cadets were required to do duty in any part of the United States the President might direct. They made their own arrangements for food and lodging.[2] There were no requirements concerning the age or ability of the cadets. Some were barely in their teens while one was a middle-aged gentleman who lived in Putnam county, had a wife and several children, and attended the Academy for more than seven years without graduating.[3]

Classes began in April, 1802. The teachers were Captains William Amhurst Barron and Jared Mansfield. Barron was a Harvard graduate, where he had been a classmate of John Quincy Adams, and had tutored in mathematics at the Cambridge University. Cadet Swift found him to be "of a social temper and kind nature." Mansfield was acting professor of natural and experimental philosophy. He had been on the faculty at Yale, had published a study of the motion of bodies in free space, and was a friend of Jefferson. His work illustrated the relationship between science and military affairs. Although he had never been in the army, his *Essays, Mathematical and Physical,* published in 1801, which dealt with problems in algebra, geometry, calculus, and nautical astronomy, had a chapter on gunnery and fundamental ballistics problems. Mansfield pointed out the importance of air resistance, not only as a retarding force but also in its effect on the projectile.

[1] Swift, *Memoirs,* 35; E. D. J. Waugh, *West Point* (New York, 1944), 50–51.
[2] Barnard, *Military Schools,* 723; *CWP,* I, 226; Boynton, *West Point,* 245.
[3] Robert H. Hall, "Early Discipline at the U. S. M. A.," *Journal of the Military Service Institution,* II (November, 1882), 448–74. Hereafter cited as *JMSI.*

He was the first scientist to treat the gyroscopic phenomenon—previous investigators studied projectiles without considering the effect of the medium through which they passed.

At West Point the texts were C. H. Hutton's *Mathematics,* W. Enfield's *Natural Philosophy,* both introductory works, Marshal S. de Vauban's *Traité de fortifications,* and H. O. de Scheel's *Treatise of Artillery.* No attempt was made to teach civil engineering, but practical instruction was given in the use of surveying instruments.

The differences between West Point and the well established colleges, and indeed, the young struggling ones, were great. Neither Latin nor Greek was taught, nor was a knowledge of the ancient languages required for entrance. There were no religious test, no course in moral philosophy, no preacher-president. There was also a qualitative difference. The cadets rarely went beyond their texts, and most did not know the difference between the ditch and the glacis of a fort. As late as 1815 two cadets graduated into the Corps of Engineers who had not gone beyond Hutton's work.[4] Those cadets who wished to extend their studies could not do so because the library was as superficial as the courses. Despite Williams' pleas, the War Department refused to purchase new scientific books because, it said, so many changes in scientific thought were occurring that none could be sufficiently up to date to be useful.[5]

Still, some work was done. In the summer of 1802 Williams had the cadets survey the area around West Point. By the use of a series of triangles they found that Crow's Nest summit was 1,480 feet above the Plain, the Break Neck 1,500, Anthony's Nose 900, the Sugar Loaf 700, and Fort Putnam 400 and that the Plain itself was 190 feet above the Hudson.[6]

There being no regular schedule, cadets could take examinations for graduation whenever they and their instructors felt they were ready. On September 1, 1802, Swift, who had been at West

[4] Swift, *Memoirs,* 32; Barnard, *Military Schools,* 735; *CWP,* I, 276.
[5] *DAB,* XX, 281.
[6] Swift, *Memoirs,* 35.

Point less than a year, and Cadet Simon M. Levy took the first public examination held at the Academy. Williams, Barron, and Mansfield questioned them on Hutton, Enfield, Vauban, and de Scheel. Both cadets graduated and received commissions, and both stayed on at West Point as members of the garrison. The next year, when Francis de Masson came to teach French and topographical drawing, they attended his classes. Professor de Masson, an emigrant from Santo Domingo who had lost his plantation in the slave revolt there, began what would become one of West Point's strongest departments, giving the cadets a grounding in the language of science and military art. He did not do as well in his other subject, as the drawing class progressed only to plain right-line drawing.[7]

Superintendent Williams was the ranking officer on the post, but he found he had little power. The line officers in the garrison refused to obey his orders on the grounds that he could only command his fellow engineers. Williams appealed to the War Department; in an effort to avoid direct encounter with the problem the Department ordered the non-engineering officers of the garrison to Norfolk, Virginia. This left only 44 army personnel at West Point, 32 engineers and cadets, Professor de Masson, 2 artillery sergeants, 8 artillery privates, and a surgeon's mate. The men in the Artillery Corps were willing to accept Williams' authority, but the principle remained at issue. Most of the engineers had previously held commissions in other branches and had been selected for the Corps of Engineers because of their superior abilities and wider experience. They resented any attempt to deprive them of their former prerogatives and contended that when artillery, infantry, and engineering troops were serving together the ranking officer should command. President Jefferson, however, upheld a War Department ruling that engineers could not command troops of other corps because, he said, the engineers were engaged in scientific pursuits and did not have time for ordinary army matters. Williams, who had recently received a promotion to lieutenant colonel, had only the cadets, a few engi-

7 *Ibid.*, 36–40.

neers, and his faculty to command. So frustrated was he that on
June 20, 1803, he resigned.[8]

His successor as head of the Corps of Engineers and the Academy was Colonel Decius Wadsworth. The new Superintendent
made a feeble attempt to bring some system to the school. He
"hoped" that the "Gentlemen Cadets" would "eagerly embrace
and improve the opportunity which is offered them of making
such advances in Military sciences as may qualify them to discharge with applause the duties of the several stations to which
they may be called." Wadsworth ordered punctual attendance of
both the officers and the cadets at classes. Barron would teach
mathematics in the mornings, while de Masson would instruct in
French and drawing on alternate afternoons. Mansfield would also
teach in the afternoons. Further, Wadsworth decided to hold a
parade and roll call in front of the Academy at nine each morning,
which "all the officers, cadets and privates of the Corps of Engineers (except the French instructor and the waiters) will be pleased
to attend."[9]

The officers refused to attend the parades, and Wadsworth, who
found he could do nothing about it, grew discouraged in his turn.
"I find myself to be wasting the best of my days in the service of
my country which professes to make no provision for the gray-
headed soldier," he told Williams. "I gain nothing but a bare
livelihood, and I feel willing that some one should take my place."
The engineers, meanwhile, wanted Williams back. One member
of the Corps wrote him in October, 1804, "Never was West Point
so much in want of you as at this moment. Everything is going to
ruin. Morals and knowledge thrive little and courts-martial and
flogging prevail." The War Department also wanted him to return
and was doing what it could to remove the "delicacies on both
sides." Then Wadsworth, in February, 1805, after he had been
"buried alive in snow at West Point" all winter, received orders to

[8] Dearborn to Williams, July 5, 1802, Henry Dearborn Papers, USMA
Library; Jacobs, *Beginning U. S. Army,* 304–5.

[9] Wadsworth order of July 20, 1804, Misc. Mss., USMA Library.

spend the summer in New Orleans. He immediately resigned.[10] The Academy was without a Superintendent, and Jefferson joined the War Department in urging Williams to return. After receiving some concessions as to his rights and status, Williams did.

As soon as he returned to West Point, Williams revived an organization he had founded earlier, a scientific society that drew on the secular learned societies of the past, such as the Academia Secretorum Naturae, for its inspiration. In the English-speaking world, the most important of these societies was the Royal Society of London, organized in the middle of the seventeenth century. The Royal Society met weekly to discuss such subjects as physics, anatomy, geometry, astronomy, navigation, and natural history. A number of Americans belonged to the Royal Society, for although colonial Americans did not think science properly belonged in a college curriculum, they were not opposed to the subject as such when its purpose was to reveal God's wondrous universe. They also organized their own societies. The first, the American Philosophical Society, was one of Benjamin Franklin's many children. He organized it in Philadelphia in 1743 and attended meetings where members discussed questions of natural philosophy, moral science, history, and politics and carried on investigations in botany, medicine, mineralogy, mechanics, chemistry, mathematics, and agriculture. In short, like Franklin, the Society was interested in all fields of knowledge.

The same was true of the American Academy of Arts and Sciences, which John Adams began in Boston in 1780. As with the American Philosophical Society, the Boston Academy was most concerned with applied science; in its articles of incorporation the members set forth as one of its objects, "to determine the uses to which the various natural productions of the country may be applied [and] to cultivate every art and science which may tend to advance the interest, honor, dignity and happiness of a free,

---

[10] Wadsworth to Williams, August 12, 1803, *ibid.;* Major E. A. Denton, "The Formative Years of the United States Military Academy," unpublished Ph.D. dissertation, Syracuse University, 1963, pp. 40–43.

independent, and virtuous people."[11] Thus the vacuum created by the classics-oriented colleges, which offered at best an occasional course in natural science, was filled by voluntary organizations. It was in this spirit and tradition that Superintendent Williams, who had been vice-president of the American Philosophical Society, had established a scientific society at West Point.

In November, 1802, when the cadets went home on vacation for the winter months, Williams had organized the officers of the garrison into the United States Military Philosophical Society. He revived the organization when he returned in 1805. Williams made the engineers and cadets members of the Society by right and allowed civilians to join upon application and election. He hoped it would become the major scientific society in the country, a place where Americans could absorb the scientific knowledge previously considered the exclusive reserve of the Europeans and add to it from the unique American experience. "The theories of Europe are undoubtedly the basis of a military education," he thought, "but the practice of our own warriors in our own country, the experience and observation of men, who have had local circumstances in view, are far more essential." The Society's special emphasis would be on military affairs, but, true to the spirit of the age, it would not consider military science to be divorced from general knowledge, and its orientation would be broad. Specifically, Williams wanted the Society to supplement the Academy or, considering the sad state the Academy was in, replace it. The Society could meet the general purpose of the Academy of preparation of the militia for war through the dissemination of military science throughout the country and the advancement of applied science. The bulk of the Society membership was civilian.

The Society held meetings twice a month in a classroom at West Point. Williams read papers describing observations of a solar eclipse, the construction of a floating battery, and experiments on the proper length of a musket barrel. Professor Barron described the Falls of the Ohio at Louisville. The Society examined some French hand-guns, decided that a piece loaded at the breach was

[11] Ralph S. Bates, *Scientific Societies in the United States* (Boston, 1945), 1–10.

superior to the muzzle-loading musket, and recommended its adoption by the United States Army. Lieutenant Alden Partridge, who in 1807 became an assistant to the mathematics professor, presented the results of some meteorological observations, as well as experiments in artillery fire. One of his tests determined the time in which a field piece could be loaded and fired, another the time in which ball cartridges could be fired. Professor de Masson, who was involved in an ambitious program of translating into English all European knowledge of engineering, lectured to the Society on his project. In 1807 Ferdinand R. Hassler, a Swiss, replaced Barron as professor of mathematics. He brought with him a valuable collection of European standards of weights and lengths, including a standard meter bar only recently made in France. He outlined for the Society the need for a coastal survey of the United States, and in 1810 Hassler resigned his West Point position to become the first superintendent of the United States Coast Survey, where he used the meter bar as the unit of length.

The Society did more than listen to lectures. It became the semi-official archives for the Corps of Engineers, receiving the General Return of Fortifications for the United States. The Society's library contained the finest collection of technical works in the country, the core being Williams' private collection, much of which he had inherited from Benjamin Franklin. The library also held the only known copy in America of Montalembert's ten-volume work. When he was minister to France, General John Armstrong presented to the Society Baron Henri Jomini's *Traite de Grand Tactique*. Bacon, Newton, Marshal Saxe, Vignola, Villeneuve, and others were represented. The manuscript collection included eight volumes of General Anthony Wayne's orders issued during his Indian campaign.

Under Williams' direction, the Society prospered. The membership expanded, and when meetings were held outside West Point, it became the first peripatetic society. When the Society met in New York City, Mayor DeWitt Clinton provided the city hall and himself attended the session. In Washington, the Society met in the War Office. Members included Thomas Jefferson, James Madison, John Quincy Adams, James Monroe, John Marshall, Thomas

Chusing, Benjamin Latrobe, Charles Cotesworth Pinckney (who was the Society's vice-president), Robert Fulton, Eli Whitney, and Bushrod Washington. By 1807 the United States Military Philosophical Society was a center of scientific activity in America.[12]

But the Society was the only institution prospering at West Point. Williams devoted little time to the Academy. When he was not doing the work of the Society, he was usually absent from West Point on visits of inspection of the fortifications on the East Coast, as a part of his duties as head of the Corps of Engineers. In his absence Professor Barron served as Superintendent. Instruction remained superficial, and faculty personnel changed frequently—the mathematics teacher changed five times in ten years. The first to go was Barron. In 1807 the Superintendent charged him with "suffering prostitutes to be the companions of his quarters and table—(testimony does not look into the chamber), thereby setting an example injurious to the morals of the youth and disgraceful to the institution." Given a choice between resignation or standing trial, Barron resigned. Jared Mansfield, professor of natural philosophy, was lost to the Academy when Jefferson made him surveyor-general of the northwest territory. Williams and Swift found it impossible to set up a definite course of study because the only entrance requirement was that a cadet had to be male. Some came to West Point with college degrees and left the Academy with their commissions after six months; others had barely emerged from reading and writing classes and remained six years or more. Even after that length of time, they had no assurance of a commission; for that, they needed both the approval of the Superintendent and the existence of a vacancy in the army.[13]

In March, 1808, Colonel Williams explained to Secretary of War Henry Dearborn the Academy's difficulties. The greatest was

---

[12] *Ibid.*, 42; Jacobs, *Beginning U. S. Army*, 303–4; Sidney Forman, "The United States Military Philosophical Society, 1802–1813," *William and Mary Quarterly*, 3rd series, II (July, 1945), 273–85; *Extracts from the Minutes of the United States Military Philosophical Society*, pamphlet in the Library of Congress; Richard S. Kirby and Philip G. Laurson, *The Early Years of Modern Civil Engineering* (New Haven, 1932), 7–8.

[13] Jacobs, *Beginning U. S. Army*, 306; Swift, *Memoirs*, 67; Denton, "Formative Years," 54.

that officers in the Corps of Engineers were required to build America's seacoast fortifications and at the same time "constitute a military academy." They could not do both, unless the Corps, consisting of sixteen officers, were increased in size. Another problem was that nobody was responsible for the institution. The President had no direct authority over it, and Congress, supposedly the governing body, contented itself with passing vague laws from time to time. Williams recommended that the Academy be placed under the definite authority of the President and that it be moved to Washington, an idea which Jefferson endorsed and which he was often on the verge of recommending to Congress. Williams also wanted the faculty to be given definite rank, pay, and allowances and to be made permanent, and he asked for buildings, scientific apparatus, and a library.

Williams' point about moving the Academy to Washington was well taken. Both physically and intellectually West Point was so isolated it might as well have been in the remote corners of Canada. Only a few poor post roads ran near the Academy, and although the Hudson River provided a convenient means of transportation during the summer, the tiny dock at West Point could only handle the smallest of ships. Teachers, engineers, and cadets, shut up in their ramshackle quarters for many months of the year, with no news of the outside world to relieve the monotony, passed the time by constant bickering. They often reached a point in which no one spoke to anyone else. As Williams remarked in 1805 about one of his professors, "Barron loves solitude and at West Point he must this winter have enjoyed it in supreme degree."

Meanwhile, the nation had forgotten its Academy. The generation that founded the institution was gone. The men now leading the United States had not been military leaders during the Revolutionary War and had never come in contact with the Steubens, the Kosciuskos, and the French officers who had so impressed Knox, Washington, and Hamilton. There had been threats, war scares, and battles with Indians, but since the turn of the century the United States had not had to face any of the European powers. The sense of urgency that the veterans of the Revolutionary War had felt when they established the Academy was gone. In its place

[33]

there was confusion, or worse, indifference. Congress had lost sight of the educational and military purposes of the Academy and was only concerned with its cost; within the army hard-bitten infantry and cavalry officers scoffed at the engineers and their puny institution. At the Academy itself no one could agree on what to do. Wadsworth had emphasized military education but had a vague idea that he wanted to retain some educational features. Williams wanted to emphasize science while retaining some military features. As one engineer officer put it, "The Military Academy, instead of being the seat of knowledge and the place of application, is fast turning into that of ignorance and idleness." [14]

Perhaps, Williams thought, some meaning could be restored to the Academy if it brought itself to the attention of the government. After moving the Academy to Washington, he would increase the number of cadets and turn the Academy into a national scientific institution, somewhat along the lines of the Military Philosophical Society. He would welcome to it any young man who wanted a scientific education. Upon completion of his studies, the cadet could take a commission in the army or the navy, or none at all. In the latter case, the graduates could become officers in the militia. "There is nothing more fascinating to youth than excellence in arms," Williams said, "and a little knowledge will create a desire to acquire more." After a few years of such a program, the army, the navy, and the militia would all have professional military men to lead them. In contrast with this plan, Williams summed up the current state of affairs: "The military academy, as it now stands, is like a foundling, barely existing among the mountains, and nurtured at a distance out of sight, and almost unknown to its legitimate parents." [15]

Dearborn referred Williams' report to Congress, which created a committee to recommend changes in the law. The fate of the Academy immediately became a political issue. Most Republicans were opposed to the school because Williams was a Federalist,

[14] Denton, "Formative Years," 43, 54.
[15] *American State Papers: Military Affairs,* I, 229; for the removal of the Academy to Washington, see Secretary of War to Williams, January 13, 1803, E. S. H. Archives.

while southerners wanted a school of their own in the South. Politicians generally were hostile because they wanted to have the exclusive right to grant commissions. President Jefferson did not help matters when, in recommending Williams' report to Congress, he pointed out that "as these youths grow up and take their stations in society, they will naturally become militia officers and in a few years, in the ordinary course of events, we should see a uniformity in our militia, resulting from a spirit of emulation, which the reputation of having received a military education would naturally excite." From the congressional point of view, all that meant was fewer militia commissions the political parties could use as patronage—a practice that would plague West Point until well into the twentieth century. The rise of organized political parties, with their insatiable appetite for rewards for the faithful, stood in the way of a large, efficient academy. The result was that Congress ignored almost all of Williams' proposals, although on April 12, 1808, it did raise the number of cadets to 156. The increase was less a result of Williams' report, however, than it was a response to America's growing troubles with France and England.[16]

In any case, the increase was only theoretical. James Madison's Secretary of War, William Eustis, had no use for professional soldiers and did nothing to encourage the appointment of new cadets. Consequently, in 1810, there were still only forty-seven cadets at West Point, three less than the total authorized in 1802.[17] Eustis did issue regulations on entrance, regulations which would remain in effect for most of the century. After April 30, 1810, no cadet would be admitted who was under fifteen years of age or over twenty. The candidate for admission must be in good health and well versed in the English language, in writing, and in arithmetic. Williams was delighted, but then Eustis softened the joy when he ordered the Superintendent to assign cadets who had completed "their Academical education" to infantry and artillery companies, where they could perform the "Duty as Soldiers in the

[16] Boynton, *West Point,* 197; *American State Papers: Military Affairs,* VII, 1–107.

[17] *American State Papers: Military Affairs,* I, 248.

Lines" and become "Candidates for promotion to Commissions." Williams protested that such an action would be highly unfair to the cadets, who expected commissions upon graduation, and persuaded Eustis to drop the order. Eustis finally agreed to give cadets who had completed the course preference for commissions for vacancies in the army. In effect, this meant that cadets could now count on an army career. In all other areas, however, Eustis, like Congress, ignored Williams' suggestions. Most important, the Secretary of War appointed no new cadets.[18]

In December, 1810, the President tried to get some action out of Congress. Madison asked for money to provide more professorships and a better library at West Point and possibly to establish another academy. In justification, he reminded Congress of the importance of scientific operations in modern war, then recalled one of the original purposes for the founding of the Academy. Trained officers made for the cheapest public defense, he said, and "In a country, happily without the opportunities [for practice in war], seminaries where the elementary principles of the art of war can be taught without actual war, and without the expense of extensive and standing armies, have the precious advantage of uniting an essential preparation against external dangers, with a scrupulous regard to internal safety."[19]

Congress did nothing, and the Academy continued to flounder. An order from the Secretary of War to Mansfield in 1810 illustrated the problems the War Department and the Superintendent faced. Eustis pointed out to Mansfield that the need for instructors at West Point and the importance of the Academy to the public interest required the services of all officers in the Corps of Engineers at the post. He therefore ordered Mansfield to settle his affairs in the northwest territory and return to West Point. "But should a compliance with this order be incompatible with your views," Eustis was forced to continue, "you will perceive the neces-

[18] Eustis Regulations of April 30, 1810, Misc. Mss., USMA Library; White, *Jeffersonians,* 253; Eustis to Williams, May 18, 1810 and June 5, 1811, E. S. H. Archives.

[19] *American State Papers: Military Affairs,* V, 349.

sity of relinquishing your commission in the Corps for the purpose of enabling the Executive to avail itself of some other person."[20]

In 1812 war came, and Williams asked for command of Castle Williams on Governor's Island in New York Harbor, which he had built. The War Department refused to give him the position, and for the second time he resigned from the army in a fit of rage. The other engineers went to posts throughout the country, leaving the Academy without a staff. There were few cadets anyway. In November, 1813, with Williams gone and the members scattered, the United States Military Philosophical Society held a skeleton meeting at Washington Hall in New York City and voted to disband.[21]

[20] Secretary of War to Mansfield, January 4, 1810, E. S. H. Archives.
[21] Forman, "Military Philosophical Society," 283.

Chapter III

Alden Partridge

In the hectic months before the declaration of war against Great Britain, Congress desperately tried to create a strong army. Wanting one that could seize Canada and defend the eastern seaboard, it instructed President James Madison to add thirteen regiments to the Regular Army, raising it to twenty-four in all, to accept 30,000 volunteers in the service of the nation, and to require the state governors to hold in readiness 80,000 militia. To supply the troops, Congress created the Quartermaster's, Commissary, and Ordnance Departments. If Madison could find recruits for the Regular Army and enough volunteers and if the governors met their obligations, the United States would enter the war with more than 145,000 soldiers. To supply the officers to lead this huge aggregation, the United States Military Academy had graduated a total of seventy-one cadets.[1]

By 1812 it was too late to rectify the situation for the imminent war, but obviously Congress would either have to make some changes at West Point or else resign itself to appointing civilians to the officer corps, not only in this but in all future wars. Suddenly aware of the inadequacy, indeed the failure, of the Academy, Congress turned its attention away from preparations for war long

[1] Emory Upton, *The Military Policy of the United States* (Washington, 1902), 91–93.

enough to provide a new base for the institution. On April 29, 1812, it passed a bill reorganizing the Academy. To Emory Upton, the first serious student of American military policy, the law was, "next to the [one] which created the Military Academy . . . the most important in its history."

The immediate need was for a permanent and enlarged faculty. Congress provided for a professorship of natural and experimental philosophy, a professorship of mathematics, and a professorship of engineering. Together with the teachers of drawing and French and the Corps of Engineers, the professors constituted the Military Academy. The law required that each cadet "receive a regular degree from an academical staff," a provision that served as the basis for the formation of the Academic Board, made up of the permanent professors and presided over by the Superintendent. The Board supervised the academic program, examined the cadets, and made recommendations for degrees and commissions.

Congress also provided for more graduates by increasing the number of cadets to 250. It reaffirmed Eustis' entrance requirements: candidates had to be between the ages of fourteen and twenty-one and "well versed" in reading, writing, and arithmetic. These requirements were laughably below those of the American colleges, whose students had to be able to read Greek and Latin to enter, but that discrepancy merely emphasized the difference in aims between the Academy and the colleges. Cadets who met the requirements received warrants appointing them to the Academy under the Corps of Engineers. When they finished the course, they received a degree from the Academic Board and a commission in any corps for which the Board deemed them competent.

To introduce the cadets to the practical side of soldiering, Congress ordered the Superintendent to draw up regulations for the Academy and place the cadets under them. He should organize the cadets into companies, and for three months each year send them into an encampment, where they would be taught "all of the duties of a private, a noncommissioned officer, and officer."[2]

[2] *Ibid.*, 94; Barnard, *Military Schools*, 729; Sidney Forman, *West Point: A History of the United States Military Academy* (New York, 1950), 36–37.

Upon Williams' retirement, Colonel Swift gained a star and moved up to command of the Corps of Engineers and thus of the Academy. He quickly recruited faculty for the new posts authorized by Congress. Swift had first offered the post of professor of engineering to Pierre Charles L'Enfant, the planner of the District of Columbia. When he declined it, Lieutenant Alden Partridge, who had been serving since 1810 as acting professor of mathematics, became professor of engineering. Andrew Ellicott, who had been the astronomer of the United States, followed Partridge as professor of mathematics. Jared Mansfield, who had left West Point in 1803 to become surveyor-general of the northwest territory, returned to assume the professorship of natural and experimental philosophy.[3]

Despite these organizational advances, the war years at the Academy were chaotic. While the school tried to reshape itself under the terms of the bill, it had also to provide officers for the army, erect new buildings, and strengthen the academic program, all without the aid of the Chief Engineer, who was so busy with his duties that he hardly ever came to West Point. During his absences, Swift delegated his authority to the senior member of the Academic Board, Captain Partridge. Partridge was an energetic officer who tried to improve the Academy, but he had little to work with. For the tactical instruction of the cadets he had some 300 muskets, one 18-pound gun, one $10\frac{1}{2}$-inch mortar, and a $5\frac{1}{2}$-inch howitzer, but no artillery officers were present to give lessons. In 1814 there were 150 cadets at West Point, but the demands of the war were so pressing that as soon as a cadet absorbed a smattering of technical knowledge he went off to active service. The enlisted garrison, a company of bombardiers, sappers, and miners numbering 94 men, served as waiters and did fatigue duty until May, 1814, when it went north to join General Jacob Brown's army. The buildings were inadequate; Professor Mansfield taught in the parlor of his house, while Professor Ellicott and his assistant held classes simultaneously at either end of a small, dark room above the mess hall. In 1814 construction of

[3] *CWP*, I, 233–43, 261–64.

three buildings was begun, a refectory, a barracks, and a combination library, experimental laboratory, and lecture room. Finished in 1815, they were coldly functional, but they did establish the pattern of locating buildings on the southern edge of the Plain, leaving the northern part open for the parade ground.[4]

The caliber of classroom instruction was low, not because of the quality of the teachers—Mansfield and Ellicott were among the best men in the country in their fields and the others were competent—but because of the quality of the equipment. Ellicott's only text was Hutton's *Mathematics,* "a plain, simple, easily understood beginning book." Still, he impressed his pupils. One of them later remembered that Ellicott looked and acted "precisely like the old-fashioned school-master, of whom it was written,

> 'And still they gazed, and still the wonder grew,
>
> That one small head could carry all he knew.' "

Mansfield's apparatus, with which he was expected to teach what would later be called physics, consisted of a field transit and a clock.[5]

Alden Partridge's course in engineering was typical of the work going on at the Academy during the war. "The most common genius could complete it in one week," a disgusted cadet thought, and he asked, "Is it the intention of the government that the most essential science for an officer should be thus treated?"[6] Partridge had only two texts available, and although he made the cadets master both, that required little effort. As soon as Partridge thought a student knew the material, he would excuse him from attending classes and recommend him for a commission, which was usually granted, the need for officers being what it was. Most cadets could graduate in less than a year. Ordinarily Partridge

---

[4] Boynton, *West Point,* 213; Barnard, *Military Schools,* 734; Forman, *West Point,* 38; Secretary of War to Swift, April 13, 1813, E. S. H. Archives; David W. Gray, "The Architectural Development of West Point," Misc. Mss., USMA Library.

[5] *CWP,* I, 233–43, 261–64; Florian Cajori, *The Teaching and History of Mathematics in the United States* (Washington, 1890), 115; E. D. Mansfield, *Personal Memories* (Cincinnati, 1879), 65.

[6] Stubb to Perkins, September 8, 1815, in the Partridge Court-martial of 1816 record, Office of the Judge Advocate General, GCM-K3, National Archives. Hereafter cited as PC16.

would have, in one room, a few cadets just starting his course, a few half-way through, and a few about to finish.[7]

Partridge did draw upon his knowledge of military history to make one contribution that had a lasting influence on the curriculum. After covering a principle of engineering or a particular type of fortification, he would illustrate his point by turning to some notable campaign, perhaps in Napoleon's wars, where the technique had been used. Often this would launch him into a discussion of the campaign itself. In effect, he was soon giving a course that combined engineering with military history.[8] His successors as professor of engineering followed the same pattern, until eventually the department was designated the Department of Military Art and Engineering. Its course was the most popular at the Academy, for it introduced the cadets to the history of their chosen profession and gave them their only insight into strategy. Perhaps this aspect of Partridge's teaching was what Swift had in mind when he told the Secretary of War that Partridge "deserves much commendation for a systematic and zealous discharge of his duties."[9]

In 1815 the war ended, with American hopes for the conquest of Canada crushed. The Military Academy had failed to play a great role in the conflict. The only West Pointer to die in combat was Lieutenant Alexander J. Williams, the son of the former Superintendent, who fell on the ramparts of Fort Erie. Another graduate, William Partridge, Alden Partridge's brother, had been assigned to General William Hull's army at Detroit. When he heard that Hull was about to surrender his superior force, Partridge, so weak from a fever he could hardly stand, stumbled into Hull's quarters, broke his sword, and threw it at the feet of his timorous superior. Hull surrendered anyway, and Partridge died six weeks later, a prisoner.[10] One hundred four other

[7] Testimony of numerous cadets in the Partridge Court-martial of 1817 record, Office of the Judge Advocate General, GCM S-50, National Archives. Hereafter cited as PC17.

[8] Lt. McNeil testimony, PC17.

[9] Swift to Secretary of War, April 25, 1815, Joseph G. Swift Papers, USMA Library.

[10] Waugh, *West Point,* 54.

Academy-trained officers participated in the war, but none rose to high rank. Two young officers, Winfield Scott and Jacob Brown, did display courage and ability, excite the public's admiration, and emerge as heroes, but both had received their commissions directly as civilians.

But if West Point's performance in the war failed to make a great impression, that of the militia, and especially of its officers, was worse. In truth, except for the Battle of New Orleans, the militia conducted itself miserably. As after the Revolutionary War, American leaders suddenly became aware of the need for trained officers. In December, 1815, Madison tactfully but firmly told Congress: "If experience has shown in the recent splendid achievements of the militia the value of this resource for public defence, it has shown, also, the importance of . . . skill in the use of arms, and familiarity with the essential rules of discipline, which cannot be expected from" the present system. Congress was busily reducing the size of the Regular Army, which made the need for professional soldiers greater. Knowing that the few West-Point-trained officers available during the war had generally done better work than the untrained lieutenants whose commissions had been granted while they were still civilians, Madison urged Congress to enlarge the Academy and establish others in various sections of the Union. A bill was introduced in the House for the latter purpose but failed to come to a vote.[11]

Still, the President was impressed with the potential of the Academy. Even though its graduates had suffered under a haphazard training program in an insufficiently equipped and poorly administered institution, they had fought well, if not brilliantly. If the Academy were improved, they might be expected to do better in the next war. Madison took a step in the direction of improvement when in 1815 he provided that "A Permanent Superintendent shall be appointed to the Military Academy, who, under the direction of the Secretary of War, shall have exclusive control of the Institution and of those connected with it, and who will be held responsible for its conduct and progress; he will direct the

[11] Boynton, *West Point,* 200–1.

studies, field exercises, and other academic duties." Madison thereby recognized that Swift had been trying to do too much and that the man who actually ran the Academy in his absence needed the support of formal authority. The President was also recognizing the importance of the Academy, which would no longer be a forgotten branch of the Corps of Engineers but would now have a nearly independent existence. General Swift, the Chief of Engineers, became the Inspector of the Academy, standing in the chain of command between the Secretary of War and the Superintendent.[12]

The first officer to be chosen specifically for the position of Superintendent, and not as Chief Engineer first and head of the Academy incidentally, was Captain Alden Partridge. Thirty years old, Partridge had made a favorable impression on Colonel Williams and the faculty during his cadet days. After a year at West Point, he was given a commission as a first lieutenant of Engineers, one of the few cadets before the Civil War to receive a rank higher than the lowest commissioned grade. Williams kept him on at the Academy as a teacher of mathematics; later Partridge rose to professor of engineering.

Partridge had the body of a penguin and the head of a hawk, with sharp, pointed nose, square, jutting chin, and tightly set mouth. He strutted about the Academy grounds in a coat that was always buttoned and a cocked hat with a black silk cockade and yellow eagle on it, flashing his sword and sash. He was an austere man. His home and furniture were unostentatious, his associates limited to Academy personnel, his life marked by "strict propriety." No one ever saw him out of uniform, and it was commonly believed that he owned no civilian clothes. He was jealous, vain, and something of a busybody, but he was intelligent and remarkably energetic. He loved drill, both infantry and artillery, and had the cadets marching at every opportunity. Behind his back the cadets called him "Old Pewter."

But neither new laws, no matter how well-intentioned, nor a new Superintendent could make a successful academy. Money and a sense of purpose were needed. Congress could supply the first,

[12] *Ibid.*, 213–14; Monroe to Partridge, January 3, 1815, E. S. H. Archives.

and the Superintendent the second, but neither did. After the war and the Battle of New Orleans, Congress again lost interest in the Academy and forgot its responsibilities. At one point Swift saved the Academy from foreclosure only by obtaining a private loan of $65,000 at 7 per cent interest.[13] Partridge, meanwhile, was irritating all the officers on the post. He had a low opinion of his professors and the attached engineers and refused to delegate authority to them. He never asked for suggestions, refused to listen to recommendations, and insisted that all problems were his and made his solution final. In short, in the words of a cadet, "he did everything." Still, his dogmatism only hid the uncomfortable fact that he had no firm idea where the Academy should be heading. He wanted to act the role of a college president, directing a curriculum that was purely military and technical. But he had neither the scientific knowledge nor the imagination Williams possessed, and for him a military education seemed to consist of constant drill. Both Swift and the faculty favored a broader approach, which only made Partridge more determined to narrow the course. The result was a continuation of the same confusion that had made the program of the school an academic hodgepodge.

The faculty disliked and mistrusted Partridge as much as he did it. And, like him, it had a substantive complaint. The professors thought Partridge was making West Point too military, and at one point they asked the Secretary of War to add Latin and Greek to the curriculum to redress the balance. Swift had also been thinking along those lines and had suggested to Secretary of War Henry Armstrong that the Academy include courses in English and classical reading. Armstrong declared that "such books as Gibbon are luxuries of leisure, the mushrooms and truffles of literary sensualists," and refused. Professor Mansfield complained that he had come to the Academy thinking it would become the outstanding school in the country. He had given up an excellent position, one that was in fact a sinecure, only to find at West Point that the professors "have no rights or privileges, even in their own depart-

[13] Swift, *Memoirs,* 139–40.

ments." Partridge interfered in everything the faculty did, to an extent not allowed "even in the greatest of despotisms."[14]

Under Mansfield's guidance, the Academic Board proposed a complete change. It would establish two more academies, one at Washington and the other at Pittsburgh, with 150 cadets at each. These schools would concentrate on military matters, and the cadets there would be boys who wanted to make a career for themselves in the army. West Point, meanwhile, would become a national scientific university, with 250 students who would pay for their education and study history, astronomy, geography, natural history, botany, literature, chemistry, ethics, and natural philosophy. It would have no connection with the army and its students would not join the service upon graduation. The proposal was based on one Swift had made in 1814, when he had felt the time was ripe to add "the branches taught at the Universities to acquirements in Military Science," and to expand the Academy. Expansion was important, he believed, "as it does not appear that the United States have the constitutional power to establish either colleges or universities."[15] Outside the Academy staff, however, the proposal received little attention, partly because no one in the government could see any practical benefit to be derived from a school such as Swift and the Board proposed but mainly because everyone was getting a little tired of the bickering between the Superintendent and his faculty.

So the question of what the Academy ought to be remained unresolved. Meanwhile, Partridge at least was able to bring some semblance of order and discipline to the cadets' lives. He began his regime by issuing a series of regulations. Cadets would rise at 6:00 A.M., attend roll call, return to their rooms, sweep and air them, make the beds, arrange the furniture, and stand inspection. Breakfast would be at 7:00 A.M., with mathematics class beginning

[14] *American State Papers: Military Affairs*, I, 838; Denton, "Formative Years," 95; Mansfield to Monroe, June, 1817, National Archives, Record Group 77, Military Academy Papers, Office, Chief of Engineers. Hereafter cited as NARG77.

[15] The proposal, dated May, 1815, and signed by the Academic Staff, is in E. S. H. Archives; Swift's suggestion is summarized in Denton, "Formative Years," 112.

at 8 and lasting until 11. The French class would meet from 11 until dinner time at 1:00 P.M. From 2:00 to 4:00 P.M. the cadets would attend drawing and engineering classes, then drill until 5:00 P.M. After that they would study until sunset, when an evening parade would be held, to be followed by supper. Partridge emphasized that during the hours set aside for study every cadet was required to be in his room. He forbade gambling, swearing, scuffling, unnecessary noise, and "all immoral conduct" and warned the cadets that "neatness in dress is required." Cadets could not trade or purchase articles, wash in quarters, or leave the post on Sundays without the Superintendent's permission. He solemnly reminded the cadets that they were "by law liable to perform any duty that a soldier may be commanded to perform" and announced a rising scale of punishments, beginning with a private reprimand and ending with confinement or possible dismissal, for violations of the regulations.[16]

Partridge also set a standard of behavior for the mess hall. The cadets would march by files to and from their meals, maintaining the "utmost order and silence." "Perfect order" must be observed at the table, with no talking allowed. When the meal was finished, all would rise from the table at the command of the officer in charge, form files, and march out.[17] The menu itself was Partridge's:

Breakfast. Good Coffee with a sufficient quantity of Milk and Sugar; Fresh Bread & Butter, Smoked beef or ham or cold meat. Radishes & Cucumbers may be substituted occasionally for the relish of meat for breakfast in the season of them.

Dinner. Fresh Meat either Beef, Pork, Veal or Mutton well roasted, with good bread & Potatoes & two of the following kinds of vegetables: Beets, Onions, Turnips, Cabbage or Carrots . . . in their season dried Beans may be given, but not to exceed once in every six days; there shall always be proper sauce or gravy for the meat.

Supper. Tea of good quality with Milk & Sugar; fresh bread and butter.

[16] Regulations issued April 1, 1814, PC16.
[17] Regulations for commons, 1815, Alden Partridge Papers, USMA Library.

In addition, the steward should serve, once a week, pie for supper and a pudding for dinner.[18]

Partridge's minute supervision of the cadets did not make him a martinet. He saw his duties as comparable to those of the small college presidents, and like them he personally supervised every phase of the Academy's life. He ate in the mess hall with the cadets. On Sundays, he gave the sermon in chapel, after which he made announcements, reviewed the proceedings of the past week, and gave a short lecture on the progress of the school. He was often seen on the Plain drilling the cadets, and during study hours frequently he toured the barracks, looking into every room to make sure the cadets were working. At such times the alarm resounded, "Old Pewter coming!" and idle cadets scampered to their rooms, seized their books and slates, and frowned in concentration. He was fondest of artillery practice, and in winter he often ignored deep snow drifts and turned the cadets out to haul an 18-pounder over to the river, where they tried their skill at ricochet firing on the ice. He was a great talker, and while the cadets were practicing, he sometimes regaled them with stories of the usefulness of artillery fire in past campaigns and battles. Cadets looked forward to his battalion drills because he always made them interesting and instructive by forming his students into diminutive armies and re-enacting renowned battles. While the cadets maneuvered, he shouted out a lecture to them on "how fields were won."[19]

Partridge made a number of permanent improvements. By pointing out that music would improve cadet drill and raise morale, he induced the War Department to assign a band to West Point, and he designed red uniforms with yellow braid for the members. In 1815, hearing that a bookstore in Philadelphia had ninety copies of Tousard's *Artillerist* which the owner would sell

[18] Bill of Fare, May 13, 1816, NARG77.
[19] Partridge to Swift, September 27, 1815, Partridge Papers; George D. Ramsay, "Recollections of the United States Military Academy at West Point, 1814–1820," Misc. Mss., USMA Library. I have drawn heavily on these recollections for my understanding of Partridge. Parts of Ramsay's manuscript are printed in George W. Cullum, *Biographical Register of Officers and Graduates of the United States Military Academy* (New York, 1863), III, 612–32, but Cullum omitted all paragraphs praising Partridge.

at $10.00 a copy, or $6.00 a copy cheaper than the retail price, Partridge found the funds to purchase the volumes and make the text available to the cadets. He set up, at least on paper, the first requirements for graduation and a commission: in mathematics, each candidate had to be well versed in arithmetic, logarithms, elements of algebra, geometry, mensuration, planometry, surveying, artificers' work, and conic sections; in French, to pronounce the language "tolerably" and be able to translate; in tactics, to understand the manual exercise with the musket, the management of a field piece, and the evolutions of infantry and artillery.[20]

In his attempts to introduce some order and discipline Partridge received no help from the War Department; rather, it made his task more difficult. Supposedly, after the law of 1812 was passed, cadets were required to be over the age of fourteen and to pass an entrance examination, but Partridge soon found that the officials in Washington had no intention of limiting appointments to qualified boys. Thus from time to time a twelve-year-old would show up, and Partridge could not deny him admittance. Once a one-armed boy from Pennsylvania joined the Corps, and another cadet from the same state brought his wife along with him. He put her up at a nearby boarding house and visited her at night. The candidates came up to West Point as soon as they received their appointments, which might be any time of the year, and the War Department required Partridge to examine them immediately. The result was that not only did he have an age group ranging from twelve to twenty-five years old, but new cadets joined the Corps all the time. Under the circumstances, no semblance of regular course work could be maintained; Partridge was likely to find in the same class one cadet who knew arithmetic but nothing else, another who had progressed to geometry, and a college graduate ready for advanced surveying. Necessarily, he had to forego any group instruction and give each student individual attention.

[20] Ramsay, "Recollections"; Partridge to Swift, September 27, 1815, Partridge Papers; Regulations for commission, 1815, PC16; S. H. Lang to Partridge, July 18, 1815, Partridge Papers.

Both during and after the war Partridge was swamped with demands for officers from the various corps of the army. Despairing of meeting the calls and still maintaining a rigid system, Partridge recommended cadets for commissions without making them undergo the examination before the Academic Board, as required by law. Another problem was that he had no instructors to assist the professors with the more than two hundred cadets. He therefore sometimes asked the more advanced cadets to teach their less advanced brothers. As they received no pay or official recognition from the government for their services, Partridge rewarded them by recommending them for commissions.[21]

Nearly every cadet, or so it must have seemed to Partridge, brought with him to the Academy a letter from someone of importance in politics, enjoining the Superintendent to look after the boy and take good care of him. The Academy was gaining a certain degree of popularity not only because Partridge had made it an excellent place for a young man to learn some discipline and not only because it was free but because it did, after all, teach some engineering, which was more than most other colleges in the land were doing. The Secretary of State took a great interest in securing appointments and closely watched the progress of his protégés; the Secretary of War sent three of his sons to West Point; the Vice-President had a son there, as did the governor of Connecticut and the former governor of New York. The cadets promptly reported to their sponsors or fathers any infraction of their rights, especially Partridge's attempts at discipline, which elicited from these directions a barrage of letters to Partridge protesting his conduct.[22] Sometimes the cadets addressed Partridge personally. The company of bombardiers had returned to West Point at the end of the war, and the veterans soon took to making fun of the cadets. They threw exaggerated salutes or imitated the cadet's march, hooted and hollered, or fell down laughing when

[21] Partridge to Secretary of War, July 6, 1817, and Peters to Hitchcock, October 1, 1814, Ethan Allen Hitchcock Papers, Library of Congress; Morton to Partridge, July 22, 1815, Partridge Papers.

[22] William Simmons to Ellicott, August 17, 1815, PC16; Ramsay, "Recollections."

one of the beardless youths waiked by in his fancy martial uniform. In a petition, the cadets complained to Partridge: "The
soldiers here are insolent to us, insult us by actions and words.
The respect due to us as superiors is entirely obliterated."[23]

Partridge was determined to impose order, but withal he had
great sympathy for the cadets. "I have ever considered these
youths, nearly as my own family, almost as my own children," he
said, "and have endeavored to treat them accordingly; that measures of severity are sometimes necessary for the preservation of
order and discipline, amongst more than two hundred young men,
of the ages they generally are at this Institution, I believe every
one will be convinced who has the charge of them." He added,
"I presume cadets are sent to the Academy for the purpose of
acquiring a military education, and I would be neglecting my duty
if I did not by every reasonable means endeavor to impress upon
their minds in the strongest manner possible that their first duties
as soldiers are obedience, regularity of conduct, and strict attention to duty."[24]

The Superintendent's first step was to ask General Swift to
impress upon the War Department the importance of having new
cadets report at one time of the year and one time only. Swift
agreed, but the War Department after a short period of co-operation
soon drifted back to its former practice.[25] Next, on the grounds
that the cadets needed more time to study, that their health would
be injured, and that he could not maintain discipline under the
circumstances, Partridge took it upon himself to ignore the three-
month encampment required by the law of 1812.[26] He then
informed the cadets that they could not apply for leaves of absence
for the purpose of going to Newburgh to attend parties or balls,
nor could they accept invitations to such events anywhere, nor
could they hold dances at West Point. He pointed out that "every

[23] Petition, 1815, Partridge Papers.
[24] The statement could have been written by the president of Brown,
Dartmouth, Harvard, or any other college; all were trying to instill the same
virtues in their students. Partridge to court, April 9, 1816, PC16.
[25] Swift to Secretary of War, April 25, 1815, Swift Papers.
[26] Partridge to court, April 9, 1816, PC16.

Cadet will find as much as he can possibly attend to if he does his duty correctly, and makes the necessary progress in his Studies."[27]

As a teaching device and as a means of keeping order Partridge required the cadets to rotate duty as officer of the day among themselves; as a part of their responsibilities, they had to report their fellows for infractions of the rules. When a cadet did violate the regulations, Partridge would have a long talk with him, urging the boy to try harder. If the offense was repeated, Partridge's punishment was swift. His biggest problem was with the younger cadets, those between twelve and fifteen, who were incapable of studying for more than a few minutes at a time and could usually be found gathered in one room, telling stories and laughing. The Superintendent decided to separate them from the others and at the same time punish them. Some he had sit in isolation with their backs stiffly straight in front of the barracks; others he had straddle a gun carriage and study there. More serious offenders he "drummed around the Plain"; these cadets were marched at quick time up and down before the Corps. The extreme cases—cadets guilty of fighting, refusal to obey an order, attempting to burn down the barracks—Partridge confined to the "Black Hole," a cave in the ground about eight feet square with a wooden lid, which the cadets found "filthy and uncomfortable." He never left them there for more than one-half hour.[28]

The cadets, who generally venerated Partridge, sometimes objected to his punishments, on the grounds they were degrading. Others accused him of nepotism. The bombardier company was made up in large part of Partridge's Vermont neighbors, and its commander, Lieutenant John Wright, was his nephew. The Superintendent's uncle, Isaac Partridge, was the Academy steward and merchant, and cadets had to buy their personal items from him. Partridge gave all his relatives special privileges. One November, when the Academy was out of funds, a great snow storm blocked the roads and brought with it a bitter cold wave. He had

[27] Orders, February 23, 1815, Partridge Papers.
[28] Ramsay, "Recollections"; Partridge to court and testimony of Captain Douglas, General Swift, and R. Blean, PC16.

no wood on hand, so he set the bombardiers to cutting timber from the public lands. Later, when he had no money to pay them, he gave the soldiers permission to cut more wood and sell it for themselves on the open market. As for Isaac Partridge, he had a flock of sheep which he grazed on the Plain. The animals suffered from a disease known as the "rot," which gave them an unusually repulsive odor. When the steward served mutton in the mess hall, the cadets immediately rose from their seats and marched out of the room. "This muttonous manoeuvre was construed into mutinous by Capt. Partridge," a participant with a penchant for the bad phrase reported, and the Superintendent marched the cadets back into the mess hall. A compromise was reached, and the cadets ate bread, butter, and molasses that night. Thereafter, whenever a cadet found one of the sheep near the edge of the Plain, he nudged the animal closer to the cliff, and the flock was soon extinct.

Rumors began to spread at West Point that Partridge and his relatives were defrauding the government. The bombardiers, so it was said, were making small fortunes in the wood-cutting business, and the steward, Isaac Partridge, a large one in his catering pursuits. In February, 1816, General Swift and President Madison came to the Academy to investigate. Although the general did not entirely approve of Partridge's novel method of paying the bombardiers, he decided that on the whole the Superintendent "has discharged his duties honestly and to the best of his capacity." He pointed out that Isaac Partridge's appointment had been approved by both himself and the Secretary of War. The President was not impressed either by Partridge or his work, perhaps because he could not sympathize with the Superintendent's problems as Swift could, but he accepted the Chief Engineer's conclusions.[29]

One of the officers was not satisfied. Captain Samuel Perkins, the assistant quartermaster general at West Point, hated Partridge because he thought the Superintendent had blocked his advancement. Perkins had already begun slandering Partridge, whispering to all who would listen that the Superintendent, his brother, and

[29] Testimony of J. Morrison, I. Hoyt, J. D. Orr, and Perkins to Crawford, December 19, 1816, PC17.

[53]

General Swift were a "pack of damned Robbers" engaged in a gigantic speculation. He also drew up a petition damning Partridge and circulated it among the cadets. He told the boys he would guarantee its effect if they would sign it, but few did. Finally, he informed the Secretary of War that Partridge forced the cadets to buy their personal items from his uncle, whose prices were outrageous, and the soldiers to cut wood for him, which the steward did not need and which he sold on the New York market to his own profit. Further, the Superintendent allowed the steward to live on the public land.[30] It was these charges that Swift and Madison went to West Point to investigate. After they left, Perkins continued his agitation and finally got the Academic Board to sign a letter addressed to Swift, complaining in detail about Partridge's behavior. The faculty made some additions to Perkins' charges; the Superintendent, they said, allowed cadets to miss classes, ignored the requirement that graduation be preceded by an examination, tried to teach all classes himself, and never consulted the faculty on any decision.[31]

Hoping to clear the air, Swift called for a court of inquiry to investigate the entire situation. It met at West Point from March 16 until April 12, 1816. The president was Colonel Henry Atkinson, with Lieutenant Colonels James House and Joseph G. Totten and Captain John M. O'Connor as members. Before the court, most of the faculty said that Partridge's Superintendency had been at least adequate.[32] Cadets also appeared; one, John D. W. Orr, said he thought Partridge had played favorites with the cadets, especially in recommending commissions. Partridge, who handled his own defense, asked Orr: "Did I state publicly to the Cadets last summer, that I had my favorites among them, and that they consisted of all those Cadets who performed or were disposed to perform their duties correctly, and observe the regulations?" Orr admitted that he had. The Superintendent next had Orr tell the court of the cadets' reaction to his return to the Academy after a brief visit to Washington in the fall. "They expressed great joy," Orr

[30] *Ibid.*, Academic staff to Swift, n.d.
[31] *Ibid.*
[32] For example, see Ellicott testimony, PC16.

admitted, "by illuminating the Barracks and huzzaing."[33] Finally, Partridge showed the court a circular written by the Corps adjutant, Cadet Thomas Ragland and signed by 109 cadets. Partridge's "treatment towards us has ever been such as to cherish that independence of spirit which every American soldier should possess," the cadets said. The charges against him were made by "enemies to virtue, and such whose minds are too contracted to possess a principle of honor." Specifically, Captain Perkins had acted "in such a manner as to entitle him to our contempt which he sincerely has."[34]

The court found Partridge innocent on all counts, although it reproved him for certain actions. The Superintendent had no authority to allow soldiers to cut wood on the public lands; the "Black Hole" was too extreme a disciplinary measure; Partridge should have held the three-month encampment while trying to convince the President that it was too long (the court agreed that it was). Most of all, the court "pointedly disapproved" of Partridge's recommending cadets for commissions without giving them an examination. But, everything considered, the court found "it is clearly proven that Captain Partridge has been extremely attentive to and solicitous about the *Health, Morals and Improvement* of the Youths under his charge; and that in the correction of faults and offenses he has been *uniform, punctilious, Dispassionate and Forbearing.*" Finally, the court declared that Captain Perkins had encouraged discontent and even opposition to legal authority merely "to gratify personal animosities."[35]

Even while the court was sitting, the War Department was taking steps to improve the Academy. In March, 1816, William H. Crawford, Madison's Secretary of War, issued a new set of rules and regulations. Henceforth, there would be a general examination of all cadets twice a year in July and December. New cadets would enter in September only. A four-year course of study would be followed by each cadet, with no exceptions. First-year cadets would study English grammar, French, algebra, geometry, and

[33] Orr testimony, PC16.
[34] "Majority of Corps of Cadets" to Atkinson, April 7, 1816, PC16.
[35] Court decision, unanimous, PC16.

logarithms; in the second year, French, geometrical construction, mensuration, trigonometry, conic sections, and drawing; in the third year, natural and experimental philosophy, astronomy, and drawing; in the fourth, engineering, geography, history, and ethics. To report on the progress of the Academy and its cadets, Crawford created the Board of Visitors, to consist of "five gentlemen versed in military and other science" and chaired by the Superintendent. They would attend the examinations and, with the Academic Board, ask questions and send a report to the War Department on the state of the Academy. Crawford also ruled that under no circumstances would a cadet receive a commission without completing the course of studies and passing an examination. At the end of the four years and after the final examination, the Academic Board would rank the cadets in order of general merit; the cadet's position in the ranking would determine the corps to which he would be assigned.[36]

Other changes were being made. Two new stone barracks were going up to add to the physical plant.[37] Partridge also designed a new uniform, the color being "Cadet Gray," in honor of the extemporized gray uniforms Winfield Scott's regulars had worn in the Battle of Chippewa. The stockings were black silk; the shoe rose about the ankle joint; the pantaloons buttoned on the sides and were gray in winter and white jean in summer; the vest was single-breasted, gray, with yellow brass bullet buttons (it was white in summer); the coat was also a single-breasted gray, with three rows of eight yellow brass bullet buttons, a collar that rose to the tip of the ear, and buttoned cuffs. The high-pointed hat had a black silk cockade and yellow eagle; the sword was a cut-and-thrust, yellow-mounted, with a black grip in a frog belt of black morocco.[38]

But drills and ceremonies continued unabated. On New Year's Day, 1817, Partridge turned out the Corps to fire a twenty-four-gun

[36] *American State Papers: Military Affairs*, II, 77; Barnard, *Military Schools*, 733; Boynton, *West Point*, 214; Denton, "Formative Years," 101, says there is some doubt that this order was published.
[37] Dupuy, *Where They Have Trod*, 111–12.
[38] Swift, *Memoirs*, 151.

salute. Disaster struck when eighteen-year-old Vincent M. Lowe of New York was ramming home the powder and his gun fired prematurely. Lowe fell, unmarked but killed by the concussion. The funeral the next day was a dismal occasion. The Corps marched across the Plain ahead of a riderless horse that bore a pair of reversed boots in the stirrups, while a gusty snow storm blew, alternately concealing and exposing the party in its route.[39]

The old controversy between Partridge and his professors continued as well, and the Superintendent was convincing himself that the professors had formed a cabal against him. He knew that Swift was on their side and expected to be ousted from his command. In November, 1816, he made a statement to the "Gentlemen Cadets," saying that he would shortly be forced to leave them. "I should do an injustice to my own feelings were I to be entirely silent upon so interesting an occasion," he declared. Partridge assured the cadets of his constant solicitude for them, and asked them to ignore "attempts . . . made to impose upon your minds a belief that Capt. Partridge is a severe and unjust Commander, and in his conduct towards you actuated . . . by personal enmity and prejudice." He advised them to work hard, to be "gentlemanly in . . . deportment."[40]

Nothing happened, but Partridge's relations with his faculty continued to deteriorate. In the course of the following spring he still refused to ask the teachers' opinions, did not hold the required examinations, appointed cadet assistants to help teach courses without consulting the professors in charge, and made recommendations for commissions against their advice. Mansfield once again complained to the President, then James Monroe, and in June, 1817, Monroe came to West Point to investigate. He had hardly arrived when the faculty presented him with a sealed communication, signed by the entire Academic Board. It was an indictment of the existing regime, with all the old charges. Partridge, the professors said, substituted "drill & Mechanical maneu-

[39] *Ibid.*, 146–47.
[40] Partridge to cadets, November 24, 1816, NARG77.

vers" for a sound curriculum. They charged Partridge with making the Academy into a narrow military drill school.[41]

Because of their attitude, their complaints to outsiders, and the interference of the War Department in his work, Partridge felt persecuted. He saw himself as the only man capable of running the Academy, beset by associates who, for reasons of their own, were trying to sabotage all his work. As evidence of his ability, Partridge could point to the cadets, most of whom thought he was an excellent teacher, a fair and just administrator, and most of all obviously devoted to them. But when Monroe read the Academic Board's charges against Partridge he ignored this other view and flew into a rage. He told Swift, who accompanied him on the inspection, that Partridge must be court-martialed and a new Superintendent found. Swift talked to Partridge, telling him he could either choose any duty he wanted or take a leave until the court could be convened. Partridge decided to go on leave. The President and the Chief Engineer then left, to prepare for the change and to inspect the fortifications on the East Coast.[42]

By now the whole affair was taking on all the elements of a badly written farce. After his superiors had departed Partridge went into a rage of his own. Certain that his rights had been violated, that his beloved Academy was to be taken from him, and that all his work to be set aside, he put the blame on the faculty. He refused to go on leave, arrested every professor on the post for participating in a cabal, and proceeded to teach all the courses himself.

Meanwhile, Monroe had decided on the new Superintendent, and on July 17 Swift told Captain Sylvanus Thayer (who held the brevet rank of major) to proceed to West Point to take charge.[43] When, later in the month, Thayer journeyed to West Point and walked up the hill onto the Plain, Captain Partridge, who was his senior in the Corps of Engineers, met him. "You are reporting to me, Brevet Major Thayer?" Partridge asked. Thayer silently took a letter from his coat and handed it to Partridge. It was from

[41] Academic Board to Monroe, June, 1817, NARG77.
[42] Swift, *Memoirs*, 153–58; Dupuy, *Where They Have Trod*, 118.
[43] Dupuy, *Where They Have Trod*, 119–20.

Swift to Partridge: "On receipt of this you will deliver to Major Sylvanus Thayer, U. S. Engineers, the command of the Post of West Point and the superintendence of the Military Academy."[44] Partridge read it, then stomped off. He left West Point the next day.

Thayer set about investigating the situation. He held a court of inquiry for the arrested professors, found them innocent, and had them released. He ordered all vacationing cadets to return to the Academy by September 1, and he received from acting Secretary of War George Graham the strongest possible support. "As Superintendent of the Military Academy you are amenable to, and subject only to, the orders of the President, thro' this department," Graham told him. "I flatter myself," he added, "that under your auspices, those feuds and dissentions which have so materially injured the institution, and harassed the government, will cease; and that the Military Academy will be brought to a degree of perfection corresponding with the views of the government, and the expectations of the public. . . ."[45]

The Secretary's hopes were too easy, for neither Partridge nor the cadets were willing to submit. It was an age in which men, *young* men included, had a keen sense of their rights. When a college president announced new regulations governing student life, if the students did not approve, he might expect a protest on the lawn outside his house. Similarly, a junior army officer being court-martialed for insulting a superior was apt in court to distinguish nothing wrong in his having called his superior a scoundrel and perhaps a poltroon. Even senior officers protested strenuously when their quarters did not reflect their positions, or whenever they felt they had otherwise been slighted by the War Department. This was the atmosphere when Thayer replaced his senior in rank in the Corps of Engineers, a man who was in addition loved by most of the cadets.

Thayer had been at West Point only six weeks when, on August 29, 1817, Partridge returned. Several cadets who were waiting idly by the landing when he arrived rushed up to shake

[44] *Ibid.,* 122–24.
[45] *Ibid.,* 125; General Orders, 26 September, 1817, NARG77.

hands with him. They then escorted him up the hill, where more cadets were collected who, when they saw Partridge, threw their hats in the air and cheered. Partridge stayed with an old friend on the post that night, and the band gathered around and serenaded him. He had gone to Thayer during the day and asked to have his old quarters back, but Thayer had refused. The next morning Partridge walked over to Thayer's headquarters and again had his request for his quarters turned down. He returned an hour later and handed Thayer a communication: "Orders: Captain Partridge having returned to West Point in conformity with the provision of the Law establishing the Military Academy, taking upon himself for the present, the Command and Superintendence of the Institution as Senior Officer of Engineers present." He signed it, "A. Partridge, Capt. of Engineers, Comdg." He told Thayer he only wanted his quarters back and in any case would only hold the command until Swift, expected shortly, arrived. Thayer reported the mutiny to Swift by letter and left the post. He made no attempt to resist, because he was convinced the cadets would support Partridge.

The regime lasted but two days. Then Swift's aide-de-camp arrived, in company with Thayer. He took Partridge's sword from him and placed him under arrest. In the ensuing court-martial, presided over by General Winfield Scott, Partridge was found not guilty of eight charges which concerned his conduct as Superintendent but guilty of disobedience of orders and mutiny. The court ordered that he be cashiered but, "in consideration of the zeal and perseverance which the prisoner seems uniformly to have displayed in the discharge of his professional duties, up to the period of August last," recommended clemency. The President remitted the sentence and gave Partridge an opportunity to resign, which he did.[46]

By now Partridge was convinced that throughout the army there was a conspiracy against him. He had devoted himself to the Academy for a dozen years and had made many permanent improvements—now he found himself thrown out by men who

[46] See PC17, especially the testimony of Thayer and Davies.

were not even aware of the problems he had faced. But he would not allow the "efforts of . . . contemptible foes" to discourage him and set about to redress the wrong done him. He told the new Secretary of War, John C. Calhoun, that his trial had been unfair and demanded the arrest and trial of Thayer, so that justice to both parties and to the army could be done.[47] When Calhoun ignored him, he made a whole series of charges against Swift, accusing the Chief Engineer of having wasted the public funds, censured cadets without cause, and acted in an unmilitary manner by advising him to arrest the professors at West Point because of their cabal and then, the deed done, backing away and disclaiming any connection with it. In reply, Swift said he had advised Partridge to arrest the professors if he could prove the existence of a cabal, which he could not. Again, Calhoun paid no attention to the charges.[48]

On October 20, 1818, Partridge told Swift that he intended to form a "Literary, Scientific and Military Academy" which would soon replace West Point as the chief source of the nation's officers. It would surpass the Military Academy because it would not be subject to the control of men who "are ignorant of the first requirements both of military and every other Science." Referring to his trial and his treatment at the hands of the army, Partridge gave Swift fair warning: "I am now thirty three years of age, and should I live to be Seventy, this subject shall never within that time be abandoned unless justice be done."[49]

[47] Partridge to Calhoun, December 13, 1817, in E. Edwin Hemphill (ed.), *The Papers of John C. Calhoun* (Columbia, S. C., 1963), II, 14.

[48] Calhoun to Swift, April 11, and Swift to Partridge, May, and Partridge to Swift, March, 1818, all in Swift Papers.

[49] Partridge to Swift, October 20, 1818, Partridge Papers.

Chapter IV

Sylvanus Thayer

In the nineteenth century the most important single element in the life of any American college was its president. He dominated all. The success or failure of an institution depended directly upon him. He was the executive who administered the government, carried out the decisions of the trustees, and selected and guided the faculty. He prescribed the course of studies. He was the public relations director, responsible for the image of his college. He was the treasurer, either begging or borrowing the funds to keep the school open. He had charge of discipline, and with the aid of his faculty maintained order, drew up regulations, and punished offenders. He was the architect responsible for the physical development of the school. He was the spiritual counselor of the students entrusted to his care, concerned not only with the problems of the school as a whole but with the individual problems of the students.

The old-time American college presidents could and did do almost anything. At Dartmouth, Eleazar Wheelock put up the college building, two barns, and a malthouse, cleared over seventy acres, and raised crops of hay and corn in order to contribute to the support of his school. He was also a scholar who taught courses and a minister who preached on Sundays. Samuel Doak founded the first college west of the Alleghenies, became its president, and went east to buy a small library, which he loaded upon pack horses and carried five hundred miles to his college in the wilderness. At the University of North Carolina President Joseph Caldwell took nightly walks in order to catch students violating his rules. At Princeton John McLean chased offenders to their rooms and up trees. While praying in chapel at Miami, President Bishop always kept one eye open. If he saw a student causing a disturbance, he made a flying leap from the platform onto the back of the malcontent, pommeled him into submission, and then with great dignity walked back to the rostrum and resumed his prayers.[1]

At West Point the Superintendent served as the president, except that he did not teach a course and ordinarily did not have the pressing financial problems of his civilian colleagues. He found it even more difficult to get along with his board of trustees, the United States Congress, than the other presidents did with theirs. He could agree wholeheartedly with President Francis Wayland of Brown University, who said in 1829, "How can colleges prosper directed by men, very good men to be sure, but who know about every other thing except about education. The man who first devised the present mode of governing colleges in this country has done us more injury than Benedict Arnold."[2] For the rest, the Superintendent's problems were those of the presidents, and West Point would prosper or not according to the abilities of its ranking officer.

From 1817 to 1833 that man was Sylvanus Thayer. During that period it was he who shaped the Military Academy. The methods and techniques he introduced are, for the most part, in effect today, the course of studies he outlined is still essentially the same, his disciplinary measures are the basis of those in use today, while his aims and goals are those of the present West Point. He was the "Father of the Military Academy."

Sylvanus Thayer was born on June 9, 1785, in Braintree, Massachusetts, the fifth of seven children. The male members on both sides of his family had taken part in the Revolutionary War. His

[1] George T. Schmidt, *The Old Time College President* (New York, 1930), 11, 54–59, 92.
[2] Rudolph, *American College,* 172.

[63]

father, Nathaniel Thayer, was a farmer and part-time carpenter. Sylvanus received little formal schooling, but it was of a high order, and he learned easily. In 1803 his father was able to give him a little money which, along with what he could pick up in odd jobs, allowed him to enter Dartmouth College in Hanover, New Hampshire. At Dartmouth, Thayer stood at the top of his class and in his sophomore year made the Greek oration at commencement. He was a member of the "United Fraternity," one of Dartmouth's two debating societies. His closest friend, both at Dartmouth and in later life, was George Ticknor, who was to become one of Boston's outstanding citizens, a great educator at Harvard, where he introduced many new ideas, and a leading abolitionist. Thayer's tastes were military; since childhood he had been fascinated by the soldier's life, partly because of stories about the Revolutionary War he heard at home and partly because of his worship of Napoleon, whose campaigns he followed faithfully. Of all the student body at Dartmouth, Thayer was the only one to subscribe to the Washington *National Intelligencer;* he did so because "it contained the completest accounts he could get of the movements of Bonaparte." Already, Thayer knew Napoleon's Italian campaigns "by heart."

In 1807 Thayer graduated from Dartmouth, but he was not present to give the commencement address, as he had already gone off to West Point. General Benjamin Pierce, a family friend whose son, Franklin Pierce, would one day be President of the United States, had persuaded President Madison to give Thayer a cadet warrant. After four years at Dartmouth, Thayer found the studies at the Academy easy and received his commission in one year. He joined the Corps of Engineers and became an inspector of fortifications in New England. In 1810 he served as assistant professor of mathematics at West Point, and he compiled a creditable record in the War of 1812.[3]

Thayer was a careful observer of developments during the war, and he was convinced that the shoddy performance of the American army was a result of poor preparation. Officers had little or no

[3] Dupuy, *Where They Have Trod,* 9–19, 43.

training, maintained few standards, and knew nothing about European methods. The Military Academy, with its tiny faculty and smattering of books, could not correct the situation. The American army, Thayer felt, would have to swallow its pride and go to Europe to learn to make war.

Others agreed with Thayer. Chief of Engineers Swift and President Madison had already discussed the possibility of sending some young officers to France for study and to purchase European books on the art of war for the Academy. Thayer, who had a high reputation in the Engineering Corps, was one of those Swift suggested. Thayer may have known of this conversation—the idea of a European tour was widespread in the army—when he wrote Swift on March 23, 1815, requesting a "furlough to visit France for my professional improvement."[4] The advantages, he said, were obvious. Swift's answer was prompt and encouraging. Not only would Thayer go to Europe, accompanied by Lieutenant Colonel William McRee, one of the army's outstanding officers, but he would receive the brevet rank of major, make the trip in an official capacity at the government's expense, and most important, receive a $5,000 credit in order to purchase books, maps, and equipment for the Academy. His formal instructions from the Secretary of War arrived on April 20; he was to go to France "and prosecute enquiries and examination, calculated for your improvement in the military art. The military schools and work-shops, and arsenals, the canals and harbors, the fortifications, especially those for maritime defense, will claim your particular attention."[5]

By May 11 Thayer was in Boston, ready to sail on a navy squadron fitting out for the Mediterranean, where it would challenge the Algerine pirates. An altercation with the navy, however—the commander of the squadron refused to receive any orders from the Secretary of War, who had ordered him to transport Thayer and McRee—prevented his departure until June 10, aboard the *Congress*.[6] He arrived in Europe on July 12, shortly

[4] Thayer to Swift, March 23, 1815, in West Point Letters, USMA Library. Hereafter cited as WPL.

[5] Secretary of War to Thayer, April 20, 1815, E. S. H. Archives.

[6] Thayer to Swift, May 13, 1815, WPL.

after his hero had lost the Battle of Waterloo. A fervent Francophile, Thayer was incensed at what he saw in France, where the allied armies were lording it over the conquered populace. A professional soldier, he was even more upset because the military schools he wished to visit had been closed and he was not permitted to see French fortifications.[7] Still, the bookstores of Paris were open, and after a careful survey Thayer and McRee began making their purchases. They eventually obtained some one thousand volumes, many charts and maps, and a few models of fortifications, all for the Academy. These were the basis for the first real military library in the United States.[8]

Early in 1816 the École Polytechnique, the most famous scientific military school in the world, reopened, and Thayer and McRee were allowed to study its operation. They also met many of its graduates, one of whom would soon join the faculty at West Point. Later they were allowed to visit the artillery school of application at Metz, although they could not inspect its fortifications.

At the time Thayer was in Europe, his friend George Ticknor, along with Edward Everett and George Bancroft, were in Göttingen studying the pedagogical methods and academic standards there. They wanted to apply what they learned to Harvard University and, like Thayer and McRee, were purchasing books and other materials for the Harvard library.[9] The two groups came back to America with two entirely different notions. Ticknor, to the horror of most college teachers, was impressed with German liberalism, intellectual freedom, and the elective principle in curriculum organization, and with some success he applied these principles to Harvard. Thayer approved the French method of prescription and a heavily scientific course for prospective officers. In France prescription dominated not only military education but also the University of France, founded by Napoleon, where the state ministry of education laid down the entire course and com-

[7] Thayer to Swift, October 10, 1815, *ibid.*

[8] McRee to Swift, December 18, 1815, and Thayer to Swift, August 12, 1815, *ibid.*

[9] Morison, *Harvard*, 225, 266.

pelled attendance at lectures.[10] The difference in pedagogical views never affected the friendship of Thayer and Ticknor for each other, and both were impressed by the achievements of the other; nevertheless, it was of the greatest significance for the development of American education. After a long struggle most schools adopted a form of the German system created by Ticknor at Harvard, while West Point retained the one Thayer brought back from France.

In May, 1816, Thayer returned to the United States. The next month President Madison visited West Point and decided to remove Partridge as soon as possible. He considered either Thayer or McRee the logical successor and decided upon Thayer because, although he was junior to McRee, he had done the major share of their work in France. The next year the change was completed, and after Partridge's attempted mutiny was put down, Thayer was entrenched as West Point's fifth Superintendent.

Thayer's greatest contribution to the Academy was the system he created, but he was able to introduce that system only through the strength of his own character. The impression he made upon cadets, the faculty, congressmen, and the public generally gave him the trust and support he needed in order to inaugurate his reforms. His personal appearance was majestic. Although he was thin, of medium height, and had soft features, he carried himself with such dignity and dressed with such care that he looked the ideal professional soldier. His habits added to the impression. He lived in solitude, except for an orderly, "with perfect neatness, order and comfort, in all his arrangements." His punctuality was unfailing and legendary. He arrived in his office on the stroke of the bell, at dinner parties at the exact hour of the invitation, at meetings at the precise moment of the calling to order. The annual June examinations of the cadets, a part of Thayer's system, were held before a group of distinguished civilians known as the Board of Visitors. They began at eight each morning. Thayer would

[10] C. Henry Wood, "The General Education Movement and the West Point Curriculum," D.Ed. dissertation, Teachers College, Columbia University, 1951, 28–29.

arrive at the examination room when the bugle sounded, take off his hat, and inquire if the president of the Board were ready. If he were, Thayer would conduct him to the examination with great ceremony; if he were not, Thayer went in without him. At the stroke of the one o'clock bell Thayer terminated the examination, often in the middle of a cadet's answer.[11]

Most men described Thayer with words like unbending, aloof, and even cold. Certainly he never showed a sense of humor and seldom relaxed. His contemporaries saw him as a single-minded, almost fanatic soldier. But the aura of pomp and dignity with which he surrounded himself was assumed; Sylvanus Thayer was basically a shy and humble man, fearful of contact with the world. The manner he assumed helped him avoid it. It also helped him create an impression which allowed him to institute the reforms at West Point in which he believed fervently.[12]

He never married; the Academy was his only love. For it he worked unceasingly. During the June examinations, which lasted for two weeks, he arose at 5:30 A.M., went to his office at 6:00, to breakfast at 7:00, to the examination at 8:00, to dinner at 1:00 P.M. where he entertained the Board of Visitors, back to the examinations at 3:00, and to parade at 7:00. From 7:30 until 8:00 he met with cadets who had business with him, and then from 8:00 until 11:00 with the faculty. Throughout the day he was always prompt, always courteous, and always looked as if he had just shaved, bathed, and dressed. During the regular session his schedule was only slightly less strenuous.[13]

Like all the good college presidents, Thayer made the cadets feel the strength of his intelligence, his character, and his discipline. One cadet commented that "his comprehensive mind embraced principles and details more strongly than any man I ever knew." Thayer, he continued, wanted to produce gentlemen

[11] E. D. Keyes, *Fifty Years' Observation of Men and Events* (New York, 1884), 191–92; George Ticknor, *Life, Letters, and Journals* (Boston, 1877), I, 373–75.

[12] W. A. Croffut (ed.), *Fifty Years in Camp and Field: The Diary of Major-General Ethan Allen Hitchcock* (New York, 1909), 49.

[13] Ticknor, *Life*, I, 375.

and soldiers, "and he illustrated in his own person the great object he sought to accomplish." The Superintendent made each one of the cadets feel "that his eye was ever on them, both in their rooms and abroad, both in their studies and on parade."[14]

Thayer not only knew every cadet by name but had a general idea of where each stood in his class and of how good, or poor, his behavior had been. What he did not know, he made sure was immediately available to him. The Superintendent received the cadets in the basement of his quarters, sitting behind a large desk which had deep pigeonholes invisible to the visitor on the other side. In the pigeonholes Thayer had his clerk paste weekly abstracts of debts, demerits, and grades. He would receive from the cadet the required written request or requisition, read it, glance at the abstract, then say, "Sir, you are in debt so much," giving the exact amount, "and will have to make do with the coat you have," or, "Sir, you have so many demerits, and cannot have a pass." The cadets swore the Superintendent had a most remarkable mind.

Thayer's discipline was stricter even than that imposed upon students of civil colleges, and it was administered impartially and without fail. Still, he refused to stoop to spying on his charges and was scrupulously honest. Once, when at a dinner party on the east bank of the Hudson, Thayer met a cadet who had illegally absented himself from quarters to attend. Thayer was courteous and formal with the boy and even ceremoniously exchanged toasts with him. After staying a polite but miserable hour, the cadet fled back to West Point, where he waited for a delinquency report which never came. His absence had not been noted by the officer regularly detailed to check the cadet quarters, and Thayer would not take advantage of the accidental meeting. Rather, the Superintendent's wrath fell on the officer who by his negligence had allowed the incident to occur.[15]

[14] George Woodbridge to Cullum, October 25, 1872, George Washington Cullum Papers, USMA Library.

[15] Dupuy, *Where They Have Trod*, 156–59. Dupuy's work is in large part a biography of Thayer and is much the best account of the man available. My understanding of Thayer is based heavily on Dupuy's study.

When Thayer came to the Academy, he had already given his reform program careful thought. He based it on his observations in France, but rather than break completely with the immediate past of the American institution he decided to consult the faculty about their proposals for change, especially since most of the members were holdovers from the Partridge era and thus particularly sensitive about Superintendents who acted on their own, without obtaining advice. Thayer's first action was to ask the faculty members to give him a detailed description of their courses. He wanted to know what textbooks were used, what books were needed, how much time was spent on a subject, how it was taught, and what suggestions for improvement the faculty might have. On the basis of these reports, and through individual and group conferences, he then began to lay out a four-year course.[16]

Meanwhile, most of the cadets were absent from West Point on an unlimited vacation; Thayer ordered them all back.[17] He then examined them and began ridding the post of "Uncle Sam's bad bargains," as local parlance had it, cadets who had been around for years without advancing beyond the first year's course of study. In all, he dismissed forty-three cadets, "most of whom are deficient in natural abilities and all are destitute of those qualities which would encourage a belief that they can ever advance."[18] Finding that the cadets were in the habit of running down to New York City, where they would sell their pay vouchers "in order to support their extravagance," Thayer made it illegal for them to leave the post except with his permission and prevented them from receiving any more vouchers.[19] He also forbade them to bring money with them to West Point or to receive any from home, so that all cadets, rich or poor, lived on the same income—the $18.00 a month the government paid them. Observing that many cadets were using the Academy merely to gain a free education by resigning their commissions immediately after graduation, Thayer

[16] Thayer to Academic Board, August 1, 1817, WPL.
[17] Thayer to Secretary of War, August 4, 1817, *ibid.*
[18] Thayer to Secretary of War, September 27, 1817, *ibid.* See also Academic Board to Thayer, September 28, 1817, NARG77.
[19] Thayer to Secretary of War, August 19, 1817, WPL.

made them all sign a pledge to serve at least one year in the army.[20] Troubled by the lack of discipline in the enlisted company of bombardiers, who behaved as if they were "composed of fugitives from justice and the refuse of society," Thayer replaced them with local men or married soldiers who were more responsible and sedate. In 1821 the company of bombardiers was disbanded, to be replaced by various companies of artillery.[21]

In order to introduce the cadets to the soldier's life and to keep a closer watch on them, Thayer abolished the practice of annual vacations and instituted a summer encampment, during which time the cadets lived in tents, participated in drill, and practiced tactical movements. Thereafter, only members of the Third Class would enjoy a summer furlough, which was the one time a cadet left the post during his four years at West Point.[22] The Superintendent also added to the cadets' practical training by forming them into two companies, each with its own officers and noncommissioned officers selected from the upper two classes. Thus, before graduation most cadets had an opportunity to serve as a corporal, sergeant, lieutenant, company adjutant, and company commander.

From the War Department, thoroughly frightened by the conditions that prevailed in Partridge's last year, Thayer received strong support. One of his great needs was a larger staff. Thayer requested, and received, a captain of infantry to act as instructor of tactics, a lieutenant of artillery to superintend the artillery drills, a quartermaster, and a subaltern to act as his personal aide. Finding that the French language was "imperfectly taught"—a notable lack since most of the books he had purchased for the library were in French and since the language "may be considered as the sole repository of Military science"—he obtained an assistant for the professor of French.[23]

Professor Mansfield, who had complained so bitterly about Partridge, reported to the Secretary of War in October, 1817, "all's well

[20] Macomb to Thayer, February 11, 1822, *ibid.*
[21] Forman, *West Point*, 47.
[22] "Early Discipline at the USMA," *JMSI*, 467.
[23] Thayer to Secretary of War, August 1 and 28, 1817, WPL.

in contrast to the old regime. Favoritism is now banished and the road opened for the advancement of Merit, whether it be found in the son of a beggar, or a King." When Partridge was Superintendent, Mansfield claimed, the cadets were "absolute dunces, little short of idiocy, and . . . deficient in moral qualities," but all that was now changed.

Mansfield soon changed his mind and was damning Thayer as energetically as he had Partridge. It was an ingrained habit with Mansfield; his wife once said of him, "it would be happy for me and for him if with his complaints he had lost the habit of complaining, but I fear it is an infirmity which time cannot remove. . . . If the present day is cloudless, the future is an inexhaustible source of misery; and a distempered fancy can select and combine . . . images of sorrow and suffering which would destroy the bliss of Eden."

In 1819 Mansfield informed the Secretary of War that "we need less military and more civilian influence here," and he hoped that the authority of the Superintendent would be lessened and that Congress would "at least put this Institution on a footing of Academies of despotic countries"; that is, would give the faculty more influence in decisions. Both Thayer and the Secretary ignored Mansfield, and the Superintendent retained his power.[24]

When he came to West Point one of the things that had shocked Thayer's systematic mind was the casual manner in which cadets reported for duty, attended classes, took examinations, and graduated. They could do any of these things at any time that seemed convenient to them. The fault was more the War Department's than it was Partridge's, and Thayer made it clear to the Secretary of War that he would not tolerate such practices. Under his rule, candidates reported before June 25, in time for the summer encampment, and at that time only. He set up two formal examinations, one in January and one in June, at which all cadets were tested; only after the June examination could any cadet graduate,

---

[24] Mansfield to Calhoun, December 30, 1819, NARG77; Denton, "Formative Years," 101; Lester A. Webb, *Captain Alden Partridge and the United States Military Academy* (Northport, Ala., 1965), 157–58.

and then the whole of the First, or senior, Class would go into the army. Or at least those who passed would.[25]

Thayer was horrified by the lack of system in recommending cadets for this or that corps of the Army. Whether a cadet went into the aristocratic engineers, the fiery cavalry, the respectable artillery, or the prosaic infantry depended entirely upon the whim of the Superintendent when he made his recommendation. His personal likes and dislikes therefore colored a man's entire career, for once in a certain arm it was almost impossible to get into any other. The Academy's first responsibility was to supply trained officers to the nation, but it also had a responsibility to place its charges in the proper positions. Neither responsibility could be met by an arbitrary system of recommendation. Thayer wanted a system whereby he could eliminate the subjective opinions of the professors and himself in making corps recommendations for the graduates, while still being able to retain control of placement within the army.

His solution was his most important contribution to the United States Military Academy. It remains the heart of the West Point system. It was the merit roll, a device which allowed Thayer to rank each cadet within his class, so that at the end of four years he could say that the cadet ranking second in his class should be an engineer, while the cadet ranking thirty-first ought to be in the infantry. The idea of ranking cadets had originated with the War Department during Partridge's Superintendency but had never been carried out. Thayer appropriated the idea and so constructed the merit roll that it eliminated practically all subjective feelings, while it took into account nearly everything a cadet did for four years, both in and out of the classroom. In truth, except for his one summer furlough in four years, there was no way a cadet could escape it. It was the most complete, and impersonal, system imaginable.

Every cadet was graded on every activity, in the classroom and on the drill field in a positive manner, and in every other way negatively. In his subjects, the cadet received marks ranging from

[25] Boynton, *West Point,* 222–23.

3.0 for perfect to 0.0 for complete failure; the more points he had, the higher he stood. But no matter how brilliant he was, his class rank could be low if his behavior was poor, because Thayer set up a system of demerits for each infraction of the regulations, and the demerits lowered a cadet's standing. Everything was weighed before the final roll was made up, with academic work counting most but not so heavily that the cadets could afford to ignore their demerits. Further, Thayer automatically dismissed anyone who received more than two hundred demerits in a single year. The new Superintendent continued the punishment tours that Partridge had used to maintain discipline, but his demerit system and merit roll proved much more effective in keeping order.[26] In the classroom, where except for illness attendance was absolutely required, each cadet was graded every day and ranked every week. He was also marked on his performance in the semi-annual examinations. Each subject was weighed in compiling a final academic standing, with mathematics counting most. At the end of each year the Superintendent and his Academic Board thus had a huge amount of data on which to base the final class rankings. Their personal opinions of this or that cadet mattered not at all; only his marks and demerits counted.

Thayer was determined that all cadets would be treated alike, and for him that even included the members of the Fourth, or freshman, Class, the plebes. During his term as Superintendent there was nothing like what would later be politely called "hazing," the deviling and harassment of new cadets. Later, when Thayer's graduates saw what was going on at West Point in this regard, when they saw plebes being berated, forced to do menial tasks, and driven from dawn to dusk, they bitterly denounced the practice. In my day, one said, anyone doing what is now done as a matter of course "would have been expelled from the corps" by his fellow cadets. For, he noted, under Thayer everyone

[26] As Cadet Ulysses S. Grant commented, "Any special excellence in study would be affected by the manner in which he tied his shoes." Lloyd Lewis, *Captain Sam Grant* (Boston, 1950), 75.

admitted to the Corps was regarded as a member of a brother-hood.[27]

This was the way Thayer wanted it. As one of his cadets remarked, "West Point constitutes the only society of human beings that I have known in which the standing of an individual is dependent wholly upon his own merits so far as they can be ascertained without extraneous influence." The poorest and humblest cadet stood equal to the richest and proudest. All sub-mitted to the same discipline, wore the same clothes, ate the same food, slept in the same rooms, studied in the same classes, and were graded by the same teachers in the same manner. "Birth, avarice, fashion and connections are without effect to determine promotion or punishment."[28] The cadets thoroughly believed this, and they seldom tried to get ahead through their influence, their person-ality, or tricks. In any case it did them little good to try, for it was true that Thayer's West Point was scrupulously fair.

Aside from eliminating favoritism, one of Thayer's aims was to encourage an active competition among the cadets. By making it clear to them that the higher they stood, the better the corps they could get into, he succeeded. He gave them an added incentive by persuading the Secretary of War to publish the names of the first five cadets in each class in the annual Army Register.[29]

Thayer had returned from France agreeing with Ticknor on one principle of education, the one principle on which Germans and Frenchmen also agreed. It was that students should be taught in small sections, divided according to ability. Thayer was deter-mined to introduce the system at West Point, with the additional requirement that every student recite in every class every day. This method could only be applied in small sections, and these in turn could be obtained only if more instructors were added to the staff. Thayer wanted a system which would free the professors from teaching altogether, allowing them to concentrate on direct-

[27] Albert E. Church, *Personal Reminiscences of the U. S. Military Academy* (West Point, 1879), 133.

[28] Keyes, *Fifty Years'*, 190.

[29] Barnard, *Military Schools*, 738; Calhoun to Thayer, February 10, 1818, in Hemphill (ed.), *Calhoun*, II, 130.

ing the work of their assistants in the section rooms. The additional instructors Thayer needed should be, he felt, army officers who were recent graduates of the Academy, which was in accordance both with the medieval tradition that the best teacher for the undergraduate was a young graduate and with the practice at Harvard.[30] That this system might lead to inbreeding was a problem Thayer ignored; in any case, few other colleges were turning out graduates with the necessary scientific training for the task. Fortunately for the Superintendent, Secretary of War John C. Calhoun was both a friend and an admirer, and he gave Thayer the men he wanted.[31] From then on each cadet received an assignment from the text each day, upon which he recited and was graded the next. The teaching was intensely practical, with little or no attempt to impart the theory of a subject. Many found the method deadly, while others prospered under it; for Thayer the important point was that it seemed the most thorough system for imparting knowledge.

While Thayer was instituting his reforms, he had the day-to-day life of the Academy to supervise. Like the college president, he found that the students were constantly testing him. Shortly after he became Superintendent, he had the drum beaten one evening for parade. At the time Colonel Webb of the Engineers was walking past some cadets. They asked if it were to be a dress parade, and when Webb did not reply began to call out, "Oh! Webb, let it be undress! let it be undress!" Others laughed and added, "Oh! Webb, where is the use? it is so wet!" Thayer held the parade, announced punishments for the offenders, and the next morning reprimanded the entire Corps: "Gentlemen must learn it is only their province to listen and obey."[32]

[30] Morison, *Harvard*, 32.

[31] Calhoun was an outstanding Secretary of War, the best of the pre-Civil War era and the first to bring to the task dedication and imagination. He did a great deal for the army and for West Point. Without his presence in the War Department Thayer would have had a much more difficult time of it and possibly would not have succeeded. Certainly Calhoun gave Thayer more support than any previous Secretary of War had given to a Superintendent.

[32] "Early Discipline," *JMSI*, 458.

In his first years as Superintendent, Thayer was not popular with the cadets, especially those who had been at West Point under Partridge. In numerous ways they made their feelings known. Once, when Thayer was offering some advice to a high-ranking graduate who had his choice of corps, the cadet cut him off with "Major Thayer, when I want your advice I'll ask you for it!"[33]

Thayer made no attempt to ingratiate himself with the cadets, for he was not concerned with his personal popularity. He did continue a stern performance of his duty, for he felt it was imperative that the Superintendent be respected. As long as Partridge's cadets were at West Point, however, the task was difficult, and in 1818 he had to face a major mutiny inspired by the same cadets who had so joyfully welcomed Partridge back to his post the year before.

One of Thayer's first acts as Superintendent had been to appoint an army officer as Commandant of Cadets. His duties were to impart tactical training to the cadets, take charge of their discipline, and assign demerits. The nature of his duties required the Commandant to keep the cadets under constant observation, and they hated both him and his position. In 1818 the Commandant was Captain John Bliss, a strict disciplinarian who in numerous ways angered the cadets. On November 22, 1818, a climax came. During a parade Cadet Edward L. Nicholson constantly and deliberately marched out of step. Captain Bliss had a fiery temper and, after Nicholson ignored repeated orders, ran into the ranks, grabbed the cadet by the collar, and "shook, jerked, and publicly damned" him. When Nicholson hotly asked if this were the manner in which a gentleman should be used, Bliss shouted, "Yes, God damn you."

That night, in quarters, the cadets elected a committee of five to present their grievances to the Superintendent. They wrote out a bill of particulars—among other offenses, they claimed Bliss had thrown stones at them—emphasizing the Commandant's actions against Nicholson. Some 180 cadets signed the petition, and the next day the committee of five, all but one of whom had been

---

[33] *Ibid.*, 473.

Partridge's cadets, went to Thayer's quarters to present the document. Dispassionately but firmly Thayer told them that, although they could make complaints as individuals, they had no right to form a combination and present a petition and ordered them out of his office. The cadets met again that night, wrote out a longer set of charges against Bliss, and the next day the committee of five attempted to present it to Thayer. The Superintendent immediately ordered them off the post and published an order to the Corps to desist these round-robin proceedings. When he learned that the five were hanging around a tavern adjoining the post, he gave them one hour to leave, which they did by rowboat, complaining they were only "waiting the arrival of the steamboat in the evening, and in the morning on which the order was issued it was raining very fast." They went on to Newburgh, where they published a pamphlet denouncing Thayer and demanding a congressional inquiry.[34]

Thayer, in asking the Chief Engineer for a court of inquiry, analyzed the various causes of the mutiny, the most important being "the erroneous and unmilitary impressions of the Cadets . . . that they had rights to defend." He added, "So long as these impressions shall remain the Academy will be liable to combinations and convulsions."[35]

The court of inquiry upheld Thayer's action, and a congressional investigation, held at the request of the committee of five, found that although Bliss did maltreat Nicholson, nevertheless, the combination formed by the cadets was "wrong and mutinous."[36] Later a court-martial met to try Cadet Thomas Ragland, one of the leaders of the mutiny and one of Partridge's favorite cadets. The court found it had no authority to try Ragland because cadets were not under military law. President Madison overruled

[34] Thayer to Armistead, November 30, 1818, E. S. H. Archives. The Commandant would "watch over and report their conduct and inflict the punishments for all minor delinquencies." *Exposé of Facts, concerning Recent Transactions, Relating to the Corps of Cadets of the USMA, at West Point, New York* (Newburgh, N.Y., 1818), 13–20; Charles Radcliff to uncle, April 5, 1820, Misc. Mss., USMA Library.

[35] Thayer to Armistead, November 30, 1818, E. S. H. Archives.

[36] *American State Papers: Military Affairs*, II, 138–39.

their action when his Attorney General, William Wirt, issued an opinion that "the corps at West Point form a part of the land forces of the United States, and have been constitutionally subjected by Congress to the rules and articles of war, and to trial by courts-martial." Wirt's opinion settled the status of the institution and of the cadets once and for all.[37]

A more important result was that the authority of Thayer, who throughout the crisis had kept the Academy operating on its regular routine, had been upheld. Secretary of War Calhoun, after dismissing Captain Bliss for being too strict, sent Thayer his approbation of his actions and his promise of firm support.[38] So Thayer, far from relaxing discipline, appointed two assistants for the Commandant, junior officers in the army who would serve as assistant tactical instructors and live in the barracks with the cadets, where they could be in twenty-four-hour contact with the Corps and report any infractions and assign demerits immediately. The cadets did not love their Superintendent, but he had made them fear and respect him. His consistency was something they could count on, and never again did they make a serious attempt to test him.

Thayer's duties were not only internal, to the cadets and the faculty; he was also responsible for the public image of the Academy. After two attempted mutinies in as many years, one by Partridge and one by the cadets, the image was alarmingly bad. Thayer's attempts to improve it were many, but they all centered around the Board of Visitors. This group, provided for by Secretary of War William Crawford in 1816, was originally designed to meet annually at West Point and report on conditions there to the War Department.[39] Under Partridge, however, it met only once and was thereafter ignored. Thayer, in reviving it, decided to use it not only as a source of competent outside criticism but also to improve the popularity of the Academy, by appointing as members outstanding men from every part of the country, includ-

[37] General Order, Adjutant General's Office, November 10, 1819, WPL.
[38] Calhoun to Thayer, February 10, 1818, in Hemphill (ed.), *Calhoun*, II, 130.
[39] Boynton, *West Point*, 214–15.

ing critics as well as friends of the Academy. He also gave wide publicity to the Board's reports, which were nearly always favorable and frequently ecstatic. Those who served on the Board at one time or another included De Witt Clinton, governor of New York, Oliver Wolcott, governor of Connecticut, Sam Houston of Tennessee and later Texas, and Ticknor. After about 1825 Thayer concentrated on southerners and westerners, and often had no one from New England on the Board, because as a cadet noted the "New Englanders are enough in favour of the Institution now."[40]

Thayer convened the Board on June 1, the day the examinations began, and it remained in session throughout the two-week period of examinations. The Visitors attended all the examinations and were invited to ask questions. Thayer, and his professors, all in full uniform, sat at one large table, with the Board at another. In front of this awesome group there were three large blackboards set up on easels. Thayer called in six cadets at a time, assigning two to each board. While one cadet recited orally, the others prepared their answers. Thayer designed the examinations to impress the Board, and they were as thorough as possible. In all, every cadet went through at least five hours of grilling, covering all his courses. Ticknor, himself an educator, was tremendously impressed with what he saw. He attended the examinations in 1826, and after watching the lowest section of one class "under the screw" for four hours, during which time he asked a number of questions himself, he reported "it was as nearly perfect as anything of the kind ever was." Even more remarkable to the Harvard professor, "the young men have that composure which comes from thoroughness, and unite to a remarkable degree, ease with respectful manners towards their teachers."[41]

In 1833 Joel R. Poinsett was president of the Board of Visitors. One morning a class passed a splendid examination, answering every question correctly, and at dinner that day Poinsett casually remarked that he had never heard better examinations. It was difficult for him to believe, he said, that any students could do so

---

[40] Bailey to mother, May 5, 1830, Jacob W. Bailey Papers, USMA Library.
[41] Ticknor, *Life,* I, 374.

well without knowing the questions beforehand. A member of the faculty heard Poinsett's remark and passed it on to Thayer. The Superintendent immediately ordered each professor to draw up a synopsis of the subjects he taught and have it ready by that afternoon. He then directed the class to report to him and the Board of Visitors and, when it had assembled, told it of Poinsett's remark. Turning to Poinsett, Thayer said that such an opinion was inevitably a reflection upon the institution and that he had therefore called the class back to be re-examined on everything that it had studied. Then he laid before the Board the synopsis each professor had prepared and requested the Visitors to go ahead and ask any further questions they desired. Poinsett flushed, rose, and made a full apology, protesting that he had not meant his remark as a reflection but rather as a compliment. He asked that the class not be made to submit again to the ordeal. Thayer was inflexible, and the examination was resumed. The cadets all did their best to uphold the honor of the class, and again not a question was missed. Thereafter Poinsett was a great friend of the Academy.[42]

Thayer had other means for impressing influential men. Across the river from West Point, at Cold Spring, Gouverneur Kemble had organized the West Point Foundry, the largest east and north of Pennsylvania. Rich and hospitable, Kemble entertained many prominent men at his mansion. On Saturday nights he held an open house, to which Thayer often went. There the Superintendent met and talked with such men as George Bancroft, Edward Everett, Hugh S. Legare, Washington Irving, Martin Van Buren, and others of the East Bank Hudson patroons.[43]

Thayer introduced the cadets to the general public through a series of summer marches. In 1819 the Corps went to Hudson, New York; in 1820, to Philadelphia; in 1821, to Boston, where the cadets ate at Harvard College and in Faneuil Hall; and in 1822, to Goshen, New York. His official reason for the marches was that they improved the health and added to the practical

[42] Francis H. Smith, *West Point Fifty Years Ago* (New York, 1879), 6–7.
[43] Dupuy, *Where They Have Trod*, 177–79.

[81]

experience of the cadets, but his real reason was publicity. Thayer knew that the American people were fascinated with fancy uniforms, martial music, and expert drill, and that most towns had their own crack drill teams, usually the local militia company. He also knew that none of these could compare with the cadets, for the Corps easily constituted the best marching unit in the country. With his summer marches Thayer reached and impressed people who neither understood nor cared about the curriculum at West Point.

Thayer also worked to improve the physical appearance of the post. He built a new, and still standing, Superintendent's quarters and four stone houses for the faculty, the beginning of Professors' Row. He added the convenience of running water by drawing on a mountainside reservoir through iron pipes, established a cadet hospital, built a new hotel, and supervised the planting of trees on the edge of the Plain.[44]

The various methods Thayer used to make the Academy popular were successful. Commenting on one of them, the *North American Review* in October, 1826, said, "It is scarcely possible for any troops to attain the power of manoeuvring with greater precision. . . . The institution has acquired a wide and honorable reputation, and is deservedly in favor both with the people and the government."[45] His academic standards impressed the Board of Visitors, and they generally looked with favor on his entire system. As the Secretary of War put it in 1828, "The Military Academy . . . has conquered all the prejudices against it."[46] Perhaps the most gratifying praise came from Horace Mann, who served on the Board of Visitors after Thayer was no longer Superintendent but while his system was still intact. "The committee," Mann said, "would express the opinion that when they consider the length of the course and the severity of the studies pursued at the academy, they have rarely, if ever, seen anything that

[44] Forman, *West Point,* 48.
[45] *North American Review,* XXIII (Oct., 1826), 271–72.
[46] White, *Jeffersonians,* 258.

equalled either the excellence of the teaching or the proficiency of the taught."[47]

Thayer's success at the Academy created some problems, but they were happy ones. Before he came to West Point no one had been particularly concerned with the system of appointment of cadets, because few were interested in sending their sons to the Academy. After Thayer made West Point an elite school, however, it seemed that every father in the land wanted his boy to have the benefit of a free scientific education. The President selected the cadets, upon the advice of the Secretary of War, and a suspicion began to grow that the appointments were being given to "the sons of the most wealthy or most influential persons."[48] The Secretary of War protested that such a charge had no basis in fact. The criteria that weighed most heavily with him were the applicant's poverty and the service the boy's family had rendered the nation—that is, young men whose fathers had fought in the Revolutionary War and possessed no wealth had a decided preference. Politics forced him to make some changes; in 1828 Secretary of War James Barbour reported that "in making selections, I have received, and treated with great respect, the recommendations of the members of Congress," and he tried to appoint one cadet from each congressional district.[49] Congressmen, ever alert to patronage possibilities, soon saw to it that this custom became a *de facto* law.

From Thayer's point of view the trouble was that in making their selections the politicians took into consideration every qualification except intellectual ability. The result was that even with the low entrance requirements—they were kept low so that poor boys, without the benefit of a formal education, would have an opportunity to get into the Academy—Thayer had to reject 30 per cent of the applicants, and sometimes as many as 60 per cent. And of those who did pass, less than one-half ever graduated. All this despite an examination so easy that one cadet was asked only to define a fraction, to read two and one-half lines from a history

[47] *Ibid.*, 259.
[48] *Niles Register* (March 16, 1822).
[49] White, *Jeffersonians*, 255–56.

[83]

book, and to write a dictated sentence on the blackboard.[50] Every cadet who had the equivalent of a high-school education passed with no trouble, but most American boys of the period had, at best, only a little common schooling.

One of Thayer's major aims was to treat every cadet alike, which was never easy and was sometimes nearly impossible. In 1824, for example, he refused to admit a candidate named Martin, who it turned out was a family friend of General William Henry Harrison, who was soon to be President. Harrison asked Thayer to reconsider, since Martin's father had fought for General Washington and the first President had "thought highly" of him. The family was now destitute, and Martin had no education. But although these things counted in the making of appointments, they did not sway Thayer in admitting a candidate, and Martin did not become a cadet.[51]

Other prominent men asked favors. In 1823 Martin Van Buren sent his son to the Academy, and the New York politician and future President asked the Superintendent to do what he could for the boy. Van Buren did tell his son that his future depended on his own "industry and fidelity," but others were not as careful.[52] General Andrew Jackson, for example, had two nephews at the Academy, and he requested that Thayer ignore the regulations about the merit roll and appoint one to the engineers and the other to the artillery.[53]

Thayer had other problems. In 1821 Congress indulged in one of its periodic cuts in the size of the army, and one result was that the Academy was now graduating more men than the army could use. The supernumeraries became brevet second lieutenants, which was not very satisfactory from anyone's point of view. The congressional solution came on February 16, 1821, when a motion was made to abolish the Academy. Using arguments supplied by Thayer, President Madison and Secretary of War Calhoun came to

[50] "Memoirs," Samuel Wragg Ferguson Papers, Archives, Louisiana State University.
[51] Harrison to Thayer, August 12, 1824, WPL.
[52] Van Buren to Thayer, May 30, 1823, *ibid.*
[53] Van Deventer to Thayer, June 3, 1820, *ibid.*

West Point's defense. Calhoun, who had already told Congress that "in the present condition of the world" military science could not be "neglected with impunity," recommended that Congress, far from abolishing the Academy, should create a second one, "placed where it would mutually accommodate the South and West."[54] Madison told Congress that the Academy "forms the basis, in regard to science, on which the military establishment rests."

The motion was defeated, but the problem of too many graduates remained. Madison had suggested that the extra men might well retire to private life, where they could give the benefit of their training to the state militia.[55] This was of course one of the original purposes of the Academy, but Thayer had built too well. He had imbued the cadets with a love for and pride in their profession, and most of them were contemptuous of the militia. As one of Thayer's cadets put it, "They talk about 'these young gentlemen becoming officers of *militia!*' Hem! . . . If they ever see a Cadet among the militia, I am very much mistaken."[56]

In the end, however, that is essentially what happened. The army did not need all the graduates, and a large percentage of them, disgusted with the snail's pace rate of promotion, resigned their commissions to take up lucrative civilian pursuits—pursuits for which their Academy training fitted them well. But when war came, in 1846 and in 1861, most of them returned to fight for their country, either as officers of volunteers or militia. As Jefferson had hoped it would, the Academy had provided a reserve of trained officers on which the country could call in time of need.

Aside from supplying its young officers, the Academy helped the army in other ways. One of these was providing a testing ground for tactical innovations, a practice that continued through the nineteenth century. It was a time of rapid and unexpected change in weaponry. At the beginning of the century men used weapons that were similar in all their essentials to those in use three hundred years earlier, while by the beginning of the twentieth century

---

[54] *American State Papers: Military Affairs*, I, 834, and II, 76.
[55] *Ibid.*, V, 350.
[56] Bailey to mother, December 11, 1830, Bailey Papers.

the rapid-firing rifled weapon was everywhere in use. Each change in weapons required a change in tactics, and each change in tactics required experiments. In nearly every case, the War Department appointed a board of army officers to meet at West Point, where the cadets would be employed in carrying out the experiments. Usually, the Commandant of Cadets was a prominent member of the board.[57]

By the mid-1820's Thayer, with the help of the War Department, had completed his reforms. West Point had finally become an institution the nation could be proud of, an institution that was pre-eminent both in science and military affairs. The Academy could look forward with anticipation and confidence.

[57] For examples, see Macomb to Thayer, July 8 and 21, 1824, WPL.

Chapter V

Thayer's Curriculum and Faculty

Sylvanus Thayer's most durable monument was the curriculum he instituted. Resisting the temptation to turn the Academy into a narrowly based military institution, he made it into a great scientific school. The cadets learned to be soldiers on the drill field, in barracks, and in summer encampments; in the classroom Thayer and his faculty saw to it that they learned practical science. In so doing, the Superintendent met one of the original aims of Jefferson and other early supporters of the Academy, who had wanted it to be a national scientific institution, and at the same time he rejected the dominant trend in American education.

The pre-Civil War American college was a stagnant, self-satisfied, superficial institution, dead and deadening. The core of the curriculum remained what it had been for centuries, Latin and Greek. Students studied these languages, and these only, for three years. Upon this scaffolding the colleges plastered a thin layer of rhetoric and mathematics, natural philosophy, logic, metaphysics, and ethics. The crowning glory of the structure was the senior year course in moral philosophy, consisting of the president's lectures on the evidences of Christianity. In their classes students sat on hard, straight-backed chairs in stuffy rooms sonorously answering the same questions on Virgil and Homer that their grandfathers had answered. In the midst of a young and expanding America that lived only for the future, the colleges remained firmly rooted in the past.[1]

There were challengers to the system. At Harvard, George Ticknor forced modern languages into the program, divided his classes into sections so that the brighter could progress more quickly, and tried to make the process of learning interesting. At the University of Nashville, Philip Lindsley attempted, ultimately without success, to develop a program to educate "the farmer, the mechanic, the manufacturer, the merchant, the sailor, the soldier." Jacob Abbott tried, at Amherst, to introduce specialized and practical courses, including some in the science of education, to no avail.[2] All these great teachers rejected the notion that the only things an educated man needed were the classics, disciplined thinking, and a strong Christian faith.

The wrath of the righteous fell on them, and the citadel of righteousness, Yale College, gave the ultimate answer to their heresy. In 1828 the faculty of Yale issued a report on the proper course of study for a young man, a report so thorough and so unanswerable that for the next half century it was cited in defense of the course in classics, mathematics, and moral philosophy. Princeton agreed with the report, and Princeton, along with Yale, supplied the college teachers for the hinterland—liberal Harvard's influence was limited to the Boston area. Together, Princeton and Yale dominated the higher learning of young American males until after the Civil War.

The Yale faculty, in its report, was firm in its rejection of radicalism. It was no business of the colleges to adjust themselves to the character of the nation. Rather, the purposes of a college education were disciplining the mind, the creation of a "proper *balance* of character," and the provision of a substitute for "parental superintendence." At Yale, and therefore everywhere else, classics would remain the core of the curriculum, for nothing else quite so effectively disciplined all the mental faculties—memory,

[1] Schmidt, *Old Time President*, 95–96; Rudolph, *American College*, 130.
[2] Rudolph, *American College*, 118–24.

judgment, reason, taste, and fancy. Mathematics would still be used to "sharpen the intellect, to strengthen the faculty of reason, and to induce a general habit of mind favorable to the discovery of truth and the detection of error." Yale would continue to use textbooks and the recitation method, an arrangement obviously superior to any that sent the students into the library where they could read the sources and consult conflicting authorities, for "the diversity of statement in these, will furnish the student with an apology for want of exactness in his answer." [3]

Thayer was not in complete agreement with either the reformers or the Yale faculty. Unlike Ticknor, he believed in the textbook-recitation method. But he was a strong supporter of practical instruction, especially in scientific courses, and he had a number of advantages in instituting such a curriculum at West Point. In the first place, West Point was expected to be a scientific institution. Secondly, Thayer did not have to answer to a board of trustees who insisted that the alma mater remain just as it had always been. Thirdly, he was not dependent on the local community for financial support, and a Yale- or Princeton-trained clergyman in a nearby pulpit could do him little harm, no matter how much the minister might disapprove of Thayer's material and modern orientation. If anything, there was more pressure on Thayer to become more practical in his curriculum than the other way round. The Board of Visitors in 1826, for example, recommended an end to the studies useful merely for the "character of an accomplished citizen," such as grammar, geography, rhetoric, national law, and ethics. It should be noted that all these subjects were taught by one man and consumed less than 3 per cent of the cadet's time. [4]

Thus, in spite of the Yale Report and the prevailing mood, Thayer was able to emphasize science, to the total neglect of the classics and lesser neglect of the art of war. The most important subject was engineering, especially civil engineering, and for a

[3] *Reports on the Course of Instruction in Yale College* (New Haven, 1828); for a full discussion of the Yale Report and its influence, see Frederick Rudolph, *Mark Hopkins and the Log* (New Haven, 1956), 42–44.

[4] White, *Jeffersonians*, 254.

time West Point was turning out better engineers than soldiers. General John E. Wool complained to the Secretary of War that the army looked in vain to West Point for professional soldiers, for the school was one of mathematical science and "the mere solution of a problem never yet made a General competent to command armies." Mathematics could not teach human nature, "yet a General without that knowledge would not be master of his profession."[5] Thayer disregarded Wool's criticism and held his course; time would show that West Point was capable of turning out both engineers and generals and that of the two the engineers were of more immediate importance and brought greater recognition to the Academy.

The twin pillars of Thayer's course were French and mathematics. French was important primarily because many of the advanced texts were available only in that language; mathematics was the basis for training in engineering. In his first, or Fourth Class, year a cadet studied French, algebra, geometry, trigonometry, and mensuration. In his Third Class year he continued the same subjects, adding drawing. The importance Thayer attached to each subject was evident in the weight he assigned; mathematics counted for three as compared to the French one and the drawing one-half. In his Third Class year the cadet studied analytical geometry and fluxions. The Second Class cadet studied topographical drawing, natural philosophy (the Aristotelian term for physics), and chemistry. Natural philosophy bore the weight of three, while drawing and chemistry weighed one each. The major course in the First Class year and the crowning embellishment of the curriculum was engineering, with the emphasis on civil engineering; in addition the cadet studied mineralogy in the department of chemistry and took one course in rhetoric and moral and political science.[6]

---

[5] Wool to Calhoun, 1819, Misc. Mss., USMA Library.

[6] This course description is general, and there were variations on it. It is taken from various editions of the annual *USMA Regulations and Register*. A glance at a number of these illustrates the changes through the years. Mensuration is the branch of applied geometry concerned with finding the length of lines, areas of surfaces, and volumes of solids from simple data of lines and angles; fluxion, in infinitesimal calculus, is a differential.

To teach this program Thayer gathered a great faculty; in the fields of physics, engineering, and mathematics the best in the United States. Thayer was at West Point long enough so that by the time he left every member of the faculty was his personal selection. Most were Academy graduates; all were dedicated to learning and teaching. Their influence spread far beyond the borders of West Point and far beyond the confines of the small Regular Army. Every engineering school in the United States founded during the nineteenth century copied West Point, and most found their first professors and president among Academy graduates. Many of the great canals, railroads, and public buildings in the United States built in the nineteenth century were constructed by men who had received their training on the banks of the Hudson. Textbooks written by Thayer's faculty dominated American mathematics, chemistry, and engineering. In matters scientific, the tiny faculty at this small school tucked away in rural New York led the way.

Thayer's courage and his willingness to fly in the face of the usual were most emphatically revealed in the selection of his faculty. The Superintendent rejected the American practice of choosing teachers on the basis of their piety and nationality and instead concentrated on their knowledge. Thomas Jefferson tried to do the same thing at the University of Virginia when he recruited a faculty that included four Englishmen and a German, all of them noted only for their scholarship. Thayer, who also recruited foreigners, could enjoy the reaction of an indignant Connecticut newspaper which observed, "Mr. Jefferson might as well have said that his taverns and dormitories should not be built with American brick," and that of a Philadelphia newspaper which pointed out that Jefferson had insulted the American people.[7]

At West Point the French department laid the basis for all the future studies of the cadets, even though the teacher, Claudius Berard, had to stay at the Academy thirty-one years, from 1815 to 1846, before he was designated professor. A Frenchman, Berard had purchased a substitute to serve in his stead in Napoleon's

[7] Rudolph, *American College,* 158.

army, then fled France when the man was killed in Spain and he was once again liable to conscription. He taught at Dickinson College, Carlisle, Pennsylvania, before going to West Point. His responsibility to the cadets was simple—Thayer required him to teach the boys to read and translate French. If they learned to speak the language, fine, but it was not necessary. What they did need was an ability to read their texts. Berard was a hard-working scholar with excellent taste. He published his own grammar, which was the basic text, and in addition had the cadets read *Histoire de Gil Blas* and Voltaire's *Histoire de Charles XII*, both of which Ticknor was using at Harvard.[8]

Cadets spent most of their time studying under the direction of the department of mathematics, which was blessed with a series of brilliant teachers. Andrew Ellicott (1813–1820) and David B. Douglass (1820–1823) began the tradition; in 1823 Thayer's man, Charles Davies, took over, to become America's best-known mathematician. He was not an original thinker, but as a teacher and compiler of textbooks he was unsurpassed, and most nineteenth-century American boys learned everything from adding and subtracting through the calculus from a Davies text. In all he wrote over a dozen, which taken together constituted a connected mathematics course, beginning with primary arithmetic and progressing through calculus. It was in large part because of his work that a historian of mathematics could say, "For several decennia West Point was unquestionably the most influential mathematical school in the United States."[9]

Davies was an 1815 graduate of the Academy, where he remained as an assistant professor until he took over the mathematics department. John H. B. Latrobe found him to be a remarkable man, both personally and mentally. Of medium height, he had a bright, intelligent face marked by projecting upper teeth, which caused the cadets to nickname him "Tush." He was filled with nervous energy; his fearless activity at a fire in a room in the barracks in

[8] Douglas Southall Freeman, *R. E. Lee: A Biography* (New York, 1936), I, 59; Forman, *West Point*, 52–54.

[9] Florian Cajori, *The Teaching and History of Mathematics in the United States* (Washington, 1890), 118–20.

1819 added the name "Rush" to the other, and he was thereafter known as "Tush-Rush." He was a frequent visitor to the section room, where he watched his assistants at work and occasionally asked questions. When a cadet muttered an imperfect answer, he would lean forward, smile, and say quietly, "How's that, Mr. Bliss?" Eventually, overwork caused a bronchial infection, and he had to retire from the Academy, later to become professor of mathematics at Trinity College, at New York University, and at Columbia College.[10]

His successor was one of his former pupils, Albert E. Church, assistant professor of mathematics from 1828 to 1837 and full professor from 1837 until his death in 1878. Dry as dust, Church had none of Davies' personal magnetism; his only love seems to have been calculus, which he considered the only respectable way to solve a mathematical problem.[11] One cadet remembered him as a "short, stock, brown-eyed, broad-faced man, with a complaining voice" and felt "there never was a colder eye or manner than Professor Church's." He seemed "an old mathematical cinder, bereft of all natural feeling."[12] The only time Church ever became disconcerted was on being told by a cadet that the reason for $+$ becoming $-$ on passing through zero was that the cross-piece got knocked off in its passage. Church arrested the would-be wit. He taught mathematics in a drill-room atmosphere. The philosophy of the subject held no charms for him, and he treated the calculus as a machine whose results were indisputable but whose mechanism was a mystery. He published four textbooks, on calculus, analytical geometry, trigonometry, and descriptive geometry. All were widely used in the colleges.[13]

In the mathematics department, as elsewhere, the students were divided into small sections according to ability. The lower sections never progressed as far as the upper ones, and the bottom one

---

[10] *Ibid.;* John H. B. Latrobe, "West Point Reminiscences," *Eighteenth Annual Reunion of the Association of Graduates* (East Saginaw, Mich., 1887), 29.

[11] "Memoirs," Ferguson Papers.

[12] Morris Schaff, *The Spirit of Old West Point* (Boston, 1907), 68.

[13] Cajori, *History of Mathematics*, 123.

usually went only half as far as the top one.[14] Under the direction of Davies and Church, the best cadets could progress through calculus and upon graduation obtain a position teaching mathematics anywhere in the country.

In their Third Class year cadets added drawing, a most practical course for future engineers, for in it they learned the elements of topography and map-making. In addition, the instructor usually tried to teach them free-hand drawing of the human figure, with uneven results. In the twenties the teacher was Thomas Gimbrede, an amiable French miniaturist and engraver. He usually gave his classes an introductory lecture, telling the unbelieving and stiff-fingered cadets, "Every one can learn to draw. There are only two lines in drawing, the straight line and the curve line. Every one can draw a straight line—and every one can draw a curve line—therefore every one can draw." In 1833 Thayer induced Robert W. Weir to come to the Academy and become the drawing teacher. Weir, who had been studying in Italy, was to stay for forty-two years, with the Academy acting more or less in the role of his patron. While there, he established himself as one of the notable American painters of the century; his "Landing of the Pilgrims" is in the rotunda of the National Capitol.[15]

In 1820 Thayer established a course in chemistry for Second Class cadets, although the teacher of the subject did not become a professor until 1838. In the early years the position was held by an army medical officer, who doubled as post surgeon. In 1829 one such instructor-surgeon, William M. Mather, helped found the American Association for the Promotion of Science, Literature,

[14] *CWP*, I, 241–43.

[15] At the time, French mathematicians were superior to those of England, but only Harvard and, to a greater extent, West Point, recognized this. Until his own works began to appear, Davies used the outstanding volume by Adrien Legendre, *Éléments de Géométrie,* and Pierre L. M. Bourdon's *Éléments d'algèbre.* Davies inscribed one of his books, "To Colonel Thayer; In the organization of the military Academy under your immediate superintendence, the French methods of instruction, in the exact sciences, were adopted; and near twenty years experience has suggested few alterations in the original plan." See David E. Smith and J. Ginsburg, *A History of Mathematics in America before 1900* (Chicago, 1934), 77–79; Francis H. Smith, *West Point Fifty Years Ago* (New York, 1879), 12; Forman, *West Point,* 55.

and the Arts, an organization that included among its members many of the cadets and most of the West Point faculty. Branch organizations were soon formed at Union College, Miami University, Rochester, New York City, Newport, and elsewhere. Designed somewhat as a successor to the United States Military Philosophical Society, the Association would, its founders hoped, become the American counterpart to the Royal Society of London. It failed quickly, however, although many of the West Point graduates among its members soon took leading roles in the formation of the American Association for the Advancement of Science.[16]

The Second Class cadets also studied natural philosophy, where until 1828 that unhappy holdover from the Partridge period, Jared Mansfield, held sway. Professor Mansfield always thought the Academy too military in its approach, and was always looking, unsuccessfully, for something better. When Thayer came, Mansfield's equipment was practically nonexistent. Gradually Thayer was able to make purchases for Mansfield, so that eventually he had enough equipment to teach statics, dynamics, hydrostatics, hydrodynamics and hydraulics, pneumatics, machinery, optics, and even astronomy, thanks to a crude telescope.[17] His successor was Edward H. Courtenay, who was overshadowed by his assistant professor, William H. C. Bartlett.

An 1826 graduate of the Academy, Bartlett became professor of natural philosophy in 1834. He was perhaps West Point's most brilliant nineteenth-century graduate. During his four years at the Academy he stood first in every class and never received a demerit. George Ticknor was present at his final examination of his First Class year and considered Bartlett the best student he had ever seen. Writing to his wife while Bartlett was answering questions, Ticknor commented: "It is a pleasure to look upon him, and listen to the beauty and completeness of all his examinations. Thayer says he has heard him at common recitations about a hundred

[16] Sidney Forman, "West Point and the American Association for the Advancement of Science," *Science,* CIV (July 19, 1946), 47–48.

[17] *CWP,* I, 261–64; Samuel Peter Heintzelman Diary, May 22, 1825, Library of Congress.

times, and never knew him to miss a single question."[18] After graduation Bartlett served as an assistant professor and, from 1832 to 1834, as assistant to the Chief Engineer. As professor at West Point he became one of America's foremost astronomers. After a trip to Europe, where he studied astronomical observatories, he returned to West Point to build his own observatory. He and his assistants, most notably his son-in-law, John M. Schofield, a future lieutenant general, made a number of important observations. In 1854, during a partial solar eclipse, Bartlett used photography for astronomical measurements—the first time this had been done in America. He was also the author of a series of popular college textbooks, on acoustics, optics, astronomy, mechanics, and molecular physics.[19]

Cadets agreed that the Second Class year was the hardest, mainly because of Bartlett. The course itself was difficult, and Bartlett made it more so because, owing to a nervous temperament and a poor digestion, he was not a good teacher.[20]

In their First Class year the cadets took the only course Thayer introduced in which he bowed to the American tradition. Essentially it was moral philosophy, although history, grammar, and geography were also included. The teacher was also the chaplain, the Reverend Thomas Picton, a Presbyterian. At most colleges the president taught the course, which was designed as the capstone to a man's education, for it reconciled natural law and modern science with the old theology and Christian law. It was so universally taught that one historian has said it was "as common a feature of the average American college as the president's house and the treasury deficit."[21] The cadets hated it. They complained that the course was too long, uninteresting, and merely repeated truisms they had learned as children.[22]

[18] "West Point in 1826," *Annual Reunion of the Association of Graduates of the USMA* (East Saginaw, Mich., 1886), 5.
[19] Edward S. Holden, *Biographical Memoir of William H. C. Bartlett* (Washington, 1911), 176–78.
[20] Oliver O. Howard, *Autobiography* (New York, 1908), I, 55.
[21] Schmidt, *Old Time President,* 108–9.
[22] *Report of the Commission,* Senate Document No. 3, Thirty-sixth Congress, Second Session (Washington, 1860), 51–98. Hereafter cited as *RC.* See

West Point's most famous department, the one towards which all other study was aimed, was engineering. The Academy was the only institution in America teaching the subject; Rensselaer Polytechnic Institute was not founded until 1824 and did not teach engineering until 1828.[23] Some engineers learned their profession on the job—in this respect the Erie Canal was especially prominent for the men it educated—but West Point stood pre-eminent. A graduate who did not want to be a soldier or a mathematics teacher could always find a lucrative position as a civil engineer.

Thayer's first professor of engineering was Claude Crozet. A graduate of the École Polytechnique, Crozet had served as an artillery officer under Napoleon. After Waterloo he fled France and came to the United States, where with Thayer's blessing—the Superintendent met him in France—he became assistant professor of engineering and in 1817 full professor. Crozet began his first class in engineering confidently enough but quickly found the students did not understand a word he was saying. His English was miserable, and Mansfield's son, a cadet, reported that "with extreme difficulty he makes himself understood and with extreme difficulty his class comprehends that two planes at right angles with one another are to be understood on the same surface of the blackboard, on which are represented two different projections of the same subject." Compounding the problem, the mathematics instruction at the Academy had not yet progressed beyond algebra, and Crozet found that he would have to teach mathematics before he could teach engineering. Young Mansfield remarked that "the surprise of the French engineer, instructed in the Polytechnique, may well be imagined when he commenced giving his class certain problems and instructions which not one of them could comprehend and perform." Bravely, Crozet tried to teach geometry but found there were no suitable textbooks, either in French or English, available to the cadets. He had carpenters build him a blackboard and taught from it until 1821, when he completed his

---

also the comments of Henry A. du Pont, in letters to his mother in the Winterthur Manuscripts, Eleutherian Mills Historical Library, Wilmington, Delaware.

[23] A. Riedler, *American Technological Schools* (Washington, 1895), 660–61.

Treatise on Descriptive Geometry. It was the first English work on the subject to exhibit to the student Pascal's Theorem. Unfortunately, as Crozet realized, its grammar often confused rather than elucidated, and it was soon supplanted by a Davies text. Still, it served the purpose, and Crozet was able to move on to engineering proper.[24]

His course was comprehensive. He divided it into the general areas of field fortification, permanent fortification, science of artillery, grand tactics, and civil and military architecture. He taught the cadets to build batteries and redoubts, fortified lines, field works, military and civil bridges, and forts. He made sure they understood the amount of labor, time, and material needed for construction of a project. He showed them the principles of gunnery and how to attack and defend fortified places, to construct and use mines. He gave the cadets their only introduction to their profession, outside what they learned on the drill field and from the tactical instructors, in a series of lectures on organization of armies, conduct of marches, preparation of orders, and combat tactics. Continuing a tradition begun by Partridge, he often used anecdotes from his own experience and from history to illustrate his points. When he showed the cadets a certain type of fortification, he was often reminded of its use in a past campaign, and soon he would be immersed in the details of one of Napoleon's battles. Eventually, strategy and the history of warfare became an integral part of the engineering course.[25]

In addition to everything else, Crozet taught architecture, where he dealt with the elementary parts of buildings and their construction, the design of arches, canals, bridges, and other public works, and the machines used to build them. His texts included S. F. Gay de Vernon's *Treatise on the Science of War and Fortification,* which the cadets were horrified to find cost them $20.00, Hackett's *Traité des Machines,* and Szannin's *Programme d'un Cours de Construction.* De Vernon's work had first been translated in 1817, by Captain John H. O'Connor, who was on special duty

[24] Cajori, *History of Mathematics,* 116; Barnard, *Military Schools,* 736–37; E. D. Mansfield, *Personal Memories* (Cincinnati, 1879), 64–76.
[25] Latrobe, "West Point," 30; Cajori, *History of Mathematics,* 116.

at the Academy at the time. He appended to it extracts from the military classics, and it was an excellent rendering of an excellent book. This was the initial attempt to develop a textbook specifically for the Academy.[26] In 1823 Crozet left West Point, later to become the chief engineer for the state of Virginia; thanks to his abilities, Virginia soon had the best mountain roads in America. He also was a founder of the Virginia Military Institute, of which a West Point graduate was the first Superintendent.[27]

Crozet's successor was David B. Douglass, a Yale graduate who had served with distinction as a young engineer during the War of 1812 and later headed the mathematics department at West Point. He was a conscientious man who tried his best to carry on the traditions of Crozet, while making some improvements. One of these was to send young graduates to Europe, where they could perfect their knowledge of civil engineering.[28] During the summers he served as a consulting engineer for the state of Pennsylvania. His standards and reputation were high, and he had an eye for good assistants, one of whom was Bartlett.[29] Another was Dennis Hart Mahan.

During the past two centuries the United States Military Academy has been blessed with scores of fine teachers and many outstanding ones. One of the most influential was Dennis Hart Mahan, who was Thayer's personal choice for the most important position on the faculty and who served as professor of engineering from 1832 to 1871.

Mahan stood first in his graduating class of 1824, then taught mathematics for two years at the Academy. Ranking officers in the army, most especially Thayer, thought that Mahan could become

[26] Freeman, *Lee,* I, 76–77. One student, trying to lower the cost of his copy of de Vernon's work, bought a used copy from a graduating cadet. Still he was charged for a new one, and when he appealed to Thayer the Superintendent told him that no graduate should dispose of his military textbooks, as he would need them in the military service, and ordered the used copy returned to its original owner. Smith, *West Point Fifty Years Ago,* 5.

[27] Latrobe, "West Point," 30; Cajori, *History of Mathematics,* 116; William Couper, *One Hundred Years at V. M. I.* (Richmond, 1939), I, 4–38.

[28] Douglass to Swift, January 31, 1825, Swift Papers.

[29] Freeman, *Lee,* I, 77.

a great teacher and theoretician, so they arranged a European tour for him. He spent four years at the School of Application for Engineers and Artillery at Metz, studying both civil engineering and European military institutions. He returned to West Point in 1830 to assume a post as assistant professor of engineering. Two years later he attained the rank of professor, a position he held until his death. He prepared all his own textbooks, which were used at West Point for over forty years, were reproduced in England, and were translated into several foreign languages. They included *A Treatise on Field Fortification, Notes on Attack and Defense, Notes on Mines, Notes on Architecture,* and his most famous work, *Course of Civil Engineering,* first published in 1837 and immediately accepted as the best text on the subject in the English language.[30]

Like Crozet and Douglass, Mahan devoted the major part of his course to civil engineering, but his contributions as a tactician and strategist were to be more important. Through the years he continually increased his teaching burden by adding to the material on the nature of war he included in his course, which was entitled, by 1843, "Engineering and the Science of War." Over the next two decades most of the men who would lead the major units in the Civil War learned the art of war from Mahan.

He never devoted more than a week to the subject, which was easily the most popular at the Academy, and through the years cadets always complained because Mahan did not spend more time on the art of war.[31] Further, the textbook he wrote for the subject had a misleading and horrendous title: *An Elementary Treatise on Advanced-Guard, Out-Post, and Detachment Service of Troops, and the Manner of Posting and Handling Them in the Presence of an Enemy. With a Historical Sketch of the Rise and Progress of Tactics, etc., etc.* But his was the only formal instruction available

[30] W. D. Puleston, *Mahan: The Life and Work of Captain Alfred Thayer Mahan* (New Haven, 1939), 5–9; Dupuy, *Where They Have Trod,* 183–204. In 1860 Mahan told an investigating commission that the textbooks were now so much clearer and easier to study than those formerly in use that they made the course too easy. They lowered the mental standard of the cadets, who could readily acquire and recite on their lessons by cramming. *RC,* 138.
[31] *RC,* 91, 112.

in the United States in strategy, and his book—usually called *Out-Post* and first published in the forties—was popular not only with Academy graduates but with other army and militia officers. It was read at the Virginia Military Institute, and during the Civil War, much to Mahan's displeasure, pirated editions were printed in New Orleans and Richmond for distribution to Southern officers. Mahan never commanded troops in action, never saw a battle, and always carried an umbrella when he went for a walk, but through his teaching and writing he was responsible for the manner in which much of the Civil War was fought.

Out-Post reflected Mahan's belief that the soldier could learn the art of war through the study of history. Beginning with the Greeks, he gave a brief account of the military experience of the various peoples and ages of Europe, ending with Napoleon, whom Mahan saw as the perfect soldier. After Napoleon, Mahan simply believed there was nothing new to be learned. "The task of the present [is] to systematize, and imbody in the form of doctrine, what [Napoleon] largely traced out." Mahan's interpretation of Napoleon was based on the theories of Baron Henri Jomini, Swiss military historian. Unlike his contemporary, Karl von Clausewitz, Jomini taught that Napoleon's success stemmed from the use of principles established by Frederick the Great rather than from the innovations which von Clausewitz emphasized. Jomini wanted to introduce a rationality and system to the study of war, and, to make war less barbarous, he created rules that emphasized speed of movement rather than the destruction of the enemy's will to fight, as von Clausewitz did in his doctrine of total war.

Following Jomini, Mahan stressed the importance of speed, maneuver, and a strong base of operations, not the attack. The ideal base included an interior line of communications emanating from a fortified position and lying between the two bodies of the enemy. From an interior line a soldier could, after the fashion of Frederick the Great, strike first one enemy force and then another before they could join forces. Interior lines simplified mobilization and supply while facilitating concentration on the battlefield. Napoleon's only mistake, Mahan thought, was in neglecting fortifications and entrenchments, an error which led the First Consul to make audacious and foolish attacks.

Mahan taught that, following the establishment of the base, the wise commander then concentrated his forces at the decisive point, which was usually a city or town. He believed that the occupation of territory or strategic points was more important than the destruction of enemy armies. It was his teaching that led to the emphasis placed by Civil War commanders on the capture or defense of Richmond, Vicksburg, Chattanooga, Atlanta, Corinth, and other cities.[32] His favorite student was Henry Halleck, of the class of 1839. Halleck wrote the only work that competed with *Out-Post,* entitled *Elements of Military Art and Science.* Like Mahan's work, Halleck's rested largely upon Jomini, and it helped to reinforce Mahan's views.[33]

Mahan was a short, slightly built man with a high, thin voice. Tully McCrea, who took engineering in the early days of the Civil War, found Mahan "the most particular, crabbed, exacting man that I ever saw. He is a little slim skeleton of a man and is always nervous and cross." He inspired respect, but never love. A rigid cross-examiner, Mahan was noted for his ability to find the one unprepared cadet in a section and cause him to display his ignorance. In the 1880's, General in Chief William T. Sherman still shuddered when he thought of being caught unprepared by Mahan.[34]

Mahan, Douglass, Davies, Church, Berard, Weir, Bartlett, Crozet—these were the men who made up Thayer's faculty. They were all secure, dignified, impressive. Whatever their army rank when they came to West Point, or even if they came as civilians, on the post they enjoyed the rank, pay, and privileges of a lieu-

[32] D. H. Mahan, *An Elementary Treatise on Advanced Guard, Out-Post . . .* (New York, 1847). There were several editions. Stephen E. Ambrose, "Dennis Hart Mahan," *Civil War Times,* III (November, 1963), 30–34.

[33] Stephen E. Ambrose, *Halleck: Lincoln's Chief of Staff* (Baton Rouge, 1962), 5–7.

[34] Ambrose, "Mahan," 33.

tenant colonel. When they were all together, in full uniform, accompanied by the Superintendent, they were an imposing sight.

Or so Thomas J. Jackson found them when he arrived, a shambling ex-constable from the hills of western Virginia, to take his entrance examination. Jackson had not progressed beyond a common school, knew little grammar, and according to one cadet "could add up a column of figures, but as to vulgar or decimal fractions, it is doubtful if he had ever heard of them." He had big, clumsy feet, homespun clothes, and a coarse wool hat, but he was in complete earnest about getting into and graduating from the Academy. The spectacle of Jackson before the faculty at his entrance examination was long remembered by a classmate. "His whole soul was bent upon passing. When he went to the blackboard the perspiration was streaming from his face, and during the whole examination his anxiety was painful to witness. While trying to work out his example in fractions, the cuffs of his coat, first the right and then the left, were brought into requisition to wipe off the perspiration." Finally one of the faculty told Jackson that he had passed and could take his seat. As he gratefully did so, "every member of the examining board turned away his head to hide the smile which could not be suppressed."[35] They had stretched the rules a little, but their faith was justified. Jackson worked harder than any other cadet, piling his grate high with anthracite coal at night so that when it was time for lights out he could study by the ruddy glow from his fire. He steadily moved up in his class and eventually graduated near the top.[36]

It was an easy, sedate life the professors led, and they loved it. Many of them remained on the faculty until their death. Their sons had the run of the post, while their daughters were wooed by the unmarried professors and cadets alike.[37] Their recreation was simple; for the most part it consisted of rowing over to Kemble's on Saturday nights, having dinner, and playing whist.[38]

[35] Lloyd Lewis, *Captain Sam Grant* (Boston, 1950), 88–89.
[36] Dabney H. Maury, *Recollections of a Virginian in the Mexican, Indian, and Civil Wars* (New York, 1894), 22–23.
[37] Davies married one of Mansfield's daughters. Latrobe, *"West Point,"* 34.
[38] Holden, *Bartlett,* 188.

Their assistants were not as happy. Most of the young officers detailed from the army to West Point were restive and ambitious and saw no chance to win glory or promotion for themselves at the Academy. Further, their commanding officers did not like to lose them from their regiments for two or three years and often made it difficult for the Superintendent to get them. Those who did enjoy teaching were quickly discouraged, for the professors never seemed to leave or die, and the chances for advancement were small. Another problem was that the army never detailed an instructor to West Point for more than three years and usually for only two. Thus just as he was becoming an effective teacher, he would rejoin his regiment, and a new man would take his place. Thayer did what he could to alleviate the situation, but the problem would remain throughout the nineteenth century.[39]

Another aspect of the same problem was the absence of any continuing intellectual stimulation in the army. As General in Chief Jacob Brown pointed out, "inaction and the want of competition" were turning the army into a stagnant institution. There was no opportunity for study, and no incentive to do so, as every officer was promoted when his turn came, regardless of record. Thayer realized that this lack of the possibility for education contributed to a scornful attitude towards it among officers, which made it even more difficult for him to obtain instructors. He had shown the benefits of military training; Brown and members of the War Department wanted to extend them to post-graduate work, and the Superintendent threw West Point's prestige behind the movement to create such schools of application. Calhoun had raised the issue as early as 1819 and in 1824 established the first army service school, the artillery school at Fortress Monroe, Virginia. The results were highly satisfactory, but because of congressional parsimony it was decades before the service school movement expanded.

[39] *American State Papers: Military Affairs,* II, 663, and IV, 678; Hitchcock to Thayer, April 15, 1829, National Archives, Record Group 94, Office, Adjutant General.

Meanwhile, the burden of teaching the army rested on West Point. That the Academy was able to carry it was due to Sylvanus Thayer and the faculty he selected and directed. As George Ticknor remarked, "I do not believe there are three persons in the country who could fill his place; and [General Joseph] Totten said very well the other day, when somebody told him . . . that if Thayer were to resign he would be the only man who could take his place—'No; no man would be indiscreet enough to take the place after Thayer; it would be as bad as being President of the Royal Society after Newton.' "[40]

[40] "West Point in 1826," *Association of Graduates*, 11.

Chapter VI

The Jacksonians
and the Academy

The great celebration which accompanied the inauguration of Andrew Jackson as the seventh President of the United States in 1829 marked the beginning of an era. To the horror of dignified and proper men everywhere, General Jackson's followers helped the first man from west of the mountains enter the White House in their own style. The drunken and disheveled farmers and mechanics, with their unseemly reveling, were announcing to a startled world that the age of the common man had arrived. The time had come to shake off the shackles of aristocratic pretension in America, to dispose of the powdered wigs and fancy knee-britches, and to substitute for them the homespun manners of common folk.

The Jacksonians aimed to destroy the system which gave special privileges to the few and replace it with one in which political freedom was matched by social and economic equality of opportunity. Every man should have a chance to get ahead, with every man for himself. The government should neither help nor hinder, except by assuring that all have an equal chance. That the result might be a greater inequality even than existed in the days of the old aristocracy, no one cared or thought about. The important thing was to ensure that every man have a chance to get rich, that he do it on his own merits, and that no one receive any extra help. Whatever else it was, Jacksonian Democracy was "a war on privilege, on artificial or accidental advantage."[1]

Privilege the Jacksonians found everywhere. While the talents of the people, which needed only proper encouragement to develop into qualities previously undreamed of in the world, were shamelessly ignored, the rich and well born, already enjoying an unfair start in life's race, were receiving special favors in education, in politics, in their relations with the government. This favoritism was especially present in those exclusive institutions, the colleges. In 1825 the governor of Kentucky denounced the tradition of state support to private colleges, because "the State has lavished her money for the benefit of the rich, to the exclusion of the poor; . . . the only result is to add to the aristocracy of wealth, the advantage of superior knowledge." In 1837 all the states made their hostility to the colleges unmistakably clear; when they distributed the federal treasury surplus that year, they gave money for common schools, roads, and banks, but not a cent went to the colleges.[2]

But in general only negatively, by withholding money, could the politicians please the people by punishing the colleges. Any institution with enough wealthy alumni or with proper church support could continue to struggle along. Not so West Point. It was dependent upon the government, and thus of all the privileged institutions in America it was the easiest to hit. It was obviously aristocratic, with its lily-fingered cadets in their fancy little uniforms who received money for their free education and became upon graduation snobbish officers in a caste-ridden army that was hostile to democracy or, worse, who resigned their commissions in order to cash in on the mathematical and engineering knowledge the government had given them. The very existence of the Academy infuriated the more fanatic Jacksonians, who held as dogma

[1] The phrase is Rudolph's, in *American College,* 202.
[2] *Ibid.,* 206, 213.

that the great body of the people constituted a huge storehouse of talent and skill. In military affairs, the militia was the storehouse, and it was an insult to the civilian soldiers and a waste of money to maintain an academy emphasizing specialized, professional training. So the Jacksonians mounted an attack upon West Point, one that came extremely close to destroying the Academy.

The first to fall was Sylvanus Thayer, and he fell to the President himself. A self-taught soldier, Jackson was suspicious of the very premise on which the Academy was built. Further, he was a man of strong opinions who often allowed his personal feelings to dictate his official actions. Although in 1823 he had said of West Point, "I believe it the best school in the world," he had since changed his mind.[3] In part this was because of his agreement with the general hostility his political followers felt towards the Academy, but personal relations played a larger role. Thayer was a friend of John C. Calhoun, whom Jackson hated; Thayer had supposedly mistreated Andrew Jackson Donelson when the latter was a cadet, and Donelson, now Jackson's private secretary, had signed the petition against Captain Bliss and supported the committee of five; Thayer had a warm admirer in General Winfield Scott, whom Jackson despised. After he became President, Jackson recommended and patronized some three or four cadets, all of whom Thayer later dismissed for negligence and misconduct. The boys went to the President and convinced him that Thayer's treatment of them had been tyrannical. Jackson "conceived the most extreme dislike of Col. Thayer" and restored the cadets to duty. He then began annulling all the decisions handed down by Thayer's court-martial boards and restoring to duty every cadet who appealed to him.[4]

A climax came with the case of Cadet H. Ariel Norris. A native of New York, where according to the new Commandant of Cadets, Ethan H. Hitchcock, he had "acquired his political tendencies and habits among the lower class of people in the city," Norris was an

[3] John S. Bassett (ed.), *Correspondence of Andrew Jackson* (Washington 1926–1935), III, 191.

[4] W. A. Croffut (ed.), *Fifty Years in Camp and Field: The Diary of Major-General Ethan Allen Hitchcock* (New York, 1909), 64–65.

ardent Jacksonian, so much so, in fact, that one night he planted that symbol of Jacksonian Democracy, the hickory pole, in the middle of the parade ground. Thayer rebuked him for it, whereupon Norris, certain that he had been insulted, complained to Old Hickory himself. Jackson praised the cadet for his action, which left Thayer with a nearly impossible discipline problem. When Hitchcock offered to go to Washington to talk with the President, the Superintendent agreed.

The conversation did not go well. Hitchcock emphasized the importance of the regulations at the Academy; he urged Jackson to study them and if he disapproved to change them, but in all events to support them. Jackson hardly listened. When Hitchcock finished, the old general rose from his chair and began stomping about the room, muttering about the "tyranny" of Sylvanus Thayer. Suddenly swinging his arms in a rage, he shouted, "Why, the autocrat of the Russias couldn't exercise more power!" Hitchcock also rose, stepped in front of the President, and announced, "You are misinformed on this subject and do not understand it."

Jackson looked sharply at the brazen young captain, seemed about to say something, but sat down. Then, slowly, he pointed out that Cadet Norris had only done what people in New York and everywhere else were doing. Just as calmly, Hitchcock replied that it was not proper to do it at the Academy. The President ended the interview by promising to read the regulations; a few weeks later he told Thayer that no changes were needed. But shortly thereafter he resumed his old habits and once again restored all discharged cadets who appealed to him.[5]

Jackson's attitude soon became common knowledge among the cadets, who practically ordered the Academy staff to treat them favorably or face a report to the President. Cadet William Frazer, who felt that the professors showed favoritism, started a rumor that Jackson was "going to clear every officer off the Point, professor and all." The President, Frazer announced, "is not agoing to have the cadets treated like a parcel of dogs, by these lazy

[5] *Ibid.*, 65–67.

drunken officers, which has been the case too long."[6] During
Jackson's second term the First Class sent a petition to the Secretary of War, complaining that Professor Mahan was too dogmatic,
that he used a French textbook, and that he was "much behind the
times," and demanded his dismissal. This time Jackson ignored
them.[7]

In the fall of 1832, after another series of dismissals and rein-
statements, Thayer wrote Secretary of War Lewis Cass, "I am led
to believe that there is something at this institution which does not
altogether meet with the President's approbation, but I am at a loss
to conjecture whether the dissatisfaction . . . relates to persons or
things." He asked if there were any specific incident of malad-
ministration that had prejudiced Jackson against him; if so, he
wanted it investigated, for "I am certain that the President is too
just and generous to pass sentence of condemnation on any one
without a hearing, or to have formed unfavorable opinions respect-
ing the administration of the Academy from information derived
from interested and prejudiced persons." After a long delay Cass
sent Thayer what he hoped would be a soothing reply. Jackson
has "not the slightest shade of unkindly feeling towards you," he
said, and although the President was not altogether happy with the
regulations, he did not blame Thayer for them.

The Superintendent was not satisfied; it seemed to him that his
authority had not been upheld. On January 19, 1833, Thayer sent
in his formal resignation. After some temporizing, Cass accepted it.

West Point was stunned. Hitchcock immediately requested
relief from his assignment, but Thayer talked him out of it, and
the Commandant stayed to help Thayer's successor, Major Rene
E. DeRussy. The members of the First Class called individually
on the Superintendent, and the faculty decided to have his portrait
painted. Professor Davies called on Thayer to inform him. "I
cannot permit such action," Thayer replied, according to one
account, with tears in his eyes. "Under the circumstances it could

[6] Frazer to brother, June 21, 1833, Misc. Mss., USMA Library.
[7] Petition by First Class to Secretary of War, 1834, Misc. Mss., USMA
Library.

be considered only as a reflection upon President Jackson." On July 1, 1833, he left West Point, never to return.[8]

Thayer's downfall did not satisfy the critics. A year after he left, Representative David Dickinson, of Tennessee, made a speech on the Academy's annual appropriation bill which fully illustrates the nature and the basis of the attack on West Point. Dickinson urged his colleagues to vote against the bill, an action that would have the effect of abolishing the Academy. Here the usual pattern was followed. Ordinarily West Point's critics did not propose changes in the curriculum or regulations or deal with any substantive matters but rather indulged in fiery rhetoric to satisfy the voters at home and in a proposal to abolish the institution altogether.

Dickinson's attack was typical in that he included nearly every charge that had ever been made against West Point. The institution, he said, was unconstitutional. The United States had nothing to fear from foreign nations and thus did not need an army. West Pointers monopolized the officer corps and degraded enlisted men. There were more Academy graduates than the army could use. The cadets went to West Point for a free education, not to learn how to be soldiers. The Academy was aristocratic in its make-up. It cost too much to run. It was unnecessary because the militia "of the country is its best and noblest and most trust-worthy defence in time of war."

Jacksonians tended to think that the government that governed least governed best, that the smaller the government the better, and that the Constitution ought to be strictly construed. A good place to start restricting the size and activities of the federal government, Dickinson thought, was West Point. "I fear, Sir, unless this excrescence shall be lopped off, that the segacious and observant enquirer will say that there is but little reliance to be placed in the promise of gentlemen to co-operate in restoring the government and the constitution to their original republican simplicity, and in hedging in all attempts and practices which go beyond the safe and clear warrant of the Federal compact." Dickinson was so pleased with his speech, and so certain of its popularity,

[8] This account is based on Dupuy, *Where They Have Trod,* 219–27.

that he had it printed at his own expense and distributed to his constituents.

Opponents of the Academy included more than just Jacksonians. Many anti-Jacksonian politicians, including David Crockett of Tennessee, were among those who wished to abolish West Point.[9] Their opposition was neither as bitter nor as emotional as that of the Jacksonians, but it was very real. Their objections were many. West Point was the only school the government maintained which put professional soldiers in a different (and higher) class than doctors, lawyers, or other professional men. The country needed ministers just as badly as it needed soldiers—in view of the protection afforded by the Atlantic Ocean and the absence of a strong threatening power on either American continent, the ministers were probably more necessary—but it did not give potential preachers a four-year scholarship. Even if the need for professional soldiers was granted, there was no guarantee that West Point would provide them, since a large percentage of graduates resigned from the army shortly after leaving the Academy. Most important, those West Point graduates who did remain in the army were gradually assuming control of that agency, which was becoming in effect a closed corporation, one which could be entered only through an Academy education. Thus America, which had hoped to extend its political revolution into all areas of life, was finding itself maintaining an army that, far from reflecting the hope and uniqueness of the American Revolution, was becoming more and more like the European armies. The only difference seemed to be that in Europe certain families controlled the officer corps, while in America West Point did.

George Washington, John Adams, Thomas Jefferson, and the others who had helped found the Academy had hoped that it would provide trained officers to lead the militia, thus giving America a revolutionary, democratic military establishment with leaders well versed in military science. That hope had never been realized, partly because of the failure of the militia system, partly

[9] *Speech of the Hon. David Dickinson in Opposition to the Military Academy* (Washington, 1834); *Reports of Committees,* Senate Document No. 201, Twenty-first Congress, First Session (Washington, 1830), 115–16.

because of the failure of West Point. The contempt at the Academy for the militia was so great that those graduates who went into civilian life almost never joined their local militia company; if war came, they planned either to return to the Regular Army or, failing that, join volunteer units. The only way the country could get the military establishment it wanted, or so it seemed, was to train its soldiers in private schools, just as members of other professions were trained, and then feed the graduates directly into the militia.

That was the program critics of West Point advocated, and in their attacks on the Academy they were able to add expert opinion to the advice of hostility and opportunity, and their expert was a former Superintendent. Following his enforced retirement from the army, Alden Partridge had returned to Vermont, where in 1820 he opened the American Literary, Scientific and Military Academy. He directed the school for over twenty years; in 1834, when it became Norwich University, he remained as president and retained ownership of the school property. During all that time he constantly criticized Thayer and West Point, called for the abolition of the standing army, and advocated a system of private military schools such as his throughout the country.[10] At first there was little response, but the rise of the Jacksonians gave Partridge a more receptive audience. Soon the demand to abolish the Academy was at its height; at West Point, isolated as it was, cause and catalyst were confused, and Professor Mahan declared that every attack could be "traced to the agency of that malicious old man, Capt. Partridge."[11]

"A little stir has been made here lately," Cadet George W. Cullum wrote a friend in 1830, "by the appearance of a pamphlet under the title of 'Military Academy Unmasked, or Corruption and Military Despotism Exposed.' "[12] Partridge was the author. He addressed the first section to congressmen, pleading with them to abolish the Academy, for "there is not on the whole globe an

[10] Daniel H. Calhoun, *The American Civil Engineer: Origins and Conflict* (Cambridge, 1960), 44.
[11] Couper, *V.M.I.*, I, 121.
[12] Cullum to Huidekoper, March 15, 1830, Cullum Papers.

establishment more monarchial, corrupt, and corrupting than this," which built a military aristocracy and, by filling all the vacancies in the army, created a little oligarchic club. Partridge addressed the second section to the President; in it he denounced Thayer, primarily for receiving credit for bringing system to West Point when in fact Partridge himself had done that and partly for Thayer's treatment of the cadets, which was "tyrannical, unjust, and even barbarous." Finally, Partridge spoke to the people of the United States, telling them that they paid the bills for this *"effeminate* and *pedantic"* institution so that it could shackle the mind and kill any spark of genius it found. West Pointers "sit high in authority and exercise command, while you and your sons, who pay $200,000 annually for their education, must approach them cap in hand, and move at their nod." Only the sons of politicians or influential men could become cadets, while "you and your sons are to march in the ranks; to carry the musket and knapsack; to be drudges, yea, the mere pack-horses of military service."[13] The only solution to an intolerable situation was to abolish the Academy and the standing army with it and rely upon the militia, officered by graduates of private military schools.[14]

As the organ of the people and the official expression of their military genius, the militia was popular. It was assumed to be democratic, although actually it was easier to obtain a commission in the militia on the basis of wealth and influence than it was in the army. Habitually and despite all previous experience, politicians flattered the militia. In his first inaugural address Andrew Jackson declared that "the bulwark of our defense is the national militia, which in the present state of our intelligence and population must render us invincible."[15]

By law, all young males were members of the militia, required to appear at the frequent militia days or pay a fine. Militia func-

[13] Alden Partridge, *The Military Academy, at West Point, Unmasked: Or, Corruption and Military Despotism Exposed* (Washington, 1830).

[14] Alden Partridge, *Capt. Partridge's Lecture on National Defence* (n.p., n.d.).

[15] James D. Richardson, *A Compilation of the Messages and Papers of the Presidents* (New York, 1911), II, 438.

tions were so numerous that Professor Mahan commented, "militia conventions seem to be the mania of the day." And, he sadly noted, their chief function seemed to be to listen to some diatribe or other on West Point, usually written by Partridge, and then to petition Congress for its dissolution.[16] In New York, a militia unit asked of the Academy, "Is it not a charity institution for the sons of broken down politicians, or the support of cringing sycophants for office?" and demanded that it be abolished, for it was "obnoxious to all our notions of equal rights." That could be done safely, for Captain Partridge's scholars were superior to West Point graduates and they could lead the military forces.[17] In Philadelphia the *Citizen Soldier* protested against "this *aristocratic excressence*" and asked Congress to abolish the Academy, giving the money it saved thereby to the states so that they could build their own military schools. Then the poor as well as the rich, the "people—the yeomanry—the mechanics—the laboring classes—the *producers*" could become officers.[18]

The Jacksonians usually centered their attack on two issues: the monopoly on the officer corps of the United States Army held by West Pointers, and the large number of resignations by Academy graduates from the army. Jackson's Secretary of War, John H. Eaton, declared in 1830 of the enlisted man, "He may become a corporal or a sergeant, but with that humble advance his hopes and his ambition terminate" because only West Pointers could become officers.[19] Senator Thomas Hart Benton of Missouri accused West Pointers of lording it over enlisted men. Encouraged by the politicians, in 1837 a group of noncommissioned officers petitioned Congress to authorize the appointment of some lieutenants from their ranks. The sergeants declared that the West Point monopoly was *"contrary to the true spirit of our country, and in opposition to all our Republican institutions"* and declared

[16] Mahan to Spencer, November 10, 1841, Dennis Hart Mahan Papers, USMA Library.

[17] *New York Military Magazine,* October 30, 1841.

[18] *The Citizen Soldier,* March 1, 1843.

[19] Richard L. Watson, "Congressional Attitudes Toward Military Preparedness, 1829–1835," *Mississippi Valley Historical Review,* XXXIV (March, 1948), 617.

that exclusion from the officer ranks was the cause "for the present abandoned and degraded condition of the American soldiery." Congress was happy to meet the sergeant's request, as it was to meet a similar demand from civilians who wanted commissions. In 1838, when Congress authorized some new regiments, it declared that the officers would have to come from civilian circles.[20]

Many a young officer must have wondered why anyone wanted a commission. An army career was unappealing, and morale in the service was low. Except on the frontier the people and the government were contemptuous of the army. In 1837 the *Army and Navy Chronicle* spoke of "the contempt in which the military service is held by Congress."[21] Ulysses S. Grant, an 1843 graduate, later remembered the first time he put on his uniform. He proudly rode through the streets of Cincinnati, "imagining that everyone was looking at me," when "a little urchin, bareheaded, barefooted, with dirty and ragged pants held up by a single gallows ... turned to me and cried: 'Soldier! will you work? No, sir-ee; I'll sell my shirt first!!' " This, Grant said, "gave me a distaste for military uniform that I never recovered from."[22]

The nation had no potential external enemy. The Indians were there, and to be sure they constituted a serious and continuing menace, but hardly one calculated to excite the imagination of a potential Napoleon. The officer might have been able to ignore the low esteem in which the nation held him if there had been compensations within the service, but there were not. The young graduate of West Point found himself on the very edge of civilization with a few resentful privates to command and a few savages to fight. Or, if he was lucky, he could get a post on the East Coast, where he would almost surely be given a quartermaster's duties— for which he had received no training—and would spend his days adding figures, proving to the auditors that he had not lost a single horseshoe and feeling very much like a common clerk. His pay was $25.00 a month; his possibilities practically none. Line officers received their promotions on a regimental basis; a second lieuten-

[20] Leonard D. White, *The Jacksonians* (New York, 1954), 187.
[21] *Ibid.*
[22] Ulysses S. Grant, *Personal Memoirs* (Cleveland, 1959), 17.

ant could move up to first lieutenant or a lieutenant colonel to colonel only when a vacancy occurred in his own regiment. There was no compulsory retirement law, and most officers stayed in the army, and thus in theory in command of their outfits, until they died. Many lieutenants had to wait twenty-five or thirty years for their captains to die before they could be promoted.[23] Excellence, devotion to duty, heroism—all counted for nothing.

The result was that few men of talent and ambition stayed in the army. With their knowledge and skill they were in demand for work on America's rapidly developing railroad and industrial empire; as engineers or architects or surveyors, West Point graduates could command a high salary and much prestige. In a single two-year period, 1835–1836, nearly 120 officers resigned their commissions. Many were recent graduates of the Academy, so in 1838 Congress required candidates for West Point to engage themselves for eight years instead of five, which meant four in the army after graduation.[24] That merely slowed down but could not stop the flood of resignations.

These facts seemed to the Jacksonians conclusive proof that the government was spending public money to promote private gain. The state legislature of Tennessee, finding the Academy "repugnant to the great and fundamental principles of our Government," therefore instructed its senators and requested its representatives to vote against appropriations for it.[25] Other legislatures soon chimed in, and in response the House of Representatives set up a series of committees to study the question of abolishing the Academy. The congressmen centered their attention on the problem of the graduates who resigned their commissions. Friends of West Point had maintained that this was all to the good, because their skills were made available to the people and in an emergency they would fly to the colors and save the Republic. One committee rejected this argument by saying that if a man could be educated at the public expense "upon the alleged possibility of a con-

---

[23] Stephen E. Ambrose, *Upton and the Army* (Baton Rouge, 1964), 142.
[24] White, *Jacksonians*, 197.
[25] *American State Papers: Military Affairs*, VII, 89, and V, 307.

tingency" that might some day render his services "necessary and useful," then "it is difficult to discover why others may not be educated in like manner . . . with special reference to a possible contingency that may render *their* services, also, necessary and useful." If soldiers could receive an education from the government without promising to serve it, why could not heads of departments, clerks, and accountants? The point was that young men were going to West Point not to get into the army and serve the Union but to get an education. One could only speculate on any future service they might render, and in any case it was obvious that in an emergency civilians would join the army as fast as Academy graduates. And these citizen-soldiers, heroes of so many battlefields of the Revolutionary War, would be discriminated against, for "the officer educated at West Point will cherish . . . a sense of personal superiority over another of his own grade, or even of a higher grade, . . . who has entered the army through some other avenue and with less imposing pretentions."

In view of all this, one committee recommended that the Academy change its orientation, that it no longer teach the elementary and theoretic sciences but become instead a school of application giving instruction only in purely professional matters.[26] With this system, only those who really wanted an army career would go to West Point, for they could learn nothing there that would help them in any other occupation. The House did not adopt the committee's recommendation, because enough members of the Congress recognized the basic errors in the approach. Most American colleges were not teaching the elementary sciences, and besides there was no way to separate military science and civilian knowledge. Whatever a man learned in the army he would be able to use in civilian life, especially in the field of engineering but in others too.

Enemies of West Point were disappointed, but they refused to give up. They continued their clamor, and in 1843 another committee, this time headed by Hamilton Fish of New York, met in response to more petitions to abolish the Academy. Fish, a staunch

[26] *Ibid.,* VII, 1–19.

Whig and more of a friend of the Academy than most politicians, based his final report primarily on information he solicited from Joseph Totten, the Chief Engineer. Generally it was favorable to the Academy, praising West Point for its accomplishments. In reply to the charge that the Academy was a breeding ground for an aristocracy, Fish quoted some figures Totten had supplied: the number of cadets at West Point whose parents were in moderate circumstances numbered 156; those with parents in reduced circumstances, 26; those with parents indigent, 6; and of the independently rich there were only 6 representatives. Fish also pointed out that while it cost $118.40 a year to educate a cadet at Woolwich and $89.00 a year at Sandhurst, the cost per cadet at West Point was only $70.70.

But even Fish had his doubts about how efficiently the nation was spending its money at West Point. He recommended that costs be reduced—the total cost of the Academy in 1843 had been $130,-380.25, or some $20,000.00 more than it had been thirty years earlier—by cutting the professors' salaries. Bartlett was receiving $2,266.00 per year, Mahan $2,013.00, and the others a little less than $2,000.00. Fish wanted them all pared down to $1,794.00, and Congress agreed. The resentment and outrage voiced at West Point obscured the essential victory Fish had won for the Academy; at least it was still in existence.[27]

It would stay in existence, for a number of reasons. Through the years, by his official acts and through his personal relations, Thayer had made influential friends and defenders of the Academy, including some Democrats, such as Gouverneur Kemble. Even congressmen who complained most about West Point usually ended up voting for it, since its elimination would deprive them of an important source of patronage. The Board of Visitors, with its annual report, played a part in making the Academy popular, although its praise was sometimes too fulsome and its language

[27] *Report on the Military Academy,* House Document No. 476, Twenty-eighth Congress, First Session (Washington, 1844); *American State Papers: Military Affairs,* III, 818.

too high-blown to be convincing, as for example the conclusion of the report for 1830:

> Inheriting from our varied ancestry the discordant character-istics of every people on the globe, it yet remains to form a specific and all pervading character for the American nation; nor do we conceive any surer method of stamping upon the yet glowing wax a more majestic form, than by sending into every district young men emphatically the children of our country, trained to the manly exercise of arms, and imbued with the tastes of science and literature; instructed in the principles and action of our political system, and the living exemplar from which sound education may rear the social edifice.[28]

But the real reason the Jacksonians did not destroy the Academy was that it was doing a job no one else could do, a job the Jacksonians wanted done more than they wanted anything else. As a congressional committee pointed out, the railroads that connected Boston with the interior, the harbors in Rhode Island and Connecticut, the Susquehanna and Baltimore and the Baltimore and Ohio Railroads, new roads in Michigan and Arkansas, harbor improvements on the Gulf Coast and Mississippi River—all were the products of civil engineers trained at West Point. "These are some of the enduring memorials of the usefulness of the Military Academy, and of the returns it has made for the care, and time, and money which have been bestowed upon it," the committee, which was otherwise hostile, reported.[29]

It was the most effective argument possible. Whatever else may have divided the American people, they were agreed on the necessity of building up and settling the continent. Although politically they might divide on how or where to build the canals, harbors, and railroads, nothing else was as important to them as internal improvements, and those who were capable of directing the building commanded respect. This conviction was especially felt by the Jacksonians, who with all their emphasis upon equality knew that equality without opportunity was meaningless. And every new

[28] White, *Jacksonians,* 197.
[29] *American State Papers: Military Affairs,* IV, 347–55.

railroad or canal or harbor or wilderness road opened up countless new opportunities.

Since the landings at Jamestown, Americans had been engaged in a gigantic struggle with their continent. In the seventeenth and eighteenth centuries they had made great strides towards conquering the area between the mountains and the Atlantic Ocean, but much still remained to be done on the East Coast, and west of the mountains only an occasional path through the wilderness testified to man's presence. Internal improvements would open up this area and its great wealth; the problem was who should undertake the task. As Albert Gallatin, Secretary of the Treasury, pointed out in 1808, the utility of roads and canals was universally admitted, but no one could agree on who should build them. Gallatin argued that private capitalists could not do it, both because of the scarcity of capital and the extent of the territory involved, so the task rightfully belonged to the federal government, which should undertake it to foster the general good. Besides leading to a growth in trade, such an operation would enhance unity: "No other single operation, within the power of Government, can more effectually tend to strengthen and perpetuate that Union which secures external independence, domestic peace, and internal liberty."[30]

Political conflicts in Congress, usually centering around the choice of the area in which canals or roads should be built, whether North or South or West, prevented any major action from that direction. The first step towards an effective national program of internal improvements came from the army, which in 1816 established the Board of Engineers for Fortifications, under the command of an immigrant French engineer, Simon Bernard. For the next eight years Bernard's Board, along with the Topographical Bureau, established simultaneously with the Board, engaged in projects of interest to mercantile and manufacturing groups as well as to the army—surveys in Albemarle Sound, for instance, and the development of rivers and harbors, navigation canals, and roads. In the General Survey Act of 1824 Congress had recognized the army's contribution and had authorized the

[30] *American State Papers: Miscellaneous,* I, 724–41.

President to use army officers as advisors to private groups building roads and canals of national importance. This Act led to the establishment of the Board of Engineers for Internal Improvements, made up of Chief Engineer Joseph Totten, Bernard, and a civilian engineer, with some twenty army officers attached to it. Under the General Survey Act the army provided engineers for many state and private internal improvement programs, including the Chesapeake and Ohio Canal, the Morris Canal, the Delaware and Raritan Canal, the Baltimore and Ohio Railroad, and the Western and Atlantic Railroad. Just as the program was at its height, however, and the railroad boom in full swing, the Jacksonians took office, and they expressed their hostility to government officials' aiding private firms by abolishing the Board of Engineers for Internal Improvements and later by repealing the General Survey Act. One of the immediate results was to encourage the private firms to offer lucrative salaries to army officers, with an immediate rise in resignations from the army.[31]

Almost to a man the army engineers who worked on these projects were West Point graduates; the importance of the Academy to the early development of American roads, canals, and railroads cannot be overstated. Until the Mexican War, with the single exception of Rensselaer Polytechnic Institute (founded more than two decades after the Academy), West Point was the only institution in the country training civil engineers.[32] Its only real rival was the Erie Canal, but by the thirties West Point was much more important than the Erie as a supplier of engineers.[33] In 1833 some 25 West Point graduates were serving as civil engineers; by 1836 the number was up to 39, and in 1838 it was 120. In all, 231 Academy graduates had worked as civil engineers by 1837 (out of a total of 940 graduates) on one project or another.[34] Thus did the Academy meet one of the hopes Thomas

[31] Calhoun, *American Civil Engineer*, 38–39.

[32] Charles R. Mann, *A Study of Engineering Education* (New York, 1911), 3–5.

[33] Richard S. Kirby and Philip G. Laurson, *The Early Years of Modern Civil Engineering* (New Haven, 1932), 47; Calhoun, *American Civil Engineering*, 43.

[34] Calhoun, *American Civil Engineer*, 43–53.

Jefferson had expressed when he founded it; thus did it supply, albeit only partially, the national direction for internal improvements Gallatin had dreamed of.

The graduates who did the work were well equipped for the task. From the first the course in engineering included material in civil engineering; by 1826 the course included roads, tunneling, inland navigation, railroad construction, and artificial harbors. In 1831 the course was again expanded, as evidenced a little later by the emphasis in Mahan's *Elementary Course of Civil Engineering*.[35] In 1829 the Board of Visitors noted that Mahan was teaching more civil than military engineering, a fact that the Board of 1830 applauded. "We consider, then, that this academy is designed to furnish . . . a corps of engineers, capable of giving wholesome direction to the spirit of enterprize which pervades our country." The Board predicted "that the pupils of West Point will deliver the country from that quack engineering which has, in divers instances, inflicted deep wounds upon our system of internal improvement."[36] The Academy had the largest engineering library in the United States, with 692 volumes, of which 308 dealt with civil engineering, including books in Latin, Italian, German, French, and English.[37]

Many West Point graduates who did not themselves become civil engineers became the teachers of students who did; the Academy's influence in the pedagogic aspects of civil engineering at least equaled its influence in the actual building process. Rensselaer Polytechnic Institute used texts written at West Point; Lawrence Scientific School at Harvard and the Sheffield Scientific School at Yale both used Academy graduates as their first teachers. Other schools followed their example; by 1870, of the nineteen technical schools in the United States, ten had direct West Point ancestry and the others were strongly influenced by it. The Colum-

[35] Dennis H. Mahan, *An Elementary Course of Civil Engineering for the Use of the Cadets of the United States Military Academy* (New York, 1837).
[36] *American State Papers: Military Affairs*, IV, 603; Calhoun, *American Civil Engineer*, 40–42.
[37] Sidney Forman, "The First School of Engineering," *The Military Engineer*, II (March–April, 1952), 109–12.

bia University School of Mines asked three Academy graduates to give it "a thorough mathematical foundation for engineering studies characteristic of West Point." The American Society of Civil Engineers, established in 1852, had four West Point graduates as charter members, and of the six honorary members, four were Academy men—John J. Abert, Alexander D. Bache, Mahan, and Totten.[38] But perhaps greater praise had come two years earlier, when President Francis Wayland at Brown declared, "The single academy at West Point has done more toward the construction of railroads than all our . . . colleges united."[39]

In truth, West Point was becoming more of a civil engineering school than a military academy. One cadet summed up the mood when he told an English traveler, "We must get up early, for we have a large territory; we have to cut down the forests, dig canals, and make railroads all over the country."[40] All of this put the Jacksonians in a tight position. They complained again and again about this development, about the government's training men to use their knowledge for gain supposedly private, and about the national flavor West Point gave to the internal improvement program, but in the end it probably was because of this program that they had to abandon their attack on the Academy. No matter how many Maysville Road vetoes General Jackson might issue, the fact remained that nothing was more popular with the people than internal improvements. The most exciting news to any community was that a railroad was going to come through town; next to that, even Jackson's stirring messages paled. Usually, the railroad was being constructed by a West Pointer. Meanwhile, the Jacksonian movement was losing its steam and American politics moving into a new era, one in which internal improvements, expansion, and sectional controversy, not questions of privilege, were the issues. Occasionally in the forties the old Jacksonian attack flared up again, but the record of the Academy graduates in the Mexican War, coming in the second half of the decade, stilled almost all criticism. Because of these things the Academy was saved.

[38] *Ibid.*
[39] Rudolph, *American College*, 238.
[40] *Ibid.*, 67.

Chapter VII

The Golden Age, 1840-1860

The years from 1840 to 1860 marked West Point's greatest age. They began with the conclusion of the Jacksonian attack and they ended with a war that was to make West Pointers famous throughout the world. In between, the United States fought its first successful war of expansion, winning an unbroken series of victories, thanks in large part to the skill of young West Pointers. The country settled all the continent east of the Mississippi River and a large part of the area to the west of it. In the process, America built an enormous number of roads, canals, and railroads. West Point men protected the settlers moving west while building the communication facilities that carried them there. In academic affairs West Point's influence continued to spread, as it improved its courses and remained pre-eminent in science. Morale at the Academy was unsurpassed; under the direction of a series of brilliant professors and Superintendents, cadets worked and studied harder than the students at any of the American colleges. Passing through the institution during those years were men whose names would one day be household words—Lee, Jackson, Beauregard, Grant, Sherman, and McClellan, among others.

Two Superintendents dominated the period, Robert E. Lee and Richard Delafield, who between them headed the Academy for thirteen of the twenty years. Lee (Superintendent 1852–55), son

[125]

of a Revolutionary War hero and member of one of Virginia's first families, had graduated second in his class and gone on to serve with great distinction in the Corps of Engineers. He compiled an outstanding record during the Mexican War and was considered the most promising officer in the army. He was just about everybody's favorite. General Winfield Scott thought he was certain to become the General in Chief. His Superintendency was a great success, adding to his already high reputation. Delafield was neither as well known nor as capable as Lee, but during his two terms as Superintendent (1838–45 and 1856–61) he was able to conserve the gains others had made.

The two officers were much different, both in their habits and appearance. Lee was a man of dignity and grace, strikingly handsome, quiet, and patient. One of his charges reported that "by his generous, manly and consistent conduct he has won the respect and esteem of every Cadet in the Corps."[1] Delafield was a pudgy little man with an enormous nose (which led to some very bad cadet poetry) and a nervous temperament. He was constantly bustling around the post, instituting changes, looking for troublemakers, investigating petty occurrences. His habit of making sarcastic puns earned him the nickname "Dicky the Punster."[2]

Both men were devoted to the Academy and to the Corps of Engineers, and both fought successfully to prevent the War Department from taking the Superintendency of West Point away from the Engineers. The idea of opening the Superintendency to the army as a whole, so that cavalry, artillery, or infantry officers could share in running the Academy, had originated with John C. Calhoun, who as early as 1820 had pointed out that West Point was much more than a training school for engineers. It had some two hundred and fifty cadets, of whom usually less than twenty-five went into the Corps of Engineers. Since it was training men for all branches of the army, the Academy ought to be separated from the Corps of Engineers and taken under the direct control of the

[1] Hartz to father, November 18, 1852, Edward L. Hartz Papers, Library of Congress.
[2] Morris Schaff, *Old West Point,* 37; Keyes, *Fifty Years',* 193.

War Department, which would then choose the Superintendent from any branch of the army.[3] Through the decades the agitation continued, with most of the non-Engineers in the army supporting the proposed change. The Superintendents were hostile to the idea, and they defended the monopoly of the Engineers by citing West Point's record and averring that its improvement could not have taken place without the support of the Engineers. In the end the prestige of the Engineers was powerful enough to block any change.[4]

Throughout the period relations between the armed services and Congress improved, not so much because of a changed attitude on the part of the politicians, although that was there, but more because both army and navy officers and the civilian Secretaries of the services were becoming more adept at getting what they wanted from the government. One example was the United States Naval Academy. For years the navy had wanted something similar to West Point, but despite the poor record of navy midshipmen, who received their training on board naval vessels, the navy had never been able to get any action from Congress. George Bancroft, historian and politician, finally solved the problem by presenting Congress with a *fait accompli*. As Secretary of the Navy he had the power to send midshipmen to a specified place to await orders and to direct instructors to teach them, so in the summer of 1845, when he was acting Secretary of War as well as Secretary of the Navy, Bancroft in the first capacity agreed to loan Fort Severn at Annapolis to the navy and in the second capacity ordered the midshipmen and four instructors there. He installed Commander Franklin Buchanan as Superintendent; within six months Buchanan had dismissed two midshipmen for insubordination, four for drunkenness, and one for delirium tremens. When Congress came back in session, the Naval Academy was a going concern, so congressmen gave in and began appropriating the money to support it.[5]

[3] *American State Papers: Military Affairs,* II, 75.

[4] *RC,* 143. Barnard to Board of Visitors, June 6, 1856, Superintendent's Letter Book, Archives, USMA. Hereafter cited as SLB.

[5] White, *Jacksonians,* 249–50.

When it asked for appropriations, West Point also benefited from better relations with Congress. There were no spectacular increases, but some extra money came in for a building program, and the Academy was in the happy position of being able to count on its annual appropriation. The important legal achievement of the period was the law Congress passed in 1843 which regularized the method of appointment of cadets. For decades it had been the practice of the Secretary of War to appoint one cadet from each congressional district, but the tradition had no legal foundation. In 1843 Congress ordered that the Corps of Cadets should consist of one man from each district (in theory the selection remained with the Secretary of War, but in fact he chose the man recommended by the local congressman) plus ten "at-large" cadets— young men appointed by the President of the United States.[6] For the army the latter provision proved a godsend, for it early became traditional for the President to appoint officers' sons to the Academy. For most army officers, moving from post to post with no roots or political connections within the states, this was the only way they could get their sons into their old school.

In return for this gift, Congress insisted on keeping the "eminently popular, republican, and equal conditions of admission"; in other words, on keeping the entrance requirements at an absolute minimum, so that few of the appointees need worry about being embarrassed by flunking the examination. All the Superintendents and faculty members and many of the cadets argued that the nation was wasting its money on incompetent boys. Through the years fewer than one-half of the cadets admitted to West Point graduated, and in the class of 1859, of one hundred and three admitted, only forty-one graduated. The politicians, however, argued that a higher standard of admission would result in the "success of the *best instructed,* wholly irrespective of capacity. . . . . The plan secures the services of dull mediocrity, well instructed; and excludes genius, without opportunities of development. It gives the very advantage to the rich over the poor, which the genius of our institutions prohibits."[7] So the examinations con-

[6] *CWP,* I, 3.
[7] *RC,* 8.

tinued in the old way. A cadet who took them in 1854 reported that he wrote down a few lines read out from a book, read aloud a page himself, and then was admitted to the Academy.[8] Edward Hartz left the best account of the examination; like most cadets he seems to have found the most difficult part of it facing up to the Academic Board. "About 3 o'clock, the 1st section of new cadets . . . was marched to the Library building. When there we were obliged to confront the most rigid, cold and merciless looking set of men I ever before beheld. They seemed so much oppressed by the weight of dignity that rests upon them, that a kind look was as much a stranger to their faces, as good living has been to me since I have landed here. There were about twenty of us marched in at once. The mathematical examination consisted of questions in vulgar and decimal fractions. . . . We were then called upon to read, I read an extract from Blair which was satisfactorily done. I was then called upon to write [a sentence]. This I done and was sent to my seat. This closed the examination."[9]

Despite the level of the examination, a large percentage of the candidates, sometimes over one-half, could not pass it. Most of the failures were from the South and West, which was a point often used to defend the existing situation—if the standards were raised, West Point would become almost exclusively an eastern institution, since boys from other areas could not receive a proper preparation. As things stood, the Academy already had an eastern orientation, because a higher percentage of southerners and westerners were "found," or dismissed for academic deficiencies, and because easterners were more apt to stand at or near the top of a class and thus return as assistant professors. In 1840 all the professors were easterners, and twelve of the seventeen assistants and instructors were from the East.[10]

Thus despite all the statements and all the efforts of the authorities at West Point, the Corps of Cadets did constitute an aristocracy. The course of studies was so rigorous that only those with

8 Cushing to uncle, June 22, 1854, George William Cushing Papers, USMA Library.

9 Hartz to father, June 25, 1851, Hartz Papers.

10 Lewis, *Grant*, 66–67.

outstanding ability or excellent preparation could stay in the school. Further, because of the method of congressional selection, the cadets tended to come from families of importance in the district, for it did a politician little good to select a boy whose parents could not help him in the next election. The only congressmen who might make a sincere attempt to appoint the most intelligent young men in their districts were westerners, because many of the western districts had never had an Academy graduate, every cadet from the area having been "found." Sooner or later local pride would assert itself, and the congressman would try to find a boy who could make it through West Point. From the East and the South, however, sons of the best families regularly appeared to take the oath as a cadet; in 1858 there were a Washington from Virginia, a Buchanan from Pennsylvania, a Breckinridge from Kentucky, a Huger and a Mordecai from South Carolina, a du Pont from Delaware, and a Hasbrouck and a Vanderbilt from New York. [11]

These boys, along with the officers, set the tone at West Point, which was one of haughty contempt for civilians, militiamen, and enlisted men. Once Cadet Oliver O. Howard found that one of his neighbors from back home was a sergeant in the company of school troops stationed at West Point, so he called on him and spent an afternoon talking with him. The officers and the cadets roundly criticized Howard for this, and the adjutant called him in and said, "You must remember that it will be for your own advantage to separate yourself from your friend while he is in the unfortunate position of an enlisted man." Within the Corps, too, there had developed over the years a definite graduation in status that all respected. Each class bowed to the one above it, while all worshipped the First Class, so much so that one cadet, when he became a member of that class, reported, "we acquire that air of importance, that show of dignity and condescension to our inferiors which forms the great characteristic of First Class Men." [12]

[11]Schaff, *Old West Point*, 80–81.
[12] Oliver O. Howard, *Autobiography* (New York, 1908), I, 50–51; Hartz to father, September 7, 1854, Hartz Papers.

But if to the outside world the cadets presented a solid front of superiority, within their own class, birth, wealth, manners, and position counted for nothing. There they were expected to fight each other for higher rank, based solely on their academic standing and demerits. "Little favoritism is shown and everyone starts with a fair chance to excel in his classes," Cadet Cullen Bryant told a younger friend who was about to enter the Academy. "This is probably more the case here than at any other institution in the country."[13] The principle of pure competition, the fighting for higher standing and rank, permeated every aspect of Academy life. Indeed, competition was raised to the level of a virtue in and of itself.[14] That it generally made the cadets work harder and produced good results there can be no doubt; Cadet Hartz pointed out another development when he told his sister, "I cannot find as good open hearts" among the cadets as among the young men at home. "There is a species of lurking selfishness hanging around cadets," he said, for "in class every man is in a degree jealous of his neighbor, in some greater or less according as the feeling is called forth by circumstances of position."[15] Inasmuch as there was a weekly posting of grades and inasmuch as a man's career was hanging on the result, it could hardly have been otherwise.

The difficulty and the thoroughness of the curriculum added to the keenness of the competition. Every cadet, in every subject, every day—that was Thayer's dictum, and hundreds of cadets could testify that it had not been forgotten. Those who had been to other colleges before coming to West Point were amazed at how much they were expected to know and how well they were required to know it. Students back home, one cadet wrote, "have not the faintest idea of what hard study is." "You can not and you dare not slight anything" at West Point, he said, for you may be called

[13] Bryant to Sweete, May 2, 1860, Byrant Family Papers, New York Public Library. In contradiction, Cadet Hartz maintained, "There is much favouritism at West Point, and Cadets with nothing to depend upon but themselves have much to contend with which perhaps it would not be proper for me to write. . . ." Hartz is the only cadet the author knows of who made this charge. Hartz to father, February 1, 1852, Hartz Papers.

[14] See *RC*, 32.

[15] Hartz to sister, July 30, 1852, Hartz Papers.

on at any time, on any aspect of the course. One sufferer, Cullen Bryant, took time from his studies to report home that he "was expected to come to the section room with a thorough knowledge of the day's lesson, and to be ready when called upon to go to the board and to take any part of it which may be given and discuss it thoroughly." West Point, Bryant observed, covered more ground in one month than the ordinary college did in three, and the level of the work was higher. "Indeed," Bryant said, "I find that a recitation which would very easily pass for perfect with Mr. Smith might be almost a failure before Lt. Howard or Prof. Church."[16] Cadet Henry A. du Pont found West Point at least twice as difficult as the University of Pennsylvania.[17]

Mathematics was by far the most important subject, both because it was the basis for later study in natural philosophy and engineering and because it counted most in making up the academic merit roll. No cadet could graduate high in his class unless he stood well in mathematics, and as one cadet reported, "in the history of the Institution no one has ever stood head [of his class] but he who has an extraordinary talent for Mathematics."[18] This emphasis infuriated the bulk of the cadets, because only down-east Yankees had the preparation necessary to handle the advanced mathematics. So Richard S. Ewell remarked, observing that southerners and westerners could never surpass the Yankees, and thus nearly always the head of the class was an easterner.[19] Mathematics was also responsible for most of the failures at the Academy, and Professor Church, a kindly man, had many sleepless nights during examinations because he was responsible for the majority of the "found" men.[20]

To those who had difficulty with the subject, mathematics became an obsession. Cadet George Cushing told his father, "I can't write as good a letter as I used to—as I am always thinking of

[16] Bryant to father, October 6, 1860, Bryant Family Papers.
[17] Du Pont to mother, October 17, 1857, du Pont Papers.
[18] Hartz to father, January 25, 1852, Hartz Papers.
[19] Ewell to Rebecca Ewell, August 29, 1836, Misc. Mss., USMA Library.
[20] William P. Smith Diary, entry of January 31, 1855, Archives, Louisiana State University.

Math. —I have a nightmare every night almost of it. —Gigantic X's and Y's, +'s and —'s squat on me—and amuse themselves in sticking me with equations, and pounding me on the head. . . ."[21] Cadet James J. Ewing expressed his feelings more succinctly when he inscribed on the fly-leaf of his calculus book, "God damn all mathematics to the lowest depths of hell!!"[22]

The cadets could not neglect their work all semester, then study intensively for finals, and come through with a good grade. Still, the January and June examinations were traumatic experiences, for they did weigh heavily in the final standings. Cadets approached them with trepidation, took them in a state of extreme nervousness, and finished them with huge sighs of relief. "Oh! Lord," Cadet Cushing wrote his parents immediately after his January examination in 1855, "I was examined to day and passed the best of any in the section."[23] After the June examination of the previous year Cadet Hartz bragged to his father, "I write with a feeling of exultation and true gratification. I have passed the second class June examination upon the most extended and difficult course of philosophy, comprising mechanics, acoustics, Optics, astronomy and magnetism, taught at any institution in the World."[24] Questions might be either general or specific, and they ranged over the entire area of the course. One cadet was required to discuss the subject of friction, give its laws, and find a value for the coefficient of friction by means of the inclined plane.[25] Another mathematics question was to prove that the logarithms of the same numbers in different systems are to each other as the moduli of those systems.[26] In natural philosophy, Cadet Hartz was asked to draw a cross section of the human eye and to explain its construction and the optical principles upon which its efficiency depended.[27] In his final examination of his First Class year, Hartz was required to "show the method of constructing a Crown work

[21] Cushing to father, November 28, 1854, Cushing Papers.
[22] Forman, *West Point*, 86.
[23] Cushing to parents, January 3, 1855, Cushing Papers.
[24] Hartz to father, June 8, 1854, Hartz Papers.
[25] Hartz to father, January 15, 1854, *ibid.*
[26] Cushing to parents, January 3, 1855, Cushing Papers.
[27] Hartz to father, June 8, 1854, Hartz Papers.

for the defence of a bridge head and to show the dispositions which would be made to secure the passage of the river to a large army in the face of an Enemy," and to demonstrate the proper positions of flankers and rear guards in a march. In ethics he had to discuss the subject of "justice as it respects reputation, and the moral law applicable thereto"; in mineralogy, to give an account of the formation of coral reefs and peat moss "and the agencies which have led to the consolidation of loose material on the surface of the earth." He also took examinations in artillery, infantry, and cavalry tactics.[28]

The tactical questions were based on work done in the summer encampment, which was almost completely in the hands of the Commandant and his tactical department. In the three months allotted to them these officers tried to teach the cadets as much as they could about every aspect of practical soldiering. They set up a laboratory, where they gave instruction to First Class cadets in manufacturing all types of ammunition and flares. In the field, the cadets made gabions, fascines, sap rollers, and so on, as well as bridges; in the summer of 1854 the First Class made a pile and a trestle bridge. It was also in the summer of their last year that cadets learned advanced artillery practice. They operated the mortar battery, the siege, light, and mounted batteries, and the huge seacoast pieces, the Columbiads. Wrestling with these pieces, a cadet from the coal regions of Pennsylvania reported, was "as much like work as Coal breakers, pump shafts, etc. ever was." A few hours every afternoon were devoted to theoretical artillery.[29]

The junior classes spent the summer learning infantry tactics and the duties of camp life. Each Commandant jealously guarded the Corps' reputation as a marching unit, and the cadets spent hours each day drilling. They all liked to show off, especially when a delegation of militia officers came to observe them. Whenever the army wanted to test a new drill system, one adopted in response to some weapons change in order to introduce more speed and maneuverability, it would automatically experiment on

[28] Hartz to father, June 8, 1855, *ibid.*
[29] Hartz to father, August 15, 1854, *ibid.*

the Corps of Cadets. After they had learned it, delegations of army and militia officers would come to West Point to see it work. The cadets would proudly demonstrate the new system, as in 1854 with a Chasseur drill, and "astonish all the gaping Cit soldiers. . . ."[30] As long as weather permitted, drill continued during the regular sessions, to the disgust of the cadets. It was at this time that the Commandant usually introduced a new system, and being eager to demonstrate it, he made the cadets work long and hard hours on it. Cadets often returned from the parade ground after dusk, too tired to study.[31]

In 1839, at Delafield's urging, the Secretary of War sent a sergeant, five dragoons, and twelve horses to West Point, and the first instruction in horsemanship was soon under way. The next year Delafield purchased thirty additional horses and secured a harness for a light artillery battery.[32] In 1846 the Riding Hall was completed, which allowed the cadets to ride all year long. They began by riding bareback and progressed through intricate group cavalry drills. The Riding Hall also served as a classroom for Monsieur Pierre Thomas, the Master of the Sword, who taught fencing.[33] One of the most memorable days in the Riding Hall came in the early forties. The finest horse at West Point was York, a chestnut-colored animal, seventeen hands high, with a strong will. York would not tolerate an inferior rider and would throw him off, then go through the remainder of the drill alone, never making a mistake. His favorite rider was a young Ohio cadet who had a way with horses, Ulysses S. Grant. Once, before the Board of Visitors and a large crowd of spectators, the riding-master had one of his dragoons hold a pole at arms' length above his head, the other end resting against the wall, and signaled Grant, mounted on York, to jump it. They cleared the pole, "coming down with a tremendous

[30] Hartz to father, October 16, November 3, 1854, *ibid.*

[31] Smith Diary, entry of October 26, 1854; C. C. Jesup to sister, October 29, 1854, Misc. Mss., USMA Library; Harris to father, February 28, 1858, William H. Harris Papers, New York Public Library.

[32] H. Irving Hancock, *Life at West Point* (New York, 1906), 13–14.

[33] William H. Baumer, *West Point: Moulder of Men* (New York, 1942), 187–88.

thud" in a din of applause. The crowd called for a repeat, and the team of Grant and York did it three more times.[34]

The Commandant exercised general supervision of the riding program. In many ways he was a man more important to the cadets than anyone on the faculty, because he directed the tactical program and was responsible for discipline. His influence spread throughout the army; as one faculty member remarked in the late fifties, "The Commandant of the Corps exercises a more important influence on the military character and opinions of the junior officers of the Army than any other individual." In the forties and fifties West Point had a series of able Commandants, men who would make their reputation in the Civil War, such as Charles F. Smith, Robert S. Garnett, William H. T. Walker, William J. Hardee, and John F. Reynolds. They came from all the branches of the line. One of the infantrymen, Lieutenant J. Addison Thomas, was a favorite among the cadets because of his penchant for getting himself into impossible verbal situations. Cadet George B. McClellan reported one of his speeches, given just before a battalion drill. "After invoking our military spirit and a few other little eccentricities he wound up by saying, 'You are not common soldiers! You are gentlemen—gentlemen of manners, of politeness, of education. The United States looks to you! The country looks to you! The Army looks to you—and—aah—ahemm—ahemm—By Company right wheel! Head of column to the left, guide right! Quick March!!!!!' "[35]

The most ambitious Commandant was William J. Hardee, of the Second Cavalry. He thought students at the country's only military academy should have more instruction in the art of strategy than they were getting and offered to have the tactical department provide it. Thayer had once made the same proposal. Professor Mahan protested that he was already teaching the subject in his engineering classes, and it was true that this section of Mahan's course was the most popular at West Point. The trouble

[34] Oliver E. Wood, *The West Point Scrap Book* (New York, 1871), 289.

[35] McClellan to Mrs. English, September 10, 1842, McClellan Papers, Library of Congress; Nathaniel C. Hughes, Jr., *General William J. Hardee: Old Reliable* (Baton Rouge, 1965), 59.

was that Mahan spent so much time on military and civil engineering that he only had a few days left over for strategy.[36] It was the unanimous opinion of the cadets that the course was too short.[37] In 1860 Hardee, pointing out that "the course on strategy has, perhaps, more attractions for the cadet than any other pursued at the institution," gained Secretary of War Jefferson Davis' support, and got it transferred to the tactical department. He continued to use Mahan's *Out-Post* as the text. But the next year, 1861, Hardee went off to fight for the Confederacy, and Mahan quietly brought strategy back into the engineering course.[38]

Extracurricular activities at West Point were limited. They centered around the two debating societies, the Dialectic and the Amosophic. Both were modeled on those at other American colleges, where the tradition was long established of having two rival debating societies, with names like Philanthropic, Diognothian, Atheneum, Philodemic, and Philonomosian. At the colleges and at West Point the clubs took the place of courses in political science, for in their debates the students discussed both theoretical political questions—"Ought freedom of thought to be granted to all men?" and "Do the talents of men deteriorate in the Western Hemisphere?"—as well as immediate and national ones—"Is the Missouri Compromise constitutional?" and "Does a protective tariff serve the interest of the people?"[39] At the society's request, Superintendent Delafield once asked Benjamin F. Butler to speak to the Dialectic Society.[40] When it did not have an outside speaker, the Dialectic assigned four of its members to declaim and six to debate at its Saturday evening meetings.[41]

[36] See Hartz to father, March 21, 1855, Hartz Papers; Denton, "Formative Years," 199.
[37] *RC*, 95.
[38] *Ibid.*, 95, 137; Hughes, *Hardee*, 55.
[39] Rudolph, *American College*, 137–38.
[40] Delafield to Butler, April 28, 1839, SLB.
[41] "By Laws of the Dialectic Society," George B. McClellan Papers, Library of Congress.

Both the Dialectic and the Amosophic tried to build up a library by appropriating money from the monthly dues of the members, but neither was very successful.[42] Perforce, the cadets had to fall back on the Academy library for their reading, with varying results. Some thought it excellent, some denounced it as ridiculously poor. Ulysses Grant, a tanner's son, was impressed by the library, while Henry A. du Pont, after a few unsuccessful ventures, never bothered to visit it.[43] James Harrison Wilson came from an Illinois family with some pretensions to culture and thus represented something of a middle ground. He thought the twenty-thousand volumes in the library were good enough as far as they went but that the orientation was too heavily military and foreign. The library did not subscribe to any of the magazines or reviews of the day, had only a few historical works, and aside from a few novels contained no light reading. The curator was Andre Fries, whom Wilson remembered as a "kindly old man who was there for years . . . and who was most helpful in introducing me to the treasures of the library. He influenced me most of all the men I knew."[44]

The crowning jewel of intellectual life at West Point was the Napoleon Club, an organization composed of the instructors, assistant professors, and professors. Mahan, who worshipped Napoleon, was president, and the members included McClellan, G. W. Smith, Superintendent Lee, and Dabney Maury. Lee gave the club a room in the academic building, and on the walls the members painted large maps of the theater of Napoleon's campaigns in Spain, Italy, and Germany. It was generally referred to as the "Napoleon Room," and occasionally officers would take cadets into it and lecture on a battle or a campaign. At their meetings, the members of the Napoleon Club discussed and argued over Napoleon's movements. All of them had studied under Mahan and regarded Napoleon as the consummate military

[42] Latrobe, "West Point," 23.
[43] Grant, *Memoirs*, 16; see Henry A. du Pont's correspondence with his family in du Pont Papers.
[44] James H. Wilson, *Under the Old Flag* (New York, 1912), I, 9–10; *RC*, 9–10; Smith Diary, entry of November 25, 1853.

genius. Most of them would fight in the Civil War, where they always tried, usually without success, to emulate the Corsican's moves. The most active member of the Club was George B. McClellan.[45]

The years proceeded at West Point, with little to distinguish among them except for changes in the physical plant. In 1836 West Point erected its first chapel, which was the first ambitious architectural undertaking at the Academy. A Roman basilica with a Grecian portico, it set the tradition of using local quarried stone for Academy buildings. Two years later the first academic building burned down (all the Academy records went with it); its replacement was, like the chapel, in the classic style. A trend towards classical buildings seemed well under way, but when Delafield arrived he stopped it short. Delafield did more building than any other nineteenth-century Superintendent. He was interested in architecture, had strong opinions on the subject, and designed the buildings himself. His style was English Tudor, with heavy emphasis on castellated towers and sally ports. During his two terms he built the library, the Riding Hall and cavalry stables, and a new cadet barracks and influenced the construction in 1851 of the new cadet mess, now Grant Hall.[46]

Captain Henry Brewerton, a most unpopular Superintendent with the cadets (1845–52), did much to add to the convenience of life at West Point. He graded the surface of the Plain, built the South Wharf and the road to it, enlarged the water supply, and constructed several cottages for the officers and their families.[47] In 1850 he persuaded a telegraph company to run a line from New York and establish an office at West Point.[48]

The greatest excitement of the period came in 1846, when the United States declared war on Mexico. "Hip! Hip! Hurrah!"

[45] P. S. Michie, *General McClellan* (New York, 1901), 24; Maury, *Recollections,* 50–51; Harris to father, April 4, 1858, Harris Papers.

[46] Gray, "Architectural Development of West Point." Misc. Mss., USMA Library.

[47] Boynton, *West Point,* 245.

[48] Brewerton to Gillett, March 30, 1850, SLB.

Cadet McClellan exclaimed. "War at last sure enough! Aint it glorious! 15,000 regulars and 50,000 volunteers!"[49] McClellan did not have to be told what the war would mean to a cadet. He might look forward to battle and the chance to distinguish himself and perhaps receive a brevet or even a regular promotion. And even if he did not get to the scene of hostilities, the expansion of the army meant that he could count on a commission as a regular second lieutenant upon graduation, not just a brevet rank.

In the second half of the nineteenth century and throughout the twentieth century, civilian soldiers would complain about the way in which West Pointers dominated the army, especially its upper ranks. In 1846, however, West Point had not yet established itself within the army, and none of the generals were Academy men. The best of them, however, Winfield Scott and Zachary Taylor, recognized the abilities of the young West Pointers and used them extensively. Nearly all the men who would rise to high command positions in the Civil War fought in Mexico and with scarcely an exception distinguished themselves there. Of the 523 graduates who fought in the war, 452 received the equivalent of medals for gallant conduct (the army did not issue medals at the time) in the form of brevet promotions.[50] But the finest praise of all came from General in Chief Scott, whose campaign against Mexico City ranks as one of the greatest in the annals of warfare. Scott said, "I give it as my fixed opinion, that but for our graduated cadets, the war between the United States and Mexico might, and probably would, have lasted some four or five years, with, in its first half, more defeats than victories falling to our share; whereas, in less than two campaigns, we conquered a great country and a peace, without the loss of a single battle or skirmish."[51]

Nothing else matched the Mexican War for excitement, but there were other memorable days at West Point. In the fifties various foreign dignitaries visited the post, including the Prince of Wales, who reviewed the Corps and then shook hands with the

[49] McClellan to sister, May 3, 1846, McClellan Papers.
[50] Forman, *West Point,* 72.
[51] *RC,* 176.

cadet officers.[52] General Scott was a frequent and most welcome visitor, and he too usually reviewed the Corps. In 1854 the Secretary of War, Jefferson Davis, a West Point graduate, spent several days with Superintendent Lee and met and talked with many of the cadets.[53] In 1856 the American Association for the Advancement of Science held its annual meeting at West Point.[54]

Lee's career as Superintendent was marked by the first major change in the West Point system since 1820. In 1854, at Lee's urging, Congress allowed the Academy to extend its course to five years. Lee wanted the extra year in order to have more time for English, military law, and field instruction and to add a course in Spanish—the army had found during the Mexican War that hardly any of its officers spoke Spanish. The Superintendent made the switch to five years by dividing the Fourth Class into two equal groups according to age, then starting the youngest on the five-year course.[55] There was a great deal of grumbling and much letter-writing to congressmen—so much, in fact, that in October of 1858 the Secretary of War yielded to political pressure and returned the Academy to the four-year scheme. Six months later he yielded to pressure from West Point officials and switched back. In June, 1860, Congress appointed a high-level commission to investigate the five-year curriculum and report on its success. Senator Jefferson Davis was president of the commission; members included Senator Solomon Foot, Congressmen John Cochrane and Henry Winter Davis, Major Robert Anderson, and Captain A. A. Humphreys. The committee, after an exhaustive study—its report constitutes the best description of pre-Civil War West Point available—recommended the retention of the five-year course.[56] The war that began less than a year later, however, brought an end to the experiment.

In the fifties West Point's reputation was high, both because of its academic excellence and because of the record of its graduates

[52] Ambrose, *Upton*, 15.
[53] Hartz to father, November 3, 1854, Hartz Papers.
[54] Bernard to Buche, August 21, 1855, SLB.
[55] Lee to Totten, September 8, 1854, *ibid.*; Boynton, *West Point*, 248–49.
[56] *RC*, 1, 71.

in civil and military affairs. Still, there were critics. Some old Jacksonians still spoke bitterly of aristocracy and monopoly, but most of the critics of the forties and fifties made comments that had more substance to them. Most knowledgeable men thought it disgraceful that congressmen could make appointments to the Academy on whatever basis they chose, especially since hardly ever was mental capacity taken into account. Candidates were still admitted who had no chance of progressing through the course.[57] Cadets and army officers complained about the habitual practice of the Secretary of War in returning discharged cadets. Delafield pointed out that in one year he had discharged nineteen cadets; ten were reinstated with no penalty and nine were put back one year and returned to the Corps.[58] Cadet James H. Wilson said he did not know of a single cadet dismissed in two years that the Secretary did not reinstate, which in Wilson's opinion offered "a premium for improper conduct."[59]

Another common criticism was directed at Thayer's ranking system. Under it cadets near the top of a class studied hard, in order to get into the corps they wanted, and cadets near the bottom did so for fear of being found deficient, but the cadets in the middle of their class did just enough to get by—they knew they were destined for the infantry whether they stood twentieth or thirty-fifth in their class.[60] Morris Schaff and his roommate were both in the middle of their class, so they spent night after night talking, rambling "from topic to topic as two little idle, barefoot boys might ramble along an old dusty road."[61] Ulysses Grant was in the same position, never read over a lesson more than once despite the existence of academic demands far greater than those of non-military colleges.[62]

Graduates felt that instruction in foreign languages was so poor as to be one of the Academy's major failings. Edward O. C. Ord

[57] See J. H. Wilson to John Logan, December 26, 1859, John Logan Papers, Library of Congress.
[58] *RC*, 157–58.
[59] Wilson to Logan, December 26, 1859, Logan Papers.
[60] *RC*, 162.
[61] Schaff, *Old West Point*, 110–11.
[62] Grant, *Memoirs*, 14.

said that in his four years at West Point he never spoke French or heard it spoken. "I have since learned more Spanish from Mexican senoritas in two months than I did French at the Point in two years."[63] Testifying before the Davis Commission in 1860, Cadet Adelbert Ames said that after finishing the French course, he still could not read the language "with entire facility" and could not speak it at all. His knowledge of Spanish was even less adequate. Ames was no sluggard; he stood seventeenth of fifty in Spanish and thirteenth of fifty-two in French.[64]

All graduates criticized West Point for failure to prepare them in any way for life in the army. Theophilus Holmes told the Davis Commission something which Davis himself already knew: "I think the sudden transition from the highest state of mental tension to one of perfect inactivity, which occurs in most cases on the graduation of a cadet, is exceedingly injurious." It left a void that was filled either by "an undue gratification of the licentious passions, or else by the trashy literature with which our country is flooded." He might have mentioned the third, and most common, method of filling the void—resignation from the army. Holmes' solution, one that would be offered by many others over the next half-century with no effect whatsoever, was to teach the cadets something of the nature of their duties on an isolated frontier post.[65]

The most telling criticism of West Point was that it tried to do too much. Forward-looking officers maintained that in an age of specialization no one school could prepare a cadet for all three arms of the line, and not only did West Point try to do that but it also prepared its charges for the scientific corps and for staff duty. This criticism would be heard more often and more loudly after the Civil War; then, as in the fifties, West Point's defenders answered that the fault lay not with the Academy but with the army's system of education. What was needed were post-graduate schools in all branches. This was the conclusion of the Davis Commission, which admitted that West Point was not as good as Metz in fortification, nor as good as St. Cyr in cavalry and infantry,

[63] *RC*, 334.
[64] *Ibid.*, 109.
[65] *Ibid.*, 173–74.

nor as good as the École Polytechnique in engineering, but argued that it was better than any of the French schools in turning out a rounded officer who was ready to become an expert in any of these fields. The trouble was that there was no place in the United States where he could get the extra knowledge he needed.[66]

Another defense of West Point's system was based on a hope, not a fact. Chief Engineer Totten argued that Europeans maintained specialized schools because, given the size of their armies, they needed a large number of officers in each branch. The American army was so small that frequently the Corps of Engineers, for example, did not need a single graduate for two or three years in a row. The American army did need officers with skills in all branches, because it was organized on the "skeleton principle"; in time of war, the nation would build its armed force around the cadre of the Regular Army, and its officers would have to serve in many varied capacities.[67] In point of fact the army only wished that the nation would use it as a skeleton force; except for John C. Calhoun, when he was Secretary of War, no one of authority in the government had accepted the principle. The United States really relied not on the Regular Army but on civilian-officered militia and volunteers for its defense.

Another aspect of the problem of a too-diversified training was that cadets had no real idea of what a particular corps did, but once they made their selection—or had it made for them—they were usually stuck for life with it. Stephen Ramseur suggested to the Davis Commission that the solution was to assign recent graduates to a temporary position in each corps and then to have an army review board decide where each would best serve. Cadets who heard of this suggestion were horrified; as Cadet Ames testified, the only incentive to hard study and high standing was the opportunity to select a corps upon graduation. Professor Mahan thought the system necessary to maintain ambition and standards.[68]

[66] *Ibid.,* 55.
[67] Totten to Black, January 26, 1844, Misc. Mss., USMA Library.
[68] *RC,* 93, 141. Ames commented, "The effort to stand high is prompted almost wholly by the prospect it holds out of selecting one's own corps, and being able to enter one of the scientific corps."

Ramseur was right in suggesting that the army needed more flexibility, that it should allow its officers to transfer from one corps to another. The only permanent solution, however, aside from radically changing the nature of the Academy, was post-graduate education. The only advanced school the army maintained was the artillery school at Fortress Monroe. Colonel Harvey Brown suggested in 1860 that the army create similar schools for infantry and cavalry, and eventually for the scientific corps—no one had yet thought of staff schools or war colleges—, and that West Point revert to a four-year course. Cadets could then spend the fifth year as second lieutenants at the advanced schools, learning the intricacies of their respective arms.[69]

This idea of post-graduate schools on the European model was very popular in the army during the period, and with only a few more dollars from Congress the War Department would have built an extensive post-graduate system. Ironically it was not congressional parsimony that forced the army to wait nearly fifty years for its completion but the success of West Point graduates in the Civil War. So many of them did so many different things so well—Emory Upton of the class of 1861, for example, successfully commanded an artillery battery, an infantry division, and a cavalry division—that there seemed to be no reason to change or add to the army's educational program.

Unlike the Jacksonians, most of the critics of West Point of the forties and fifties were friendly; in fact, most were graduates. The Academy was an institution to which most Americans looked with pride. The Davis Commission, in its summary on the value of West Point, spoke for many:

> Nearly all the great public works of the country, the river and
> harbor works, the lighthouses, and even the public buildings,

[69] *RC*, 193. In a sense, West Point did give specialized training, because the higher sections always progressed further in their studies than did the lower ones. Thus a cadet who stood third in his class would have been in the first section in mathematics and would therefore have gone much further in the subject than a cadet who stood fortieth and was in the fourth section in mathematics. The high-ranking cadet would go into the Engineers or Ordnance in possession of much more knowledge on these subjects than his lower-ranking classmate.

have been directed by its graduates; they were the pioneers in the construction of railroads, and among the teachers of that art; and the great scientific works of the government have been chiefly conducted by them. The military services of its graduates have been ever more conspicuous than those in engineering and science. The fortifications, the improvements in ordnance and small arms, the conduct of the geographical and other scientific labors carried on in connection with the operations of troops, equally attest the character of the instruction imparted at West Point. Ever since the organization of the government, perpetual Indian warfare has kept the larger part of the Army in active operation on the frontier and in the barren plains and mountains of the interior. The duties are harassing, and entail great privation and exposure; they call for the exercise of all the best qualities of the soldier, which, tried by this severe test, the graduates have been found to possess in an eminent degree.[70]

Within the year Davis would be the head of a new government making war on the United States, and graduates would have an opportunity to prove the truth of his words.

[70] *RC,* 56–57.

Chapter VIII

Cadet Life

The pre-Civil War American college faculties were preoccupied with the development of character. They pushed, pulled, shaped, and hammered the boys into the accepted mold of a Christian gentleman. Their methods were simple: required attendance at church, minute regulation of daily life, cold rooms in winter and hot ones in summer, inferior food, and no recreation.

At West Point, character building reached its apogee. The Academy faculty was trying to turn out not just Christian gentlemen but Christian soldiers, so the virtues of duty, loyalty, honor, and courage were emphasized more at West Point than anywhere else. For the cadets, the regulations were stricter and the living conditions worse than for the college students. Jacksonian charges of high-living encouraged the Superintendents and their faculties to make the system even harsher. In 1843 Cadet William Dutton took note of their success in a letter to his sister: "All I want of those Editors who say—that 'lily fingered cadets lounge on their velvet lawns—attend their brilliant balls and take pay for it' as I saw in a paper yesterday—is that they may go through but one . . . encampment."[1]

West Point made life hard for the cadets in order to turn out finished soldiers. The Academy, in the words of one nineteenth-

[1] Dutton to sister, February 18, 1843, Misc. Mss., USMA Library.

century official there, "exacts of every individual rigid conformity to its standard. . . . It stands *in loco parentis* not only over the mental but the moral, physical and, so to speak, the official man. It dominates every phase of his development. . . . There is very little of his time over which it does not exercise a close scrutiny, and for which it does not demand a rigid accountability." In all this, West Point differed only in degree, not in kind, from other institutions. What made four years at West Point especially difficult was that, in addition to everything else, "it's minimum standard is proficiency in every branch of study taught in its curriculum, and . . . it dominates . . . every moment of [the cadet's] academic existence."[2]

The most obvious manifestation of the Academy's concern for its charges was the schedule. Seldom did the cadet enjoy more than seven hours' sleep. During the summer encampment of 1856, Henry A. du Pont reported that he rose at 5:00 A.M., policed the grounds till 5:30, drilled until 6:30, prepared for inspection, ate breakfast at 7:00, went to parade at 8:00 and to artillery drill at 9:00, policed again, ate dinner at 1:00 P.M., attended dancing class from 3:00 to 4:00, policed again, and went to infantry drill at 5:30, to evening parade and inspection at 7:00, to supper at 8:00, and to bed at 9:30. In barracks that fall he rose at 5:30 A.M., studied from 6:00 to 7:00, attended classes until dinner time at 1:00 P.M., studied from 2:00 to 4:00, read or wrote letters until supper at 6:00, and studied from 7:00 until taps at 9:30. Like many other cadets, he often put a candle under a propped-up blanket and continued to study until midnight. "To tell the truth," another cadet said, "I don't like this mode of life at all; it is too much like slavery to suit me."[3]

When the cadets did have some time off, as on Sunday afternoons, the authorities did their best to see to it there was nothing to do. There were no organized activities, and the only voluntary associations permitted were the debating clubs. No lectures were

[2] *CWP*, I, 472. These observances were made in 1902 but apply equally well to the ante-bellum period.
[3] Du Pont to mother, July 14, 1856, du Pont Papers; *RC*, 6; Bryant to father, June 17, 1860, Bryant Family Papers.

allowed, and cadets could subscribe to no more than one periodical a month. Cadets could not go off the post, and the Superintendent habitually turned down requests for leaves to go to New York City. In any case, the cadets had no money to spend. They never saw their pay of $28.00 a month (raised to $30.00 in the fifties); they could only draw on it at the commissaries, and the only items available there were clothes, mirrors, razors, and other essentials. The monthly pay was never high enough to keep the cadets out of debt at the commissaries, and they could not deposit money to escape their debt. Indeed, they could not receive any money from home. Superintendents often used indebtedness as an excuse to deny an application for leave; for two years Cadet du Pont could not leave the post because he was in debt at the commissaries.[4] Except for their two-month furlough at the end of the Third Class year, the cadets lived on the post and followed the established routine.

The cadets endured it, but not without complaint. Time and again they apologized to their families for not writing or for writing short letters and explained, "There is absolutely nothing unusual to tell you in this monotonous life."[5] In 1840 Cadet James Schureman told his sister, "At West Point all is monotony. What is said of one day will answer for it almost years after."[6] As if to prove Schureman's point, fourteen years and three days later Cadet Edward Hartz told his sister that West Point, isolated as it was, with nothing to do, no one to talk to, no new faces to see, and no breaks in the routine, was oppressively dull.[7]

At West Point the students were not "boys" but "men," and their superiors said they expected them to act as such. The rules and regulations, however, expressed a different view; they assumed the cadets were wild youngsters who had to be watched and from

[4] Du Pont to mother, October 16, 1856, du Pont Papers; Lewis, *Grant,* 71; Lee to Shewep, February 3, 1855, and Brewerton to Totten, February 10, 1846, SLB.

[5] Du Pont to mother, November 15, 1856, du Pont Papers.

[6] Schureman to sister, October 14, 1840, James Wall Schureman Papers, Library of Congress.

[7] Hartz to sister, October 17, 1854, Hartz Papers.

whom temptation had to be removed. As the Board of Visitors of 1828 noted, "The moral discipline of the institution is perfect; the avenues to vice are closed, and the temptations to dissipation . . . have been vigilantly guarded against." Thayer and his successors forbade the cadets to drink, play cards or chess, gamble, use or possess tobacco, keep any cooking utensils in their rooms, participate in any games, read novels, romances, or plays, go off the post, bathe in the river, or play a musical instrument. Thayer would not allow the officers themselves to play cards in their homes, for fear the cadets would be tempted. Cadets could possess only certain items, and each of these had to be in its assigned place in their rooms. They could not send a challenge or participate in any other way in a duel, enter into any "combinations," or write anything for publication about the Academy.[8]

Supervision was minute, although the Superintendents had to compel the faculty to vigilance, for most army officers found the spying distasteful. Indeed, this was one major reason the Superintendents had difficulty obtaining and retaining instructors and assistants. Cadet James Burbridge reported that "Old Thayer is as cunning as a fox if he suspects [anything] he spares no pains in obtaining" evidence.[9] The usual punishment for violations was, in addition to demerits, extra tours of duty. Cadet George Cushing walked guard all one September Sunday for "defacing public property"—he had been caught with his feet propped on the table in his room.[10] Other cadets suffered similar punishment for having cards or liquor in their rooms, kicking a horse, throwing bread in mess hall, "concealing self in fireplace to evade Officer of the day," visiting after taps, and using profane language. On one day in January, 1825, Thayer dismissed one cadet for fighting, another for playing cards, another for neglect of duty as orderly in allowing card playing, another for showing disrespect to the Superintendent, and several for drinking in their rooms. All were, however,

[8] Military Academy Regulations, No. 1408–13, Archives, USMA; "Early Discipline" *JMSI*, 465.

[9] White, *Jeffersonians*, 258; Burbridge to Hawkins, June 10, 1827, Misc. Mss., USMA Library.

[10] Cushing to family, September 12, 1854, Cushing Papers.

reinstated, either by Thayer himself because of former good conduct or by the Secretary of War. One cadet, suspended by Thayer until June for bringing wine into his quarters, had his sentence suspended "on account of his youth."[11]

As did nearly every other college in the country, West Point required its charges to attend Sunday chapel. Cadet Hartz wondered why, for "all excesses are without our reach and in fact we are every where so hemmed in that it is almost as difficult to sin here as it is to do well in the world at large."[12] The chaplain was usually an Episcopalian, representative of a faith regarded as ideal for an officer and a gentleman. The cadets, especially those from western states, considered chapel a chore. George W. Cullum, remembering that at home he looked forward to going to church, where he could see his friends "and particularly my female acquaintances," complained that at West Point he was required to sit for two long hours on a backless bench, squeezed among his fellow sufferers, punched in the ribs by his side arms, listening to a dry discourse.[13] Cadet Grant thought there were two things wrong with chapel; it was an Episcopal service, and he had to march to it. This was "not republican." Few went willingly, for as one noted in 1820, "there is not one here who professes Christianity. The two who did have left."[14]

Occasionally the cadets would rebel, and Thayer would have to issue warnings against shuffling, groaning, or otherwise creating a disturbance during services. Sometimes cadets would take advantage of the protection from supervision chapel afforded to chew tobacco. In 1840 the Commandant pleaded with them to cease the practice, for they were leaving so much tobacco spittle on the floor

[11] White, *Jeffersonians*, 258; Heintzelman Diary, entries of January 8, 25, and March 11, 1826.

[12] Hartz to sister, December 11, 1852, Hartz Papers.

[13] Cullum to Huidekoper, November 22, 1829, Cullum Papers.

[14] Lewis, *Grant*, 71; Canfield to family, June 9, 1820, Misc. Mss., USMA Library.

Sunday morning that the chapel could not be used Sunday afternoon.[15]

Revivals were neither as frequent nor as intense at West Point as they were in other American colleges. The Superintendent, the faculty, and the chaplain felt they were in bad taste. For the religious there were, instead, prayer meetings, held on Wednesday nights and Sunday afternoons. Usually the cadets organized and ran these meetings themselves, but an occasional instructor took an interest. While he was a member of the mathematics department, Oliver O. Howard, later to be known as the "Bible General," led a weekly prayer meeting which fifteen cadets attended. Officers as well as cadets were required to attend chapel. In the late twenties three instructors protested to Thayer that this requirement violated their constitutional rights. The Superintendent sent their remonstrance on to Washington. The Secretary of War replied that he "was farthest from any desire to interfere in the least with their conscientious scruples, and would, therefore, send them where attendance upon Divine service would not be deemed necessary." All three were assigned to frontier posts.[16]

The judgment of Cadet Emory Upton probably reflected the true state of religious affairs at West Point. In 1858 he declared that West Point "is a hard place to practice religion; though few scoff at it, yet a great majority totally disregard it."[17]

Superintendent Thayer knew that constant supervision, a full schedule that removed temptation, and moral exhortations were not enough to make a soldier. Like the presidents at other colleges, he wanted the cadets to learn to do without unnecessary comforts. The cadet's furniture consisted of an iron bedstead, a table, a straight-backed chair, a lamp, a mirror, a mattress and blanket (which were folded when not in use), and a washstand. Running water was introduced in 1826.[18] Ventilation was poor,

[15] Lewis, *Grant*, 82.
[16] Schaff, *Old West Point*, 70; Church, *Reminiscences*, 156–57.
[17] Ambrose, *Upton*, 7.
[18] Dutton to cousin, February 18, 1843, Misc. Mss., USMA Library.

and the heating system—open fireplaces—defective. In 1860 a congressional commission found that some of the rooms were so cold in winter the cadets could not study in them, while others were so hot the occupants got headaches.[19]

The uniform, which was basically Partridge's design, was usually ill-fitting and always constraining. The color was "Cadet Gray." The shoes were heavy and clumsy; they rose above the ankle joint and were worn under the pantaloons. The stocks were silk, and the pantaloons, which included an understrap, were gray cloth in winter and white jean in summer. The vest was single-breasted, as was the coat, which had three rows of eight yellow brass bullet buttons in front. There was a cadet verse about the coat:

Your coat is made, you button it, give one spasmodic cough,

And do not draw another breath until you take it off!

The crowning adornment was a bell-crowned black leather cap, seven inches high, with a polished leather visor and an eight-inch black plume. Cadet John Pope complained that the cap weighed five pounds and "hurt my head extremely."[20]

The pantaloons had many hidden puritanic discomforts, chief of which was that they opened at the side. Rebellion came in 1840, when Cadet Pope swaggered in from his furlough wearing pants that buttoned down the front. Faculty wives were shocked at his bold recognition of the male anatomy, but Superintendent Delafield praised the new style for its economy and practical utility and ordered the tailors henceforth to make cadet pants open in front. In turn, Mrs. Delafield exercised her authority and announced that "cadets thus dressed should not come in person to the house."[21] Delafield's dedication to economy did not always work to the cadet's advantage. During his second tour as Superintendent,

---

[19] *RC,* 6.

[20] Du Pont to father, July 7, 1856, du Pont Papers; Freeman, *Lee,* I, 51; Dupuy, *Where They Have Trod,* 112, 186; Pope to mother, July 7, 1842, Misc. Mss., USMA Library; Joseph B. James, "Life at West Point 100 Years Ago," *Mississippi Valley Historical Review,* XXXI (June, 1944), 24. Superintendent Lee changed the cap, because it was too heavy and caused "headaches and dizziness." Lee to Totten, March 15, 1853, SLB.

[21] Lewis, *Grant,* 79.

in order to save twenty cents per cadet, he had the lining removed from the overcoats.[22]

All of the hardships of West Point life paled beside the food. Nothing helped the fledglings recognize so quickly that they had left the nest as the meals. Mr. Cozzens, who ran the hotel, supplied the food, and he did his best to keep it as cheap, unappetizing, and unnourishing as possible. His menu was short and to the point: boiled potatoes, boiled meat, boiled pudding, bread, and coffee. In the sober words of a congressional commission which made an unannounced visit to the mess hall, the food "was neither nutritious nor wholesome, neither sufficient nor nicely dressed." Cadet Adelbert Ames reported that although he had become accustomed to the sight, and even the smell, of the boiled fish, in four years he had never been able to eat it.[23]

Sometimes the food got so bad that cadets complained to the Superintendent. Cozzens saved money by using stale bread and other leftovers in his pudding; once the captain of the mess hall found in his pudding a nest of three mice. He carried the bowl to Thayer, who remarked that accidents easily happened and dismissed him. For a month thereafter, however, the cadets feasted on roast goose and turkey. Things were soon back to normal, and about a year later another cadet found a comb in his pudding. Through the years the diners became accustomed to sour molasses, rancid butter, bugs in the sugar, and cockroaches in the soup.[24]

There was one escape. The Misses Thompson were daughters of a Revolutionary War soldier who, because of their destitute condition, Thayer had allowed to live on the post in General Washington's old log headquarters and prepare meals for a few cadets. A "place at the Misses Thompson's" was a prized possession—they had room for just twelve cadets—and was willed by a graduating First Classman to a friend in a lower class. At the Misses Thomp-

[22] Du Pont to mother, October 26, 1856, du Pont Papers.

[23] *RC*, 6, 110–11.

[24] *Ibid.*, 110–11; Oliver E. Wood, *The West Point Scrap Book* (New York, 1871), 34–35.

son's cadets did not have to march to meals, could eat slowly and quietly "instead of bolting down one's food in the midst of an intolerable din," and could dine free from the searching eyes of the first captain. Most important, the food was edible. Cadets who were not fortunate enough to eat at the Misses Thompson's occasionally would steal a goose or duck from a local farmer and roast it over the fires in their rooms. Such a meal was called a "hash." Usually several cadets, walking in stocking feet and carrying silver borrowed from the mess hall, would gather in a room, roast the meat over the grate fire, and bake potatoes in the ashes. After the meal, pipes were lighted and graduation and assignment prospects discussed. William T. Sherman had the reputation of being the best hash-maker in the Corps.[25]

Some cadets simply refused to conform to the West Point mold. One was James McNeill Whistler, who entered the Academy in 1851, left in 1853, and later became one of America's best-known artists. Whistler was an irrepressible, witty youngster, called "Curly" by his classmates, who usually stood first in drawing class and last in everything else. He was a dreadful horseman; one day when he pitched forward over his horse's head, the riding instructor called out, "Mr. Whistler, I am pleased to see you for once at the head of your class!" During a history recitation, Whistler confessed he knew nothing of a Mexican War battle. "What!" said the instructor, "you do not know the date of the battle of Buena Vista? Suppose you were to go out to dinner and the company began to talk of the Mexican War, and you, a West Point man, were asked the date of the battle. What would you do?"

"Do?" said Whistler. "Why, I should refuse to associate with people who could talk of such things at dinner!"

Even in drawing class Whistler had some trouble. Professor Weir, himself an excellent artist, often grew impatient with the best efforts of his students and touched up their drawings. Once when Whistler was doing an India ink drawing, Weir came up

[25] Du Pont to mother, August 4 and 21, 1857, du Pont Papers.

behind him, looked over his shoulder, strode forward to his desk, filled his brush with ink, and started back towards Whistler. When Whistler looked up and saw Weir coming, he raised his hands as if to ward off an attack and called out, "Oh, don't sir, don't! You'll spoil it!"

Whistler's end came in a chemistry section in 1853 when the instructor asked him to discuss silicon. Curly started out boldly enough: "I am required to discuss the subject of silicon. Silicon is a gas. . . ." The instructor interrupted, "That will do, Mr. Whistler." Shortly afterwards he was found deficient, dismissed, and had his appeal turned down by Superintendent Lee. Years later Whistler claimed, "Had silicon been a gas, I would have been a major general."[26]

Edgar Allan Poe was another cadet who could not live with the West Point system. Before he came to the Academy in 1830, Poe had served for a time as an enlisted man in the army, so he was a little older in addition to being a great deal more sensitive than his fellow cadets. Poe thought the Academy intellectually stagnant. The dreadful monotony of the place nearly suffocated him; the intensity of the section room, with all its repetition, drove him to poetry. In a sonnet he asked "Science"

> Why preyest thou thus upon the poet's heart,
> Vulture, whose wings are dull realities?

and demanded

> Has thou not torn the Naiad from her flood,
> The Elfin from the green grass, and from me
> The summer dream beneath the tamarind tree?

While he was a cadet, Poe completed a book of poems and showed the manuscript to Colonel Thayer. The Superintendent liked them and urged Poe to publish. The poet pointed out that he would need a subscription list of advance purchasers before a publisher would undertake the work, so Thayer suggested that Poe get his fellow cadets to subscribe seventy-five cents each by implying that the poems were humorous verses directed against

[26] James, "Life at West Point," 35; E. R. and J. Pennell, *The Life of James McNeill Whistler* (London, 1908), I, 31–37.

the staff. Poe did so, the cadets put up the money, and in 1830 *Poems, by Edgar A. Poe,* appeared.

Poe was a free spirit and always drew a great number of demerits. A heavy drinker, he suffered from a lack of funds. To supply himself, he would trade for brandy at a local tavern blankets, candles, or whatever else he had available. His nemesis was Lieutenant Joseph Locke, of the tactical department, who delighted in reporting Poe. The poet's retaliation was swift:

John Locke was a notable name;

Joe Locke is a greater; in short,

The former was well known to fame,

But the latter's well known 'to report.'

After less than a year at the Academy, Poe left one day without explanation or permission. He never returned.[27]

Whistler and Poe were only extreme examples of the common reaction of cadets to West Point. Few young men could survive four years on the post without some kind of outlet for their energies—Robert E. Lee was one of a small number who went four years without a single demerit. Legally, one of the few breaks in the cadet's routine was a two-month furlough at the end of the Third Class year. The "furlough class" looked forward to the summer with great excitement and prepared for it by practicing the most rigid economy. Even the officers would look the other way when a Third Classman appeared in a ragged shirt or had a hole in his stocking, because it was recognized that he was being as stingy as possible in order to save enough money to buy "cit" clothes for his furlough.[28]

All through the winter and spring of his furlough year, Cadet Schureman thought of it during the day and dreamed of it at night. "It is," he told his family, "the climax of [the cadet's] wishes and the boundary of his imagination, it is a period calculated to awaken the strongest idea of human happiness, it is liberty sweetened by confinement, and ease enhanced by previous labours. Long and ardently have I wished for that happy moment

[27] Hervey Allen, *Israfel: The Life and Times of Edgar Allan Poe* (New York, 1934), 218–44.

[28] Hartz to father, September 19, 1852, Hartz Papers.

to arrive when I can say farewell O West Point. . . ."[29] Cadet Ulysses S. Grant later recalled that his ten furlough weeks "were shorter than one week at West Point."[30]

Even those not going on furlough looked forward to the summer, for the encampment, despite its physical demands, was a welcome respite from the section room. Moreover, the activities in camp had a more obvious relation to the business of soldiering. Some summers the cadets marched to nearby cities, such as Boston or Philadelphia, and camped there for a few days. Summer was also the period for hazing, which before the Civil War was confined to the encampment and consisted of well worn tricks played on the plebes. The favorite was to grab a sleeping plebe by his heels and jerk him off his bed. Another was to cut the tent ropes in the middle of the night, enveloping the plebes in the canvas. Cadet John Schofield was a notorious hazer; he loved to steal the plebes' clothes at night, so that in the morning the victims had either to absent themselves from roll call or else to appear wrapped in a blanket. In either case the officers reported them. Schofield and his cohorts also plagued the plebes the first time they stood guard, so much so that one complained, "The cadets are . . . excessively given to a petty teasing habit." Generally the authorities paid little notice to the pranks, which ended when studies began.[31]

Summer was the social season, as girls went to the Point from the South and New York City to escape the heat. Hops and balls marked the week ends, and a dancing master was available to give lessons, at $2.00 a month, to those cadets who wanted them. The season began on July 4, with the climax coming at the end of encampment, when a grand ball was held.[32] The dancing began

[29] Schureman to sister, February 14, 1840, Schureman Papers.

[30] Grant, *Memoirs*, 15.

[31] Francis Sullivan (ed.), "Letters of a West Pointer, 1860–1861," *American Historical Review*, XXXIII (April, 1928), 600; Joseph Wheeler, "West Point Fifty Years Ago," *The Golden Age*, XII (February, 1906), 68; Hartz to sister, June 14, 1851, Hartz Papers; Brewerton to Totten, July 8, 1852, and Bowman to Stanton, September 18, 1863, SLB; Thomas Rowland, "Letters of a Virginia Cadet at West Point, 1859–1861," *South Atlantic Quarterly*, XV (May, September, 1915–16), 4.

[32] Heintzelman Diary, entry of July 25, 1825; Rowland, "Letters," 208–11.

at nine, and the four hundred people present wheeled back and forth to the cotillion, Spanish dances, galopades, and waltzes. At midnight refreshments, "consisting of all the luxuries which New York could afford," were served. Then the dances resumed, to continue until four in the morning.[33]

Another custom associated with the end of encampment was less elegant. The day after the ball the cadets struck their tents, then gathered around the tent floors with clubs and brooms. Two cadets took hold of each corner and, at a signal, jerked up the floor. "Instantly," Cullen Bryant reported, "about a thousand and one rats go scampering about in every direction. Then comes the fun, and such a yelling, chasing and slaughter of rats it never was my fortune to behold heretofore."[34]

In comparison with their compatriots in the colleges, the West Point cadets were well disciplined. With the exception of the incident Thayer had to face shortly after he took command, Academy Superintendents avoided that distinguishing mark of other institutions, the student rebellion.[35] But if the cadets seldom rebelled or even indulged in an evening's riot, they were nevertheless young men who, during the short days and long nights of the interminable winter months, often found a release for their energies and an escape from their boredom in activities other than those permitted in the rules and regulations. In December, 1853, six Third Classmen dressed themselves in "cits" and, about midnight, sneaked out of their quarters, crossed the Hudson in a rowboat, and attended a ball at a village one mile up the river. While they were dancing, an inspecting officer "hived"—cadet slang for found or discovered—their absence, despite the stuffing they had arranged in their beds, and sat down to await their return. When the cadets got back about 5:00 A.M., the officer arrested them. They were tried before a general court-martial, found guilty, dismissed, and reinstated.

Cadet Thomas Phoenix was the most notorious cadet of the forties. He was often found guilty of drunkenness, of dressing in

[33] Schureman to sister, September 9, 1839, Schureman Papers.
[34] Bryant to father, August 30, 1860, Bryant Family Papers.
[35] Rudolph, *American College,* 119.

civilian clothes and attending balls at Newburgh or Cold Spring, of card playing, and of other such offenses, but his great moment came near Christmas of 1846, when he induced two prostitutes to come up from New York and sneaked them into his barracks room, where they spent the night. He was caught but not dismissed—to avoid scandal the Superintendent allowed him to resign.[36]

The most frequent violations of the rules were fights. They usually occurred during the winter months and, especially in the fifties, involved a southern and a northern cadet. In March, 1855, Cadet William Hartz, of Pennsylvania, acting in his role of First Captain, reported a southern classmate for a breach of the regulations. The southerner assumed that Hartz was acting out of regional prejudice and the next evening strode into the room where Hartz and five other Yankees were talking. The southerner announced he wanted to give Hartz his opinion of him. Hartz told him to do so, the southerner did, and Hartz pitched into him, bloodying his nose and knocking some teeth loose. A half-hour later one of the defeated cadet's friends waited upon Hartz with a written challenge demanding satisfaction in a duel. Hartz, who came from coal country where dueling was not only illegal but was looked upon as aristocratic pretension, was unimpressed. He returned the note with a warning that the next time he was challenged he would turn the case over to the authorities. With satisfaction, Hartz later noted that his opponent "has been quiet since."[37]

Another duel did bring bloodshed. In the late fifties Cadet Wade Hampton Gibbes, of South Carolina, made some offensive remarks about Cadet Emory Upton's supposed intimacies with Negro girls at Oberlin College, which Upton had attended for a year. Upton demanded an explanation, Gibbes refused to give one, and the two arranged to fight with swords that night. A large crowd gathered on the first floor of the cadet barracks while Upton and Gibbes went upstairs into a darkened room. While the sentinel, a Fourth Class cadet, called for the corporal of the guard and the cadets cheered for their favorite, Upton and Gibbes

[36] Hartz to sister, December 22, 1853, Hartz Papers.
[37] Hartz to father, March 24, 1855, *ibid.*

fought. Soon they staggered down the stairs, Upton with a cut on his face.[38]

Growing sectionalism merely provided an extra excuse for, and was not in itself the cause of, fighting. Conflict often arose just because someone was bored. This was the case with Archibald Gracie, Jr., a New Yorker who decided one day to enliven a parade by treading on the heels of the cadet in front of him, Wharton Green. When Green swore, quietly but furiously, that Gracie was going to get a drubbing, Gracie laughed and answered, "Not from you." As soon as the review ended, Green turned and threw a punch at Gracie. The fight lasted a few minutes, with Gracie getting the worst of it, when an instructor stopped it. Green ran off, but Gracie was caught. When asked the name of his opponent, he replied, "You will have to ask him, for I'm no informer." He was arrested.

The next morning Green reported to Superintendent Lee and said, "Mr. Gracie was yesterday reported for fighting on the parade ground, and the 'other fellow' was not." "Yes, sir," Lee replied, "and I presume you are 'the other fellow.' " "I am, sir, and I wish to submit the case in full for your consideration. Don't you think it very hard on him, Colonel, after getting the worst of the fracas, to have to take all the penalty incidents?" "Admitted," said Lee, "what then?" "Simply this, sir. Whatever punishment is meted out to him, I insist on having the same given to me." "The offense entails a heavy penalty," Lee warned. "I am aware of the fact, Colonel," Green replied, "but Mr. Gracie is not entitled to a monopoly of it." Lee agreed, then said he would cancel the report altogether and punish neither cadet. "Don't you think," he continued, "that it is better for brothers to dwell together in peace and harmony?" "Yes, Colonel," Green said, "and if we were all like you, it would be an easy thing to do."[39]

"Tobacco is prohibited" at West Point, Cadet George Cushing told his uncle in 1854, "but I never saw so much used before."[40]

[38] Schaff, *Old West Point*, 142–48.
[39] Freeman, *Lee*, I, 337–38.
[40] Cushing to uncle, June 22, 1854, Cushing Papers.

He was probably right. Like most other Americans, cadets displayed their newly achieved manhood by either chewing or smoking tobacco at every opportunity. Chewing was especially popular because, if a suspicious officer approached a cadet who was indulging himself, he could destroy the evidence by swallowing. Smokers kept a pipe in their rooms and, when all was quiet, opened a window and lighted up. The tactical department went to great lengths to catch smokers. Lieutenant Cadmus Marcellus Wilcox put rubber soles on his shoes so that he could sneak into a room unheard, which led to an "Ode" that ended:

> I hear the old rascal upon the stairs;
> In spite of his rubbers, I hear him there.
> He stole! He stole!
> He stole my pipe away![41]

An even worse violation than smoking, the authorities thought, was drinking. They especially thought so before the Civil War because of the pressure on West Point officials from the Americans of the era who were greatly concerned with the evils of Demon Rum. Throughout the country newly formed prohibition or temperance societies demanded that the national academy be dry. The societies, which were strongest in New England and upper New York State, also encouraged the cadets to use that favorite device for insuring good behavior, the voluntary pledge. In 1824 a majority of the cadets signed one such pledge: "We the undersigned, conscious of the alarming degree to which the drinking of spirituous liquor has been carried in the Corps, . . . do set our Countenance against it, and do pledge our word and honor that we will not in anyway use wine or Spirituous liquor. . . ."[42]

Thayer was himself an anti-liquor man, but he allowed its use by the cadets on one day a year, the Fourth of July, so that they could properly celebrate the nation's birthday. The day included a thirteen-gun salute, a reading of the Declaration of Independence, a bad oration, an excellent meal, and liquor.[43] The temperance movement, however, began to put pressure on congressmen and on Thayer to put a stop to the imbibing at the Academy,

[41] James, "Life at West Point," 36; Wood, *Scrap Book,* 137.
[42] Pledge, February, 1824, Misc. Mss., USMA Library.
[43] Heintzelman Diary, entry of July 4, 1825.

even a single day of it. In 1826 Thayer gave in and prohibited all liquor at all times.

Illegal drinking increased. Thirty years later Cadet Cushing told his father he had never seen so many or such drunken men as he had on Christmas Day at the Academy. Turkey with the trimmings was served in the mess hall, but it went for naught as most of the Corps had spent the day drinking at local taverns and showed up "as drunk as rot gut could make them." Cadets jumped on the tables, where they danced, sang, and kicked the food off. New Year's Day that year was even worse. A fight broke out, carving knives were used, and several men were stabbed.[44]

There were a number of taverns near the post where a cadet could get liquor. The most popular was Benny Havens', located in Highland Falls. As a young man Benny had worked for a sutler but, having been discovered selling rum to a cadet, was fired. In 1824 he set up his own tavern, which he continued to run until long after the Civil War. It became the most famous establishment in all West Point history, honored by song, story, and hundreds of cadet visitors. Mrs. Havens did the cooking, specializing in buckwheat cakes and roast turkey. Benny himself was a great talker who had a deep sympathy for the plight of the cadets—he often extended credit or took blankets and other stolen items for his excellent flip. Edgar Allan Poe, who went often, thought Benny "was the sole congenial soul in the entire God-forsaken place."[45] Enterprising cadets sometimes brought a barrel of whiskey to Benny when they returned from furlough, and Benny obligingly stored it for them and tapped it whenever they could get away from the post. The Havenses enjoyed the unique honor of being the only two American citizens forbidden to set foot on the post of West Point. Thayer had issued the order when he caught them running liquor to the cadets.[46]

[44] Cushing to parents, December 29, 1854, and January 3, 1855, Cushing Papers.

[45] Robert J. Wood, "Early Days of Benny Havens," *The Pointer*, February 26, 1937.

[46] "Memoirs," Ferguson Papers; Brewerton to Totten, March 13, 1848, and February 12, 1847, SLB.

Thayer had only himself to blame for Havens' popularity. In the twenties Gridley's was the place to go, but it proved too much of a nuisance to Thayer, and in 1825 he persuaded Congress to appropriate $10,000 to purchase Gridley's property. Gridley accepted the money and went to Newburgh to live, and his house was converted into a cadet hospital. But the chief result of the move was to give Benny Havens a monopoly, and Gridley spent the rest of his life complaining to one and all about what a fool he had been to let the government get off with so small a sum.

For fifty years Benny provided for hungry or thirsty cadets. The roster of his clients reads like the roster of the generals in Blue and Gray.[47] Cadet Jefferson Davis was a frequent visitor; indeed, he was a member of the first group of cadets to be court-martialed for drinking at Benny's. During the summer encampment of 1825 Davis and some friends found they had a thirst and "ran it" to the tavern where, after a few hours' drinking, they were discovered by an officer. At his trial, Davis protested that he had only been drinking beer, which he did not understand to be liquor. Nevertheless, he was found guilty, dismissed, and then, as usual, reinstated.[48]

Less than a decade and a half after it was established, Benny's was an institution. In 1838 Lieutenant Lucius O'Brien recognized its status with the first verses of "Benny Havens, Oh!," set to the tune of "Wearing of the Green":

> Come, fill your glasses, fellows, and stand up in a row;
> To singing sentimentally, we're going for to go;
> In the army there's sobriety, promotion's very slow,
> So we'll sing our reminiscences of Benny Havens, oh!

> Oh! Benny Havens, oh! oh! Benny Havens, oh!
> So we'll sing our reminiscences of Benny Havens, oh!

The most effective weapon the authorities had against Benny was the class pledge. Whenever they could court-martial a cadet for drinking, they told the cadet's classmates they could rescue him

---

[47] Church, *Reminiscences,* 136; see also Smith Diary and Heintzelman Diary for references to visits by cadets to Havens'.

[48] Hudson Strode, *Jefferson Davis, American Patriot* (New York, 1955), 42.

from dismissal and eternal disgrace by pledging never to drink at West Point. Everyone in the class had to sign. "It goes pretty hard with some of them," one pledger reported, "but they all sign rather than suffer a classmate to be dismissed." The cadets honored their pledge—except on furlough, when it was not binding—so Commandant John F. Reynolds was delighted when, in January, 1861, he had all but one of the classes signed up. Reynolds still was not satisfied; he announced he would get the last class signed up "if he had to drink one of them drunk himself."[49]

In March, 1861, the cadets who were on pledge were put to the test. Fire broke out in Cozzen's Hotel and the Corps, which had its own fire machines and periodically engaged in fire drills, rushed out of the mess hall and down to the scene of the blaze. There the cadets found the machines could not throw the water high enough and had to content themselves with saving what they could. The first items they dragged out were the bottles in the wine cellar. It was dark, so one class set to drinking, while the others looked on helplessly—they were all on pledge.[50]

But there was one way even a pledged class could satisfy its thirst. Professor Kendrick took pity on the cadets, and every Saturday afternoon he held open house for all cadets on pledge. Kendrick served peaches spiked with brandy and became a hero to many a grateful cadet for his invariable polite question, "May I help the members of the class to more peaches?" Kendrick, an old bachelor, made the occasions even more memorable by serving waffles and maple syrup.[51]

Most of the members of the faculty knew how abominable the food in the mess hall was and did what they could to help. Whenever he could, Professor French bought a hickory-chip and corn-cob smoked Virginia ham, invited a few cadets to his home, and shared it with them. Decades later Cadet Morris Schaff remarked, "I can see yet the delicious, cherry-red slices falling from his

[49] Rowland, "Letters," 206.
[50] Sullivan (ed.), "Letters," 608.
[51] Joseph P. Farley, *West Point in the Early Sixties* (Troy, N. Y., 1902), 69; Hugh T. Reed, *Cadet Life at West Point* (Chicago, 1896), 185.

knife."[52] Once a week Professor Bailey's wife baked pies and cakes, which her son delivered to the cadets. Like the old-time faculty members elsewhere, the West Point professors knew that their charges were something less than men, and they did what they could to ease the burden of homesickness.[53]

The Superintendents felt they should know each of their charges personally, but unlike the college presidents they did not teach a class, so that they had to find some other method of meeting and talking with the cadets. Usually, they invited the cadets in small groups to dinner. Colonel Lee was most noted for the practice, and his own manner and bearing, as well as that of Mrs. Lee, greatly impressed the cadets.[54] Cadet Hartz was fortunate enough to attend twice; the first time he professed to find the whole affair a great bore, although he admitted that the food was good. The second time Lee thrilled his young guests, including Hartz, by using General Washington's personal silverware.[55]

But despite anything that the Superintendent or the faculty or Benny Havens might do, the fact remained that life at West Point was dull. Two things sustained the cadets: West Point's beauty, and the promise of a commission and a career in the army. Whenever they became particularly depressed, cadets would hike up to old Fort Putnam, look down on the Hudson and out upon the mountains, and daydream. The view was one few forgot. "This prettiest of places," Cadet Grant said of it, "the most beautiful place I have ever seen."[56] But most of all, the cadets could console themselves with their graduation hopes and by singing "Army Blue":

> We've not much longer here to stay,
>   For in a year or two,
> We'll bid farewell to 'Cadet Gray,'
>   and don the 'Army Blue.'

[52] Schaff, *Old West Point*, 104.

[53] *Ibid.;* William Whitman Bailey, "Recollections of West Point," Misc. Mss., USMA Library.

[54] Smith Diary, entry for February 10, 1855.

[55] Hartz to family, March 26, 1853, and November 3, 1854, Hartz Papers.

[56] Lewis, *Grant,* 70.

Chapter IX

Civil War

On April 12, 1861, at Charleston, South Carolina, General P. G. T. Beauregard, Confederate States of America, West Point graduate and one-time Superintendent of the Academy, ordered his gunners to open fire on Fort Sumter. One of those to pull a lanyard was Wade Hampton Gibbes, who had graduated less than a year before. The Union commander at Fort Sumter was Major Robert Anderson, an Academy graduate who had been Beauregard's artillery instructor at West Point.

The United States Military Academy, like every other institution in America, was torn apart by the Civil War. The Academy was one of the last to divide. After the Democratic Convention of 1860, the Academy and the Catholic Church remained as the only truly national institutions left in the United States. It was not surprising that this was so, for as the "national academy" it had consistently tried to eliminate sectional prejudice and foster national sentiments. As early as 1824 the Board of Visitors had reported that "cadets coming from every section of the country contribute much . . . to the extirpation of local prejudices and sectional antipathies."[1] Five years later Secretary of War John H. Eaton advised President Jackson that the Academy "may be

[1] *American State Papers: Military Affairs,* II, 716.

looked to as one of the strong bonds of our union."[2] The cadets felt a sense of obligation to the federal government for their education; as First Classman Joseph Ritner put it in a Fourth of July address in 1829, "We are the children of the Union . . . and should ever faction raise the fire-brand of sedition, and spread conflagration, turmoil and confusion through our devoted land, then let it also be recorded, that from her army, at least, our country received a firm, devoted support."[3]

At the Academy the common experience of all cadets, regardless of social or sectional background, together with a feeling of solidarity they shared as future members of a neglected and even despised profession, strengthened the ordinary bonds of college classmates. West Point was small enough to allow everyone to know everyone else and to know the names and reputations of many of those who had earlier attended the Academy. In the army, and even more at West Point, the graduate or cadet was isolated from the rest of the world. His friends and acquaintances were men who had shared the same experiences, and the result was a feeling of comradeship stronger, for example, than that in most college fraternities (which were not allowed at West Point). That comradeship overcame nearly all social, religious, and political differences. Even during the Civil War some friendships born at West Point endured; one thinks of Grant sending congratulations across Petersburg's trenches to George Pickett on the birth of his child.

The authorities did all they could to prevent politics from dividing the Corps. In the forties, Delafield dissolved the Dialectic Society for a year because it was debating subjects such as "Has a State under any circumstances the right to nullify an act of Congress." When he allowed it to re-organize, he limited it to non-controversial topics.[4] The Corps of Cadets, however, represented all sections of the country, and in the fifties, as political passions rose, divisions did begin to appear. Fights, especially during elec-

[2] *Ibid.*, IV, 152.

[3] Joseph Ritner, *An Address Delivered before the Corps of Cadets* (Newburgh, N.Y., 1829).

[4] Forman, *West Point*, 115–16.

tion periods, became more frequent. In the aftermath of John Brown's raid on Harpers Ferry in 1858, there were many heated arguments and at least one duel. A Georgia cadet, Pierce M. B. Young, hanged Brown's body in effigy from one of the windows at the barracks.[5] In a Fourth of July address the next year, First Classman William W. McCreery condemned the outbreaks, maintained that the "noble Union" would not dissolve, and concluded, "Let us put from us the seeds of sectional strife and draw closer and closer the bonds of this glorious union." Two years later Lieutenant McCreery resigned from the army and joined the forces of his native Virginia. He died in action at the Battle of Gettysburg.[6]

In September, 1860, an unknown group of cadets held a mock Presidential election in the Corps. Some 214 of the 278 cadets voted, 99 of them for the Southern Democrat candidate John C. Breckinridge, 47 for the Northern Democrat Stephen A. Douglas, 44 for the Constitutional Union candidate John Bell, and 24 for Republican Abraham Lincoln. Southerners were jubilant, Yankee cadets furious. Second Classman Emory Upton of New York claimed that southerners had prevented northerners from voting, there was talk that all the tellers were southerners, and the Yankees dismissed the whole thing as a southern project.[7]

The final break began four months later, when the first southern cadet resigned to join the forces of his native state. Henry S. Farley, a political fire-eater with appropriate red hair, left the Academy on November 19, a month and a day before his state, South Carolina, seceded. Four days after Farley's departure another South Carolina cadet, James Hamilton, resigned. In December the remainder of the South Carolina contingent, along with three Mississippians and two Alabamians, also left. One of the Alabama cadets was Second Classman Charles P. Ball, first sergeant of Company "A,"

[5] Lynwood M. Holland, *Pierce M. B. Young: The Warwick of the South* (Athens, Ga., 1964), 27.

[6] W. W. McCreery, *An Address . . . on 4th July, 1859* (Newburgh, N.Y., 1859).

[7] Schaff, *Old West Point*, 164–65; Holland, *Young*, 32; Upton to sister, September 30, 1860, du Pont Papers.

heir to the first captaincy of the Corps and one of the most popular cadets. When he was about to leave, he revived an old custom, calling the cadets to attention in the mess hall and saying some parting words. A classmate remembered that his voice was "clear and strong" as he called out, "Battalion, attention! Good-bye, boys! God bless you all!" Thereupon the members of his class hoisted him onto their shoulders and carried him to the wharf.[8]

Resignation came hard to most southern cadets, even those who had no qualms about secession. After his state seceded, Pierce Young, first classman from Georgia, told his parents, "You and others down there don't realize the sacrifice resigning means." He reminded them that "it is a hard thing to throw up a diploma from the *greatest* Institution in the world when that diploma is in my very grasp and you know that diploma would give me preeminence over other men in *any* profession." He was hurt because Georgia had offered him only a second lieutenancy in her state forces. "The idea of giving me a second lieutenant when in a year I would have been offered the same position in the most aristocratic and highly educated army in the world is indeed hard." His father advised him to stay on at West Point and graduate, then resign his commission and join the Confederate forces. Young was going to do so but when the war began decided he could wait no longer and resigned.[9]

For a brief period during the secession crisis the Superintendent was a southerner, Captain P. G. T. Beauregard. He relieved Delafield on January 23, 1861. A day or so later a cadet from his state of Louisiana called on Beauregard and asked him whether or not he should resign. The Superintendent replied, "Watch me; and when I jump, you jump. What's the use of jumping too soon?"[10] As soon as the Secretary of War, Joseph Holt, heard rumors that Beauregard intended to resign when Louisiana left the Union, he relieved him, and on January 28 Delafield once

---

[8] Schaff, *Old West Point,* 175; Farley, *West Point,* 24–25.

[9] Holland, *Young,* 43.

[10] Schaff, *Old West Point,* 196. This story has often been disputed, but Beauregard's latest and most competent biographer, Dr. T. Harry Williams, thinks it is probably true.

again assumed the duties of Superintendent. It was his third term. He served for six weeks until a replacement, Alexander H. Bowman, could relieve him.[11]

Until the second week in April, most of the attention at West Point centered on southern officers and cadets, as everyone speculated on which ones would resign and which would not. Perhaps to hide their own doubts and misgivings, the southerners tended to proclaim their views often and loudly, and they assumed that most if not all of the officers and cadets agreed with them. The idea that the army and West Point were pro-slavery was popular throughout much of the South. In February, 1861, Lieutenant Oliver O. Howard, an instructor at the Academy, received an offer of a professorship in North Carolina, with the final words, "As an officer of the army, I presume, of course, that you entertain no views on the peculiar institution which would be objectionable to a Southern community." And when Lieutenant Alexander McCook accepted the colonelcy of an Ohio regiment, a Kentucky officer at the Academy said in McCook's hearing, "A West Point man who goes into the volunteers to fight against the South forgets every sentiment of honor!"[12]

The firing on Fort Sumter changed everything. Northern cadets who had been indifferent to or had even sympathized with secession suddenly began to understand the implications of secession. A meeting was arranged by word of mouth, and that night all the northern cadets met in the room of William Harris, where they sang "The Star-Spangled Banner" so that it could be heard across the river. It was, Morris Schaff remembered, "the first time I ever saw the southern contingent cowed. All of their Northern allies had deserted them, and they were stunned."[13] The next day all the professors, including Virginia-born Mahan, made patriotic

[11] Beauregard felt the action stemmed from Holt's political differences with Senator John Slidell, Beauregard's brother-in-law. Gouverneur Kemble to Scott, 1861, Misc. Mss., USMA Library; Hamilton Basso, *Beauregard, the Great Creole* (New York, 1933), 61. A persistent and possibly true story has it that Beauregard intended to return to Louisiana before handing in his resignation, then ask for a travel reimbursement.

[12] Howard, *Autobiography*, I, 105.

[13] Schaff, *Old West Point*, 220.

speeches, and Dr. French offered all the money he had to strengthen the government exchequer.[14] A few days later, when a Union officer who had been at Fort Sumter visited West Point, he was joyously serenaded.

By this time southerners were leaving nearly every day, including two instructors, Lieutenants Fitzhugh Lee and Charles W. Field. But the old ties were still there; one cadet remembered later that "between the men of the several sections of the country there was no bitterness manifest, nothing but expressions of sorrow and disappointment."[15] This attitude was especially true in the case of Lee who, like his famous uncle, left only after his native Virginia had seceded and then with great regret. A big, cheerful, smiling man who had almost been dismissed on several occasions during his cadet career because of his pranks, Fitz Lee was the most popular officer at the Academy. On the night of his departure the officers of the post serenaded him and the entire Corps of Cadets stood, hats in hand, in front of the barracks as he went past.[16]

By May, 1861, most of the southern cadets were gone. Out of a total Corps of two hundred and seventy-eight, there were eighty-six southerners, of whom sixty-five resigned. The new Superintendent, Major Bowman, noted that the remaining twenty-one were discontented, restless, and neglecting their studies—but for that matter so were the Yankees, the excitement being what it was. Bowman was convinced most of the twenty-one were merely waiting for permission from their parents to resign, and to force them out before they could "cause a commotion," he ordered all cadets to sign an oath of allegiance.[17] Some of the southerners from the border states hesitated, causing New Yorker Upton to remark, "The Government will know who are loyal and who are traitors." Eventually all signed and fought for the Union.[18] Later, in

[14] Howard, *Autobiography*, I, 100.

[15] Farley, *West Point*, 24.

[16] Forman, *West Point*, 120; R. Ernest Dupuy, *The Compact History of the United States Army* (New York, 1961), 123.

[17] Bowman to Totten, April 26, 1861, SLB.

[18] Peter Smith Michie, *The Life and Letters of Emory Upton* (New York, 1883), 34.

August, Bowman held another oath-signing ceremony, this time
with the words, "I will maintain and defend the sovereignty of
the United States, paramount to any and all allegiance, sovereignty
or fealty I may owe to any State, county or country whatsoever."
Two Kentuckians refused to sign, including plebe John C. Singleton, and were thereupon dismissed. Singleton went home, joined
the Union army, and was killed in action.[19]

In the first weeks of the war the cadets felt an acute sense of
isolation. "I suppose there is a great deal of stir and preparation
for war going on in the country," Cullen Byrant wrote his father,
"though I have as yet seen but very few evidences of it. We are
almost completely secluded and shut out from the rest of the
world." The war news from all over the country was intensely
exciting, but at West Point, now that the southerners had left,
all was quiet and normal—maddeningly so. All over the North
volunteer companies and regiments were being formed, men were
marching off to war to the tune of "The Battle Hymn of the
Republic" with pretty girls' kisses on their cheeks, and the great
crusade was under way. But at West Point, nothing. The young
heroes, eager to save their nation, were ignored. In retaliation they
ridiculed the more fortunate. Cadet Bryant sneeringly told his
father he did not expect the volunteer companies at home were
much to look at, and he supposed the officers were "rather poor
specimens." Bryant, who had been at the Academy for ten months,
pontificated that "experience only can make an efficient officer.
I am afraid our volunteer companies would make a rather poor
show in a fight with disciplined troops."[20]

The cadets often announced their contempt for civilians turned
soldiers, so they were dismayed when they saw high rank in the
volunteer regiments going to untrained men when the best they
had to look forward to was a second lieutenancy in a regular
regiment, and even that would probably be a brevet rank. They
watched with envious eyes as their southern classmates became
captains or more in state forces, ranks a Regular Army officer could

[19] Dupuy, *Where They Have Trod*, 298.
[20] Bryant to father, May 5, 1861, Bryant Family Papers.

hardly hope to reach before he was forty. And they were absolutely furious when they discovered that the Secretary of War, in expanding the Regular Army, was giving commissions in it to mere civilians. Those who received the appointments would permanently rank ahead of the First Classmen, who would not graduate and receive their commissions until June, for in the army a man's position, and thus his promotions, depended upon his date of appointment.[21] The system of cadet rankings had taught the students they were expected to fight for higher rank, and they learned the lesson well. Many wrote complaining letters on the subject to their congressmen, including William Harris, whose father was a United States Senator, but the letters did no good.[22]

Some cadets listened closely to the enticing offers of the state governors, men who realized that their volunteer forces needed at least a smattering of professionalism. The governors offered a captaincy or a majority or in a few cases even a colonelcy to home-state cadets. For the young men the temptation was great but so were the drawbacks. They would be commanding citizen-soldiers, and they had an ingrained prejudice against such warriors. To accept such an appointment, they would have to resign from the Academy, which First and Second Classmen found difficult, especially since General in Chief Scott had made it clear he did not want any regular officers joining the volunteer forces. Scott argued that this would so weaken the Regular Army that it would never recover, and he forced officers to resign their Regular Army commissions before they could join the volunteers.

It was a crucial decision, one that did incalculable harm to the Union cause. For half a century the United States had maintained a military academy to provide professional leaders for citizen-soldiers in time of war, but when war came, Scott decided it was more important to preserve the integrity of the Regular Army. In the preceding generation West Point had graduated about thirteen

[21] "They are filling up the vacancies in the Army with citizen appointments as usual," one disgusted First Classman wrote, "a great outrage to our class but nothing else can be expected from politicians." Henry A. du Pont to father, March 21, 1861, du Pont Papers.
[22] Harris to father, February 17, 1861, Harris Papers.

hundred cadets, at least half of whom served in the Union army. There were not enough West Pointers to provide even one per regiment, therefore, but nevertheless they could have been used for training purposes, as the members of the class of 1861 were for a short time, with excellent results. There were more than enough West Pointers available to put one in every brigade, but under Scott's policy whole divisions went into battle without a single professional soldier among the line or staff officers. In the Confederacy, where there was no regular army, West Pointers were scattered throughout the outfits, and at least part of the South's early success was the result of this policy. The North, on the other hand, went into the opening battles with little more than armed mobs, except for the Regular Army regiments, which were the equivalent of elite troops. The trouble was that nowhere were there enough of them.

Later in the war, after Henry Halleck had replaced Scott, he encouraged regulars to join the volunteers, hoping thereby to improve the citizen-soldiers' efficiency, and many did so. Under the Halleck system they retained their grade and position in the Regular Army, while rising as far as their abilities could take them in the volunteers. For example, Emory Upton, an 1861 graduate of the Academy who in late 1862 joined the New York volunteers, was still a lieutenant in the regulars when he was a brevet major general in the volunteers.[23] More important, the West Pointers made valuable contributions to the volunteer regiments.

In early 1861 all the possibilities presented endless topics for discussion, as cadets marveled over the colonelcy one had received, what another had been offered, and what a third intended to do. A number sent in their resignations after accepting a volunteer commission, but to their disgust the Superintendent refused to receive them. Major Bowman argued that they were not ready to represent the Academy in the field, although he admitted that they would probably do better than most of those already serving as volunteer officers, and he feared that if he accepted any resig-

[23] Ambrose, *Upton,* 12.

nations to permit cadets to serve with the volunteers, the entire Corps would resign.[24]

Like most Americans, the cadets assumed the war would consist of one gigantic battle, with the winner marching on and capturing the loser's capital. The inactivity and isolation at West Point, the continuation of regular classes, and the seeming blindness of the authorities who refused to call them immediately into active service—all made the cadets frantic. They were certain the great battle would be fought without them. America was facing its greatest crisis, and the nation needed all the help it could get, but the authorities were blindly ignoring the hundreds of potential Napoleons at West Point. Cadet Bryant complained about being "completely secluded" and commented bitterly that "we might as well be at some frontier post a thousand miles from any settlement."[25] When they heard in March that the midshipmen at Annapolis were going to graduate early and go to war, the First Classmen held a series of informal meetings and decided upon a course of action. The cadets each wrote their congressmen, asking that they urge the Secretary of War to graduate the First Class early. As a group, they sent a petition to the Secretary of War himself, pointing out that the Secretary of the Navy had ordered the first class at Annapolis into the active service and arguing that they were just as ready and willing to assume their responsibilities.[26] The Secretary, Simon Cameron, responded favorably, and on May 6, 1861, without benefit of either graduation ceremonies or the traditional furlough, the First Class went off to war—or, in actual fact, to Washington, where they spent the next month drilling volunteers.[27]

Encouraged by their predecessors' success, the new First Class also petitioned Cameron, once again with success, and on June 24, a year early, the cadets were examined, graduated, and ordered to Washington. They received their commissions in General Scott's office, with President Abraham Lincoln present for the ceremony,

[24] Bowman to Totten, September 5, 1861, SLB.
[25] Bryant to father, May 5, 1861, Bryant Family Papers.
[26] Du Pont to father, April 14, 1861, du Pont Papers.
[27] Ambrose, *Upton*, 12.

then went out in the field to serve as drill masters. By July both classes had done so well in their tasks that Cameron ordered the new First Class, the third of that year, to begin recitations and prepare for graduation. Three days later, just as it began to appear that West Point would soon have no cadets at all, Cameron rescinded his hasty decision and postponed the graduation until the next year. For the rest of the war classes graduated at the regular intervals.

Throughout the war the Academy had to make adjustments to the emergency. One problem was the scarcity of equipment, officers, and enlisted men. Early in 1861 Captain Charles Griffin took the light battery off to war. It became Battery "D" of the Fifth U. S. Artillery, the West Point battery, and it fought with distinction at the first big battle, Bull Run, and at most of the later battles in the eastern theater. Shortly after Griffin's departure the engineering detachment of enlisted men and officers went off to war, taking with them the few horses Griffin had left.[28] By September of 1861 Superintendent Bowman was complaining that instruction in artillery and cavalry had been totally suspended at the Academy, because of the absence of officers, horses, and guns.[29]

Bowman was also unhappy over the rapid changes in the academic and tactical staff. In 1861 alone some thirteen officers applied for and received service in the field. Eventually every able-bodied officer at the Academy went into the active service, but after the first few battles Bowman had no great difficulty replacing them—there was a whole host of disabled officers he could choose from.[30] The Cadet Corps was also changing. In 1864 Congress made it possible for men up to the age of twenty-four who had war service to enter the Academy as cadets. Several who did so were bearded men who had fought at Shiloh, Antietam, and elsewhere, and some had been commissioned volunteer officers.

In 1862 the cadets had a chance to see the President, as Lincoln came to West Point to consult with General Scott about a new General in Chief. Scott, who had retired and was living at West

[28] Farley, *West Point*, 87; Forman, *West Point*, 123.
[29] Bowman to Totten, March 18, 1861, SLB.
[30] Schaff, *Old West Point*, 255–56.

[177]

Point, recommended Halleck. After Lincoln completed his business, Bowman took him on a short tour of the Academy. The President said a few words to the cadets to whom he had given an "at-large" appointment and shook hands with others. Then Lincoln went to the Napoleon Gallery, where maps of Napoleon's campaigns had been drawn on the wall. The President was impressed by the maps and asked for copies, which Bowman prepared and sent to him.[31]

Aside from Lincoln's visit and the celebrations in honor of Union victories, only once did the war upset the Academy's routine. In the summer of 1863, when conscription went into effect, there were widespread riots in New York City. A crowd that had gathered to protest the draft quickly turned into a mob. At the time, Lee's invasion of Pennsylvania had taken away the state and city militia companies, and garrison soldiers—mostly invalids—from the forts in the harbor were unable to quell the riot. Reinforcements were called for, and a detachment of fifty-nine enlisted men went down from West Point to help restore order. At the same time a rumor reached the Academy that the "copperhead" or pro-South element in New York City intended to come up the Hudson and destroy the Cold Spring Foundry, where Robert P. Parrott, a West Point graduate, was producing the famed Parrott gun. Bowman issued ball cartridges to the cadets and put them on guard duty for several days and nights, but no attack was made.[32]

The excitement was atypical. For the most part, even during the war, West Point was as isolated as ever. In 1863 Congress voted funds to build a road from the Academy to Cornwall, up the river, which would have made West Point more accessible. Bowman was horrified and insisted the work be stopped. He protested that "it would be ruinous to the morals and discipline of the Corps [to open] an easy approach to Newburgh."[33] The only contact the cadets had with the war, aside from what they read in newspapers or heard from invalid officers on the academic staff, came to members of the furlough class, who usually asked for and

[31] Bowman to Lincoln, May 6, 1863, SLB.
[32] Forman, *West Point*, 123–24.
[33] *Ibid.*

received permission to spend their furloughs with the Army of the Potomac.[34] For the rest of the cadets the new sport of baseball, supposedly invented by Academy graduate Abner Doubleday, helped pass the time. It became popular there during the war, just as it did among the armies in the field.[35]

The war changed many of the Superintendent's problems only in degree, not in kind. He continued to worry about getting good teachers for instructors, maintaining discipline in the Corps, improving facilities, and the like. And he continued to play the role of college president, with Congress as his board of trustees. In 1864 Senator Ira Harris, father of a recent graduate, helped push through a pay raise for the cadets. Bowman, in thanking him, asked his help in getting admission standards raised. Every Superintendent before him had done so, and every one after would make the same request, with the same results. Bowman tried to meet the main argument against raising standards for admission by pointing out that such a policy would not have the effect of limiting the Academy to the sons of the rich, for America now had free schools open to all. But it was no use, because no matter how many times the Superintendents complained that candidates "are unable to spell the simplest word," Congress would not open itself to the charge of favoring the rich and writing undemocratic laws.[36]

War-born legislation did add one problem for the Superintendent. In 1865 the Chief Engineer reminded him that as carpenters at the Academy received $2.00 a day, or over $600.00 per year, they were liable for income tax. He should have been withholding the proper amount from their pay, but in any case he was responsible for it, and if he could not collect the tax from the carpenters he would himself have to pay the amount due the Commissioner of Internal Revenue.[37]

Among the cadets the progress of the Union armies was the subject of most conversation. Many had their own war maps, and

[34] Bowman to Delafield, June 20, 1864, SLB.
[35] Baumer, *West Point,* 198.
[36] Bowman to Harris, March, 1864, SLB.
[37] Delafield to Cullum, December 23, 1865, SLB.

all studied the newspapers thoroughly. Victories were celebrated with speeches, proclamations, and fireworks. One hundred guns saluted the fall of Mobile Bay and Atlanta; and in December of 1864 thirty-six guns fired in honor of "General Sherman's gift to the nation of the city of Savannah."[38] The staff and the cadets were proud of the records of Academy graduates, on both sides, especially in the last two years of the war, when West Pointers dominated both armies. They knew that of the 296 graduates serving the Confederate States of America, 151 became general officers. In the Union army, 294 West Pointers gained their stars. Of the sixty most important battles, all but five were commanded on both sides by Academy graduates; of the exceptions, one side in each case was commanded by a West Pointer.

But although the names of Lee, Jackson and others were mentioned with awe, the Academy was uncompromisingly pro-Union. Like the army and the government, in the beginning West Point was divided on the best method of conducting the war, and many officers and cadets who were opposed to the rebellion were nonetheless pro-slavery. Democratic congressional victories in 1862 insured that the Corps would continue to represent something more than a monolithic political view. Still, as the war went on, the army and the Academy, which usually reflected the army's views, became more and more Republican in their orientation. As the disagreements between Republicans and Democrats increasingly tended to center around the issue of centralization and states' rights, army officers tended to support Lincoln and his wing of the party. They were servants of the central government, and as professional soldiers they wanted a more powerful Regular Army, which they saw could be achieved only through the support of a powerful nation, one in which the federal and not the state governments dominated. General in Chief Halleck, a Democrat until 1862, set the pace. He became a Republican when he realized that the Democratic states' rights position included support of the state militia and volunteer forces, while the moderate Republicans, at least in theory, were more amenable to the idea of a

[38] Forman, *West Point*, 123–25.

national, professional army.[39] At the Academy, Henry A. du Pont, James H. Wilson, and a score of other pre-war Democratic cadets followed Halleck's lead and became staunch Republicans.

Among the faculty the unofficial dean of the Academic Board, Dennis Mahan, also left the Democratic party to support Lincoln. His new faith, and that of many other officers, was tested in 1864 when the first Academy graduate to be a candidate for the Presidency, General George G. McClellan, ran against Lincoln on a platform that included a peace plank. McClellan had been one of Mahan's best pupils and had taught under him, but like Halleck, Sherman, and many other officers, Mahan denounced the Democrat's candidacy. On one occasion Mahan got into a heated argument with his old friend Gouverneur Kemble, who lived across the river in Cold Spring. Kemble supported McClellan and thought Mahan should too. Mahan replied that he was a Democrat of the "Jefferson and Jackson school, holding, with them, that there are times in a nation's existence when the safety of the state is the highest law." He said that it was shameful for the Democrats to call for an end to a struggle that was "between right and wrong." When Kemble attacked Lincoln and his policies, Mahan replied that McClellan, with the possible exception of John C. Fremont, was "the least qualified man who ever ran for the Presidency." Mahan said he based his opinion on "indisputable data," and claimed that McClellan had a "deficiency of certain cardinal moral traits."[40]

The move of army officers into the Republican party was the more remarkable because it was members of that party who were responsible for the most serious attack ever launched against the Academy, one that surpassed in scope the one made by the Jacksonians three decades earlier. These new critics, who were both radicals and moderates, used all the old Jacksonian charges about West Point's being a breeding ground for aristocracy but added to them two new ones. First, pointing to the large number of Academy graduates who were leading the Confederacy, including

[39] Ambrose, *Halleck*, 209–11.
[40] Mahan to Kemble, September 26 and 29, 1864, Mahan Papers.

most of the important generals and the President of the Confederate States of America, and to the many West Pointers leading
the Union armies who were known to hold conservative views,
such as Don Carlos Buell and McClellan, the critics charged that
Academy graduates were disloyal and that the institution itself
was pro-Southern. Secretary of War Simon Cameron led the way
in his annual report for 1861, written in June, in which he said
the resignations of the southerners in the army showed "extraordinary treachery" and wondered if they were not the result of
"a radical defect in the system of education" at West Point. He
argued that the Academy's system of discipline failed to distinguish between "acts wrong in themselves and acts wrong because
prohibited by special regulation" and that this substitution of
"habit for conscience" produced traitorous officers.[41] The second
charge was more serious. It was simply that, whatever the facts
about the Academy's loyalty might be, the important thing was
that West Pointers were poor soldiers, incapable of training or
organizing troops or of winning battles.

Friends of the Academy answered the first charge by pointing
out that, while six out of ten southern cadets, on the average,
left the Academy to fight for the C.S.A., ten out of ten southern
students did so at Harvard, Yale, and Princeton. Obviously West
Point had done a better job of showing southerners where their
duty was than the colleges had. This observation neither answered
nor satisfied the critics, for the United States government was not
providing four-year, all-expense scholarships to Harvard, Yale, and
Princeton. Still, the South had paid its share of the expenses at the
Academy and this was, after all, a civil war, and it plainly was
unreasonable to expect most southern graduates to fight for the
North.

The charge of incompetence was another matter. The war
brought into a sharp focus many traits of the American people
previously forgotten or ignored, at least by army officers, among
them the widespread hostility to a standing army and professional
soldiers. Also, the prevailing American contempt for the specialist,

[41] *Annual Report of the Secretary of War* (Washington, 1861), 27.

in this case the trained soldier, led to bitter attacks upon the generals and extensive criticism of their military operations. For a peace-loving people, Americans were remarkably fascinated with war, and most considered themselves experts in both tactics and strategy. The maddening delays of 1861, relieved only by the disaster at Bull Run, and the consistent attempts to apply Mahan's theories—interior lines of operations, a strong base of supply, fortifications, a campaign of positions, all derived from the ideal of limited war—were more than many northerners could take. Frustrated and angry, they looked for the cause and found it in West Point and its cautious specialists. On December 13, 1861, the New York *Tribune* spoke for the people when it declared, "However imperfect the civil appreciation may be as to military science, common sense is an attribute which buttons and bullion do not alone confer; and common sense is quite as competent as tactical profundity to decide the questions of hastening or deferring operations against the rebels."[42]

Ten days later a bill was introduced in Congress to increase the number of cadets. Republicans leaped to the attack. Benjamin F. Wade, John Sherman, and Lyman Trumbull spoke of West Point's treason, of the ungrateful who had taken their education from the government and then made war upon it. Others repeated the old Jacksonian charges about the aristocratic anomaly in democratic America and the snobbish closed corporation. William Pitt Fessenden thought the Academy lacked an atmosphere of moral principle, for the pupils were "educated in a narrow, exclusive, miserable spirit" and fancied themselves as the sole possessors of military wisdom. Other senators spoke of the absurdity of the government's maintaining a school to educate soldiers when none existed for doctors, ministers, or lawyers.

There was much truth in the charge of incompetence. The West Pointers running the armies, McClellan, Buell, Halleck, and later Pope, Burnside, and Hooker, were doing a poor job of it. They

[42] *New York Tribune,* December 13, 1861; for an excellent discussion of the whole problem, see T. Harry Williams, "The Attack on West Point During the Civil War," *Mississippi Valley Historical Review,* XXV (June, 1939), 492–501.

had received neither practical nor theoretical training at West Point for handling the huge numbers of men thrust into their hands, and they showed it. Politically, in the first year or two the northern generals were not in agreement with their government's policy, and some of them, notably McClellan, were remarkably free in expressing their feelings. The favoritism of one West Pointer for another became notorious; it was something no one could prove but everyone knew about. There were two famous cases. In 1863 Halleck dumped John McClernand, an Illinois politician, in favor of Ulysses Grant; in view of McClernan's record, no one complained very much about that. But the case of John A. Logan, also of Illinois, was different. He led the Army of the Tennessee to victory in the Battle of Atlanta in 1864 but was denied permanent command of that army only because of his lack of a West Point education. Most maddening of all, however, was the battlefield performance. Any man with common sense, it seemed, could do better than McDowell at First Bull Run, Halleck at Corinth, McClellan during the winter of 1861–62 and later at Yorktown, Pope at Second Bull Run, and especially Burnside at Fredericksburg.

Small wonder that the Republicans were contemptuous of specialized military training. Confident that the common man could master any profession in a short time, the congressmen boasted that the successful generals of the war would emerge from the ranks of civilian officers. Benjamin Wade maintained that the "men who will eminently distinguish themselves in this war, who will come forward and show themselves capable of commanding great armies in the field, will be men the scope of whose intellect has never been narrowed down to the rules of your military school." One reason was that in the nature of the thing West Pointers could not become great or even good generals because the curriculum at the Academy was designed to stifle all imagination. The theoretical nature of the course work produced impractical graduates, "invariably men of all theory and no execution of results," as one critic said, who were capable only of constructing defensive bases. And Senator Sherman, whose West Point–trained brother would soon add a novel dimension to war, said the professionals were only fitted "to discipline, to mold, to form lines and squares, to go through the ordinary discipline and routine of a camp." He joined with other senators to urge that the money spent on West Point be instead distributed to the state colleges for military training programs there. The moderate Republicans and some Democrats tried to answer the charges, and Professor Mahan and other faculty members wrote to the Radicals refuting their charges, but the fact remained that the West Pointers, at least in the northern army, were not doing well, and the bill to enlarge the Academy failed.[43]

In January, 1863, a time when the Union's war effort was getting nowhere, a bill for the annual appropriation for the Academy came on the Senate floor. The Radicals, beside themselves with fury at the scope of the conspiracy that had brought the Union to the edge of total disaster—and how, save by conspiracy, could the failure of the more numerous and better armed northern armies be explained?—demanded that West Point be abolished. Senator James H. Lane of Kansas suggested that when the North was defeated an appropriate epitaph would be, "Died of West Point pro-slaveryism." And even if there was no conspiracy, Senator Trumball said, the emphasis placed by the Academy on mathematics and fortifications was the cause of the Union's defeats. "Take off your engineering restraints. . . . Dismiss . . . from the Army every man who knows how to build a fortification, and let the men of the North, with their strong arms and indomitable spirit, move down upon the rebels, and I tell you they will grind them to powder in their power."[44] *Harper's Weekly,* commenting on the debate, declared, "Not that a military education naturally unfits a man for being a great soldier. But war being an art, not a science, a man can no more be made a first-class painter, or a great poet, by professors and textbooks; he must be born with the genius of war in his breast." Few such men were born, and *Harper's* thought the chances were they would not be found at West Point.[45]

[43] Williams, "Attack on West Point," 497–500; Mahan to Fessenden, March 18, 1862, Mahan Papers.
[44] Williams, "Attack on West Point," 502–4.
[45] *Harper's Weekly,* VI (January 17, 1863), 75–78.

The attempt to destroy the Academy failed by a 29 to 10 vote. Some of the Republicans who voted against the resolution realized that the Yankee armies were being defeated, after all, by West Pointers who were displaying imagination and dash, the chief culprit being former Superintendent Robert E. Lee, so that charges of incompetent training had a false ring. The North, it seemed, had just got the wrong graduates.

There was more to it than that. Southern graduates, in the early years of the war, did better than their northern classmates for a number of reasons. Their troops were better. The rural South produced soldiers who were used to firearms and outdoor living. They were on the defensive, fighting in their home country, with short supply lines and a friendly population (whenever southern armies ventured into the North they were defeated). Until 1863, morale in the Confederate army, for diverse reasons, was higher than that in the Union army. Until Halleck and Secretary of War Edwin Stanton came to the War Department, the Confederate army was better organized. Confederate cavalry was clearly superior, not only because it was better led but because southerners sat their horses better. Perhaps equally important, the leading Confederates—Lee, Jackson, and the two Johnstons—were career soldiers, men who had served as professional soldiers most of their adult lives. The leading Union officers, throughout the war, had resigned from the army after the Mexican War and followed various civilian pursuits. George H. Thomas was one of the few who remained in the army—Grant, Sherman, McClellan, Halleck had all been civilians. In 1861 they had to readjust, and it took time; the Confederates did not.

Most of this the critics did not see. What they did recognize, when it occurred, was that in the summer of 1863 the North won her two greatest victories, Vicksburg and Gettysburg, both under Academy-trained men. The war was finally being won. Grant, Sherman, Meade, Sheridan, and other professionals were becoming heroes; McClellan and Buell, the leading conservative Democrats in the army, were gone; Halleck had become a Republican. Also in 1863 Captain Edward C. Boynton of the Academy published the first history of West Point, designed to answer the charges against it. The critics thereafter left West Point alone.

Because of the record of Academy graduates in the war, charges of incompetence were seldom heard again.[46] The old question of loyalty did reappear. In 1904 Robert Bingham claimed that from 1825, the year Lee and Jefferson Davis entered the Academy, until 1850, the right of secession was taught at West Point in a text by William Rawle, *A View of the Constitutions of the United States of America*. Charles Francis Adams supported Bingham.[47] In a more or less official reply Colonel Edgar S. Dudley, professor of law at West Point, demonstrated that Rawle's work had only been used for one year, 1826, and that Kent's *Commentaries* was the text used to teach law thereafter.[48] In any case Rawle's views were neither as extreme as Bingham claimed, nor were they any different from those being taught elsewhere. In declaring for the right of secession, Rawle was careful to associate it with the final right of rebellion, enjoyed by all peoples at all times. He was, in fact, rooted in Lockean tradition. "To deny this right" to secede, he said, "would be inconsistent with the principle on which all our political systems are founded, which is, that the people have in all cases the right to determine how they shall be governed."[49] He was personally strongly opposed to secession and felt there was a "sacred obligation to preserve the union of our country," in which "we feel our glory, our safety, and our happiness." Secession, he warned, would produce "jealousies, discord, and . . . mutual hostilities," and the nation would be conquered by foreign enemies.[50]

[46] The general hostility to West Point was of course shared by civilians in uniform, who came to hate West Point officers and their closed society. The best expression of this attitude is John A. Logan's *The Volunteer Soldier of America* (Chicago, 1887). An outstanding citizen-soldier, Logan attacked West Point from its founding to the Civil War. He contended that volunteers made the best soldiers. For a further discussion of Logan's views, see 215–17.

[47] Robert Bingham, "Sectional Misunderstandings," *North American Review*, CLXXIX (September, 1904), 361.

[48] Edgar Dudley, "Secession," *Century Magazine*, LXXVIII (July, 1909), 631.

[49] William Rawle, *A View of the Constitution of the United States* (Philadelphia, 1825), 289.

[50] *Ibid.*, 299, 301.

Despite all the Academy could do to defend itself, the fact remained that as an agency of the United States government, using federal funds, it had trained men who had then used their talents to try to destroy that government. To prevent a recurrence, after the war a new oath was introduced for candidates: "I do solemnly swear that I will support the Constitution of the United States, paramount to any and all allegiance, sovereignty, or fealty I may owe to any State. . . ."[51]

While the Academy did its best to still the critics, it could not forget all the harsh comments about professional soldiers. Late in the war a group of disabled officers teaching at West Point began discussing the manner in which the conflict was reported. They all felt that the Regular Army was not appreciated, because the newspapers tended to laud the performance of their state's volunteer regiments and ignore all others. Certain that no state would erect a monument to the Regular Army after the war, they decided to form a committee and raise their own at West Point. Collections came in slowly, but by 1889 they had some $60,000 in subscriptions from Regular Army officers, and construction of the Battle Monument near Trophy Point began. In 1897 it was completed and dedicated to the officers and soldiers of the Regular Army who died in the Civil War.[52]

Sectional bitterness also survived the war. In 1868 Superintendent George Washington Cullum published the first volume of his *Biographical Register*. In it he excluded the records of all southerners after they resigned to fight for the Confederacy.[53] Later Cullum married General Halleck's widow and thus gained control of Halleck's fortune of over a half-million dollars, which Halleck had made in mining activities in California before the war. Upon his death Cullum gave the money to the Academy, to be used to build Cullum Memorial Hall on the eastern edge of the Plain. Dedicated to the deceased officers and graduates of the Military Academy and completed in 1898, it contained plaques,

---

[51] Farley, *West Point*, 23.

[52] Charles W. Larned, *History of the Battle Monument at West Point* (West Point, 1898).

[53] Cullum, *Biographical Register*.

paintings, and other rememberances of West Point's famous sons. In accordance with Cullum's wishes, however, it was marked by a complete absence of the great Confederates. Only Lee and Beauregard were there, and they in a series concerning the Superintendents.

Not many graduates shared Cullum's views. The Academy had been the last great institution to part, and it was one of the first to reunite. Grant and Lee, at Appomattox and in later correspondence, set the pace, and all over the South, as the Confederate armies surrendered, senior and junior officers who had been classmates at West Point held individual reunions. In 1869 President Horace Webster of the College of the City of New York, West Point graduate of 1818, issued a call for a meeting to form an alumni association. Graduates from both the Union and Confederacy responded, took the name The Association of Graduates of the United States Military Academy, elected Sylvanus Thayer their president, and drew up a constitution. In it they sought to avoid politics by declaring their object to be "social intercourse and fraternal fellowship of the graduates" and forbidding political discussion. Thereafter, at annual reunions Yankees and Rebels got together and talked of old times.[54]

The rest of the nation took longer, but eventually it too forgot most of the wartime hatreds and learned to live together. For the army as a whole the most obvious reunion came in 1898, during the Spanish-American War, when southerners fought alongside northerners, with officers from both the Union and Confederate armies leading them. Four years later, at Alumni Day proceedings at the West Point Centennial, General E. Porter Alexander, Chief of Artillery in the Army of Northern Virginia, gave the main speech. After praising Lee, Stonewall Jackson, Jeb Stuart, and other Rebel leaders, he said it was best for the South, the nation, and the world that the war had turned out as it did. The northern and southern graybeards in the audience rose to their feet with a mighty roar. The band struck up "The Star-Spangled Banner,"

[54] *The Association of Graduates of the USMA, Bulletin Number 1* (West Point, 1900).

then "Dixie," and the old men who had once fought against each other embraced and cried unashamedly.[55] The next day Secretary of War Elihu Root provided a fitting climax to the reunion when he said, in effect, that the War Department no longer doubted the loyalty of West Point. "No army inspired by the spirit of the Military Academy can ever endanger a country's liberty or can ever desert its country's flag."[56]

In truth the statement was superfluous, as no one had really doubted West Point's loyalty since at least the seventies. The Academy emerged from the war one of America's most hallowed institutions. Grant, a tanner's son, Sherman, an orphan, and many others made the old charges of its aristocratic nature seem absurd. Not a single graduate had made any attempt to take over the civilian government, either in the North or the South—although General McClellan did make a couple of frightening but empty statements along those lines—, and the ancient fear of military domination was lessened. Most important, Americans North and South were immensely proud of their armies, and they regarded the men who had led them as heroes, superior soldiers, so they said, to any others in the world. And the leaders were West Pointers.

[55] William Whitman Bailey, "The Centennial at West Point," Archives, USMA.
[56] *CWP*, I, 53.

Looking north up the Hudson River from the Plain.
Charles Dickens said the Academy "could not
stand on more appropriate ground and any
ground more beautiful can hardly be."

ALDEN PARTRIDGE, third Superintendent, and JARED MANSFIELD (by Thomas Sully), professor of natural and experimental philosophy. Mansfield said Partridge interfered in the faculty's work to an extent not allowed "even in the greatest of despotisms." Partridge had Mansfield arrested for engaging in a mutinous cabal.

JONATHAN WILLIAMS, the first Superintendent (portrait by Thomas Sully on facing page). He found that "the military academy, as it now stands, is like a foundling, barely existing among the mountains, and nurtured at a distance out of sight, and almost unknown to its legitimate parents."

Cadet uniforms, about 1823. A cadet verse ran, "Your coat is made, you button it, give one spasmodic cough, / And do not draw another breath until you take it off!"

A pre-Civil War examination before the Board of Visitors. Most Board members became enthusiastic admirers of the Academy.

SYLVANUS THAYER (by Robert Weir). He lived in solitude
"with perfect neatness, order and comfort in all his
arrangements," and looked the ideal professional soldier.

DENNIS HART MAHAN. "The most particular, crabbed, exacting man that I ever saw," one cadet commented. ALBERT E. CHURCH. He seemed "an old mathematical cinder, bereft of all natural feeling." WILLIAM H. C. BARTLETT. George Ticknor of Harvard thought that Bartlett was the best student he had ever seen. ROBERT WEIR started James McNeill Whistler on his artistic career.

A general view of West Point, about 1826.

The barracks and the Corps on parade, about 1840.

ROBERT E. LEE, Superintendent from 1852–55. One cadet reported, ". . . by his generous, manly and consistent conduct he has won the respect and esteem of every Cadet in the Corps."

James McNeill Whistler's conception

BENNY HAVENS. Cadet Edgar
Allan Poe, who was a frequent
visitor at Havens' tavern,
thought Benny "the sole
congenial soul in the
entire God-forsaken place."

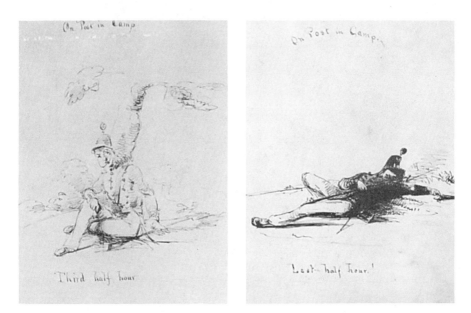

of sentry duty in summer camp.

Two cadet groups during the trying days of 1863. Note the men in mourning.

PETER SMITH MICHIE, outstanding member
of the post-Civil War faculty. A deeply religious
Scotsman, Michie threatened to find deficient any cadet
who did not believe his physics class proved the existence of God.

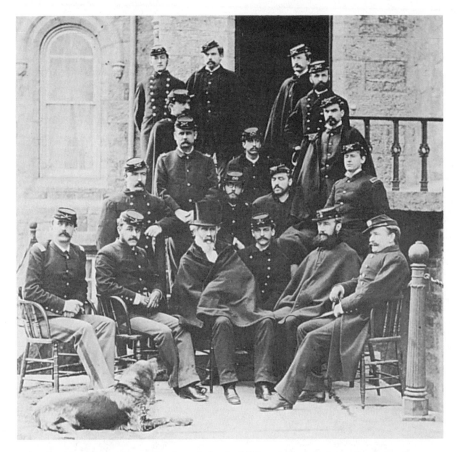

The faculty, 1870. Together they defended West Point against all encroachment, change, and criticism. In the center is Henry Lane Kendrick, "Old Hanks," wearing the tall silk hat.

Summer camp scenes. After World War I, Superintendent Douglas MacArthur temporarily abolished summer camp because he thought the fancy uniforms and formal hops had little relation to the business of soldiering. Inspection of the Guard, 1906. Lounging before tent, 1876.

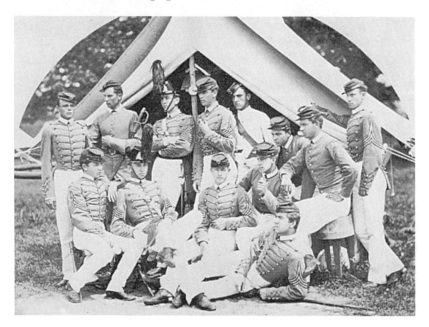

Cadet HENRY O. FLIPPER,
the first Negro graduate,
class of 1877.

On the Hudson, the Academy's first rowing team, 1887.

The Superintendent's house.

Plebes taking oath of allegiance, 1913.

An engineering class in the early 1900's.

Cadets in the dining hall, early 1900's.
The food and service had improved since pre-Civil War days.

DOUGLAS MACARTHUR, 1903.

DWIGHT D. EISENHOWER, 1915.

GEORGE PATTON, 1909.

OMAR BRADLEY, 1915.

Graduation photographs of four cadets who later
commanded the American armies of World War II.

Class of 1915, the class the stars fell on. Fifty-nine of these cadets became general officers. Three of them wore four stars, two wore five stars, and one

Cadet uniforms, about 1914.

became President of the United States. Members of this class led the largest American armies both in World War II and the Korean War.

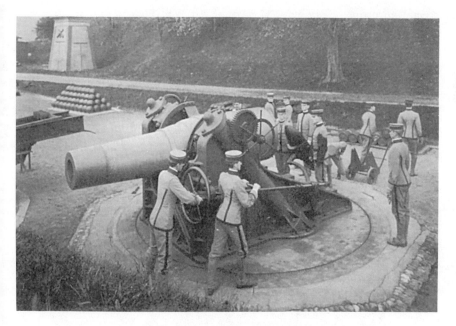

Coast artillery drill, about 1914.

Cadet room, 1917. MacArthur thought the cadets deserved a few more comforts.

Engineering instruction, about 1904. MacArthur felt West Point would benefit from less rigid, formalized instruction.

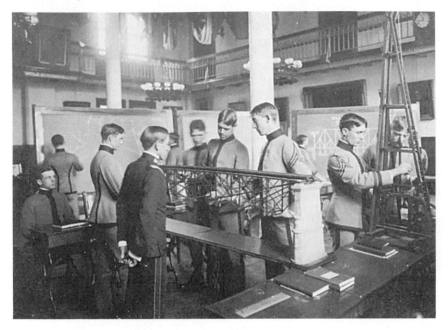

Douglas MacArthur. Cadets remembered him "gazing at distant horizons,"
wearing an unconventional and strictly forbidden uniform.
They considered him "a law unto himself."

The first Army-Navy game, 1890, won by Navy, 24 to 0. The game was played on the Plain.

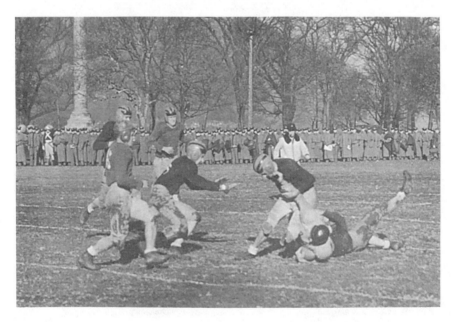

A football game between the Goats and the Engineers, about 1920, typical of the spirit of athletics MacArthur inspired.

Stars of Army's great
football teams of 1944–46:
GLEN DAVIS (41),
"Mr. Outside," and
FELIX "Doc" BLANCHARD
(35), "Mr. Inside."

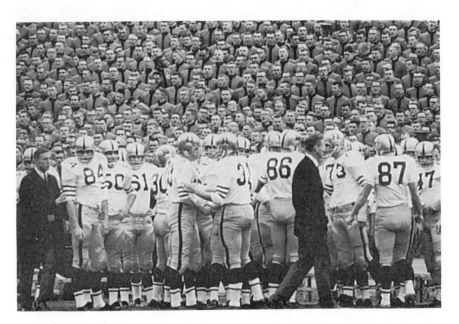

The Army-Navy game, 1964, won by Army, 11 to 8. "The Corps is always Army's
twelfth man."

An aerial view of the modern Academy.

Color Guard, carrying campaign banners,
at the 1965 Graduation exercises.

Two old graduates and former Chiefs of Staff,
OMAR BRADLEY and DWIGHT D. EISENHOWER,
at their fiftieth reunion, 1965.

The Corps of Cadets on review to honor the new Deputy Chief of Staff and former Superintendent Maxwell D. Taylor, January 19, 1952. This is the central barracks area. The Cadet Chapel rises in the background.

Summer camp training today. The Academy keeps pace with the changing requirements of national defense.

The Corps of Cadets on the Plain, at the 1965 Graduation parade.

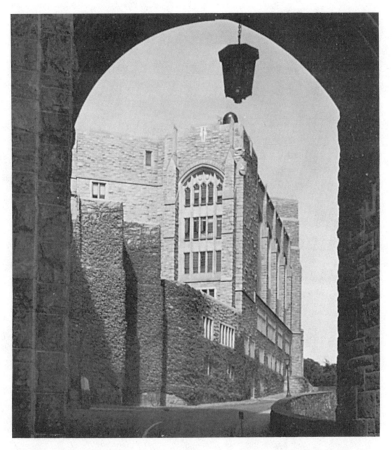

The East Academic Building, about 1913, looking through the archway that connects the Headquarters Building and Thayer Hall.

Coming in and going out.

The Cadet Chapel.

Trophy Point, looking north up the Hudson.

Chapter X

Stagnation

In 1871 James Burrill Angell, president of the University of Michigan, declared, "In this day of unparalleled activity in college life, the institution which is not steadily advancing is certainly falling behind."[1] Accepting Angell's dictum, the post-Civil War colleges became obsessed with progress. Freeing themselves from the old classical approach to education, they vied with each other in becoming modern and up-to-date. Forgetting their reverence for the past and their role as defenders of its integrity, they promised to make their graduates not classically educated gentlemen of letters but business and professional men possessing a great deal of the latest information about a very narrow field. It did not happen all at once, and in a few institutions it never happened at all, but if in general the spirit of the pre-war college was that of Cambridge, Oxford, and the Yale Report, then the spirit of the post-war institution was that of the stock exchange, the laboratory, and the professional journal. Henry Cabot Lodge remembered that when he entered Harvard in 1867, "I went in under the old system, and came out under the new. I entered the college of the eighteenth century with its 'gratulatios' and odes and elegies in proper Latin verse . . . the college with the narrow

[1] Quoted in Rudolph, *American College*, 329.

classical curriculum of its English exemplars, and came out a graduate of the modern university."[2]

The most important reason for the change was the advance in man's knowledge, an advance that the Civil War had dramatized not only with its new implements of death but also in engineering, transportation, communication, and other areas. The most convenient places to collect, collate, store, and distribute this vast amount of information were the colleges; in accepting the task, the colleges assumed for themselves a totally new role. In changing from old-line classical schools to modern, many-sided institutions, they found themselves accepting another proposition—that no longer could one person know everything worth knowing. They also found themselves unable to agree on what within each field of knowledge (for knowledge was now divided into "fields") was worth knowing or even what fields themselves were important. They met the problem by adopting, first at Harvard under President Charles W. Eliot, the elective principle, which threw onto the student the burden the faculties had been unwilling or unable to accept—the decision about what was important enough to know.

America in the Gilded Age was bold and brash, always changing, living in and for the future. New ideas, new methods, new organizations dominated. With a few exceptions, the American college reflected this spirit as much as any other institution. The major exception to the rule was the United States Military Academy. Geographically only fifty miles from the commercial and intellectual capital of the new America, New York City, it might as well have been in another country. The more the intellectual and technological developments demanded change, the more determined the Academy was to retain inviolate Sylvanus Thayer's system. It had been tried and proved; the only thing needed was to maintain what had been. The system had once been forward-looking, but in the Gilded Age it was an anachronism. And the more the Academy became estranged from national life, the more

[2] Quoted in Allan Nevins, *The State Universities and Democracy* (Urbana, Ill., 1962), 1–2.

self-satisfied it became. "The great charm of West Point is that so many things never change," a graduate could boast in 1917.[3]

Indeed they did not. The Academy continued to teach the same subjects, often with the same professors, from the same textbooks (Albert E. Church's work on descriptive geometry, written well before the Civil War, was used until the 1930's). It remained a small, tight-knit community. The Corps of Cadets, numbering 220 in 1843, increased only to 492 by 1900, in striking contrast to the growth of the colleges. The professors, instructors, and administrators came almost exclusively from the ranks of graduates, who continued to carry on the traditions. Few new buildings were added, and even cadet slang remained the same. West Point's direct response to the Civil War, the greatest single event in American history, was slight. The Superintendency was opened to all arms of the service, breaking the monopoly of the Engineers and meeting a long-standing complaint of the line, and the supervision of the Academy was vested in the War Department; the minimum age for admission for cadets was pushed up to seventeen; English grammar, descriptive geography, and American history were added to the entrance requirements.[4] That was all. For the rest, as far as the Academy was concerned, the Civil War need not have taken place.

The self-satisfaction was not complete; the Superintendents and the faculty continued to work to improve the school along lines already laid out before the war. The trouble was, neither Superintendents nor faculty looked forward; rather, they assumed the problems were still the same. As always, they demanded higher admissions standards; as always, Congress refused.[5] The Academy was still admitting nearly all the candidates, then finding half or more of the cadets deficient during the first two years of the course.

[3] Robert C. Richardson, *West Point: An Intimate Picture of the National Military Academy* (New York, 1917), 173.

[4] Beukema, *The United States Military Academy*, 23.

[5] *Annual Report of the Secretary of War, 1899* (Washington, 1899), I, 552; Schofield to Secretary of War, August 30, 1877, John Schofield Papers, Library of Congress.

In 1879 only 40 per cent of those admitted in 1875 graduated.[6] Under the system of written examinations, adopted in 1868, an even higher percentage of the candidates passed. The reason, according to one cadet, was that under the old method of an oral examination before the Academic Board many of the boys "were so badly frightened that they did not know what they said, and some who failed were graduates of good schools, or had passed splendid competitive exams for their appointments."[7] Agitation for higher standards continued throughout the period, always to be met by the same argument (in this case the speaker is General Sherman): "We don't want an increase in the entrance examination requirements, as this would virtually exclude the sons of poor parents or of those so situated as to be unable to give their sons the education required."[8] The Academy's answer—that the increase in free public high schools throughout the United States had raised educational standards generally and it was time West Point caught up—went unheeded.[9]

Another problem post-war Superintendents shared with their predecessors was congressional interference with the administration of the post. Congressmen continued to intercede with the Secretary of War whenever one of their appointees was found deficient or dismissed for a breach of discipline, and usually the Secretary reinstated the cadets. Periodically Superintendents had to send copies of the textbooks used at the Academy for congres-

[6] *Annual Report of the Secretary of War, 1870* (Washington, 1870), I, 299; George L. Andrews, "The Military Academy and its Requirements," *JMSI,* IV (August, 1883), 112–49; Peter Smith Michie, "Education in its Relation to the Military Profession," *JMSI,* I (June, 1880), 158.

[7] Hugh T. Reed, *Cadet Life at West Point* (Chicago, 1896), 73. In the introduction Reed copied some sample questions from the entrance examination: explain the difference between a common fraction and a decimal; define the parts of speech, and give their classes and properties; give and apply the ordinary rules of syntax; give the locations of the states, their boundaries, including large rivers, and all other prominent geographical features; explain the difference between the Royal, the Chartered and the Proprietary colonies; identify the remote and immediate causes of the American Revolution.

[8] Sherman to Rawlins, February 1, 1866, Misc. Mss., USMA Library.

[9] C. Willcox, "The Preliminary Examination: West Point," *JMSI,* XVI (March, 1895), 253.

sional examination.[10] Supervision could be even more minute. In 1874 Superintendent Thomas Ruger had to assure the Secretary of War that, while he followed a policy of hiring the best workmen available for the post and did not know the politics of many of them, he would not "hesitate to discharge anyone, who made himself obnoxious by his democratic sentiments." Other things being equal, Ruger promised that he would always hire Republicans as carpenters, teamsters, and for other work.[11]

The Civil War brought a revolution to warfare, and the Academy slowly adjusted to the new methods. Seven years after the war ended and five years after the weapon was adopted by the army, West Point added instruction in the use of the Gatling gun. But despite the experience of the French in the Franco-Prussian War, who found that the Gatling gun was of no use when employed as artillery because of its limited range, the authorities at West Point included it in the course in field artillery.[12] One of the problems in adding instruction in modern arms was lack of equipment. As late as 1890 *Harper's Weekly* reported an episode at the Academy that illustrated the point. Some years earlier one of the old guns of the siege battery at West Point burst. The Superintendent complained, and after a while the old battery was taken away and replaced by guns of another but still old-fashioned pattern. In 1889 one of these guns burst, that battery was taken away, and other guns were promised in its place. When the replacements arrived, they were found to be the same guns that had been removed in the first place as dangerous. *Harper's* commented, "It would be interesting to know whether the two batteries are to be used up at West Point by alternate burstings."[13]

In the field of military science the most important event of the second half of the nineteenth century was not the American Civil War but the Franco-Prussian War of 1870–71. Partly this

[10] Belknap to Ruger, September 19, 1874, National Archives, Record Group 94, Office, Adjutant General.

[11] Belknap to Hamilton Fish, June 19, 1874, *ibid.*

[12] Ruger to Secretary of War, January 27, 1872, SLB, and War Department to Ruger, January 29, 1872, *ibid.*

[13] *Harper's Weekly*, XXXIV (May 10, 1890), 367.

was because the lessons of the Civil War were ignored, even in America, but mainly it was because the Franco-Prussian War, coming later, introduced even more new techniques, organizational methods, and implements of war. The Prussian victors became the accepted models for professional soldiers everywhere, and students flocked to Berlin to study from the masters.[14] The army responded to Germany's replacement of France as the leading military nation in the world by sending its brightest officers there to observe and study and by adopting the Prussian-style helmet. Congress responded by passing a resolution recommending the addition of the German language at the Academy, but the authorities at West Point refused to make any curriculum change. Superintendent Ruger argued that German could be adopted only by increasing the course to five years or by getting better students, which would mean raising the entrance requirements to the level of the colleges, which in turn would lead to the rejection of three-fourths of the candidates. German was not added.[15]

The faculty also resisted change. One cadet, a veteran of the Civil War who had fought in a volunteer regiment, remembered the day he had an assignment from Professor Mahan on out-post duty. Since he had performed that particular duty many times during the war, he ignored the text and, when called upon, began to recite from his own experience. Mahan angrily exclaimed, "No, sir! that is all wrong!" "But, professor," the cadet replied, "that is just as I have performed that duty practically as a soldier many times during my battle service. . . ." "I don't care what you did or what you saw during the Civil War, you stick to the text!" The cadet tried to point out that under certain circumstances it was necessary to depart from the rules of textbooks, but Mahan shouted, "I want to hear nothing further from you. Sit down, sir!"[16]

West Point ignored the rest of the country to such a degree that even the Board of Visitors, traditionally friendly, was frequently critical in the post-war period. In 1879 the Board asked

[14] See Ambrose, *Upton,* 85–100.

[15] Ruger to Secretary of War, March 2, 1872, SLB.

[16] Robert G. Carter, *The Art and Science of War Versus the Art of Fighting* (Washington, 1922), 4–5.

for more variety in the methods of instruction, hoping to "relieve the course from a wearisome monotony." An occasional lecture in place of the usual recitation might "make the system more elastic, more exciting, and more efficient." It suggested that the curriculum add more history and introduce some natural science and recommended the substitution of the German language for Spanish. None of this was done.[17]

Superficially, West Point had no *raison d'être*. Almost immediately after the war it lost its scientific and engineering pre-eminence, both because of the rise of specialized civilian institutions and because of the increase in technical knowledge that was not reflected in the curriculum of the Academy. Since the Academy could not devote any more time to these subjects than it had before the war, cadets spent less time on chemistry or engineering than did the students in the specialized civilian schools, which therefore became superior to it. Academy graduates had proved their excellence on the battlefield, but there were no battles left to fight and none loomed in the future, except those on the frontier that only the frontiersmen cared about. There was intellectual ferment in the army, which itself was becoming more specialized and thus required a new type of junior officer, but West Point for the most part overlooked it. The Academy was able to disregard the mood of the age and hold to the old because no one very much cared. Just as West Point ignored America, so did America ignore West Point.

One of the chief reasons the country allowed the stagnation at West Point to continue was the Academy's success in the Civil War. America was satisfied with West Point's performance, so much so that whenever the Board of Visitors or other critics suggested a change, the response both within and outside the Academy was outrage at the possibility that the system that produced Grant and Sherman and Lee and Jackson might require alteration. This attitude was especially pronounced among the professors and Superintendents at West Point, who until 1900 were nearly all Civil War veterans. They combined to keep the memories of those

---

[17] The Board of Visitors' Report is in the *Annual Report of The Secretary of War, 1879* (Washington, 1879), I, 428.

great days from 1861 to 1865 alive, and they resisted any attempt to change the system under which they had studied.

In 1866 Superintendent George W. Cullum heard some vague rumors that Congress might propose certain changes at the Academy. He immediately wrote to Senator Henry Wilson in protest. "A system, founded by . . . General Thayer, which for half a century has borne such prolific fruits of excellence, should not be lightly changed for any new patent nostrums," he declared. "Leave well enough alone is a wise saying." He advised Senator Wilson to do nothing until he had consulted with Academy graduates in general and Thayer, Grant, and Sherman in particular.[18]

In 1879 General in Chief Sherman replied to a minister who had criticized the Academy for allowing cadets to study on Sunday. Sherman observed that the cadets were following the same schedule that had been in effect at West Point for fifty years, "during which time West Point has turned out Generals of great renown, Bishops of approved virtue and piety, Statesmen equal to all occasions, and men of honor, integrity and great purity." Why change it? "Does not wisdom suggest that we leave well enough alone? The regularity of the military system now become habitual at West Point has begotten habits of order, obedience and respect to authority, which pass directly into the army, and thence to the country, and have borne fruits of infinite value to this Democratic country, if it has not been its actual salvation."[19]

Sherman was General in Chief from 1869 to 1884, the fourth West Point graduate to hold that position—the first was McClellan in 1861, the second Halleck in 1862, and the third Grant in 1864—, and he took a much more intense interest in the Academy than any head of the army had before him. Sheridan, Grant, and other Civil War heroes were frequent visitors to the Point, but none came more often, stayed longer, or enjoyed it more than "Uncle Billy."[20]

[18] Cullum to Wilson, January 17, 1866, SLB.
[19] Sherman to Cameron, December 2, 1879, William T. Sherman Papers, Library of Congress.
[20] Sherman to Schofield, June 5, 1878, Sherman Papers.

Stagnation

General Sherman attended nearly all the graduation exercises, often with the President in tow, and usually made a speech. A high point came in 1881. The previous year, Sherman had said some kind words about the "Immortals," those at the foot of the class, telling them they no doubt had noble talents which the course of study had not brought out. The Immortals of 1881 expected the same treatment, but instead Sherman was stern with the entire class, telling it that it had only made a beginning and the members must now be prepared to devote themselves to a lifetime of study, unremitting industry, and industrious diligence. While he was speaking, former President and Mrs. Grant appeared, and everyone on the platform began inviting them to come up and take prominent seats. Instead Grant and his wife took some camp stools and sat among the crowd. A cadet reported that "Grant sat there like a graven image." Each speaker went out of his way to refer to Grant's career, to the applause of the cadets and guests, but through it all "General Grant sat there and never changed a feature." When the ceremonies were over Sherman performed his customary function of passing out the diplomas, giving a stern and soldierly glance at each graduate. But when the last man came up the General in Chief smiled at him, apologized for his speech, and explained that he had been criticized the year before for praising the Immortals too much and so had decided to change the tenor of his remarks this year.[21]

In his official capacity Sherman did all he could for his beloved cadets. In 1880 Superintendent John Schofield dismissed some cadets for being drunk on New Year's Eve. Sherman overruled the sentence, then told Schofield that "getting drunk on New Year's Eve is just the boy's way of welcoming the new year." He could not take a serious view of the situation, and advised Schofield to drill them at midnight next New Year's—they would soon be asking to be allowed to sleep. "In my day," Sherman remembered, "we always cut up on 'New Year's Eve' and the custom had a tacit recognition. In one instance the morning gun was found

[21] Williston Fish, *Memories of West Point 1877–1881* (Batavia, N. Y., 1957), I, 21–23.

on the fourth floor of the north barracks, and the drums and fifes at the top of the flag-staff. Of course there was no reveille *that* morning."²² On other occasions Sherman would remit sentences against cadets guilty of hazing; like so many other graduates, the General in Chief took the view that hazing was an integral and necessary part of West Point training.²³

Sherman had an excellent memory, and he was constantly reminding Superintendents about how things had been done before the Civil War. In 1880 Schofield became disturbed because he found he could not force cadets to attend chapel. Sherman told him to use the solution that had been applied in 1844, when a court-martial decided that chapel should be voluntary. The next Sunday the Superintendent had the Corps form up, told off the cadets who wanted to go to chapel, and then had the rest stand at attention while a stuttering clerk read the Articles of War and Army Regulations to them. The next Sunday he did the same thing; after that, all the cadets went to chapel in preference to the recitation of army regulations.²⁴

Sherman's desire to preserve the Academy in its pre-Civil War purity was only slightly tempered by his experience in the war itself and later. In 1877 he did recommend that the Superintendent teach the cadets something about the army's system of money and property accounting, and he thought a "half a dozen lectures on organization, equipment and logistics" might be in order. The course on strategy and the art of war could benefit by finding someone a little more modern than Jomini to study; Sherman had decided that "Jomini is antiquated and dull."²⁵

Through the years the cadets idolized Sherman. Even after his retirement from the army he came up to the Point for June Week, where he was always the center of attention. Cadet Charles Rhodes reported Sherman's activities during June Week of 1889. "On June 11, Genl Sherman, sitting on the hotel porch, expressed his fixed opinion that the cadet-girls were getting prettier every year;

²² Sherman to Schofield, January 6, 1880, Sherman Papers.
²³ Sherman to Schofield, January 2, 1880, *ibid.*
²⁴ Sherman to Schofield, January 6, 1880, *ibid.*
²⁵ Sherman to Schofield, March 21, 1877, *ibid.*

addressing himself to a nearby graduate in gray, he said, 'My boy, if you have not yet picked out your girl, wait! They'll be all the prettier, next year!' " The next day at the ceremonies, Sherman broke his vow to refrain from making a speech. "He talked of many things. He told them he was about to give each his diploma, that all were identical, and identical to the one he got, and all other graduates." He told them that if they were assigned to an outpost as a commissary or quartermaster they should "be ever ready to tell on the instant, the amount of money in the cash-box, or how many nails there were in a keg." When he graduated, Sherman said, West Point was just as peaceful as now, and everyone complained of slow promotion. But then came the war with the Seminoles, the Mexican War, and the Great Rebellion, and everyone got his chance to command. His conclusion was, "And always remember, to be as true to the flag, as the needle to the pole!" [26]

Less than two years later, in February, 1891, Sherman died. Superintendent John M. Wilson secured permission from the War Department for the cadets to attend the funeral in St. Louis. Then Wilson asked that the cadets be allowed to form part of the escort. "They loved General Sherman as a father," Wilson said, and "he loved them as his children." Permission was granted by the family, and the cadets proudly walked behind the casket to the burial ground. [27]

Sherman's death did not free the Academy to strike out in new directions. His successor as General in Chief, Philip Sheridan of the class of 1855, was just as determined as Sherman to prevent any change at West Point. And in any case the General in Chief was not the only one, and not even the most important one, responsible for the Academy's preoccupation with tradition. The years between the end of the Civil War and the end of World War I could be called the era of the professors. In 1839 the War Department had changed the Superintendency from a permanent position, as it was under Thayer, to a routine short tour, usually

[26] Rhodes to mother, June 13, 1889, Charles D. Rhodes Papers, Archives, USMA.
[27] Wilson to Howard, February 16 and 18, 1891, SLB.

lasting less than five years. Meanwhile the professors remained permanently at the post, and soon they were not only masters in their own departments but, collectively and through the agency of the Academic Board, of the Academy as well. Their attitude towards the Superintendents was something like that of the heads of bureaus and service corps in the army towards civilian Secretaries of War, which is to say that they merely tolerated them while making all the decisions themselves. And until after the turn of the century, nearly all of the professors were pre-Civil War graduates, just as determined as Sherman or Sheridan to hold to the past.

The Academic Board was most responsible for the Academy's ignoring technological and intellectual ferment and remaining a changeless institution in a changing age. The Board had absolute control by law over the curriculum and, through its influence with the transient Superintendents, over all other activities at West Point. The professors who made up the Board were middle-aged or old men who had not been away from the Academy for any length of time since they were seventeen years of age. Not only were they unaware of what was going on in the country at large and in the civilian colleges; they did not even realize what changes were being made in the army. They loved their quiet life at the Academy and made sure it was not changed in any way.

Professors were carefully groomed for their positions. Whenever the head of a department had a vacancy or needed an additional instructor, he would submit to the War Department a list of qualified young officers who would meet his demands. He usually named his brightest students from four or five years back. The best of the instructors stayed on as assistant professors, and the best of these eventually became professors. Thus most of the professors, from the time they entered the Academy until they died or retired, were away from West Point for only a three- or four-year tour with the line.[28] Non-graduate scholars who inquired about positions on the faculty were bluntly told, "There is no vacancy in any department here which could be filled by a civilian."[29]

[28] Parke to Adjutant General, May 20, 1899, SLB.
[29] Wilson to Mr. Earle, April 17, 1890, SLB.

West Point probably had a better record for holding onto its professors than any other college in the country. Peter Smith Michie was there as professor for 30 years, Charles W. Larned for 35, Samuel E. Tillman for 31, Edgar W. Bass for 20, Henry Kendrick for 24, and others for equal periods. All these men served as assistants before becoming professors. Most of them studied and later taught as instructors under Mahan, Church, Bartlett and the other great members of the pre-war faculty. They used the same textbooks and methods their mentors had employed, and for all intents and purposes the graduate of 1898 knew no more and no less than the graduate of 1848.

The inbreeding was something new. Thayer had gone not only outside the army but outside the country for his faculty. This endogamy was based on the conceit that only a West Point graduate was capable of handling a West Point section of cadets, and it extended into all fields. In 1876 the distinguished painter Robert Weir retired. A Thayer appointee, Weir was not a West Point graduate but had studied in Italy. The War Department announced that his successor would be Charles W. Larned, an 1870 West Pointer whose artistic experience was limited to a two-year tour as one of Weir's assistants. Before that time, Larned had been on frontier duty with the cavalry. Schofield had just become Superintendent and had not been consulted on the appointment; nevertheless, he complained to Sherman and begged him to wait until a prominent civilian artist could be found to take Weir's place. When Sherman said he could do nothing, Schofield appealed to the President. "Let us all try to build up the old Academy, and not to break it down," he begged of Grant, but to no avail. Both the General in Chief and the President thought Larned's qualifications sufficient, and he retained the appointment, to serve as professor of drawing for thirty-six years. He changed the course completely. Weir had concentrated on landscape painting, while Larned emphasized mathematical drawing and topographical work.[30]

[30] Schofield to Sherman, July 25, 1876, Sherman Papers.

The professors who dominated West Point from 1865 to 1918 were, if not as distinguished a group of scholars as their predecessors, nevertheless capable and forbidding. The oldest in point of service was Albert Church, who had been teaching mathematics at the Academy since 1828 and who served as professor of mathematics until his death in 1878. In 1871 West Point lost both Mahan and Bartlett, Mahan by death and Bartlett by retirement. Mahan's successor was Junius Brutus Wheeler, an 1855 graduate who was professor of engineering from 1871 to 1884. He taught the course in military art and engineering much as Mahan had and from the same textbook, although he did make some revisions of Mahan's works. Wheeler had served in the Corps of Engineers from 1863 to 1871 and, unlike Mahan, had had much practical experience. His course, however, was even more theoretical and less practical than Mahan's had been. In 1881 the West Shore Railroad built a tunnel under West Point; Wheeler ignored cadet requests to go out and observe the work in progress. Even when there was a huge cave-in and the cadets begged to be allowed to watch the repairing process, he refused.[31]

The professor of French from 1871 to 1892 was George L. Andrews, number one in the class of 1851 and known to the cadets as "Pop." His successor, Edward Edgar Wood, was professor of modern languages (a department, created in 1882, that included French and Spanish) from 1892 to 1910. Wood had been Andrews' assistant. As a fifteen-year-old, Wood had enlisted in the Seventeenth Pennsylvania Volunteers. He was captured in December, 1862, and exchanged in May the next year. By 1864 he was commanding a company and in 1865 served as regimental adjutant—having reached seventeen years of age by then. Immediately after the war he came to West Point where, along with other former volunteer officers who were now plebes, he found himself set upon by the yearlings and made the object of special hazing. He survived without undue difficulty, however, to remain at the Academy the rest of his life. As a teacher of French he concentrated on the grammar and made no effort to teach the cadets to speak the

[31] Fish, *Memories*, III, 863–65, and I, 10–15.

language (he did not speak it himself) or to read the masterpieces of French literature. One of his students reported that he was totally addicted to chewing tobacco and "on a good chaw would go into an ecstasy, lost in his pleasure, and noticing nothing around him."[32]

The chaplain from 1871 until 1881, John Forsyth, was a tall, portly, Falstaffian figure, much loved by the cadets for his short sermons and his pontification in geography, history, and ethics, all of which he taught. Forsyth was given to grasping his lapels, rising on his toes, clearing his throat, sonorously declaring, "Every tub must stand on its own bottom," and then dismissing his class. Other of the chaplain's activities that the cadets approved of included his tardiness for chapel owing to an interesting game of billiards at the officers' club, his ownership of a share in a brewery, and his failure ever to establish any welfare or rescue work. One cadet summed him up: "He was lazy, non-athletic, indifferent to study, and allowed ambition to seize other men."[33]

Church's successor as professor of mathematics, Edgar Wales Bass, was altogether different. He served from 1878 to 1898 and by all accounts was even more aloof than Church. Bass, one cadet wrote his parents, "is like a piece of cold steel with eyes like icicles, and a voice though soft, almost makes a fellow shudder from it's cold-blooded softness."[34] Next to Church the man who taught longest at West Point was Henry Lane Kendrick, "Old Hanks" to the cadets, who began teaching in 1835 and was professor of chemistry from 1857 to 1880. In his later years he was the finest looking man on the post, with his long white beard, handsome tailor-made black suit, black cape, and tall silk hat. He had the reputation of being exceptionally kind to new cadets.[35]

The outstanding figure on the post-Civil War faculty was Peter Smith Michie, instructor in engineering from 1867 to 1871 and professor of natural philosophy from 1871 to his death in 1901. Born in Scotland, he came to the United States as a small boy and

[32] *Ibid.,* III, 867–68.
[33] *Ibid.,* I, 199–210.
[34] Rhodes to mother, September 17, 1885, Rhodes Papers.
[35] Fish, *Memories,* I, 44–46.

received his appointment as a cadet from Ohio. He had a laugh so natural and infectious that the day he arrived on the post upper classman George Armstrong Custer gathered a crowd around him by exclaiming, "Fellows, come here and hear my fellow Buckeye laugh."[36] During his years on the faculty Michie wrote several books, among them an elementary text on mechanics, a biography of McClellan, a history of the Army of the Potomac (in which he fought), and *The Life and Letters of Emory Upton,* an outstanding volume. With his black hair and full, black beard, he looked something like Grant. He was a deeply religious man and often introduced religion into his classroom discussion. After explaining the laws of matter and force, he would ask, "And that shows, does it not, that there is a Creator who set the hosts of the skies and determined their motions?" Once, when a cadet merely nodded his assent but looked skeptical, Michie remarked that if there were a cadet in that section who did not believe what he had just said he would be found deficient.[37]

Wheeler, Andrews, Wood, Forsyth, Bass, Michie—these were the leaders of a faculty that defended West Point against all criticism, encroachment, and change. But the Academic Board could not, by itself, keep the Academy permanently rooted in the past. It needed help from the alumni, especially those graduates who remained in the army. Except for a few reformers like Upton—and even he was more interested in establishing post-graduate schools than in changing the Academy—most alumni were more than willing to do what they could to retain the old system. This inclination to defend the old was present not only in the nineteenth century but also in the twentieth and not only in officers who served out their careers on isolated frontier posts but also in generals of World War I and after who had seen a great deal of the world, generals who were involved in the most momentous political, military, and technological changes. West Pointers generally felt more deeply about their old school than civilians did about theirs and were more concerned with preserving its purity. In part, the attitude

[36] Schaff, *Old West Point,* 116.
[37] Fish, *Memories,* III, 831–33.

was the result of the appointment system. West Point was the only thing graduates had in common. There was no family tradition at the Point, and most cadets did not come from a military background. Graduates learned the traditions of their profession not from their parents or grandparents but from the Academy. The European system, by which generations from the same family held a monopoly on the officer corps, was totally absent in America. As Jefferson had hoped it would, the congressional system of appointment prevented the rise of an officer caste. It was the Academy that had imparted approximately the same experience to all. At West Point, graduates had all taken the same classes, undergone the same hazing, marched in the same formations. This common experience gave them a sense of community, of fraternity, that they could not bear to see destroyed. A change in the continuity at the Academy would have the effect of disturbing their bond. To tamper with West Point would be to tamper with the cement that held the army officer corps together.

In speaking of the honor system at West Point, Dwight D. Eisenhower once likened it to the virtue of a man's mother. It was an interesting choice of words.

Still, there were critics. Chief of these was Sylvanus Thayer, who had retained his interest in the Academy even after his retirement in 1863 from the army. In 1865 Thayer composed an extensive criticism of the institution where he was already acclaimed as "father." Thayer thought the Academy ought to have higher entrance requirements and that cadets should be appointed after an open competitive examination. "It is remarkable, and seems little creditable, that the great model Republic, of which we are justly so proud, should be the last to give up patronage, the policy of aristocratical and monarchical governments, and also the last to adopt the republican principle of open competition. . . ." Neither recommendation attacked the basic system at West Point, and nearly everyone on the post and in the army agreed with it. Not so with Thayer's third point. He thought that the course of study at West Point should be divided at the end of the Third Class year, with those cadets who were proficient in mathematics continuing in the present course while those with less aptitude for mathematics took a course "more helpful in preparing them for infantry and cavalry." If adopted, this recommendation might have started West Point down the road to an elective system and certainly would have changed the traditional West Point method.[38]

Nearly fifty years later Samuel Tillman, who was on the faculty at West Point for forty-one years and who came out of retirement to serve as Superintendent during World War I, took up Thayer's suggestion. The army expanded after the turn of the century, and Tillman thought it important that a high proportion of the officer corps should consist of Academy graduates. But with a larger army, that would be impossible unless West Point expanded, something Tillman declared would be a tragic mistake, as an enlarged West Point would lose its discipline and character. He felt the solution could be found in a modification of Thayer's suggestion for two distinct courses, and he advocated a second West Point for cavalry and infantry officers, with the original school continuing its traditional curriculum. Tillman realized that "Our Academy stands practically alone among educational institutions, civil or military, in retaining a considerable portion of its curriculum chiefly because of its value in mental discipline and development, and not at all for its utility" but argued that officers in the cavalry or infantry did not need as much natural philosophy or mathematics as engineers. If West Point were allowed to grow to fill the needs of the army, Tillman feared that it would soon follow the trend of the colleges, seeing its role as one of preparation for post-graduate education and relying on army service schools to complete the officer's education. Two schools, he felt, "each of smaller numbers—one for engineers, artillery and ordnance and one for the infantry and cavalry—can best conserve the traditions and disciplinary features, mental, moral and military, of West Point, and yet give better preparation for the requirements of the respective branches." This was the way the English, with Sandhurst and Woolwich, educated their officers.[39]

[38] Thayer's criticism is reprinted in *Annual Report of the Secretary of War, 1899,* I, 579–87.
[39] Samuel Tillman, "Is there Necessity for a Second West Point?" *JMSI,* XXXV (December, 1904), 1.

Tillman's suggestion raised a storm in the army. Lieutenant William E. Birkhimer declared, "The institution criticized is venerable in years and honors. The wisdom of that far-reaching policy which established it has been vindicated many times." He roundly declared there was no reason for any change. Most graduates agreed. There were some who supported Tillman, including former Superintendent Schofield,[40] but a number of officers thought that what Tillman feared most—that West Point would become a preparatory school for post-graduate education in army service schools—was exactly what should happen.[41] The Board of Visitors had declared in 1889, "As the college of liberal arts in civil education lays broad foundations for the future student of law, or medicine, or theology, so should this military academy be but preparatory to the post-graduate studies of advancing students in the art of war."[42]

In the army itself there was a new spirit, an intellectual ferment never before present, that was receptive to the idea of post-graduate education. The period from the end of the Civil War to the beginning of the Spanish-American War was an important one for the United States Army. During those thirty-three years its appearance changed but little, its uniforms, arms, organization, and size remaining about the same. Internally, however, the basis for a modern army was laid, with men like Upton, Schofield, Sheridan, and to an extent Sherman preparing the way for the

[40] "Comment and Criticism," *ibid.*, 123–31, and XXXVI (January, 1905), 164–67, 335. Schofield thought that the facilities at West Point should be used for the education of a larger number of young men than the army annually needed; these additional cadets would upon graduation return to their respective states for service in the organized militia. It was an old idea, but Schofield added to it by recommending that those cadets who wanted to join the militia follow a different course of studies from the one pursued by those headed for the army. The potential militia officers could take a two- or three-year course, which would qualify them to command infantry, cavalry, or even artillery, and could omit the engineering instruction. Thus there would be in effect two West Points, but they would be physically united, and the old spirit and tradition could be maintained. Schofield to Secretary of War, October 18, 1879, Schofield Papers.

[41] *Harper's Weekly*, XXXIV (May 10, 1890), 366.

[42] The Report is in *Annual Report of the Secretary of War, 1889* (Washington, 1889), 40.

great changes that came after the turn of the century. All these men were West Point graduates and retained their interest in the Academy, but none of them thought that it alone could produce the professional soldiers the army needed, and they were advocates of a complete post-graduate system, with "colleges" for each of the arms and the staff, and a "war college" as the crowning institution.

Despite congressional parsimony and public indifference, they had some success. The Artillery School at Fortress Monroe, first established in 1824, was reorganized and strengthened, and the army's chief theorist and advocate of reform, Emory Upton, taught there for a number of years.[43] The Corps of Engineers established the School for Engineers at Willets Point, Long Island, and required two and a half years of study there as a prerequisite to service in the Corps. Technical instruction included twenty-two weeks in civil engineering, ten weeks in military engineering, nineteen weeks in chemistry, and forty weeks in explosives and torpedoes.[44] At Fort Leavenworth, Kansas, the army created a two-year course for infantry and cavalry.

The late nineteenth century was also marked by the formation of branch associations, each devoted to the improvement of its arm. Most of the associations had their own periodicals. The *Cavalry Journal* began in 1888, the *Military Surgeon* in 1890, the *Artillery Journal* in 1892, and the *Infantry Journal* in 1904. All were highly professional and specialized.

Pleased though they were with the specialized technical schools and the branch associations, the army reformers were disappointed at their inability to secure the funds for a capstone institution that would concentrate on the nature of war, its philosophy, and its relationship with political affairs—on strategy, in a word. During his Superintendency, Schofield tried to fill the gap by creating at West Point "something in the nature of a 'post graduate course' for the benefit of young officers temporarily stationed here, by which they may, with the aid of the older and more experienced officers, advantageously pursue their studies in the higher branches

[43] Ambrose, *Upton*, 96–98.
[44] Riedler, *American Technological Schools*, 659.

of their profession."[45] Based upon and drawing its inspiration from the old Napoleon Club, Schofield's program included lectures, campaign studies, and discussions of the writings of the great military thinkers. It was never very satisfactory, however, both because it could not reach all the best young men in the army and because the instructors were so busy with their teaching that they had little time for their own studies.

Another problem was an absence of wholehearted faculty support. Most of the professors, if they did not scorn the post-graduate program, were much less interested in it or convinced of the need for it than officers of the line. None of them ever made the charge openly, but there was a feeling among them that the idea of post-graduate education implied a rebuff to West Point. In 1880 Professor Michie declared that the Academy "stands to-day, as in the past, an institution of faithful, thorough and efficient education, doing the very best with the material at its disposal, and it turns over to the Army young men, carefully trained in mental discipline, to the highest level of their natural capacities." He did not necessarily mean that any more education for these graduates would be superfluous, but he did feel that whatever additional knowledge they might need they were capable of picking up on their own, without any formal instruction.[46]

Besides Thayer and Tillman, another prominent critic of the post-war Academy was Morris Schaff, whose *The Spirit of Old West Point*, published shortly after the turn of the century, is one of the classics of West Point literature. Although it is essentially a book of reminiscences, in it Schaff raises a number of questions about the West Point system. He calls for a change in attitudes at the Academy, observing that it was "notorious" that the Academic Board held English, history, and other non-scientific subjects to be of minor importance. West Point must also come to

[45] Schofield to Adjutant General, November 8, 1877, SLB.
[46] Michie, "Education," 171. Michie thought it sufficient that the instructors, coming to West Point after four years in the army, brought with them to the Academy "the existing sentiment of the army," which benefited the Academy; they then found "their iconoclastic opinions . . . considerably modified, and . . . return to the Army much better satisfied with the administration of the affairs of the Academy"; Baumer, *West Point,* 133–34.

realize that the Academy no longer stood pre-eminent, that statements like Superintendent Wesley Merritt's in 1887—"I think there is no important dissent among the scientific men of the Country that the Military Academy is one of the most thorough schools in . . . sciences . . . in this or perhaps any other country"— were no longer true.[47]

The most outspoken critic was Lieutenant Elmer W. Hubbard, an 1885 graduate who served as an instructor of chemistry from 1889 to 1893. In 1895, in the *Journal of the Military Service Institution,* Hubbard published "The Military Academy and the Education of Officers," the most critical attack on West Point since the days of the Radical Republicans and one of the most competent of the nineteenth century. Hubbard thought the Academy's major fault was its method of training the cadets without any reference at all to the tasks they would be called upon to perform. West Point existed to produce soldiers who could protect the Republic in time of war; the Civil War and the Franco-Prussian War had introduced the era of mass conflict, and like it or not the army and the Academy had to accept the fact that the great bulk of the enlisted men in the next war would be hastily mobilized civilians. But in no way did the Academy prepare its graduates to command civilians in uniform. Anticipating the point that Superintendent Douglas MacArthur would make again and again after World War I, Hubbard demanded that the Academy reorient its system, freeing the cadets from their seclusion and allowing them contacts with the civilian world so that they could equip themselves to lead civilian-soldiers in time of war.[48]

Not only was the Academy doing little positive to prepare the cadets for actual combat, though that was after all its ultimate purpose, but it was actually detracting from their native preparedness because of its teaching methods and its emphasis on mathematics. Hubbard contended that work in the exact science of mathematics did not help prepare a man for war, a most inexact science, and

---

[47] Schaff, *Old West Point,* 76–77; Merritt to Commissioner of Education, May 9, 1887, SLB.

[48] Elmer W. Hubbard, "The Military Academy and the Education of Officers," *JMSI,* XVI (January, 1895), 2–6.

in fact made the cadets deficient in judgment and intuition. Further, he charged that the blackboard-recitation method of instruction, while useful in mathematics, was ruinous to all other subjects, and he thought the Academy should add laboratory work in at least the natural and physical sciences. Even Professor Mahan had once said, "The defect of our course as a whole is, perhaps, that we are too abstract and that there is not sufficient application of the theory and principles that are taught." The usual answer at West Point to this charge was that the Academy was not attempting to teach chemists or physicists and that abstract teaching was good mental discipline. Hubbard rejoined that in fact the effects of an excess of theory at West Point were clear in the army, where "we are too much given to theorizing, and practice has little attraction for us." [49]

Hubbard had other criticisms. He thought the course both too long and too difficult. For a start he wanted to drop Spanish and the drill regulations and decrease the amount of time spent on the sciences, letting the post-graduate schools add the information officers in the specialized corps needed.[50] "Briefly stated," Hubbard concluded, "West Point tries to do too much in the time at her disposal. . . . Antiquated methods of instruction prevail in some departments, and the expansion of sciences has caused her to overcrowd the course to the detriment of true education." His solution was simple: "West Point, the Army, and the post-graduate schools must divide the field, the courses be harmonized, and the officer's education stretched over a greater length of time." [51]

Hubbard's remarks raised a storm at West Point. Cornelius deWitt Willcox, who had graduated ahead of Hubbard in the class of 1885 and who was an instructor at the Academy, where he would later serve for fifteen years as professor of modern languages, answered his classmate with one sentence: "Like the house that defied the storm, West Point is built on a rock, and that rock is mathematics." During this period, cadets were spending 213,495 minutes of classroom time and preparation on mathematics and

[49] *Ibid.*, 8–9.
[50] *Ibid.*, 12–15.
[51] *Ibid.*, 24.

239,720 minutes on non-mathematical subjects.[52] Professor Charles
Larnard, noting that Hubbard was proposing "radical and sweep-
ing change," remarked that "any very sudden and violent shock
to our system may destroy its vital principle." West Point had done
well in the past—Jackson, Grant, and Lee were resurrected once
again as examples of its success—and "it is a very serious matter to
tamper with the nice adjustment of so delicate and powerful an
organism." Larned thought it ridiculous to adjust the Academy
to the post-graduate schools of the army; it was they which should
adjust to the Academy, "the parent of them all."[53] Retired Professor George Andrews thought there was some merit in Hubbard's criticisms, especially about mathematics, and made the
general comment, "Referring to the intense conservatism of the
Academy, it has been well said that there is no civic college in
the country whose professors would boast that there has been no
substantial change in the curriculum since 1840." But even
Andrews felt that any change "should be gradual."[54]

Hubbard at least had the satisfaction of eliciting a response from
the West Point faculty; usually they ignored their critics. But he
did not inspire any significant change, either radical or gradual.
Nor did John Schofield, president of the Board of Visitors in 1901.
As a former Superintendent and a retired lieutenant general of
the army, Schofield spoke with authority when he called for a new
Academy, with more versatile graduates, men who had studied
history, ethics, literature, and economics, men who could speak,
and not just read a smattering of, foreign languages. He concluded, "The time has come when those in charge of the Academy
should realize that there are other requisites to a well-rounded
education, as applied to the soldier, than those that relate to
mathematics and their application. There has been too great a
tendency to cling to old educational traditions that have influenced, if not entirely shaped, the curriculum from the foundation
of the Academy."[55]

[52] Willcox, "Preliminary Examination," 265; Richardson, *West Point,* 175.
[53] "Comment and Criticism," *JMSI,* 320–22.
[54] *Ibid.,* 316–17.
[55] Schofield's remarks as president of the Board of Visitors are in the
Annual Report of the War Department, 1901 (Washington, 1901), I, 402.

John A. Logan had already spelled out what Schofield hinted at. This volunteer officer during the Civil War who was positive he had been denied the highest commands because he was not a West Pointer was now politically powerful. A senator from and Republican boss of Illinois, he was the Republican Vice-Presidential candidate in 1884. But his criticisms, made in the late eighties, were important not because of his political position but because of their substance. Logan was trying to create for the United States a revolutionary military establishment, one that broke completely with the European models and reflected the American political achievements. His arguments, especially his attacks against the Academy, were tinged with Jacksonian suspicion of the expert, but he was more sophisticated than the Jacksonians.[56]

Logan directed three charges against West Point. The first centered around the defection of the southern cadets to the Confederacy and was essentially the old complaint about treason. Logan contended that the political system of appointments meant that the Academy and the army were filled with men whose dedication was not to the nation but to party and section. His second charge, also a favorite of the Republicans, was that West Pointers were incompetent. He came close to saying that military genius was inherent and could not be taught. The third charge was that the Academy presented a danger to democratic institutions since it confined "knowledge of the military art" to a small percentage of the people. This restriction meant that there existed a minute group who "would possess the power, even should they never entertain the inclination, to control, or to put it more broadly, to conquer the rest of the community."[57]

Logan's point about the failure to train sufficient non-regular officers had the most merit, and in his elaboration of it he showed that his was something more than an emotional Jacksonian attack on aristocracy. He pointed out, "The result of our system has been to constitute both the army and navy the closest corporations in the country. The entrance to a recognized career in either one or the other service lies only through the picket lines of West Point

[56] There is an excellent discussion of Logan in Russell Weigley, *Toward an American Army* (New York, 1962), 127–36.
[57] Logan, *The Volunteer Soldier,* 337, 439–56.

or Annapolis. All knowledge not obtained there is spurious, and all soldiers and sailors not made there are considered mere pretenders. . . ." Graduates of the service academies controlled "the whole organization of military affairs," and they "arrogated" to their own kind "the appellation of *regular* officers in opposition to volunteer officers, who by contrast have become *irregular*, and, as a consequence, pretenders in the profession of arms."[58] The government, the army, and West Point all ignored the citizen-soldiers who would have to fight the next war, just as they did the Civil War.

It was indeed true that during the Civil War officers in the Regular Army had a great deal of difficulty in adjusting to the citizen-soldiers whom they led, and during the first years of the war, when their services were most needed in the volunteer regiments, the General in Chief had kept Regular Army men segregated from the volunteers. Possibly some of the horrors of First Bull Run and Shiloh could have been avoided if the Regular Army had devoted itself to training the volunteers, instead of jealously guarding its own sanctity. Jefferson had established the Military Academy in order to have a body of men prepared to train and lead these citizen-soldiers in war, but West Point and the army had lost sight of this fundamental duty.

In effect, Logan decided that Jefferson was wrong, that the nation could not get the professionals it needed to train citizen-soldiers from West Point. He advocated abolishing the present Academy and starting over. He argued that a military education program suited to American needs must be divorced from politics, must offer commissions to all on a basis of merit, and must spread military knowledge among the people at large. He proposed that each state university add a military department to teach military science. Graduates of the program would take competitive examinations, and the winners would go to West Point or Annapolis, which would become post-graduate schools of application. Other graduates of the military course in the state universities could be offered commissions in an emergency. Both service schools should

[58] *Ibid.*, 457–58.

be enlarged, so that they would graduate more men than the army and navy needed, the remainder returning to their home states to join the militia.[59] Thus America could have a democratic, national army, officered by men in close contact with the civilian world and capable of leading citizen-soldiers. The nation's army would be shaped to the characteristics of Americans and would be superior to all the professional armies of Europe.[60]

"Practically considered," Logan said, "the nation has no army in time of peace." But "when the clarion voice of war resounds through the land, the country throughout its vast extent becomes, if necessary, one bristling camp of armed men." This was a unique event in human affairs. "It is so new that it has no precise parallel in all history; it belongs to the genius of the American Republic; and it is possible only to a government founded upon a basis substantially identical with that upon which our free institutions so securely rest."[61]

Logan's criticisms and solutions had no effect. His book, *The Volunteer Soldier of America,* was too big and the writing too turgid; few read it. He died before it was published, and thus his political influence could not assist it. Most Americans were not interested in the subject, while those who were belonged to the very group Logan was attacking. But most of all Logan had no effect because his suspicion of the expert was no longer an integral part of the American system. Nineteenth-century Americans still paid their respects to the jack-of-all-trades heritage, but, like the other peoples of the Western world, they lived and gloried in an age of specialization. Doctors, lawyers, teachers, and mechanics were all creating their own organizations and erecting educational requirements before allowing an outsider to practice their trade. Each such group was making sure it enjoyed a monopoly of knowledge. Army officers wanted the same monopoly in the military field, and most Americans thought they should have it.

[59] *Ibid.,* 604–6.
[60] For the most complete discussion of the arguments about the organization of the U. S. Army, see Weigley, *Toward an American Army.*
[61] Logan, *Volunteer Soldier,* 464.

Professional training, with all that training of the kind implies, was as important to army officers as it was to lawyers. The trouble was, West Point was not really preparing officers for their profession. The years from 1865 to 1898 were important, and those from 1899 to 1917 crucial, in the development of the modern United States Army. The young officer of 1917 found himself in a far different organization from that to which his predecessor of 1861 belonged. On the eve of the Civil War the army had been scattered in small frontier posts, and it had little time and less respect for those who advocated new methods, weapons, or ideas; on the eve of America's entry into World War I the army was intellectually alive, as the General Staff and the post-graduate institutions, capped by the newly created War College, revealed. But the plebe who entered West Point in 1917 found little that had changed since 1861. West Point, which before the Civil War had been ahead of the army in its thought and methods, was after that conflict providing instruction that was increasingly irrelevant to the needs of the army.

Chapter XI

Hazing and the Negro Cadets

Nearly all the changes that occurred at the Academy between the Civil War and World War I were introduced by the cadets themselves, and nearly all of these were devices to help pass what time was left after classes, studies, and drill, adopted without the support of the administration or the faculty. The most famous was the Hundredth Night entertainments, marking the point at which there were only one hundred days left until graduation. Each class had something to celebrate: the plebes could look forward to their elevation to the stature of Third Classmen; the Third Classmen to furlough; the Second Classmen to the beginning of their last year at the Point; the First Classmen to buying uniforms, graduation, assignment to duty, and a furlough. The Dialectic Society gave the Hundredth Night in the mess hall, and it included plays, songs, jokes, and poetry recitals. Most of the officers attended, to hear their foibles exposed by cadet mimics. In 1886 the butt of most of the jokes was the First Captain of the Corps, Cadet John J. Pershing.[1]

A particularly memorable Hundredth Night came in 1881, when the usual program was supplemented by a speech by Samuel Clemens, who delivered his typical long, rambling talk filled with ludicrous stories. Later Clemens played billiards with the officers

---

[1] Rhodes to mother, February 21, 1886, Rhodes Papers.

and beat them all; the next day he visited the barracks, swapping jokes with the cadets.[2] Clemens was a frequent visitor at the Academy, often coming over from his home in Hartford, Connecticut, for a day or so. He liked to saunter around the post, puffing on a corn-cob pipe and talking to the cadets.[3] One of his works, a piece of salty Elizabethan dialogue sometimes mistaken for pornography, was first published by his friend Lieutenant Charles E. S. Wood, an aide to Superintendent Oliver O. Howard, in a limited edition on the West Point press. Entitled *1601, Conversation as It was by the Social Fireside in the Time of the Tudors,* the original edition is referred to as the West Point edition.[4]

Another post-war tradition was the class rush; it became the custom for the cadets to rush forward to meet the returning furlough class on the Plain, throwing caps in the air, tearing clothing, and letting pent-up spirits loose. In 1886 Superintendent Wesley Merritt forbade the rush, and the members of the First Class held a meeting to decide upon a course of action. They were unable to agree, but the next day, when the furloughmen were scheduled to return, most of the class assembled on the parade ground. Hundreds of visitors were looking on, while the cadets milled about and excitedly talked about what they should do. Suddenly, the first of the furloughmen was seen at the top of the hill. Someone cheered and cried, "Come on, fellows!" With a roar, the waiting class rushed across the sentinel's post towards the furloughmen, who by now themselves were running towards the First Classmen, and the customary tumult followed. Tactical officers milled about, writing down the names of any cadets they recognized. That night Superintendent Merritt telegraphed the War Department asking authority to dismiss summarily all cadets who had taken part in the rush; he received a negative answer. The First Classmen did spend a large part of the

[2] Fish, *Memories,* I, 61–68.
[3] Rhodes to mother, May 1, 1887, Rhodes Papers.
[4] Forman, *West Point,* 147.

next few months walking punishment tours, and the rush was not repeated the following year.[5]

In 1888 it was a March blizzard that was remembered. A storm at that season was hardly unusual at West Point, but this one piled up drifts fifteen feet high and kept the post isolated from the outside world for over a week. No food could get through, and rations were cut in half. The cadets amused themselves by jumping out of second story windows in the barracks into the drifts. For the first time since Alden Partridge's day, they were allowed to walk back to barracks individually from their meals, picking their way through the drifts.[6]

For the most part life continued as it had before the war, except that the Corps was more popular and in heavier demand for parades, inaugurations, and similar occasions and with better railroad facilities available (the West Shore Railroad was completed shortly after the war) made more appearances in New York, Philadelphia, Washington, and other cities.[7] In 1892 a small bowling alley was added to the gymnasium.[8] But the schedule of drill, studies, and class remained heavy. "I tell you a fellow works for his rest here, and no mistake," Charles Rhodes reported. "I never appreciated sleep so much before." His pleasure was doubled in his last year when he could tell his mother, "Just think! Beds with wire springs have been introduced! Since the Civil War, cadets have slept on iron cross-bars, perhaps to harden them."[9]

Discipline was even stricter after than it had been before the war. From 1857 until 1881 the authorities had allowed cadets to smoke pipes in their rooms, but even that privilege was taken away. "They are awfully down on the use of tobacco here," Cadet Rhodes noted in 1885, and every few days someone was caught violating the rule and assigned six punishment tours. "One 'Tac,' known by the soubriquet of 'slop-bucket johnny,' has a habit of coming around at night with a bull's eye lantern, and peering

[5] Rhodes to mother, August 29, 1886, Rhodes Papers.
[6] Rhodes to mother, March 18, 1888, *ibid.*
[7] Reed, *Cadet Life*, 227.
[8] Wilson to Architect, March 25, 1892, SLB.
[9] Rhodes to mother, November 15, 1885, and March 3, 1889, Rhodes Papers.

into a fellow's slop-bucket to see if he can find any trace of the use of tobacco."[10] Permissible amusements were few. The library was small, and those books contained in it were, outside military science, of poor quality. Superintendent Thomas G. Pitcher felt "it does not compare favorably . . . with the 3rd class colleges in the country" and asked for a law which would give the West Point library a copy of every book copyrighted in the United States, under the same terms as the Library of Congress received its free copy. Perhaps fortunately, the law was never passed—had it been, the entire Plain would have been needed to house the volumes.[11] The only cadet societies the authorities allowed were the Dialectic and the Young Men's Christian Association.[12] Drinking had been more or less eliminated in the Corps, partly because supervision was stricter and partly because places like Benny Havens' had been closed down. Thus, in an age when most colleges were providing enormously expanded programs of extracurricular activities, West Point cadets had fewer avenues open to them for amusement or the shedding of excess energy than ever before.

Their substitute was hazing. With the positive support of old graduates and the surreptitious support of the faculty to urge them on and with only the ineffective opposition of the Superintendents to fear, the cadets turned to hazing with such enthusiasm that it soon came to be associated with the spirit of West Point.

Hazing had been practiced before the Civil War, but it was limited to summer camp and consisted primarily of harmless pranks of the kind experienced campers may play on the neophyte. In the early fifties, Cadet John Schofield had the reputation of being the worst such prankster in the Corps.[13] After 1865, however, hazing took on a new aspect. Throughout the year, upperclassmen forced plebes to do exhausting physical exercises that sometimes resulted in permanent physical damage, to eat or drink unpalatable foods, and in various ways to humiliate themselves. Soon the system had its defenders, their chief argument seeming

---

[10] Rhodes to mother, December 7, 1885, *ibid.*
[11] Pitcher to Inspector of Military Academy, January 3, 1868, SLB.
[12] Mills to Hathaway, October 14, 1901, SLB.
[13] Brewerton to Totten, July 8, 1852, SLB.

to be that they themselves had been exposed to the same hazards without injury and presumably to their benefit.

There were other reasons for the growth and continued practice of hazing. Most of the plebes did not object to it, both because they felt that the more they could take the better men they were and the higher would their status be in the eyes of their peers and because they looked forward to the day when they could do some hazing themselves. Graduates encouraged upperclassmen to "teach the plebes their manners." The plebes came to West Point all puffed up, it was said, for in their own towns they generally were the best athletes and smartest students and, in addition, had just won the coveted appointment to the Academy. The cockiness had to be suppressed. The Academic Board usually agreed with the graduates and would not co-operate with the Superintendents in their efforts to stop the practice.[14]

A reasonable justification of hazing came from a twentieth-century graduate, who described one of the methods used, the "clothing formation."

> The way it works is this, There are no elevators in West Point barracks and the plebes tend to live in the 4th floor. In the basement of most of the barracks, except the very new ones, the showers are, the washbasins and so on. On a Sunday afternoon plebes who have done something wrong or made some mistake are turned out for clothing formation. They go down in the basement and a bunch of upper classmen brace them, that is, make them stand in an exaggerated posture of attention. Then one of these upper classmen will say you have 2½ minutes to go to your room, change into full dress uniform and be back down here. Now this is a perfectly preposterous demand. It takes much longer than that to get up to your room, change into full dress uniform and come down, but if you show an indifference or any unwillingness to try to reach this impossible goal they will jump all over you and make you go to clothing formations for the rest of the year. Indifference is another thing they are trying to eradicate. There is no worse crime than indifference. Well, the cadet dashes upstairs, changes into his full dress uniform, dashes down again. He must

[14] John J. Lenney, *Caste System in the American Army: A Study of the Corps of Engineers and their West Point System* (New York, 1949), 149–50.

do this under a terrible pressure of time and when he comes down and the upper classman finds that he has forgotten something or that his belt isn't tied right, then he catches unmitigated hell. This accustoms a man to panic, to having to do things that require a lot of coordination, to remember a great many details and to do it under great time pressure. Cadets learn by this to be familiar with the feeling of panic, to control it. They learn to do things at a very fast pace, but calmly so as not to forget any details. It doesn't take much imagination to see the utility of this for a war situation. I never once saw the significance and purpose of the clothing formation when I was a cadet, but I had occasion to remember it in the war and my understanding of the significance of it came after I was actually in combat.[15]

Whatever the benefits of hazing in cultivating endurance and a cool head, the Superintendents opposed it. They did so partly because occasional events, such as the suicide of a plebe or a death resulting from hazing, led to embarrassing congressional investigations but mainly because they sincerely felt the practice, which openly violated the regulations, was wrong. Their efforts to stamp it out were fruitless, however, not only because of the attitude of the graduates and the faculty but because the plebes themselves refused to co-operate. It was a point of honor among Fourth Classmen never to reveal the names of the cadets who hazed them. Under the circumstances, no matter how strict the regulations or stern the punishment for hazing, nothing could be done. A typical example occurred in 1894, when Mr. C. W. Otwell of Independence, Kansas, complained to Superintendent Oswald Ernst that his son had reported that he was being hazed. Ernst called Cadet Otwell in and read his father's letter to him, then asked the cadet to identify the men who had hazed him. Otwell replied that he could not recognize any of them, then made the general statement that he had exaggerated the case in his letter to his father and had nothing to complain of. As Ernst wrote Mr. Otwell, "In other words, he is aiding and abetting the violation of the regulations on this subject. If new cadets are to take this stand you can readily

[15] Quoted in Morris Janowitz, *The Professional Soldier: A Social and Political Portrait* (Glencoe, Ill., 1960), 129–30.

perceive that the authorities have no easy task before them. I can only say that they will do everything in their power to protect the new cadets even against themselves."[16]

Before the Civil War plebes went directly into summer camp after reporting on the post; after the war they first spent a three-week period segregated in the barracks, with a few upper classmen there to teach them saluting, marching, and other basic elements of military life. This undertaking was soon marked more by an introduction to hazing than to the profession of arms and became known as Beast Barracks. Upperclassmen concentrated on driving all sense of self-importance from the plebes and in teaching them unquestioning and instant obedience. Beast Barracks included a great deal of bracing, double-timing, and shouting—"Get your shoulders back! More yet! More yet! Hold your head up; drag in your chin! Suck up your stomach! Hurry up, Mr. Dumbjohn!" In 1917 a faculty member described the system with some pride, adding that obedience was "the foundation of discipline, toward the inculcation of which in the new cadet, an excellent beginning is made in Beast Barracks."[17]

After Beast Barracks plebes went into summer camp, where among other things they performed menial tasks for upperclassmen. Cadet John J. Pershing was notorious for making plebes police the area in front of his tent for him.[18] More active hazing was also common. A congressional committee late in the nineteenth century was able to get cadets to admit to the following

[16] Ernst to Otwell, July 16, 1894, SLB. In 1879 Superintendent Schofield told the Secretary of War the trouble was that every time he dismissed a cadet for hazing, the War Department reinstated him. "In my opinion, the discipline of the Academy requires the prompt dismissal of every cadet who has been guilty of hazing, or of shielding the principals," Schofield said, but it did no good. Schofield to Secretary of War, July 22, 1879, Schofield Papers. In 1899 Superintendent Mills proposed to require every cadet eligible for graduation or furlough to sign a statement that he had not hazed Fourth Classmen during his cadetship; those who could not sign would have their furlough or graduation delayed one month. He later withdrew the request, possibly because this system would in effect have forced the cadets to inform on themselves. Mills to Adjutant General, September 25, 1899, SLB.

[17] Richardson, *West Point,* 124–25.

[18] Rhodes to mother, July 5, 1885, Rhodes Papers.

methods: bracing, chewing rope ends, eating soap and quinine, drinking tobasco sauce, picking up all the ants in a hill, one at a time, permitting hot grease to be dropped on the feet, reciting nonsensical stories and poems, being pulled from bed without warning, holding Indian clubs at arm's length, being thrown into a ditch when on sentinel duty, doing the Spread Eagle (deep knee bends with arms held at sides), Swimming to Newburgh (balancing on the stomach on a pole and pretending to swim), and sitting at meals with the feet raised to the bottom of the table. A favorite practice of the upperclassmen was to go to a plebe's tent after tatoo and make him stand at attention on his head, while for general nuisance value upperclassmen habitually made any idle plebe they spotted do push-ups and other exercises. Whenever they were doing nothing else, plebes were expected to brace, whether they were told to or not.[19]

A hazing incident that occurred shortly after the turn of the century was typical in all respects but one—the guilty cadet was dismissed and the dismissal stood, despite the usual congressional attempt to reinstate him. During the Gilded Age a surprising number of West Pointers rode their war records into Congress. Most of them became members of the military affairs committee, where they were able to make sure the Academy held to the old ways. They also were able to protect cadets dismissed for hazing.

During the summer camp of 1910 Cadet Chauncey C. Devore, of the First Class, accompanied by three friends, toured the post of the plebe sentinels, teasing them. One of the Fourth Class sentinels, taking his responsibilities seriously, resisted them and, after more harassment, charged them with his bayonet. They immediately told him to brace, then made him ride on a rail, which injured his groin, finally forcing him to fence with them with tent posts. Cadet Devore rapped the plebe on the head, knocked him down, and took away his rifle. A tactical officer came upon the scene and identified Devore, who was dismissed the next day.

[19] *Hazing at the Military Academy,* House Document No. 2768, Fifty-sixth Congress, Second Session (Washington, 1901), 670–72; *Hazing at USMA,* Senate Document No. 731, Sixtieth Congress, Second Session (Washington, 1909), 210–15.

Hazing

Following the custom, Devore went to Washington, where his congressman introduced a bill to reinstate him. The Senate Committee on Military Affairs held a hearing. Commandant Frederick W. Sibley, testifying before it, said that the punishment, although mandatory, was too extreme, and admitted that he had done "much more severe" hazing himself when he was a cadet. No one expressed the slightest surprise that the man charged with maintaining cadet discipline would make such a statement.

Superintendent Hugh L. Scott followed Sibley. He thought the punishment fair and urged the senators not to reinstate Devore. One senator asked Scott, "You have turned out some pretty good officers while hazing has been going on, have you not?" Scott replied, "In spite of it." "In spite of it?" "Yes." Senator Frank Briggs of Delaware, an 1872 graduate of the Academy, asked Scott, "Do you believe that the ordinary hazing, as we used to have it—where a man was made to stand at attention and obey unquestioningly any reasonable order of an old cadet—injured the discipline of the Academy?" Scott replied, "I believe if a cadet is made to do menial service, if he is browbeaten and humiliated, it is injurious to his character. It is just the same with cadets as with anybody else." Senator Henry A. du Pont, also of Delaware and an 1861 graduate of West Point, remarked that it was unfair to punish the one who got caught and let the others go. Scott replied that that was always the excuse for avoiding any punishment at all. In the end, and for one of the few times, the punishment stood.[20]

For the plebe, perhaps the worst feature of his life was not the physical hazing but the isolation. At no time was he allowed to feel a real part of the Corps, a procedure that did make becoming a Third Classman and being accepted into the community more

[20] *Hearings Before the Senate Committee on Military Affairs Relating to the Subject of Hazing at the USMA,* Senate Document No. 781, Sixty-first Congress, First Session (Washington, 1910), 14–60. In his memoirs, Scott made a clear and simple statement of his position on hazing. "The facts are that the foundation of all military discipline is obedience to orders, and that, therefore, since hazing has been forbidden by the proper authorities, it cannot be tolerated." Hugh L. Scott, *Some Memories of a Soldier* (New York, 1928), 18.

appealing but still meant that the plebe's first year was a difficult and constant test. To some extent the isolation made the plebes welcome hazing, for then upperclassmen were at least paying some attention to them; when the cadets "cut" a plebe, months would literally pass without anyone's speaking to him. Even plebes who were not cut felt something of the same coldness; towards the end of his Fourth Class year Charles Rhodes reflected, "It's a very strange thing, and I don't believe there's a place in the world where a lot of young fellows, thrown together as we are, isolated from the rest of the world and dependent on each other for many favors, could keep up the restraint and formality that is never withdrawn. The plebe and the cadet of the upper classes are separated by a gulf of infinite width."[21]

One plebe who felt the full effects of cadet ostracism was Oscar L. Booz. During summer camp upperclassmen were in the practice of designating their "Special Duty Cadets," plebes who made their beds, kept their rifles clean, filled their water buckets, and did other odd jobs. Once, after a long day of drill, Booz refused to do this work for his upperclassman, muttering something about "do it yourself." He was immediately called out to fight, which meant that the Third Class "scrapping committee" would designate a man in the Third Class who was approximately the same height and weight as Booz to fight the undisciplined plebe. The idea was that the class honor had to be maintained and plebes kept in line but that it was unfair to make a plebe fight whoever called him out. Actually, the upperclassmen usually made sure the plebe would get licked by picking an experienced boxer. If the plebe won, he was immediately called out again, and again if necessary, until some upperclassman had finally defeated him. Thereafter, at least in theory, the plebe would have proper respect.

Booz and his opponent trudged up to Fort Putnam for their fight, accompanied by a hundred or so cadets. The first round was uneventful. In the second Booz caught a solid blow in his solar plexus and fell to the ground. He refused to get up and fight again. Plebes and upperclassmen alike shouted at him to get up;

[21] Rhodes to mother, February 28, 1886, Rhodes Papers.

when he would not, they called him coward and angrily stomped off. For weeks thereafter he was humiliated by the upperclassmen, but they soon decided that ostracism was not a severe enough punishment and began a systematic hazing campaign, the chief feature of which was forcing him to drink tobasco sauce with every meal.

Booz soon decided that he could do without a diploma from the Academy and wrote his father begging permission to resign. His father came to West Point and talked to his son, who said, "The upper class men are tyrants, brutes, and bullies, and they have an eager desire to injure or pain somebody." His father allowed him to resign, and he went home. By then his throat was so badly inflamed from the tobasco sauce that he could not drink orange juice or almost any liquid except water, and within a year he died from tuberculosis of the larynx. His family charged that he contracted the disease because of the tobasco sauce, but at a congressional investigation medical testimony indicated that, while the tobasco did him no good, it could not have caused tuberculosis. Thereafter, drinking tobasco sauce was eliminated from the West Point hazing program.[22]

A contemporary of Booz's who also suffered from excessive hazing was Douglas MacArthur. In his case it was not because of any supposed cowardice on his part but because his father was a ranking general in the army. Upperclassmen made him recite over and over his father's doings at Chickamauga, Lookout Mountain, and Stone's River, but it did not end with that.[23] His special treatment included a full program of exercising at all hours of the day. One night in summer camp, immediately after dinner, he did Spread Eagles for over a full hour and was still at it when the other plebes in his tent had collapsed. Suddenly MacArthur lost control of his muscles and fell to the floor, unable to move.[24] A congres-

[22] *Hazing at the Military Academy,* Fifty-sixth Congress, Second Session, 615–1255.

[23] Marty Maher, *Bringing Up the Brass: My 55 Years at West Point* (New York, 1951), 88.

[24] *Hazing at the Military Academy,* Fifty-sixth Congress, Second Session, 916–32.

sional investigation followed; the congressmen tried to get Mac-
Arthur to admit he suffered from convulsions, but he constantly
denied it, saying he was merely exhausted and possibly had a
cramp or two. An exchange between Representative Edmund H.
Driggs of New York and MacArthur followed:

Driggs: Was it too dark for you to recognize the faces of your
hazers?

MacArthur: I do not think it would have been if I had looked at
them, but it is generally customary for fourth class men not to
look at those people who are hazing them.

Driggs: They are not even to look at them?

MacArthur: Ordinarily not; no, sir.

Driggs: Did you ever know of any cases where they did look at
them?

MacArthur: In an official capacity, always; yes, sir.

Driggs: I simply mean in these hazings. Is that one of the orders
given by the upper class men—that the fourth class men shall
not look at their tormenters, if I might use that term?

MacArthur: Yes, sir.

Driggs: Then they go in and order you to go through a physical
exercise or through hazing of that character, and the first
order is not to look up, not to look at them?

MacArthur: No, sir; I don't think you caught my meaning. The
idea is not in any way to protect themselves by the fourth
class men not looking at them. It is simply always a general
order for a plebe to keep his eyes to himself.

Driggs: Is that the very general idea that prevails among the
corps and among fourth class men?

MacArthur: It is; yes, sir.

Driggs: That they are not to look at the men who are hazing
them? That is a sort of general order?

MacArthur: Again you have not caught the idea. It is not the
men that are hazing them. They are not to look at upper
class men.

Driggs: They are not even expected to look at upper class men?

MacArthur: Not to stare at them.

Later, Driggs took up the question of hazing in general.

Driggs: Did you expect when you came to West Point to be
treated in that manner?

[230]

MacArthur: Not exactly in that manner; no, sir.

Driggs: Did you not consider it cruel at that time?

MacArthur: I was perhaps surprised to some extent.

Driggs: I wish you would answer my question; did you or did you not consider it cruel at that time?

MacArthur: I would like to have you define cruel.

Driggs: All right, sir. Disposed to inflict suffering; indifference in the presence of suffering; hard-hearted; inflicting pain mentally or suffering; causing suffering.

MacArthur: I should say perhaps it was cruel, then.

Driggs: You have qualified your answer. Was it or was it not cruel?

MacArthur: Yes, sir.[25]

Later, in his memoirs, MacArthur would say, "Hazing was practiced with a worthy goal, but with methods that were violent and uncontrolled."[26]

Cadets who were never subjected to hazing were the Negroes. White cadets left them strictly alone, and few were able to withstand four years of total isolation, stay on at the Academy, and do good enough work to graduate.

The first congressman to consider appointing a Negro cadet was Benjamin F. Butler of Massachusetts. In 1867, at a time when Reconstruction and the discussion of the freed Negroes' place in American society were at their height, Butler thought it would help the Radical Republican cause to appoint an outstanding Negro to the national military Academy. He tried to choose his appointee with the same care Mr. Branch Rickey used after another war to pick Jackie Robinson to play baseball for the Brooklyn Dodgers. Butler turned to President James Fairchild, of the integrated Oberlin College, for help but in the end could get

[25] Douglas MacArthur, *Reminiscences* (New York, 1964), 25. In his memoirs, MacArthur claims that despite great pressure from the congressmen he refused to give the names of his hazers. Actually, he divulged quite a few names, but they were all of cadets who had either already admitted their guilt or who, for one reason or another, had resigned.

[26] *Ibid.*

none, as Fairchild had no Negro students he thought capable of meeting the challenge. Those who were intelligent enough were high-strung, physically weak, or alive to an insult and would be unable to meet the non-intellectual challenges West Point was sure to throw at them; those who could meet the physical challenges were not intelligent enough to pass the course. Disappointed, Butler made no appointment.[27]

Three years later the first Negro, James Webster Smith, entered West Point. A native of South Carolina, Smith received his appointment from a carpetbagger, Solomon L. Hoge, in 1870. From the first the white cadets ignored Smith, except when the time came to assign him to a table at the mess hall (he had been given a room to himself). Those who found themselves sitting with Smith applied for a transfer to another table. Superintendent Thomas Pitcher placed two of them under arrest for refusing to sit with Smith at all and informed the rest that their "reasons for wishing such a change could not be entertained for a moment." Smith himself was something of a celebrity, and newspaper reporters, especially from Radical papers, tried to get him to make a statement denouncing the Academy. He either refused or said he had no complaints to make.[28] Still, he was unpopular and ostracized. One of his classmates charged that "all he wanted was social equality, not an education."[29] Smith struggled through four years at the Academy. He was once turned back a class and in his Second Class year was found deficient in natural and experimental philosophy and dismissed.

The next Negro at the Academy, and the first to graduate, was Henry O. Flipper, who had a great advantage over Smith in that, at least in the eyes of his white classmates, he "never pushed."[30] Flipper received his appointment in 1873 from James Crawford Freeman, a Republican in Georgia who came from an old mercan-

[27] G. W. Shurtleff to Butler, May 16, 1867, B. F. Butler Papers, Library of Congress.
[28] Pitcher to Inspector of Military Academy, July 11, 1870, SLB.
[29] George L. Andrews, "West Point and the Colored Cadets," *International Review*, IX (November, 1880), 479–84.
[30] *Ibid.*, 484.

tile and banking family. Flipper was strong enough to ignore his classmates just as much as they ignored him, go through four years of a monk's existence, and graduate fiftieth in a class of seventy-six. Upon his graduation he was placed in a Negro cavalry regiment, where he served for five years before taking up mining activities in Mexico.[31] In all, in the fifty years after the Civil War, West Point admitted some thirteen Negro cadets, of whom three graduated and one rose to the rank of colonel; all served with Negro regiments. During the same period the Naval Academy did not admit a single Negro midshipman.[32]

Throughout the Reconstruction period the treatment of Negro cadets was a popular subject for newspaper and magazine reporters. Generally the treatment implied that there was a conspiracy at West Point, one which included not only the cadets and faculty but the army as a whole, to ostracize the Negroes. In point of fact there was no conspiracy, for there was no need for one. Prejudice against Negroes was neither higher nor lower at West Point and in the army than it was throughout the nation—which meant that it was high. Still, President Grant was embarrassed by the charges, his party being so dependent on Negro votes, and to add some stature to the Academy and hopefully to quiet the critics, in 1876 he asked General Schofield to accept the Superintendency. Schofield's reputation was high; of the Civil War heroes still in uniform only Sherman and Sheridan were better known. The problem was Schofield's rank—he was a major general, and previously the post had been in the hands of colonels or lower ranking officers. Further, since Schofield was commanding the Division of the Pacific, Grant was asking him to give up a great deal to come to the small and controversial post at West Point. Working closely with General in Chief Sherman, Grant finally persuaded Schofield to come to West Point by changing it from a post to a department (the Department of West Point), assuring him that he would report directly to and take his orders only from General Sherman,

[31] Flipper wrote a book about his experiences: *The Colored Cadet at West Point* (New York, 1878).
[32] *New York Times,* April 9, 1922.

telling him it was for the good of the army, and asking him to accept the appointment as a personal favor.[33]

Under the circumstances, Schofield accepted, but he was never happy in his position. The Secretary of War and the adjutant general continued to interfere with the Superintendent, especially by returning dismissed cadets. Sherman proved somewhat less than understanding of the nature of Schofield's problems, and generally Schofield never shook the feeling that the Superintendency was beneath his dignity as a major general.

In the main matter, the treatment of Negro cadets, Schofield did his best. The year he took up his duties, 1876, a Negro cadet from South Carolina, Johnson C. Whittaker, entered. After Flipper graduated in 1877, Whittaker was the only Negro cadet. In 1879 the Academic Board found Whittaker deficient, but Schofield recommended that he be turned back a year instead of dismissed. The Superintendent confessed that "I may be influenced somewhat by the fact that he is the only one of his race now at the Academy, and has won the sympathy of all by his manly deportment, and earnest efforts to succeed." The professors doubted that he could ever graduate, but Schofield was "disposed to give him another chance."[34] Whittaker managed to struggle on, never doing well but avoiding dismissal.

Then, on the morning of April 6, 1880, a tactical officer found Whittaker bound to his bed, suffering from serious injuries around the head. Whittaker reported that three masked men had attacked him during the night. The news quickly reached New York City and the newspapers, and Whittaker's case soon acquired national importance. Schofield hired private detectives to investigate and promised that "every possible effort will be made to detect the perpetrators of this outrage."[35]

In the upshot, it turned out Whittaker had given the blows to himself, tied himself to the bed, and then invented his story—his motive, probably, was that he feared being found deficient in the

[33] Schofield reviewed the situation surrounding his appointment in a letter to Sherman, August 11, 1880, Sherman Papers.

[34] Schofield to Adjutant General, January 15, 1879, Schofield Papers.

[35] Schofield to Adjutant General, April 6 and June 21, 1880, *ibid.*

coming examinations and wanted an excuse to avoid taking them. Schofield was furious. If anything, he said, he had shown "undue kindness toward an unworthy cadet for no better reason than that he is colored."[36] He convinced himself that Whittaker was "acting under orders from some authority which he believed perfectly competent to protect him from any possible harm" and demanded an immediate court-martial.[37]

Whittaker, however, refused to admit his guilt, and throughout the country he, and not Schofield, was believed. By now Sherman was as furious as the Superintendent, and he railed against President Hayes and the Secretary of War for joining in the "cry raised by the party press, which was like a pack of hounds barking at they knew not what." Eventually Sherman convinced Washington authorities of the truth in the case, and both the President and the Secretary apologized to Schofield, but only privately. Schofield had meanwhile tried to dismiss Whittaker on disciplinary grounds, but the President would allow him to be discharged only on the grounds of deficiency in studies. All this was being done, in Schofield's view, "for the purpose, hardly attempted to be disguised, of alluring the colored vote!"[38]

Meanwhile, there was a popular clamor for Schofield's removal, and the administration was on the verge of giving in to it. Schofield was beside himself with rage. "Thus after I have been induced to submit to one humiliation by accepting an inferior command," he said, "it is proposed to complete my disgrace by turning me out of that inferior command, and that in pretended furtherance of the interests of that race for whose freedom and equal rights very few men now living have ever done as much as I!" He demanded that Sherman relieve him before he could be dismissed and further that he be given a command commensurate with his rank.[39] The latter demand embarrassed Uncle Billy, as he had no place to put someone of Schofield's rank, and he persuaded the Superintendent to stay on for a few months—he, Sher-

[36] Schofield to Adjutant General, November 11, 1880, *ibid.*
[37] Schofield to Sherman, July 31, 1880, Sherman Papers.
[38] Schofield to Sherman, August 11, 1880, *ibid.*
[39] *Ibid.*

man, would make sure Schofield was not dismissed meanwhile—
while a solution was worked out.[40]

While Sherman was trying to think of a solution, he heard a
rumor that the administration was going to replace Schofield with
General Oliver O. Howard, whose reputation among Negroes was
higher than that of any other white man in the country. Howard
had served as head of the Freedmen's Bureau, founded the university that bears his name, organized an integrated Congregational
church in Washington, and was director of a bank for Negroes.
Sherman did not know who had started the rumor about Howard
or how much truth there was in it, but thought he ought to write
Howard in any case. The General in Chief carefully explained
the Whittaker case to Howard, then delivered a lecture on race
relations. "I am willing to go as far as the furthest in this question," Sherman said (without much justification, it must be
admitted), "but I do not believe West Point is the place to try the
experiment of social equality. All else has long since been conceded. Social equality must be admitted in civil life, in Congress,
the Cabinet, and the Supreme Court before it is enforced at West
Point." Sherman then confessed that he thought Howard was
"extreme on this question" and that he preferred someone else
for the Superintendency.[41]

Six days later, on December 13, 1880, the War Department
announced that it had relieved Schofield and was assigning him to
a new division in Texas, Louisiana, Arkansas, and the Indian
Territory. Howard would be the new Superintendent. "I was not
consulted," Sherman remarked bitterly, "and wash my hands of
the whole thing."[42] Howard remained only a year and a half, to

[40] A note in the Sherman Papers, written in Sherman's hand, reveals his
thoughts. "To relieve Gen. Schofield *now*, will embarrass the War Dept.
no place to put him. But in 1882 Gen. Sherman *may* retire, having reached
the age of 62. When Lt. Col. [*sic*] Sheridan will succeed to the Post at
Washington. Then—1882—the 3 Divisions will easily and naturally fall to the
3 maj genls, Hancock, Schofield, and McDowell."

[41] Sherman to Howard, December 7, 1880, Sherman Papers.

[42] Sherman to Sheridan, December 13, 1880, *ibid.* See also Howard to
Senator Morrill, June 8, 1881, O. O. Howard Papers, Bowdoin College
Library.

be replaced by Colonel Wesley Merritt, and the Department of West Point reverted to its status of post.[43] The Negro question, meanwhile, was solved not by anything that was done at the Academy but by the country as a whole, which, following the Compromise of 1877 and the acquiescence of the North in the passage of the Jim Crow laws, no longer paid any attention to the problem. Most Americans agreed with Schofield, who contended it was unreasonable "to expect . . . Negroes to compete with whites, and a mistake to make them try."[44]

In the twentieth century, especially after World War II and the integration of the army, the number of Negro cadets increased and their position improved. An outstanding example is Benjamin O. Davis, Jr. His father, who fought as an officer of volunteers, had enlisted in the Ninth Cavalry after the turn of the century and risen from private to brigadier general. Young Davis, who graduated in the upper ranks of the 1936 class, commanded an Air Force flight group in World War II and later became a lieutenant general. His success, and that of other Negro cadets, disproved Schofield's bitter conclusion.

[43] Howard's biggest problem, in fact, turned out to be the law professor, who in Howard's words "is drinking steadily and sometimes unduly." Moreover, he was giving "strong drink" to cadets who visited his house and allowing them to gamble with cards there. Howard to Judge Advocate, October 10, 1881, *ibid.*

[44] Schofield to Adjutant General, November 11, 1880, Schofield Papers.

Chapter XII

From Cuba to France

In the twenty years from 1898 to 1918 West Point began to be less cloistered and to come into closer contact with the nation and the modern age. The two decades were marked by the Spanish-American War, the Philippine Insurrection, the Centennial celebration, an ambitious building program, World War I, and an almost imperceptible move in the direction of modernization of the academic program. On the last point little was actually accomplished—it would take a world war and Douglas MacArthur to bring the Academy more or less against its will into the twentieth century—but the foundation for change was laid.

West Point greeted the Spanish-American War with cheers. After thirty-three years of peace, broken only by an occasional Indian war (and even these had by 1898 disappeared), West Pointers finally had their chance to lead troops in combat. A generation had passed since the Civil War; during that entire period cadets were regaled by the old veterans with tales of heroism and great deeds, while they suffered through years of dreary peace without any foreseeable opportunity to emulate their predecessors. Then war came—not much of a war, perhaps, but the best that generation was to have—and it was welcomed with joy at West Point. Following the lead of the 1861 class, the First Class of 1898 demanded an early graduation and immediate assignment to the war zone. Superintendent Oswald Ernst reported that the war and the prospect of early graduation "has caused such a state of unrest among the members of the class that they find great difficulty in prosecuting their studies."[1] He recommended an early graduation, and on April 26 the War Department permitted the class to graduate and go immediately to the field. Three members of the class were killed in combat, two of them—Edmund N. Benchley and Clarke Churchman—at San Juan Hill.[2]

Meanwhile, the War Department continued to follow a policy that dated back to at least the War of 1812—giving commissions in the Regular Army to civilians. That policy infuriated the cadets, especially the members of the new First Class, since these civilians would permanently rank them in the army. They too began an agitation for early graduation, and on February 15, 1899, four months early, they received their commissions. The class of 1900 graduated on schedule, but then the Philippine Insurrection put heavier demands on the army than the war with Spain had and the class of 1901 graduated in February, 1901, four months early. Altogether, Emilio Aguinaldo's Filipinos proved much more dangerous than the Spanish; of the four classes from 1898 to 1901, some sixteen members died in the Philippines.[3]

As America settled down to administer her new colonial empire, the army assumed new responsibilities and to meet them increased its size; the Corps of Cadets, although it did not keep pace, also expanded. In 1900 each senator was allowed to make an appointment, and the President was given the authority to make thirty

[1] Ernst to Adjutant General, April 23, 1898, SLB.

[2] The praise of Secretary of War Elihu Root was welcome. "I believe that the great service which West Point has rendered the country was never more conspicuous than it has been during the past two years," he said in 1899. "The faithful and efficient services of its graduates since the declaration of war with Spain have more than repaid the cost of the institution since its foundation. They have been too few in number and most heavily burdened." *Annual Report of the Secretary of War, 1899*, 212–13.

[3] All statistics of this nature throughout this work are compiled from the *Register of Graduates and Former Cadets*, an annual publication of the West Point Alumni Foundation. The 1963 edition has been used in this instance.

at-large appointments, bringing the Corps to 533 men; in 1910 further additions made the total 580.[4]

The increased size of the Corps, coupled with the administrations's determination to retain the Thayer system inviolate, created problems in finding enough new instructors who were properly equipped to teach. Every year from 1902 on, the Superintendents asked for help; Superintendent Clarence Townsley's plea of 1913 was typical. He asked that the War Department allow the Academy to keep instructors for at least four, instead of the then current three, years. Townsley pointed out that the number of available instructors was limited because of the Academy's requirements. Instructors must be West Pointers; they were required to have been out of the Academy for at least three years, for otherwise they would be teaching men they had lived with as cadets; but they could not have been absent from the Academy for too long, for in that case they might have forgotten its system; and of course they must have excelled in the subject they were going to teach. When a professor did find an instructor who pleased him, he lost the young officer just as he was becoming a proficient teacher. Standing in the way of a four-year tour was a newly enacted detached service law, which prevented an officer from staying away from his regiment for more than three years. The law was designed to prevent an abuse of a nineteenth-century practice, when officers were sometimes on detached service literally for decades, while their regiments continued to carry their names on the rolls and they stood in the way of promotion of men actually serving with the troops. The new detached service law was not changed, and instructors who were not promoted to assistant professor continued to leave after three years.[5]

[4] *Report to the Superintendent by the USMA Committee on Service Academies* (West Point, 1949), 11–12.

[5] Superintendent's Annual Report, 1913, in *Annual Report of the War Department, 1913* (Washington, 1913), III, 128; see the report of the Board of Visitors for 1907 in *Annual Report of the War Department, 1907* (Washington, 1907), IV, 163. The Superintendents were also unhappy over a change in the Board of Visitors. In 1909 Congress decided to abolish the old Thayer system and substitute for the prominent civilians and army officers who had made up the Board a group of congressmen, five from the Senate

The increased size of the Corps provided impetus for an ambitious building program. In 1901 the Board of Visitors, with John Schofield serving as president, spoke of the condition of the Academy's plant as a disgrace and called for a "complete tearing down and a new building up." The cadet barracks, the Board said, were little better than those at the average county poorhouse; conditions were so bad that "the cadet who entered the West Point barracks the first day the institution opened its doors, nearly 100 years ago, found himself surrounded by almost as many comforts and conveniences as the cadet who entered last June."[6] In response to the report of the Board, Congress appropriated $6,000,000 for a building program. The question of architectural style arose at once. One suggestion was to follow the pattern of Cullum Hall, on the eastern edge of the Plain, which had just been completed. It was designed in the classical style, more or less after the temples of the ancient Greeks and Romans. Others advocated a return to the Tudor style. The War Department decided to hold a design competition between architects and appointed a jury to judge the results. Members included Schofield and Superintendent Albert L. Mills. In the spring of 1903 the jury announced that the winner was the Boston firm of Cram, Goodhue and Ferguson, the style would be Gothic, and the entire plant would be built according to a single integrated plan.

The idea of one basic style for a group of buildings had once been considered impractical, but it had been applied successfully at the Chicago World's Fair of 1893 and had since been copied elsewhere. The architects announced that the new buildings were intended "to harmonize with the majority of the existing buildings, prolong rather than revolutionize the spirit of the place that has grown up through many generations, emphasize rather than antagonize the picturesque natural surroundings of rocks, cliffs,

---

Committee on Military Affairs and seven from the House. Also, the new Board came to the Academy during the academic year and not during the June examinations, a variation that upset the Superintendents because it interrupted the teaching schedule.

[6] The Board's report is in *Annual Report of the War Department, 1901* (Washington, 1901), I, 401.

mountains, and forests, and be capable of execution at the smallest cost consistent with the monumental importance of the work."[7] In the next decade old structures came down while the new ones went up; the chapel and the Administration Building, the East Academic Building, the Riding Hall, and the North Barracks were all completed. Meanwhile, the department of tactics supervised the restoration of Fort Putnam, which had been falling into ruins.[8] The result was a campus distinctly masculine and military, which blended well with its background.

All the improvements were a boon to the cadets but, except by surrounding him with beauty to look on, did nothing for the visitor. The hotel remained a disgrace. Built in the nineteenth century with funds raised by selling timber and located on the north edge of the Plain, it was an old, ramshackle building that few could bear for more than a night or two. The Board of Visitors, forced to spend nearly two weeks in the hotel, was usually unable to refrain from commenting about its condition and demanding, to no avail, that the government build a new one. In 1900 the Board outdid itself. "It is, perhaps, because of the relation between cleanliness and godliness," the Board said, "that so many ungodly remarks are provoked by even a temporary sojourn in this hotel." The Board added that a public house conducted on the temperance plan might "at least provide water in abundance."[9] Nothing was done, however, until the Hotel Thayer was built in the twenties.

In the midst of the building program, during June Week of 1902, the Academy celebrated its centennial. The occasion was marked by speeches, parades, and balls. The center of activity was the newly completed Cullum Hall, where the hundreds of old graduates and distinguished visitors milled about. Foreign officers, representatives of foreign and American colleges and universities, the President of the United States, the Secretaries of War and the

[7] Sylvester Baxter, "The New West Point," *Century Magazine,* LXVIII (July, 1904), 333–39.

[8] Gray, "Architectural Development of West Point."

[9] The Board's report is in *Annual Report of the War Department, 1900* (Washington, 1900), I, 230.

Navy, and the governor of New York were among those present. President Roosevelt reviewed the Corps and afterwards, in the highlight of the centennial, presented the Medal of Honor to Cadet Calvin P. Titus, of the Fourth Class, for "gallantry at Peking, China, August 14, 1900, while a soldier of the Fourteenth U. S. Infantry."[10]

Speakers at the centennial included President Roosevelt, his Secretary of War Elihu Root, General Schofield, and West Point veterans of the Mexican War, the Civil War (both sides), and the Spanish-American War. Schofield declared that "The Corps of Cadets has always been a real American aristocracy—an aristocracy of character," but fittingly the highest praise came from Roosevelt. "This institution," he said, "has completed its first hundred years in life. During that century no other educational institution in the land has contributed as many names as West Point has contributed to the honor roll of the nation's greatest citizens. . . . And more than that, . . . taken as a whole, the average graduate of West Point during this hundred years has given a greater sum of service to the country through his life than has the average graduate of any other institution in this broad land."[11]

In the fall of 1902, shortly after the centennial celebration, West Point for one of the few times in its history was carried away by a popular movement in the educational field. The movement had had its beginnings in the seventies, when the University of Michigan began to admit without an examination graduates from public high schools in the state when the schools met certain standards. Known as the certificate movement, the method freed the university of the necessity of maintaining preparatory courses and of giving entrance examinations and had a great influence in raising standards in the high schools, as they all attempted to earn certification by the state university. The Michigan system was soon copied elsewhere. By 1890 a system of certification was in effect in all the middle western states and some others; by the turn of the century forty-two state universities had some form of the system,

[10] *CWP*, I, 4; Bailey, "The Centennial at West Point."
[11] *CWP*, I, 20, 61–62.

and throughout the country the high schools had risen to the challenge.[12] In 1902 West Point followed suit; Congress had finally dropped the 1866 entrance requirements of a knowledge of American history, mathematics, and the English language and had allowed the Secretary of War (actually, the Academic Board) to set admission requirements. The Academic Board authorized admission of candidates who presented a certificate testifying to their graduation from a public high school. Within five years the high rate of dismissal among cadets admitted through the certificate scheme convinced the Board that it had made a mistake, and in 1907 it began giving its own entrance examination.[13] The Academy's experience with the certificate movement did not induce it to look favorably on other trends in civilian education. West Point still tended to look inward, to feel that it was disastrous to tamper with perfection.

Still, this was the twentieth century, the era of the automobile and the airplane, the machine gun and quick-firing artillery. The Academy could not totally ignore it. The most important changes of the period—indeed, the most important since the Civil War—came in the tactical department, under the direction of Commandant Otto T. Hein. An 1870 graduate of the Academy, Hein had spent seven years on frontier duty and five years as the military attaché in Vienna before returning to the Academy in 1897 for a five-year tour as Commandant. His varied service, and especially his years in Vienna in proximity to the Prussian war machine, had taught him a great deal about modern war, and he was shocked to find that "tactics" at West Point had not changed in one hundred years. A cadet learned close-order drill in his first six weeks, then spent the next four years performing it over and over. He had no preparation for the duties of a second lieutenant. Hein aimed to turn out officers trained to meet every emergency of actual service; under his regime cadets learned the use of a mountain-gun battery, the Gatling gun, a mortar battery, and so on. Instead of bringing enlisted men along on the practice marches around the country-

[12] Rudolph, *American College*, 283–84.
[13] Beukema, *The United States Military Academy*, 39–40.

side to do the work for the cadets, Hein required cadets to groom, saddle, and unsaddle their own horses, raise their own tents, load the pack mules, and clean the camp site. He gave them instruction in open-order drills, attack formations of infantry and cavalry, picket and guard and reconnaissance duty, and target practice. He rotated the command duty of the cadets in the Corps, so that each had an opportunity to act as adjutant, as captain, as major, as lieutenant of infantry, cavalry, and artillery, and as officer of the day.

During the academic year, Hein's instructors gave lectures on the army's housekeeping functions. They told the cadets about the duties of recruiting officers, taught them how to make reports and returns, gave them a grounding in the mechanics of company organization, the army ration and company records, the duties of a quartermaster, and property accountability. For the first time, graduates were aware of the complexity of the army structure and wary of the pitfalls of its red tape. To further aid them, Hein summarized the lectures in pamphlets which the graduates took with them into the service; then, if ordered to act as head of the post exchange, the new officer could at least make an intelligent start by consulting Hein's pamphlet.[14]

The department of military art and engineering was also changing. It added some time to the section dealing with the art of war but more important began in 1902 a policy of taking the First Class to a Civil War battlefield. The trip usually took two days and was preceded by an extensive study of the armies, organization, strategy, tactics, and arms used at the battle. Gettysburg was the favorite site.[15] The department also took the First Class to various forts, seacoast batteries, and proving grounds for practical instruction.[16]

In one respect West Point was a leader in pedagogy; it was one of the few schools in the country with a program of physical

[14] *The Nation,* LXXI (October 18, 1900), 304; *CWP,* I, 385.

[15] Superintendent's Annual Report, 1911, in *Annual Report of the War Department, 1911* (Washington, 1911), III, 261; Mills to Boyd, April 25, 1901, SLB.

[16] Superintendent's Annual Report, 1910, in *Annual Report of the War Department, 1910* (Washington, 1910), III, 278.

exercise for all its students. The Naval Academy had introduced organized athletics in 1865, in order to keep the midshipmen out of Annapolis taverns during their free time, and Harvard built a gymnasium in 1878 for much the same purpose, but few schools offered a well organized or even a modest physical fitness program. Colonel Herman J. Koehler, instructor in military gymnastics and physical culture, with the title of Master of the Sword, gave West Point one. Colonel Koehler came from the German Turner tradition—he was a graduate of the Milwaukee Normal School of Physical Training who had won a national championship for all-around gymnasium work when he was nineteen—and he established a complete course in calisthenics of his own invention. He came to the Academy in 1885 and personally gave all the instruction; members of the Fourth Class were required to participate in his program and other cadets were allowed to. Koehler expanded it in 1892 when a new gymnasium was completed, adding riding, fencing, boxing, wrestling, and swimming to the calisthenics. In 1905 President Theodore Roosevelt, a great believer in *mens sana in corpore sano* who had observed Koehler's system and thought highly of it, ordered that all classes participate.[17]

Meanwhile, West Point, like most American institutions including the civil colleges and universities, was becoming conscious of its public relations. The post-Civil War inclination to ignore the people who paid for the Academy passed in 1906 when Superintendent Hugh L. Scott assumed his duties. He was the first head of the Academy since Thayer to strive to improve the picture of West Point in the public mind. He concentrated on relations with the New York City newspaper reporters, who since the Booz case had been hostile to the Academy. Scott used the usual methods to win them over—numerous press conferences, where he served hot coffee and good cigars, personal visits to the editors, and a general effort at co-operation. He was successful, and he considered this success his greatest contribution to the Academy. In other ways Scott improved the Academy's reputation. He invited the American public to come and visit the post, announced the

[17] Superintendent's Annual Report, 1908, in *Annual Report of the War Department, 1908* (Washington, 1908), IV, 12, and *Annual Report of the War Department, 1913* (Washington, 1913), III, 134.

time and place of parades, established comfort stations for both sexes, built drinking fountains, and soon turned West Point into a popular tourist attraction.[18]

The curriculum was also being modified. This was the era of the Johns Hopkins and the University of Chicago, of the social sciences, of the broadening of the college into the university, of the emphasis on the arts and sciences. At West Point, the Board of Visitors continued its assault on the old order. The Board of 1907 roundly declared that it was time to bring the curriculum up-to-date. It pointed out that when the Academy was founded the army offered no post-graduate education; now that had changed, and the emphasis on technical proficiency was out of place. It hinted at something even more fundamental. The United States was not maintaining a military academy in order that certain traditions could be preserved or in order to please old graduates but for the nation's benefit. Those who paid the bills deserved a return on their investment; they deserved graduates prepared to assume the duties of an officer in a modern army. The Board therefore recommended that the course of studies be broadened so that "the cadet can be graduated with an education approaching in general culture that acquired in the best American colleges."[19] The next year the Academy did make some modifications in, or rather additions to, the curriculum. The professors would not consent to drop any part of their courses as they then stood, so the Academic Board required the new cadets to report on March 1 instead of June 1 and used the extra three months gained thereby to add studies in foreign languages and history. Under this system cadets were at least introduced to social and political science and "historical geography with special reference to military geography."

The early report system was dropped the next year, but the West Point faculty was beginning to recognize that the "wider sphere of activities into which our officers have been thrown of recent years has required them to exercise functions demanding of them much more varied accomplishments and a broader range of general information than heretofore." Army officers in Cuba

[18] Scott, *Some Memories of a Soldier*, 417–60.
[19] The Board's report is in *Annual Report of the War Department, 1907* (Washington, 1907), IV, 171.

and the Philippines were exercising many civil functions—serving as the governors of towns, districts, and provinces.[20] The Academic Board made an effort to broaden the cadets' education by embarking on what seemed to it to be a revolution. In 1908 it created a new department—the department of English and history—and brought in an outsider—Professor John C. Adams of Yale—to head it.

Previously, grammar had been taught in the department of modern languages, and no effort was made to include literature. History was in the province of the department of law and history, which treated that subject in about the same way as the high schools taught their courses in civics. Professor Adams was pleased with his appointment and the challenge it presented, and he immediately set to work to bring West Point up to the level of the colleges. He began by discarding Thayer's system, eliminating the instructors and doing all the teaching himself. He was horrified by the usual West Point method, under which the professors handed each day's lesson to the instructors, who then delivered it unchanged to the sections, so that the professor could go from one section room to another and hear the same speech being given in each. Adams set the plebes to reading Shakespeare and Tennyson and used as his textbook in history *The Development of Modern Europe,* by J. H. Robinson and Charles A. Beard.[21]

Professor Adams lasted two years. In June, 1910, he left, taking many grievances with him and leaving a muttering faculty behind. He had never been invited to join the meetings of the Academic Board; he had no army rank; on the faculty he was not professor but instructor, even though he headed the department; he felt the rest of the faculty had not lived up to its promise to "dignify and broaden the subjects of history and English"; he was sure his talents were better appreciated at Yale, to which he returned.[22]

[20] Superintendent's Annual Report, 1910, in *Annual Report of the War Department, 1910* (Washington, 1910), III, 279–82.

[21] Course descriptions can be found in *Official Register of Officers and Cadets* (annually, West Point) for the appropriate years.

[22] Superintendent's Annual Report, 1910, in *Annual Report of the War Department, 1910* (Washington, 1910), III, 282.

The Academic Board's experience with Adams produced no rancor towards civilian teachers in general; rather, the Board profited from it. Adams' successor was Lucius H. Holt, also of Yale. The Board saw to it that he received the rank of lieutenant colonel and was a member of the Board with the position on the faculty of professor. Holt retained most of Adams' changes, although he did make use of instructors, and he even broadened the scope of the English course by adding Palgrave's *Golden Treasury of Poetry* and some of Stevenson's writings. In history he continued to use Robinson and Beard and added R. G. Gettell's *Introduction to Political Science.*[23] But within a year Holt too was unhappy; he wanted his department divided. "It is requiring more than should be required of one person to ask that he should keep himself an authority in two branches on such broad nature as these," he complained. "Merely to inform one's self thoroughly of the literature of the French Revolution, or of Napoleon, or of conditions in contemporary Europe, or of the principles of political science, will tax a person's efforts to the utmost, but to attempt this in addition to keeping abreast of contemporary work in literature . . . is to attempt the impossible." To the Academic Board, Holt's was a brazen demand. Their fields seemed to them just as broad as his, and they had no trouble deciding what to teach the cadets; besides, they had already given up some time from their own courses for the new department, and now Holt wanted another department and thus even more time. They flatly refused. Eventually, the administration worked out a compromise of sorts; it gave Holt some additional instructors, which relieved him of some of the burden. He remained at the Academy for more than a decade.[24]

An even more important addition to the staff than Professor Holt was Edward S. Holden, librarian from 1902 until his death in 1914. Following his graduation in 1870 from the Academy, Holden had served as a professor of mathematics at the Naval Observatory

[23] See the *Official Register of Officers and Cadets* for 1911.
[24] Superintendent's Annual Report, 1913, in *Annual Report of the War Department, 1913* (Washington, 1913), III, 147.

in Washington, D.C. (1873–81), as president of the University of California (1885–88), and as director of the Lick Observatory (1888–98). When he returned to West Point to assume the duties of librarian, chaos was waiting. There were few reference works in the Academy library, and no one knew where they were; the arrangement of the books on the shelves followed no system at all; the cataloguing was left to chance. Holden soon brought order to the library, then began a program to improve its holdings, which consisted for the most part of out-of-date military works. He added many of the standard works of literature and reference, building the resources from 46,000 to 93,000 volumes. He gave the cadets lectures on the use of a library, and altogether produced at the Academy one of the best equipped and most convenient small college libraries in the country. In his spare time he compiled a two-volume account of the centennial celebration of 1902, which included an extensive history of the Academy.[25]

The changes at West Point in the early years of the twentieth century were not extensive—most departments neither learned nor forgot anything—but they did prepare the way for what was to come. The spirit was still one of self-satisfaction. Superintendent Scott summed up the situation most accurately. He came to West Point in 1906 and later said, "I . . . brought to West Point no arrogant project of drastic reform. . . . West Point is not a subject for reform in that sense. It goes forward on its majestic course from year to year toward the fulfilment of its destiny, moving serenely under its traditions of 'honor, duty, country,' . . . without need of radical alteration." He went on to say that those who did want to make their mark through reforms were soon dismissed.[26]

For the cadets, life was about the same. General Henry H. Arnold, a graduate of 1907, could write of his cadet days in the same terms that a cadet of 1850 might have used. "Despite the legends about it," Arnold remembered in 1949, "the Point was not nearly so tough a place from which to graduate then as it is today." Like those nineteenth-century cadets who stood in the

[25] Forman, *West Point,* 161.
[26] Scott, *Some Memories of a Soldier,* 420.

middle of the class, Arnold studied little. "I had time to play football as a substitute fullback and halfback, to play on the polo squad, place in the shotput at interclass track meets, and with the rest of the Cavalry fanatics ride furiously, not only at drill, but in the Riding Hall and over the reservation. . . ." Most of all, he remembered, "we lived . . . in conformance with a code, and with daily routines which had not changed strikingly . . . since Grant was a cadet."[27]

But the changes were coming. The "Cavalry fanatics" would not long continue to dominate West Point. Hein in tactics, Koehler in gymnastics, Adams and Holt in English and history, and Holden in the library were all helping the Academy turn out graduates more useful to the modern army, and they were all breaking the way for Douglas MacArthur.

First, however, there was a war to be fought, a war that had begun in Europe in 1914 but that did not touch West Point until 1917. As far as the Academy was concerned, the first three years of the war in Europe need never have taken place. No attempt was made to learn from it or to apply its lessons to the curriculum. In the department of military art, the cadets continued to concentrate on and visit Civil War battlefields; while the French army bled to death in front of Verdun, the cadets at West Point inspected Gettysburg. In the department of tactics Hein's changes were considered quite sufficient. The instructors continued to emphasize cavalry tactics and made no attempt to teach the cadets anything about trench warfare.[28] The first mention of the war came in 1916, when the head of the department of modern languages reported, "On account of the war abroad, no request was made to send officers to Europe to study French and Spanish."[29] Even after American entry into the war, nothing changed in the academic routine and instruction—except that, owing to early graduation,

[27] H. H. Arnold, *Global Mission* (New York, 1949), 6–7.

[28] See the various Superintendents' Annual Reports for the war years.

[29] Superintendent's Annual Report, 1915, in *Annual Report of the War Department, 1915* (Washington, 1915), I, 1195.

the cadets skipped the course in the art of war altogether.[30] In September, 1917, the war was forgotten at West Point—a hazing scandal had led to another investigation.[31]

Those were dreary years, but from them came the greatest class in West Point's history, a class that demonstrated that no matter how far behind the times the Academy was, its emphasis on character and solid learning could still provide a springboard to greatness. In 1911 a remarkable group of young men came to the Academy; in 1915, 164 of them graduated. Of the 164, 59 rose to the rank of brigadier general or higher, three to the rank of full general, and two to the rank of general of the armies and the office of Chief of Staff of the Army. One became a President of the United States. Members of the class included Vernon E. Prichard, who commanded the First Armored Division in Italy in World War II; George E. Stratemeyer, Commanding General of the Air Defense Command after 1945 and of the Far East Air Forces during the Korean War; Charles W. Ryder, Commanding General of the IX Corps in World War II; Stafford Irwin, Commanding General of the XII Corps in World War II; Joseph McNarney, Governor of the U.S. Zone of Occupation in Germany after 1945; James A. Van Fleet, Commanding General of the Eighth Army in Korea; Hubert R. Harmon, the first Superintendent of the Air Force Academy; Herman Beukema, founder of the social sciences department at the Military Academy; Omar N. Bradley, Chief of Staff of the Army during the Korean War; and Dwight D. Eisenhower.

The Superintendent during the war was old Colonel Tillman, called out of retirement when Colonel John Biddle went off to war. One of his major duties was to entertain distinguished visitors. In May, 1917, just after America entered the war, General Joffre, the hero of the Marne, visited the United States and came to West Point for a day, to the delight of the cadets. Joffre reviewed the Corps, solemnly pronounced it the finest drilled and most efficient unit he had ever seen, and had lunch at the officers'

[30] *Ibid.,* 953.
[31] *New York Times,* September 28, 1917.

club.[32] An even more exciting visit came a year later, when the Blue Devils, a group of French combat veterans who did fancy drill work, visited the Point and drilled for the cadets.[33] Some of the more absurd aspects of America's entry into world conflict touched the Academy. In February, 1918, Superintendent Tillman announced that all athletic events had been cancelled and a quarantine imposed because of an outbreak of "liberty measles."[34]

Despite his age, Tillman proved to be a reformer. He had earlier been a critic of some of the Academy's methods, and as Superintendent he had a chance to make some changes. His annual report for 1918 was, in effect, a history of hazing at the Academy, with some suggestions for changes—suggestions which Douglas MacArthur later applied.[35] He brought to summer camp several professors from Harvard University to give the cadets instruction in speaking French. He forced the tactical department to change its course, dropping some instruction in cavalry tactics and adding practical work in trench warfare. He sent the class that graduated in May, 1919, after the war ended, to France for a three months' post-graduate course. The young officers lived with the occupation forces in the field and studied the armies of the Allies.[36]

But by himself Tillman could not do much, especially with the disturbances in the routine caused by the war. There were too many problems—old ones to be sure, but ones that had never really been solved. In 1917 the United States, for the first time since 1861, set about to raise a huge civilian army. The problem of finding officers to lead this aggregation was acute, for neither West Point nor the Regular Army nor the National Guard nor the preparedness camps like the one at Plattsburg, New York, could begin to supply the need. Perforce, the country turned to civilians and gave commissions to thousands of "Emergency Officers." The system used was not as openly political as that of the Civil War— Theodore Roosevelt was unsuccessful in his efforts to emulate

[32] *Ibid.*, May 12, 1917.
[33] *Ibid.*, May 7, 1918.
[34] *Ibid.*, February 8, 1918.
[35] *Ibid.*, February 17, 1917.
[36] *Ibid.*, January 13, 1917.

Benjamin F. Butler or Nathaniel P. Banks (Lincoln, one feels, unlike Wilson, would have welcomed such support from a major political opponent)—and the Emergency Officers never rose to positions as high as those reached by their Civil War counterparts. There were no John A. Logans or John A. McClernands in World War I.

Still, the Emergency Officers did make the AEF possible, as they made up the bulk of the junior officers. And they and the enlisted men made the same complaints about West Pointers as their Civil War predecessors had. They saw again in Academy graduates the closed corporation into which only fellow graduates were allowed. West Pointers, it was once more observed, made sure that choice assignments and promotions were limited to their tight little fraternity. Further, the civilians found that West Pointers understood nothing of the national character, that their discipline was rooted in Frederickian concepts rather than in the realities of the American situation, that it was, in short, "harsh and inhumane."[37] The resentment was reflected in provincial newspapers; a Jacksonville, Florida, paper proposed "throwing the military and naval academies into the scrap heap" and suggested that the "road to a commission in the army and navy be through the recruiting offices." Only thus, it felt, could democracy and respect for enlisted men come to the army. The *New York Times* thought this view a little extreme but did advocate a year's service as an enlisted man as a prerequisite to entrance to West Point or Annapolis.[38] None of these changes was made, and the attack on West Point during World War I never reached the level it had during the Civil War. The twin pillars that had supported the Radical Republican assault were now absent—there was no question of treason and little of incompetence on the part of West Point graduates.

Nevertheless, the criticism of West Pointers in the army was wide. The same pattern would reappear in World War II and in the Korean War; it had already shown itself during the Civil War and the Spanish-American War. Whenever the army has rapidly

[37] *Ibid.,* December 29, 1916.
[38] William A. Ganoe, *MacArthur Close-Up* (New York, 1962), 15–16.

expanded and West Pointers and civilians have been thrown into close contact in situations of stress, many of those civilians have become critics of the Academy. West Pointers do, after all, dominate the upper levels of the Regular Army and have done so since the 1850's. They are thus usually in positions of command in their relations with newly commissioned civilians. It is true, too, that Academy friendships may continue in the years beyond, that graduates might be expected to accommodate one another in many small but meaningful ways. What is most significant in this pattern, however, is the fact that the West Pointer and the civilian simply have had difficulty in communicating with each other. Their training has been different, they have in many cases a different set of values, and they speak a different language. There is misunderstanding on both sides, then impatience and anger. But of course it is the civilian criticisms that are publicized, for the West Pointer must keep his thoughts to himself.

In 1917 the most intense excitement and indignation was created among the Corps by the government's practice of awarding commissions in the Regular Army to civilians; these newly made officers would permanently rank all those cadets who had not yet graduated, and another old complaint was revived. Cadets argued that since the civilian appointees were given their commissions and then sent to Fort Monroe or Fort Leavenworth for instruction, West Pointers who already had the benefit of such instruction should be commissioned as first lieutenants upon graduation.[39] Nothing came of this suggestion, and the cadets turned to the practices of 1861 and 1898—demanding an early graduation—in order to get their commissions before civilians had filled all the choice positions. The need for officers was so great that the War Department soon complied; the class of 1917 graduated in April, two weeks after the declaration of war against Germany. The next class, scheduled to graduate in June, 1918, instead did so in August, 1917. Twenty-one members of these two classes were killed on the battlefields of France, while a number of others

[39] Tillman's report in *Annual Report of the War Department* (Washington, 1918), 1423–30.

received disabling wounds. The class of 1919 graduated one year early, leaving only three classes on the post.

In October the war was still in doubt, the army was increasing in size, and the need for officers continued. The War Department decided to graduate immediately the two upper classes at West Point, the classes of 1920 and 1921. The class of 1921, then, would graduate after only seventeen months at the Academy, and West Point would be left with only one class, the Fourth, on the post. The news, according to William A. Ganoe, then adjutant at the Academy, "hit the Post like a flash flood." The professors, the administration, even some of the cadets argued against it, but the War Department held firm, and on November 1, 1918, both classes graduated.[40] Even the plebes would not be at the Point long, for the War Department also ordered that the course be reduced during the war to one year, and the Fourth Class would therefore graduate in June, 1919.[41] They would take classroom instruction in the mornings, military instruction in the afternoons. In effect, the order changed the Academy from a military training university to a wartime military training camp for officers, not much different from Plattsburg or the other preparedness camps of 1915–16.

Nearly everyone associated with West Point was incensed by this recklessness, but none more so than the old graduates. It almost seemed that the preservation of the West Point system was more important to some of them than the successful prosecution of the war. Actually, the nineteenth-century problem of the nature of the Academy was at issue. The War Department and members of the government who pressed for early graduation thought West Point should be a practical, narrow military school. The faculty and members of the administration at the Academy preferred a more general educational institution. The problem has arisen in every American war and has never really been settled.

The philosophical questions did not concern one graduate who, when he heard that the cadets would not even graduate in their gray dress uniforms but in the army service uniform, could hold

---

[40] *Ibid.,* 1420; *New York Times,* May 16, 1919.
[41] *New York Times,* October 4, 1918.

his peace no longer. "You can't make a West Pointer in one year," he told the *New York Times,* "and that is all there is to it. West Point is one of the glorious things in American history, and it has taken more than a century to bring it to that point of perfection where it is the acknowledged model for all other military schools the world over. Just think of a West Point cadet who is not in gray!"[42]

The test of whether or not a true West Pointer could be molded in a year was never made, as no class graduated with only one year at the Academy. Two classes did graduate with only two years of training. That of November, 1918, contained 227 members, who among them compiled a record equal to that of most other four-year classes. Forty-three went on to wear at least one star, with a good smattering of major and lieutenant generals among them. The class of 1919, which also had only two years at the Academy, did equally well; its members include Alfred M. Gruenther, Anthony C. McAuliffe, Nathan F. Twining, and Albert C. Wedemeyer. At least for these two classes, the loss of two years of West Point training was not a disaster.

All classes did well in the war. In part the record graduates compiled may, as civilian critics charged, have been a consequence of West Point domination of the army, but that was obviously not the entire explanation. Whatever the shortcomings of the Academy in the years between the Civil War and World War I, and they were many, West Point had nevertheless managed to train men who successfully guided the American army to and through the battlefields of France. The simple truth was that army officers who received their first training in leading men in battle at West Point were better at that task than was anyone else. Graduates may not have been complete soldiers—they needed a great deal of practical experience after their four years at the Academy, and all of them profited from the army's post-graduate schools—but the Academy had laid the necessary basis. Secretary of War Newton D. Baker spoke to this point. "West Point again demonstrated its supreme value to the country in the hour of need," he said in

[42] *Ibid.,* November 3, 1918.

1919. "In all walks of life character is the indispensable basis of enduring success. West Point does many things for its men, but the highest quality it gives them is character, and in the emergency of the World War, our success rested on the character of our leaders."[43]

West Pointers dominated the high command during World War I even more than they had during the Civil War. Of the thirty-eight corps and division commanders in France, thirty-four were West Pointers. The three field armies were all under Academy men; the Chief of Staff was Peyton C. March, of the class of 1888; the Commander in Chief of the AEF was John J. Pershing, of the class of 1886. On the lower levels, too, West Pointers proved to be intrepid leaders. Losses per thousand among first lieutenants who were Emergency Officers serving in the theater of operations were 30.3; among West Pointers in the combat zones the figure was 195.0. For all junior officers, regardless of their assignment, the losses per thousand among Emergency Officers were 21.5; among West Pointers they were 41.9.[44] Recent graduates, such as MacArthur and George Patton on the battlefields, or Omar Bradley and Dwight Eisenhower in the training camps, led General Pershing to make a tribute to the Academy, recalling the one General Winfield Scott had made after the Mexican War. Pershing said the Academy had "justified itself a hundred times over in furnishing to this great American Army . . . the splendid men who have served . . . in the old West Point spirit."[45]

The war was over; peace and normalcy were returning. But at the Academy, all was turmoil. The winter and spring of 1918–19 brought gloomy days, marked by a return to excessive hazing, a cadet suicide, fights and bitterness among the cadets, and a War Department investigation of conditions at West Point. The administration remained in the hands of retired officers called back to duty for the war, officers determined to recover the past. An air

[43] Quoted in Baumer, *West Point,* 232–33.
[44] Forman, *West Point,* 173.
[45] Quoted in *Post-War Curriculum at the USMA* (West Point, 1945), 9–10.

of melancholy prevailed.[46] The old Corps was gone; in its place three distinct sets of young men marched about the Plain. One group wore the traditional gray, with bell-buttoned dress-coats and black-striped trousers, another U. S. Army officers' olive-drab blouses, and a third salvaged army privates' uniforms with canvas leggings and campaign hats.

The cadets wearing the gray were members of the one class left at West Point after the November graduation of the two upper classes. Those in officers' uniforms were the Third Classmen graduated in November, 1918, after less than two years at the Academy; the War Department had ordered them to return for an additional six months' instruction. Since they already had commissions (and, many of them, combat experience) they could not be treated as cadets and enjoyed a wholly anomalous status; uniformed and paid as officers, drilled and instructed as cadets, they belonged to neither category. The cadets wearing privates' uniforms belonged to the new class the War Department had ordered admitted in November, 1918. The Academy administration had decided that it would not be fair to put them through the regular plebe program, insofar as there would only be other plebes to haze and train them. It therefore decided to keep the two classes entirely separate, and emphasized the decision by making the newcomers wear privates' uniforms.[47] The West Point course was still officially one year in duration, but obviously that schedule would have to be changed, and the War Department was already preparing studies on whether the old four-year course ought to be re-employed or a new three-year course adopted.

In the spring of 1919 the Chief of Staff, General Peyton C. March, summoned to his office a young hero and recent graduate who had risen to the rank of brigadier general in the AEF. March, who had graduated in 1888, was worried about the Academy. He felt the problems of the war, early graduation, and the absence of the traditional Corps of Cadets could be overcome; the problem of a half-century of decay was much more serious. March knew

[46] *Assembly*, XXIII (Spring, 1964), 8.
[47] Ganoe, *MacArthur*, 13–19; Beukema, *The United States Military Academy*, 24.

that the Academy was far behind the times, that it was asleep, that it needed modernizing and a completely overhauled curriculum. He also realized that change would be difficult, that the professors (the "Old Guard" to younger advocates of reform) and the long gray line (the "DOG's," or Disgruntled Old Grads) would fight any change, no matter how small. What March needed was a young, progressive officer with an unimpeachable record who could combine the intelligence, persuasiveness, and tenacity necessary to effect a complete reform. His choice was Douglas MacArthur.[48]

When MacArthur entered March's office, the Chief of Staff abruptly told him that he was going to West Point to be the Superintendent. After MacArthur absorbed the information—he would be the youngest Superintendent since Thayer and had only graduated sixteen years before, so that many members of the Academic Board had been full professors while he was a plebe—March proceeded to tell him in some detail of West Point's problems. The Academy, he finally concluded, would have to be "revitalized." In June, 1919, MacArthur assumed the command. He found "the entire institution . . . in a state of disorder and confusion." His conclusion was the same as the one March had come to: "The Old West Point . . . had to be replaced."[49]

[48] *Assembly*, XXIII (Spring, 1964), 12–13; Ganoe to author, February 27, 1965, in author's possession.
[49] MacArthur, *Reminiscences*, 77–80.

Chapter XIII

Douglas MacArthur

"If Sylvanus Thayer was the Father of the Military Academy, then Douglas MacArthur was its savior." So William A. Ganoe decided, and there was much truth in what he said.[1] MacArthur rescued the Academy in a time of crisis; like Thayer, he changed its orientation, turning it from a self-centered institution that was oblivious of the society that created it into an institution alive to its responsibilities. MacArthur's challenge was essentially the same as Thayer's—to turn out graduates demonstrably useful to the United States. The country's needs had changed—it no longer required a public institution for civil engineers; it did need a cadre of professional soldiers able to lead civilian soldiers in war involving the large masses of society—but the principle remained the same. Still, MacArthur could not blindly follow Thayer. Most of his practical problems were entirely different from those Thayer faced. The Father of the Military Academy had the active support of the army and the West Point faculty, while his opposition came from outside the establishment. MacArthur had to overcome the intense and sometimes fanatical resistance of the old graduates and the Academic Board, while he found his strongest supporters among the ranks of civilian educators and commentators.

[1] Ganoe, *MacArthur Close-Up*, 167.

In the broadest sense MacArthur's task was more difficult than Thayer's, for Thayer did not have to struggle against the tyranny of the past. MacArthur's chief problem was not to formulate specific new approaches or ideas but to effect a general breakthrough. If he could do that, if he could get the Academy to recognize and accept the need for change, the need to throw out some of the antiquated methods, the rest would come sooner or later. He did do so, and that was his greatest contribution.

MacArthur found on his arrival a surly Corps of Cadets whose morale was faltering and an academic program that was badly disorganized. The cadets the War Department had admitted in 1918 had been promised graduation in June, 1919, but when the war ended, the date was delayed to 1921; in disgust, over one hundred members of the class resigned. The 1918 graduates who had been ordered back to the Academy for additional training as "commissioned officers unassigned" were furious and made no attempt to hide their feelings. The Academic Board favored an immediate return to the four-year course, but Congress fixed the term at three years.[2]

MacArthur's most pressing problem was the length of the course, and his first task, which was also among his easiest, did resemble Thayer's. MacArthur protested that the congressional attempt to save money by reducing the course to three years was misguided. "The government's expenditures for military needs are a form of national insurance from which come dividends year by year," he said. "A comparatively small outlay by the United States will serve in future wars to lessen the tremendous expense and the loss of blood for which no money can repay when the unforeseen tragedy is upon us."[3] For one of the few times in his career as Superintendent, MacArthur had the support of the old graduates and the Academic Board. They all urged Congress to reconsider, none more strongly than General Pershing, who firmly declared in a public letter to Representative John J. Morin, "Four years is none too great a time for the character forming . . . [that is] the greatest

---

[2] *Annual Report of the Superintendent* (West Point, 1919), 3–5.
[3] MacArthur, *Reminiscences*, 78.

advantage of West Point."[4] Congress gave in and allowed the Academy to return to the four-year course.

During the debate over the length of the course the *New York Times* raised what it conceived to be a related issue. In supporting the reduction of the course to three years, the newspaper declared, "We need less 'pipeclay' and less seclusion at the Military Academy—in one word, more democracy. During their four years' term the cadets see about as little of the world as the inmates of a convent. When they graduate they know little of human nature, and the only men they have handled are themselves."[5]

MacArthur agreed with everything the *Times* said, except that he could not see how it related to three versus four years, and the main trend of his administration would be to move the Academy in the direction the newspaper urged. MacArthur also found support for his ideas from the President Emeritus of Harvard University, Dr. Charles W. Eliot. In a far-reaching, yet detailed criticism, Eliot declared in 1920 that in the first place no American college should accept "such ill-prepared material as West Point accepts. Secondly, no school or college should have a completely prescribed curriculum. Thirdly, no school or college should have its teaching done almost exclusively by recent graduates of the same school or college who are not teachers and who serve short terms." Turning to results, which the Academy always cited as proof of the perfection of the system, Eliot charged that "during the Great War, West Pointers were unable to adapt to new methods in the fields of supply and procurement, because of their stifling training."[6]

Colonel James G. Steese, of the War Department General Staff, prepared a more or less official answer to Eliot. After taking up Eliot's points one by one ("The entrance requirements at West Point are about equivalent to those of the average college of the United States"), Steese concluded: "We admit that West Point is hard, and we admit that it is narrow. We consider that it is well that at least one institution should continue in the United States

[4] Baumer, *West Point,* 18–19.
[5] *New York Times,* May 21, 1919.
[6] *Ibid.,* May 9, 1920.

which holds that the duties of its students are more important than their rights." [7]

Someone in the War Department should have checked with the Superintendent at West Point before firing off an answer to Eliot. MacArthur, it turned out, not only agreed with the Harvard president but went further. In his first annual report, MacArthur explained his thinking. He assumed West Point's mission was to provide officers capable of leading men in future wars. At the Academy, it had always been thought that this unchanging mission could best be accomplished with unchanging methods. MacArthur disagreed. "Until the World's War," he pointed out, "armed conflicts between nations had been fought by . . . a small fraction of the populations involved. These professional armies were composed very largely of elements which frequently required the most rigid methods of training, the severest forms of discipline, to weld them into a flexible weapon for use on the battlefield." But all that had changed. "Early in the World's War it was realized to the astonishment of both sides that the professional armies . . . were unable to bring the combat to a definite decision. It became evident that war was a condition which involved the efforts of every man, woman and child in the countries affected."

The rousing of the nation to arms brought about an entirely different kind of army. Now officers had to lead men who represented the sturdiest parts, and not the scurviest, of society, men eager to fight who only had to be told where and how. Discipline was no longer a problem, so the old rules and methods no longer sufficed. A new type of officer was needed, one "possessing an intimate understanding of the mechanics of human feelings, a comprehensive grasp of world and national affairs, and a liberalization of conception which amounts to a change in his psychology of command." [8] Or, as MacArthur put it more succinctly to Ganoe, "How long are we going on preparing for the War of 1812?" [9]

As long ago as the early part of the nineteenth century, the Prussian Minister of War, Leopold von Boyen, had compared the

---

[7] *Ibid.,* May 30, 1920.
[8] *Annual Report of the Superintendent* (West Point, 1920), 3–5.
[9] Ganoe, *MacArthur Close-Up,* 30.

two approaches to war. "The old school places all its trust in the standing army," he said, while "the modern school believes . . . that the country cannot be defended by a standing army alone. . . . The old school believes that arbitrary authority and discipline alone makes soldiers, the new school that it is necessary for the army to follow changing civilian custom. . . . The old school wishes to consider military questions without the participation of the public; the new school holds that the defense of the state is impossible without the material and moral co-operation of the entire nation."

MacArthur announced that he intended to do away with cadet provincialism, increase cadet responsibility, especially so as to prevent as much as possible the automatic performance of stereotyped functions and develop initiative, bring the Academy into a newer and closer relationship with the army at large, substitute subjective for objective discipline, broaden the curriculum to keep it abreast of the best civilian thought on education, and in sum "deliver a product trained with a view to teaching, leading, and inspiring the modern citizen" in the next war.[10]

The Academic Board was astonished. No Superintendent since Lee had made any internal changes at the Academy without consulting the Board and obtaining its approval, and none since Thayer had even dreamed of such far-reaching changes. The Board liked neither MacArthur's methods nor his objectives. The members, senior men all (five had been professors when MacArthur was a plebe), felt themselves responsible for the integrity of the Academy; Superintendents came and went, but they stayed on. MacArthur soon faced the active hostility of a majority on the Board; his only supporters with any power in the administration were his adjutant, Ganoe, and his commandant, Robert M. Danford; and only Danford had a vote on the Board.

It was in the nature of the institution that the Board's opposition would be effective. Many years later Ganoe, who in the meantime had served for nearly a decade in civilian universities,

[10] *Annual Report of the Superintendent* (West Point, 1920), 3–5; Boyen is quoted in Ropp, *War in the Modern World,* 153.

said he had never discovered another "group so powerful and deeply entrenched."[11] The members had tenure, status, and an intimate knowledge of the workings of the Academy, while the Superintendent was a transient who was fortunate if he knew the right questions to ask. The Superintendent had one vote on the Board, which was therefore controlled by the professors. The Board had authority to determine the time allocated to each department, to conduct and grade examinations, to grant diplomas, to recommend cadets for commissions, to choose textbooks, and to suggest changes in the course of study or methods of instruction.[12]

Thus great power rested in the hands of the members of the Board, most of whom felt in 1919 that the only change needed was an immediate return to the pre-war system that had bred the great leaders of World War I. MacArthur himself quickly saw one reason for this attitude. "The professors are so secure, they have become set and smug," he told Ganoe. "They deliver the same schedule year after year with the blessed unction that they have reached the zenith in education." They did not have to compete for grants, promotions, or chairs; they had no need to fear deans, presidents, trustees, or regents. They retained their "highly respectable and regarded position by merely going along."[13]

Under the circumstances, MacArthur was at a distinct disadvantage. His personality did not help. A supreme egotist, he found it difficult to pay proper respect to the professors or to work a tone of deference into his voice when he talked to them. He badly hurt their feelings by announcing his intentions without consulting with them or asking their advice. He felt a strong sense

[11] Ganoe, *MacArthur Close-Up*, 35.
[12] John W. Masland and Laurence I. Radway, *Soldiers and Scholars; Military Education and National Policy* (Princeton, 1957), 174–76, has an excellent discussion of this problem. The authors point out that the Superintendent has a status comparable in some respects to that of a political minister who assumes control of a department of professional civil servants. If the Superintendent wants to make far-reaching changes, he must recognize that he may not be around long enough to see them through, and he has no assurance that they will be continued by his successors. The point is especially well taken if one thinks in terms of the minister in a European multiparty system, such as the Fourth Republic in France.
[13] Ganoe, *MacArthur Close-Up*, 88–89.

of mission and considered his program so obviously necessary that he never explained it fully to the Board; the members, consequently, saw him as a brash young man meddling in areas he did not understand. MacArthur understood what he was about, in fact, and had carefully studied the problems before coming to his conclusions, but the Board never knew this, and he never took its members into his confidence.

There was a certain aura about MacArthur that prevented people from getting close or really understanding him or his aims. One cadet of the time remembered, "Neither I nor the vast majority of my class ever saw the general, except when he was walking across diagonal walk, apparently lost in thought, his nose in the air, gazing at distant horizons as his publicity photos always portrayed him throughout his career." He shocked everyone with his unconventional uniform, which included a sloppy cap from which he had removed the wire stiffener and a short overcoat. Pershing had strictly forbidden such dress, so the impression MacArthur gave was that "he was not only unconventional but perhaps a law unto himself." MacArthur's habit of returning salutes with a casual lift of his ever-present riding crop added to the impression, especially since the Academy prided itself on being punctilious in matters of military courtesy.[14]

MacArthur's majestic bearing and his astonishing record of accomplishment intimidated people. He did nothing to dispel this attitude and allowed very few men to get close to him. Indeed, he took such pleasure in his own superiority that not many tried. One result was that the distance between the Superintendent and the Academic Board grew even greater. Another problem was that MacArthur knew he would be at the Academy for five years at best, and he felt a sense of urgency which was totally absent in the Board, whose members had been there for

[14] W. S. Nye to author, December 3, 1964, in author's possession. Colonel Nye goes on to point out, "Likely my impression is a superficial one, for by all accounts MacArthur was a man of superior intellect and great leadership ability. All that granted, I think it must be conceded that he was also a man of boundless ambition, and a great actor. All great men, generals included, need such attributes."

decades and would stay on long after MacArthur was gone. They saw no need to hurry. Neither understood the other.

The professors were not unaware that there were things wrong with West Point, that some traditions and practices could be defended only on the ground that they had always been. What the Board feared was that any tampering with the framework would bring the entire edifice tumbling down. MacArthur saw things differently; to him it seemed obvious that unless the building was shored up and repaired by making long-needed changes, the whole structure would rot away. Both the Superintendent and the Academic Board wanted to preserve the century-old system—MacArthur, when he assumed his duties, said, "We have to hold fast to those policies typified in the motto of the Academy, DUTY–HONOR–COUNTRY"—but their approach was so different that there was no possibility of their working together.

MacArthur did try; he made more of an effort to meet the Board halfway than it did to meet him, although both the Superintendent and the members strove to keep surface relations friendly. Only once did the deep but underlying hostility come into the open. One of MacArthur's proposals was to bring to the Academy as instructors Regular Army officers who had graduated from civilian institutions and gave promise of being excellent teachers. Like Eliot, he thought the inbreeding at West Point had gone much too far, and he suspected that the professors were bringing back as instructors those former cadets whom they had liked without making an attempt to secure the best teachers. He asked the War Department to prepare a list of those potential instructors who would meet his criteria. Then he explained his plan to the Academic Board. A stuffy silence followed. Finally, one of the oldest members of the Board delivered his opinion. The plan, he said, was a step backward. The instructor from outside simply could not fit into the section room, could not handle the cadets, could not appreciate the West Point system. It was bound to fail. As the professor sat down, MacArthur quietly pointed out that non-graduates were already instructing in the department of modern languages and in the gymnasium with great success. He continued to defend his idea, but the professor

[268]

began to interrupt more and more frequently. Soon he was cutting in on the middle of MacArthur's sentences. Finally the Superintendent exploded. He banged his fist on the table and shouted, "Sit down, sir. I am the Superintendent!" He looked around the room, then added, "Even if I weren't, I should be treated in a gentlemanly manner."[15]

Failing to persuade the professors by his arguments, the Superintendent decided to send them to civilian institutions to see for themselves the great strides that were being made in education. He himself did not inspect any civil schools, but he read widely— he was especially well versed in John Dewey's writings on education—and was aware of what they were doing and accomplishing. The professors resented the implication that they had anything to learn from civilians and resisted, but he required them to spend one month of each year at another school of their own choosing to observe and absorb new methods and ideas. The program was not a great success, but a few of the professors did admit that they had learned something.[16]

This was the age of the social sciences, and MacArthur hoped that the professors' observations at the civilian schools would persuade them to add a whole new series of courses. In time he asked the members of the Board for courses in psychology, sociology, economics, and political science, all designed to broaden the cadet's education and prepare him for his new responsibilities. The Board gave MacArthur a combined course in economics and political science—even that did not get under way for some years— and nothing else.[17] And, as if in reply to MacArthur's program, in 1920 the Academic Board stated in its report on the curriculum, "The Military Academy is intended to impart a specialized training for a specialized purpose, and this purpose is not the same as that of any civilian institution."[18]

[15] Ganoe, *MacArthur Close-Up*, 97–99; Danford, writing in *Assembly*, XXIII (Spring, 1964), 13, remembered MacArthur's expression as "Sit down, Sir, I'm talking."

[16] Ganoe to author, February 27, 1965, in author's possession; *Assembly*, XXIII (Spring, 1964), 18–19.

[17] *Annual Report of the Superintendent* (West Point, 1920), 20–22.

[18] Quoted in *ibid.*, 6.

MacArthur next tried visiting the professors individually in their offices and attending sections himself. Neither procedure had ever been employed before. Through these methods he was able to induce some professors to make some changes. In modern languages, he persuaded the professor to eliminate the past system of daily marking for those cadets who had no preparation for the particular language, thus encouraging the deficient cadets to make known their difficulties and permitting the instructors to help them. The English department put more emphasis on public speaking, organizing a course in the subject and a debate team. It also required each cadet to read two newspapers daily and discuss the day's news in the first ten minutes of class. In natural philosophy the professor agreed to allow the cadets to use a slide rule; in drawing, more time was spent on maps; chemistry added lessons on the internal-combustion engine; the department of military art and history abandoned the detailed study of the campaigns of the Civil War and substituted for them the campaigns of World War I; in history, more emphasis was placed on the Far East.[19]

The changes were coming too fast for the Academic Board, but MacArthur was winning some of the members over. In 1921 he got a majority of the Board to agree to recommend three changes: instructors should spend the first year of their appointment to the Academy at civilian universities, taking courses in the particular study they would teach; each professor would visit three separate institutions of higher education as an observer each year; to relieve the isolation, more general lectures by men of authority and reputation would be given to the entire Corps.[20] That was something, but in relation to what MacArthur had hoped to accomplish it was not very much. Owing to the hostility of the Board, the curriculum was the area in which he was least successful in his efforts to reform.

On other matters MacArthur did not need to consider the Board. Its authority was limited to the curriculum, and it was

[19] *Annual Report of the Superintendent* (West Point, 1921), 23–25; *ibid.* (West Point, 1922), 13.
[20] *Ibid.* (1921), 15–17.

outside that area he had his great successes. One of his first acts was to abolish Fort Clinton, the area east of Trophy Point where summer camp was held. It was a drastic break with one of West Point's oldest and most hallowed traditions. For over a century the cadets had gone to camp to do a little drilling in the morning, rest or gossip in the afternoon, and attend formal hops in the evening. It was a carefree life, a welcome respite after the academic year, marked by excellent food served by civilian waiters in a magnificent mess hall, by band concerts, and by guard duty pranks. Social life at the Academy revolved around summer camp, and the officers—and their wives—were shocked when MacArthur terminated it. But he was determined to produce soldiers, men who knew something of the army and of their profession beyond fancy uniforms and formal hops. During his Superintendency the cadets spent their summers at Camp Dix, New Jersey, training with Regular Army troops under the guidance of career sergeants who were delighted with the opportunity to put the cadets through a program of basic training. When it was finished, MacArthur made the cadets march back to West Point, with full gear and no help from enlisted men.[21]

MacArthur had another objective in sending the cadets to Camp Dix; he wanted to introduce them to at least a portion of the outside world. This was a major part of his program, and he did everything he could to accomplish it. When he went to the Academy, West Point was still following the system set up by Thayer, and the only time in four years that a cadet got away from the post was for summer furlough at the end of his Third Class year. There was no Christmas leave, no leave of absence. Cadets were allowed off the post only on horseback, and then they were on their honor not to dismount or halt. They had absolutely no contact with civilians. MacArthur himself later recalled the situation. "They had no opportunity to familiarize themselves with the mores and standards of people in the world without," he said, "so that when they graduated and mingled freely with their

[21] *Assembly*, XXIII (Spring, 1964), 11; Ganoe, *MacArthur Close-Up*, 33; *New York Times*, August 19, 1920.

Duty, Honor, Country

fellows, they had no common background of knowledge and awareness. They were thrust out into the world a man in age, but as experienced as a high school boy. They were cloistered almost to a monastic extent."[22]

Working from his premise that West Point was created and supported by the nation in order to provide leaders in war—officers, that is, who could lead citizen-soldiers—MacArthur did all he could to see to it that cadets came into contact with civilians. In large part, expanding the horizons of the cadets meant allowing them more privileges, something which brought down on the Superintendent the wrath of the old graduates. Unlike the Board, the alumni had no power and could only grumble or sometimes rant. MacArthur gave the cadets $5.00 a month in cash, to spend where and how they chose. He granted upperclassmen six-hour leaves on week ends, except during the summer months, when they received two-day leaves, a relative freedom that allowed them to go into New York City. "They acquire by their small business transactions and by their contact with the outside world," MacArthur explained, "the beginnings of an experience which will be of value to them when they graduate." During the spring term, First Classmen could walk out of the gates at will. All cadets were allowed to receive packages from home as ordinary mail and no longer had to submit them to a tactical officer for inspection. MacArthur gave First Classmen the status of junior officers in their social relations with the officers of the post, which meant they could make calls, attend parties, and even play cards with the officers and their wives. The three upper classes were allowed to organize themselves, electing a president, vice-president, and other officers.[23]

Nothing upset the alumni and the professors more than MacArthur's liberalization of the regulations. Allowing the cadets to enjoy more freedom struck, it was believed, at the very structure of the Academy. For over a century West Point had been a place of rhythm and harmony, a place where behavior was governed by

[22] MacArthur, *Reminiscences,* 81.
[23] *Annual Report of the Superintendent* (West Point, 1922), 7–8; *ibid.* (1921), 11–12; Baumer, *West Point,* 173–74.

strict regulations, a place that substituted order and the collective will for presumption and individualism. But it was not just the loss of serenity implicit in MacArthur's program that bothered the old grads, not just the painful knowledge that there would be times when no one in authority would know where the cadets were or what they were doing; rather they had a substantial objection. Order, discipline, and a sense of community were necessary to the efficient working of an army, and MacArthur seemed to be destroying them all.[24]

The principle was that in the army, and thus at West Point, the individual's needs must be subordinate to those of society. MacArthur was in full agreement with this basic dictum of the military ethic; what he feared was that West Point had gone too far and in its enforced conformity had lost sight of its, and the army's, duty to society. The dictum was true only in its broadest sense; in specific terms, West Point and the army had to recognize that the nature of war itself had changed, was constantly changing. Here was the crux of the matter, the proposition the Old Guard could never accept; to them only tactics changed. A new type of officer was needed, one who could subordinate his own needs but at the same time could lead civilians who had an advanced concept of their rights and who were reluctant to accept the military ethic. In fact, the citizen-soldiers often found their motivation in fighting the exact opposite of the military ethic.

MacArthur himself could say, "In many businesses and professions the welfare of the individual is the chief object, but in the military profession the safety and honor of the states become paramount,"[25] but in modern war it was not enough merely to state the theory. Officers had to *convince* civilians acting as soldiers of its necessity for the duration of the conflict, and they could never do so unless they understood the civilians. In turn, they would never understand the civilians unless they shared some experiences with them.

[24] Allen Guttmann, "Political Ideals and the Military Ethic," *The American Scholar,* XXXIV (Spring, 1965), 221–37, has an excellent discussion of the military ethic.
[25] Quoted in *ibid.,* 231.

All of this is not to say that West Pointers had, before Mac-Arthur, subscribed to some kind of *ancien régime* system of values, as was sometimes asserted. Graduates were, after all, Americans before they became cadets, and they represented their society. Even had it tried to do so—and it never did—the Academy could not have changed the cadets from Americans into professional European soldiers who scorned those who engaged in pursuits for profit. Grant, Sherman, McClellan, Halleck, and many others were extensively engaged in real estate, manufacturing, railroading, and other business activities before the Civil War. The concept of "honor" held by French officers shocked Eisenhower and the other American generals who dealt with them in 1942. And General Mark Clark used a commercial metaphor to describe one of those dealings: "Darlan was a political investment forced upon us by circumstances, but we made a sensational profit in lives and time through using him."[26] For the European professional, honor and glory may have sufficed; for the American soldier, true representative of his society, efficiency and results counted. General Matthew Ridgway, who graduated two years before MacArthur became Superintendent, opposed officers who wasted lives for "glory." He could also make the statement, "All lives are equal on the battlefield. . . . The dignity which attaches to the individual is the basis of Western civilization."[27] Nevertheless, before MacArthur, the emphasis had been placed on unquestioning obedience and the subordination of the individual to the group. And certainly there had been no attempt to introduce cadets to the civilian world which they served and from which the soldiers in the next war would come. This opportunity MacArthur tried to provide.

Part of his program was to turn out officers whom the ordinary citizen-soldier would respect. He had been greatly impressed during the war with how much better athletes among the officer corps performed than did non-athletes and with how much enlisted men admired athletes. The West Point physical fitness

[26] Quoted in *ibid.*, 228.
[27] Quoted in *ibid.*, 232.

program was already better than that offered by any college, but MacArthur decided to extend it, to the point that it eventually became an *idée fixe* at the Academy. Quoting John Dewey— "There is an impossibility of insuring general intelligence through a system which does not use the body to teach the mind and the mind to teach the body"—he introduced what he correctly believed to be "one of the most complete physical regimes in any institution in the world." He centered his program around competitive athletics, not the individual or group calisthenics which American boys have always hated. The key was a program of intramural athletics, with each company fielding a team in each sport—football, baseball, soccer, lacrosse, tennis, basketball, track and field, and golf and polo. All cadets were required to participate. The play was so rough, especially in intramural football, that the cadets came to call it "intra-murder." MacArthur was delighted with the results. "Nothing more quickly than competitive athletics brings out the qualities of leadership, quickness of decision, promptness of action, mental and muscular coordination, aggressiveness, and courage," he said. "And nothing so readily and so firmly establishes that indefinable spirit of group interest and pride which we know as morale." [28] Or, as he put it in the lines he had carved on the stone portals of the gymnasium:

Upon the fields of friendly strife
Are sown the seeds
That, upon other fields, on other days
Will bear the fruits of victory. [29]

MacArthur's success with the athletic program was offset by his failure in his dealings with Congress. He asked for two things— an extensive building program and a doubling of the size of the Corps of Cadets—and got neither. In both cases he was really too late; during the war, when Congress appropriated nearly any amount the army asked for, he might have received the money he needed for construction. He once told Danford that during the war everyone connected with West Point must have been sound

---

[28] *Annual Report of the Superintendent* (West Point, 1922), 11; Baumer, *West Point*, 188–89; *Assembly*, XXIII (Spring, 1964), 11.
[29] MacArthur, *Reminiscences*, 82.

asleep. "Here, while we spent billions on the Army, not a penny of it came to West Point!" He repeatedly asked Congress for money to build and in one report included extensive drawings of needed construction, but to no avail.[30]

He had the same experience in his attempts to double the size of the Corps. It had been increased in 1916 to a total of 1,334, but the army had also grown, so West Point was only furnishing one-third of its officers. MacArthur argued that, since the overwhelming trend of public opinion was opposed to a large standing army and preparations for war, it was all the more necessary to "increase the small leaven of professionally trained experts to train the great masses of the citizen soldiery which must be improvised in time of strife."[31] But Congress did not increase the Corps until 1935, when it allowed a total of 1,960 cadets.

MacArthur, supported and prodded by the Chief of Staff and remembering his own experiences as a plebe, made the elimination of hazing one of his major goals.[32] Others had tried to achieve this end before him, with no success. Superintendents Ernst and Mills had attempted to use the cadet officers of the First Class to control hazing by ordering them to make sure the Second and Third Classmen did not exert unnecessary authority upon the plebes, but the system never worked, for the First Classmen would not turn in their fellow cadets. Superintendent Scott tried to curb the practice through extremely rigorous regulations, which among other things gave him greater and more arbitrary power, but without the co-operation of the cadets he was helpless. Superintendent Tillman, who suffered through some unfavorable publicity when the Academy underwent a hazing investigation during World War I, also studied the problem closely. He knew that West Point had more trouble than civilian colleges with hazing because the authorities had countenanced the practice, and he charged that for the most part no "serious efforts" had been made to eliminate it. It was difficult to eradicate because tradition held that hazing had always been practiced, because each class knew

[30] *Assembly*, XXIII (Spring, 1964), 14.
[31] *Annual Report of the Superintendent* (West Point, 1921), 10–13.
[32] MacArthur, *Reminiscences*, 81.

that its predecessor had indulged in the practice, and because the alumni openly supported it. Tillman's idea, which MacArthur would appropriate as his own, was to put selected upperclassmen in charge of the plebes, giving them recognized and specified authority.[33]

Tillman did not have time to inaugurate his system, and when MacArthur took over, hazing was at its height. The barking, hissing, and snarling of upperclassmen to plebes was more than one cadet, Stephen Bird, could stand, and he committed suicide on New Year's Day, 1919. In trying to stop the practice, however, MacArthur met his stiffest resistance from the graduates, who had come to regard hazing as West Point's most hallowed tradition, and of the cadets themselves. One of his first acts was to meet with a selected group of First Classmen and ask them to study the Fourth Class orientation system and report on it. He charmed the First Classmen by treating them in a friendly, informal manner and even offering them cigarettes, which was against regulations, but he was not able to get what he wanted from them. Eventually they did draw up a pamphlet on plebe customs, listing "acceptable" and "unacceptable" hazing practices, but the upperclassmen simply would not abandon the "tradition." Hazing continued pretty much as it had since the Civil War.[34]

Perforce, MacArthur used sterner methods. One day in 1920 Commandant Danford came to see him and the two began talking about hazing. Danford recalled that early in his army career he had been at Fort Riley, Kansas, where he was given charge of some sixty recruits. Danford trained them just as he would have a plebe in Beast Barracks. After three days his commanding officer called him in and admonished him, "Mr. Danford, we do not

[33] Superintendent's Annual Report, 1918, in *Annual Report of the War Department* (Washington, 1918), I, 1423–24.

[34] *Assembly*, XXIII, (Spring, 1964), 9; Nye to author, December 3, 1964, in author's possession. Nye reports that one of his classmates who attended the meeting said later that "he thought MacArthur to be somewhat of a poseur and not very frank or sincere with the cadets." I am deeply indebted to Colonel Nye for his help on this chapter; he was kind enough to grant me a long interview, to put his comments in writing, and to give me permission to quote him.

handle the American soldier the way a Yearling handles a Plebe at West Point." Danford went on to tell MacArthur that Beast Barracks ought to be abolished; the system terrified incoming cadets, gave them and the upperclassmen who had charge of them a totally wrong impression of army discipline, and was a chief factor in the continuance of hazing. MacArthur agreed, and he and Danford worked out a new system. Beast Barracks would henceforth be run not by upperclassmen but by commissioned officers of the army, and only they would have charge of and contact with the plebes. It was a momentous change, and the alumni set up a howl, but to no avail as long as MacArthur was Superintendent.[35]

Another change in discipline came when MacArthur, with Danford's help, abolished the "skin list." Under the old system, whenever a tactical officer saw an infraction of the regulations or something else amiss during his inspections, he would make a note of the offense, something like, "Smith, T. H.—Grease spots on floor at ten A.M." Taken together, these "skins" made up the skin list, which was read before the Corps in the evening. If Smith had no excuse, he would accept his demerits; if he had one, he would carefully write it out in the prescribed form. A day or two later the tactical officer would just as carefully either accept the excuse and remove the skin or not, as he saw fit. In the latter case Smith could again file an excuse, on which the tactical officer would make another endorsement. Sometimes the notes went back and forth for weeks. Danford wanted to do away with the system, substituting for it a company orderly room on the ground floor of each barracks. There, at a stated hour each day, the tactical officer could handle delinquencies verbally, looking the cadet in the eye and treating him, as a means of teaching him the responsibilities of command, just as a company commander in the army treated his enlisted men.[36]

One of MacArthur's contributions to the Academy has since become West Point's proudest possession. It is the Honor Committee and the codified honor code. The honor system at West

[35] Ganoe, *MacArthur Close-Up*, 103–7.
[36] *Ibid.*, 120–21.

Point dates back to Sylvanus Thayer, who established the principle that a cadet's word is always accepted and consequently that a cadet is expected always to tell the truth. But neither Thayer nor his successors ever spelled out the code or established any investigating and enforcing agency. Sometimes cadets took matters into their own hands, as in 1871 when members of the First Class learned that two plebes had lied to Commandant Emory Upton. Fearful that the cadets would be dismissed by the Academy only to be reinstated by Congress, they took the guilty plebes outside the post, forced them to put on civilian clothes, gave them $50.00, and instructed them never to return. News of the incident soon reached Congress, which investigated, censored Upton and Superintendent Pitcher—both believed the First Class had acted badly but from commendable motives—and reinstated the plebes. Undeterred, the cadets organized a Vigilance Committee, consisting of representatives from each company, to continue the practice, and it continued for years.[37]

The esteem in which West Pointers hold the honor system was best expressed by a 1915 graduate, Dwight D. Eisenhower, shortly after World War II. "I think that everyone familiar with West Point would instantly agree that the one thing that has set it definitely apart from every other school in the world is the fact that for a great number of years it has not only had an 'honor' system, but that the system has actually worked," Eisenhower said.[38] But MacArthur realized that if the honor system were to continue it would have to be on some regular foundation—Vigilance Committees had a habit of changing rules in midstream. He therefore created an Honor Committee, selected by the cadets themselves, which interpreted the honor system to the Corps and brought violations into the open so that the guilty could be discharged by constituted authority. Its procedures and rules were codified, but it had no punitive power. It acted, in

[37] Ambrose, *Upton,* 72–75.
[38] *Report to the Superintendent by the USMA Committee on Service Academies* (West Point, 1949), 77–78.

effect, as a grand jury, reporting possible violations to the Commandant.[39]

The six general principles of the code are: (1) lying, quibbling, evasion, or a resort to technicalities in order to shield guilt or defeat the spirit of justice are not tolerated; (2) a cadet who intentionally violates the honor system should resign at once and offenders are never granted immunity; (3) anything to which a cadet signs his name means irrevocably what is said, both as to letter and spirit; (4) no intentional dishonesty is condoned; (5) every man is honor bound to report any breach which comes to his attention; and (6) the Corps, individually and collectively, is the guardian of its honor system.

In practice, the effect of the system is that when a cadet tells a tactical officer that his absence after hours is legitimate, his word is accepted; when sections take examinations, the members have their books before them, the instructor leaves the room, and no man cheats; when one section has an examination before the noon meal, which the members of that section take with members of another section that will take the same examination that afternoon, no one discusses the test.

Another MacArthur innovation, which again flew in the face of current American trends, was the military efficiency and conduct rating. In civilian institutions in the twentieth century the dedication was to scholarship, as opposed to the "whole man" concept of the pre-Civil War era, and a sharp distinction was made between academic grades and delinquency demerits, between scholarship and conduct. Harvard led the way in 1869 when it began to rank students on the basis of academic grades alone. Character no longer counted in grading. All that mattered was classroom performance.[40] MacArthur was aware of this trend, which was accepted nearly everywhere by the time he became Superintendent, but he did not approve of it. To him character, the "whole man," was just as important as classroom brilliance. Thus he continued to count demerits in the general standings,

---

[39] *Ibid.*, 78; *Assembly*, XXIII (Spring, 1964), 9.
[40] Rudolph, *American College*, 348.

but he went further. Military bearing, leadership and personality, military efficiency, athletic performance, and cadet participation in such activities as choir or the Y.M.C.A. all counted. Cadets were rated periodically by the other cadets in the company on their leadership ability and on other elements of military character, and by the tactical officer attached to the company. The results counted heavily in the final class standings.[41]

Before the Civil War, when West Point was a leading scientific institution, not much was said about character development there, especially since Yale, Princeton, and other such institutions were specializing in that field. After 1865, however, when the civilian institutions began to feel that the whole man could not be educated in traditional ways and simultaneously began to surpass the Academy as practical schools, West Point increasingly maintained that it was different from (and, though no one ever said it publicly, better than) the colleges because of its emphasis on character development. MacArthur approved of this emphasis—no one felt this aspect of the West Point mission more deeply than he did. But he also knew that character development could become a catch phrase, devoid of meaning, that it was difficult to define at best and had to have its roots in reality if it were to retain any meaning. He felt that cadets could be high-minded, clean-living men in an age that ridiculed such phrases, but only if they saw some meaning to those virtues and only if they saw some connection between what they were doing at the Academy and what they would be doing as army officers. The graduates feared that cadets would be contaminated by any contact with the outside world; MacArthur feared they were doomed without it. He was trying to preserve the best in the West Point system, but few understood this and even fewer were willing to rally to his side.

In January, 1922, less than three years after he assumed his duties, MacArthur learned that the Chief of Staff, John J. Pershing, was ordering him to duty in the Philippines. Insofar as he normally could have expected to stay at the Academy for at least four years, the order came as a shock. Immediately West

---

[41] *Annual Report of the Superintendent* (West Point, 1920), 10.

Point, the army, and to a certain extent the nation were alive with rumors. The most obvious explanation was that pressure from the Academic Board and the alumni had forced Pershing and the War Department to relieve the young Superintendent. MacArthur himself hinted as much when he told Ganoe that General Fred W. Sladen, of the class of 1890, was to be his replacement. "I fancy it means a reversal of many of the progressive policies which we inaugurated," MacArthur commented.[42] One young officer stated publicly that the traditionalists in the army were removing MacArthur because he was not Prussian enough.[43] There is, however, no evidence to support the charge.

The official War Department explanation was simple. It kept a roster of general officers available for foreign service, and when MacArthur's name came to the top of the list he was more or less automatically transferred to the Philippines. The explanation, though probably true, satisfied practically no one. In February a fresh rumor cropped up. MacArthur had just announced his engagement to Mrs. Cromwell Brooks, a Philadelphia widow (he married her on February 14 in Palm Beach, Florida). The story was that Pershing had also been a suitor for the hand of Mrs. Brooks and when he lost her decided to punish MacArthur by sending him to the Philippines.

"It's all damn poppycock," Pershing told reporters when asked about the rumor. "If I were married to all the ladies to whom the gossips have engaged me I would be a regular Brigham Young." MacArthur also vehemently denied the allegation.[44] Another story that reached the newspapers was that MacArthur was going to hand in his resignation from the army.[45] Nothing came of it, and in June MacArthur quietly turned the Academy over to Sladen.

The Old Guard may have had nothing to do with MacArthur's transfer, but they certainly welcomed it. In his first year as Superintendent, Salden did all he could to return to the old ways. He abolished the practice of sending the cadets to Camp Dix for

---

[42] Ganoe, *MacArthur Close-Up,* 157.
[43] *New York Times,* February 5, 1922.
[44] *Ibid.,* February 10, 1922.
[45] *Ibid.,* February 8, 1922.

the summer and instead rebuilt the old summer camp, rather smugly noting, "The experience of the summer has proved conclusively that the practice, prevailing for more than a century before 1920, of maintaining a summer camp at West Point for military instruction was based upon sound principles." In the English department, the required daily reading of newspapers was dropped. Sladen did away with MacArthur's practice of granting frequent leaves to upperclassmen and would not allow the cadets to possess cash. He returned Beast Barracks to the upper-class cadets.[46] MacArthur and his innovations, seemingly, had been safely laid to rest.

But that was not really so. MacArthur had brought a new spirit to the Academy, a willingness to experiment, to break with tradition, to question everything, that could never be shut out. Slowly his innovations would be restored, his ideas accepted. If Sylvanus Thayer dominated West Point in the nineteenth century, Douglas MacArthur dominated it in the twentieth. The chief difference was that Thayer had sixteen years in which to impose his personality and ideas, while MacArthur had but three.

[46] *Annual Report of the Superintendent* (West Point, 1923), 7.

Chapter XIV

Implementing the MacArthur Reforms

In the decade and a half from the mid twenties to the outbreak of World War II, West Point adjusted to the MacArthur program. In 1926 when General Merch B. Stewart, a combat veteran of World War I and later Commandant of Cadets, replaced Sladen as Superintendent, he immediately announced that he intended to carry on MacArthur's work.[1] His successors, most especially General William D. Connor, Superintendent from 1932 to 1938, followed the same policy. Connor had graduated first in the Class of 1897. During World War I he served on Pershing's headquarters staff and later was Chief of Staff of the Thirty-second Division. His appointment as Superintendent was especially significant because for the first time it brought the Academy into an intimate association with the leading army post-graduate school—from 1927 to 1932 Connor had been the Commandant of the Army War College. He was acutely aware of the demands that might be put upon army officers in the next world war and both at the War College and at the Academy did all he could to prepare them. During World War II many of the leading Ameri-

[1] Ganoe, *MacArthur Close-Up*, 192.

can soldiers, including Dwight Eisenhower, repeatedly expressed their thanks to Connor for what he had taught them in the twenties and thirties.

Stewart, Connor, and the other Superintendents of the period accepted the MacArthur thesis that West Point existed to produce leaders of citizen-soldiers. As a graduate of the thirties declared, the Academy "trains its men never to forget, in the easygoing years of peace, that they are the previous catalyst in the hour of survival that transforms a citizenry into an army." Even Superintendent Sladen came to recognize this principle. In 1923 he allowed the cadets to issue their own magazine, *The Pointer*. A typical undergraduate publication, *The Pointer* was a bi-weekly containing news, a great deal about athletics, humor, and cadet-written plays, poems, short stories, and essays. In a foreword to volume 1, number 1, Sladen declared, "And in that our new publication may well become a factor in guiding our students in the acquiring of experience, it will be one more help in obliterating the charge that our education is too remote from life." General Pershing, who also wrote a note for the first issue, went further. "Heretofore requirements of service have forced the Army officer to spend a large portion of his career out of touch with the everyday life of the American citizen," he said. "Today, however, the officer finds his principal mission to be the instruction and guidance of those patriotic fellow citizens who volunteer their services for the National Defense."[2]

Throughout the army there was a growing recognition of the uniqueness of the American military policy and of the demands it placed on the American officer corps. Modern war would inevitably be based upon the concept of a nation in arms, and inevitably officers would lead civilians into battle. The difference between the Americans and the continental European powers was not in the composition of their forces during war but in their policies during peace. In Europe, most young men were undergoing extensive training or participating in active reserve units all the time. When war came they were accustomed to the soldier's life,

[2] Baumer, *West Point,* 1; *The Pointer,* September 15, 1923.

willing to take orders and accept rigid discipline, and ready to march. Standing armies in peacetime had existed in their countries since the eighteenth century, and they expected to surrender their liberties when they were called to the colors. Their fathers had done so, and their fathers' fathers before them. In the United States both the tradition and the training were absent. American boys would not be called up until the last possible minute, at which time the army would expand enormously. Officers had to be prepared to take these civilians, train them, persuade them to accept discipline, supply them, and get them overseas before a single American unit could participate in combat. Europeans took years to accomplish all this preparation and were constantly practicing for the critical moment; Americans could only plan and hope that their officer corps was capable of meeting the emergency. In a real sense, the easiest task of all would be leading the men in combat; getting them to Europe or the Pacific combat-ready in a matter of months would be the difficult, not to say impossible, task.

Pershing put it well in 1923 (in a speech written for him by a young officer on his staff, George C. Marshall), when he pointed out to the faculty of the Army War College that "the one-time role of a regular Army officer has passed with the Indian campaigns. . . . In no other Army is it so important that the officers of the permanent establishment be . . . prepared to serve as instructors and leaders for the citizen forces which are to fight our wars."[3] The army met the challenge with its post-graduate schools. Institutions like the Industrial College, the Command and General Staff School, and the War College offered to army officers one of the most complete educational systems available to any professional group in the world. West Point made its most effective contribution in the department of economics, government, and history. One of the projects for which MacArthur had obtained Academic Board approval was a reorganization of the department of English and history into two parts, the department of English and the department of economics, government, and history. Professor Holt, head of the latter department and one of

[3] Forrest C. Pogue, *George C. Marshall: Education of a General* (New York, 1963), 220.

MacArthur's few supporters on the Board, was directed to double the amount of time devoted to his subjects and used the increase to introduce the cadets to all phases of the social sciences. Holt retired in 1930; his successor was Herman Beukema. A member of the famous class of 1915, Beukema was to become one of the most important members of the twentieth-century faculty. He had served on the Mexican frontier, had led an artillery battalion in France, had studied at the Field Artillery School and at the Army Command and General Staff School, and joined the staff at West Point in 1928 as an assistant to Holt. Beukema was to remain as head of the department until 1954, devoting himself and his staff to preparing cadets for their role as army officers, especially by incorporating as much as possible into his courses from the social science departments in civilian institutions.

Widely known as a geo-politician, Beukema strove to integrate the study of geography, international relations, and the economics of national security. West Point had never made an effort to train its cadets for duty with such army branches as Services of Supply, but Beukema realized that in any major conflict a key function of the army would be allocation of resources, procurement, and distribution. He felt that all officers should be aware of the complexity of total war and did what he could to prepare them. He introduced into the economics course Holt had created material on the vital role of strategic and critical raw materials, concentrating on the influence of raw materials on the economic, political, and military policies of nations. In a sub-course entitled "Resources for War of the Great Powers" Beukema used a text he had prepared from Army War College and Army Industrial College sources. In 1934 he expanded this program into a full course on international relations, adopting for use in it Brooks Emeny's text, *The Great Powers in World Politics.* In 1940 he added another course, "Economics of War." In history, Beukema concentrated on the two areas of potential American involvement in war, Europe and the Far East. In 1938 he expanded the government course from one which dealt only with the United States to one that covered the governments of the major foreign powers. His own textbook on contemporary foreign governments was adopted at a number of civilian colleges. He arranged for his instructors to take graduate work in universities near West Point, and by the time he retired all his instructors had at least a year of graduate training, while many of them held a master's degree in one of the social sciences.

Beukema was a dedicated social scientist who had much in common with his civilian colleagues. He was constantly trying to expand his department's function; to the wry amusement of the department of military art and engineering he once tried to pirate American military history and policy into one of his own courses. He gave a new breadth and depth to the cadet's education and helped to modify the orientation of the Academy. He did not turn it into a liberal arts institution, nor did he want to, but owing to his efforts cadets received as much or more training in the social sciences as engineering majors in the civilian colleges. As President Grayson Kirk of Columbia expressed it, "Beukema has been more instrumental than any other man in his generation in pulling up Academy educational standards. He has understood that, in these days when Army men so frequently become policy-makers on matters which go far beyond the military and technical fields, they must be well and deeply educated or the entire Nation may suffer."

The extent of the change at West Point can best be judged by comparing activities there not with those at the civilian colleges but with those at the Naval Academy. In 1937 Rear Admiral David Sellers, Superintendent at Annapolis, declared that "success or failure in battle with the fleet is in no way dependent upon a knowledge of biology, geology, ethics, social science, the literature of foreign languages, or the fine arts." The Naval Academy would continue to emphasize mathematics, engineering, and technical naval subjects. Two years later Captain W. W. Smith made a comprehensive study of the Naval Academy curriculum. He concluded that it was too crowded and recommended that the study of American government should be dropped, since the midshipmen had studied civics in high school. Annapolis should concentrate on preparing midshipmen for the duties of junior officers.[4]

[4] Masland and Radway, *Soldiers and Scholars,* 92–93.

That these sentiments were not entirely absent at West Point was evident during World War II; when the Academy adopted a three-year course of studies, the first subject the Board dropped was economics of war, and it drastically reduced Beukema's other courses. But he was able to recover the time, and more, after the war.[5]

Beukema was active in bringing distinguished lecturers to West Point, especially politicians and teachers of the art of politics. One of these, Sir Alfred Zimmern, the professor of international relations at Oxford, wrote Beukema after his 1938 lecture: "Having visited a great many Universities in the U.S. in the last twenty years, I should like to testify to the fact that I have seldom, if ever, encountered a group of students who struck me as having been better disciplined intellectually for the study of international politics." Professor Zimmern said that the discussion which followed his lecture "was one of the best that I have had with students of university rank anywhere," all of which was highly pleasing to Beukema, but everyone at the Academy could take pride in what followed. "It confirms me in the view I have long held," Zimmern declared, "namely, that concentration on exact studies, such for instance as engineering, is an excellent preparation for the study of international relations and the best antidote to the vagueness and sentimentalism that has been such an obstacle to the study of the subject during the last twenty years."[6]

Changing attitudes towards civilian institutions, while most evident in Beukema's department, were taking place in all areas of Academy life. Cadets and faculty members alike made frequent visits to neighboring universities and colleges to study educational techniques and course content. The Superintendents invited leading civilian educators to West Point to observe and comment. One result was that in March, 1925, the Association of American Universities listed the Academy as an "approved technological institution," and two years later the Academy joined the

[5] *Assembly*, X (January, 1952), 14–17, and XX (May, 1962), 80–81; John Elting to author, February 9, 1965, in author's possession; Baumer, *West Point*, 113.

[6] Quoted in *Report to Superintendent*, 55–56.

Association of American Colleges. These steps prepared the way for an even greater change. Since its founding, West Point had scorned the civilian degree; graduates received a commission in the army and nothing more. This practice led to some embarrassment, however, especially to young officers who wanted to enter a graduate school and had to explain why they did not possess a bachelor's degree. In 1933 Superintendent Connor obtained from Congress the right to confer on all graduates the degree of Bachelor of Science. The degree was also granted retroactively to all those who had graduated after the Academy had been accredited by the Association of American Universities.[7]

West Point was becoming more and more like the civilian institutions. Superintendent Stewart introduced the position of Dean, legalized smoking, gave the cadets a ten-day Christmas leave, and allowed the First Classmen six week-end leaves a year.[8] After MacArthur prepared the way by showing that the Academy could break with tradition and still retain its essential attributes, many new extracurricular activities were allowed. Literary-minded cadets could work on either the *Howitzer,* the class yearbook, or *The Pointer.* The Dialectic Society continued to put on an annual musical comedy; the West Point Players called on the talents of cadets interested in drama. By 1940 the Academy had a glee club, a cadet orchestra, and organizations dedicated to photography, oratory, debating, radio, chess, hunting, fishing, and skeet shooting. In 1931 the cadets organized a Cadet Lecture Committee, which raised funds through Corps contributions and brought to the Academy a wide variety of lecturers and entertainers.[9]

Like the civilian colleges, West Point also grew in size, and the building program became a major concern of the administration. In 1935 Congress raised the authorized strength of the Corps from 1,374 to 1,960. New buildings were needed to accommodate the cadets, and the Academy employed Paul Philippe Cret to design them in harmony with the pattern set by Cram, Goodhue

[7] Beukema, *USMA and its Foreign Contemporaries,* 33.
[8] *New York Times,* February 27, 1927.
[9] Forman, *West Point,* 200.

and Ferguson at the turn of the century. By 1939 the new North Barracks, the west wing of the gymnasium, the East Academic Building, the Armory-Field House, the Engineering and Ordnance Laboratory, and a large-scale housing project for faculty members had been completed.[10]

But despite the increasing attention to social sciences, more cadet freedom and activities, and a typical building program, West Point was not becoming another civilian college, distinguished only by the gray uniforms worn by the students. Cadets still spent most of their time studying mathematics and the physical sciences, still submitted to a rigid discipline, still maintained their honor system and took a prescribed course. It remained a professional college with no pretense of being a university, training its students for a specified and single task. While recognizing that the army's functions in the twentieth century were diversified and that officers would be called upon for all sorts of activities, West Point did not so broaden itself as to offer a variety of degrees or even electives. It continued to feel that its most important contribution was character development, and everyone connected with the Academy strove for the realization of this goal. West Point differed most sharply from the colleges in this dedication, the most obvious manifestation of which was the Academy's use of the word "mission." In contrast to the colleges, which seemed to army officers to be aimless and purposeless because they seldom took time to define what they were doing or why they were doing it, the Academy was constantly evaluating itself and declaring what it was about. Each department had a formally stated mission, as did the library, the athletic program, and every other agency at West Point.

For the Academy as a whole, the official mission was defined in 1940: "To instruct and train the Corps of Cadets to the end that each graduate shall have the qualities and attributes essential to

[10] *Ibid.*, 201–2. The increasing number of visitors to the Point had brought about another physical change. In 1925 the old hotel on the edge of Trophy Point was torn down and a new one, called the Hotel Thayer, was built on the southern edge of the reservation, next to the village of Highland Falls. *New York Times*, November 1 and December 6, 1925, and April 1, 1928.

his progressive and continued development throughout a lifetime career as an officer of the army. In general, courses of instruction and training will be designed to develop character and the personal attributes essential to an officer, to provide a balanced and liberal education in the arts and sciences, and to provide a broad basic military education rather than that individual proficiency in the technical duties of junior officers of the various arms which is of necessity a gradual development, the responsibility for which devolves upon the graduates themselves and upon the commands and schools to which they are assigned after being commissioned."[11]

The statement indicates the extent of the MacArthur revolution. West Point had come to realize its limitations and to accept the help of the army's service schools in preparing competent officers. The days of Michie, Bass, and Andrews, when the Academy felt it could do everything by itself, were gone forever. The Academic Board had recognized the complexity of the modern world and the modern army and had realized that all it could do was prepare a base on which the cadets could build.

But the Academy was not changing fast enough or completely enough to satisfy some of its critics. The most important of these was Colonel T. Bentley Mott. A graduate of 1886, he had served as an aide to General Merritt, had been an instructor at the Academy, was assigned to Pershing's staff during the war, and had been a military attaché in France and other European countries. In 1934 he published an attack on the Academy in *Harper's Magazine*. Citing his experience with foreign armies, Mott said West Point was too impersonal, disciplined, and rigid, that it lacked imagination, that it made no attempt to treat the cadets as human beings, and that its teaching by rote employed the worst possible method. He claimed that in the past fifty years only three professors—Michie, Robinson, and Holt—"have stood out from the dead level of mediocrity."[12] Mott's criticisms, while just as much to the point and just as damning as those Lieutenant Hubbard

[11] Quoted in Maxwell D. Taylor, *West Point, its Objectives and Methods* (West Point, 1947), 3.

[12] T. Bentley Mott, "West Point, a Criticism," *Harper's Magazine*, CLXVIII (March, 1934), 466–79.

had made in 1895, did not raise the storm at the Academy that Hubbard's had. The reason was simple: West Pointers had already accepted much of what Mott said and were trying to improve the Academy along the lines he suggested.

The civilian critics of the twenties and thirties were not so reasonable. After the Civil War most Americans, satisfied with the performance of Academy graduates in the conflict, had left West Point alone, deciding that the Academic Board knew best how to train soldiers. But following World War I many Americans were profoundly disturbed by the direction war was taking, by the manner in which it was conducted. They agreed with Georges Clemenceau that it was becoming too serious a business to be left to the generals. The post-war period in the United States was marked by a series of diverse attacks on the institution of war and on militarism, which the critics incorrectly thought was an attitude common to all men in uniform. In a great over-simplification, they traced most of the ills of the twentieth century to one cause, militarism—a word which few undertook to define. Their assumption was that if total disarmament were achieved and the soldiers eliminated, eliminated too would be the problems of the times.

Alfred Vagts has defined militarism as an "array of customs, interest, prestige, actions and thought associated with armies and wars and yet transcending true military purpose." It includes the parades, honorifics, and displays common to eighteenth-century European armies and is in direct contrast to the "military way," which emphasizes efficiency and results and has usually been characteristic of the American army. Militarism is often incompatible with the military way, for it rejects the scientific character of modern war and "displays the qualities of caste and cult, authority and belief."[13]

The American army contained some elements of militarism but not many and in any case was far from being the hopelessly reactionary institution some of its critics contended it was. Nor was West Point the institution Margery Bedinger described in 1930

[13] Vagts, *History of Militarism,* 11.

in "The Goose Step at West Point," which appeared in *The New Republic* and was a typical attack of the period. Bedinger sensed a conspiracy at West Point. She said the authorities who controlled every minute of the cadet's life had deliberately designed a program that would stifle imagination and individuality. She maintained that "the cadet is totally ignorant of modern trends in thought, undeveloped emotionally, motivated by set prejudices and burdened with a naive belief in his own importance." The authorities, she said, "aim to destroy every trace of independent thinking and seek to cast the cadet in the form of the traditional army officer—a man cherishing an attitude toward life that belongs to the dark ages."[14]

Eleven years later America entered World War II and the "traditional army officer" was put to the test. His professional performance was at least satisfactory, but more to the point, he was called upon to make countless political and diplomatic decisions. The results indicated that such officers were as thoroughly professional as any group in America, that they held no unitary political view, and that they were highly sophisticated men who were keenly aware of the political implications of their military movements. When West Pointers became involved in politics and civil affairs, they showed a remarkable astuteness and realism. In the handling of the occupation of North Africa, Italy, Germany, and Japan, in pushing troops through to Lubeck in April, 1945, to seal off the Danish peninsula from the advancing Russians, in working to get President Franklin Roosevelt to accept the inevitable and recognize and co-operate with Charles de Gaulle's government, in trying to soften the harsh Unconditional Surrender policy, and in countless other ways West Pointers gave the lie to both the notion that the Academy imposed a right-wing political philosophy on its graduates and to the concept that soldiers are devoid of comprehension of political issues. The honorifics of militarism were conspicuously absent from the United States Army. American soldiers felt no kinship with members of the officer corps of those powers where militarism held sway. They were

[14] Margery Bedinger, "Goose Step at West Point," *The New Republic*, LXIV (September 24, 1930), 144–46.

mildly amused by the Italian, disgusted with the German, and contemptuous of the Japanese officers. American occupation policies in Germany and Japan were the near-exclusive responsibility of soldiers. Whatever is said about Eisenhower's and Lucius Clay's and MacArthur's activities in these two countries, no one could contend that they exhibited fascist tendencies.

In World War II West Pointers like MacArthur, Eisenhower, Clark, Bradley, and Patton brought to the army a tactical brilliance and a strategic proficiency which, coupled with the abilities of men like Brehon B. Somervell in the Services of Supply and Lesley J. McNair in the Army Ground Forces, allowed America to raise, equip, train, transport, and put successfully into conflict a huge army. All these men were West Pointers, but much of the credit for their achievements was due the army post-graduate schools, where many of the top commanders of the war really learned their trade.

One result of the post-graduate system was that West Pointers did not dominate the higher ranks as they had in previous wars. Prejudice and favoritism remained in the army, but it was no longer that of one West Pointer for another but rather that of one Regular Army officer for another and, more specifically, of one War College graduate for another. West Pointers made up 41 per cent of the Regular Army officer corps; of the 155 division commanders or higher during the war, 89, or 57 per cent, were West Pointers.[15] A man who entered the Regular Army officer corps in World War II, either through the ranks, by direct commission, or through a transfer from a National Guard unit, stood nearly as good a chance of achieving high rank as a West Pointer. And of course Chief of Staff George C. Marshall, who was held in unusually high regard by nearly every officer, West Pointers included, was a graduate of the Virginia Military Institute.

During World War II the Academy was much more alive to the changing nature of war and to its responsibility to prepare cadets for modern combat than it had been in 1917. This alertness was most directly reflected in air training. As early as 1915 General

[15] *Report to Superintendent*, 17–18.

Maxwell Van Zandt Woodhull had recommended that the Academy give flying lessons, but nothing was done until 1927, when a hangar and a ramp were built.[16] The installation had an impressive name, Air Corps Activities Project, but its complement consisted of only three officers, three enlisted men, and one Loening Amphibian. It served only one purpose, to allow Air Corps officers at the post to maintain their flying proficiency.[17] Shortly after America entered the war, however, the program grew. Superintendent Francis B. Wilby, taking advantage of Stewart Field, a 220-acre plot 12 miles north of West Point that had been donated by the city of Newburgh, introduced an extensive course in air training. He divided the Corps into two parts, Air Cadets and Ground Cadets. About 40 per cent of the cadets chose to become Air Cadets. They followed a separate program, one which included 257 hours of ground instruction, 402 hours with synthetic training devices, such as the Link Trainer, and 205 hours in the air. They received their wings upon graduation and went directly into the Air Corps. All cadets participated in a short course in air observer training.

West Point purchased over 10,000 acres of surrounding land during the war, and Ground Cadets received an intensive tactical training. Techniques such as pontoon bridge building, ferrying, and assault boat attacks were emphasized. All cadets participated in full-scale maneuvers, usually with army divisions. Third Class cadets spent their summers at Fort Knox, Fort Benning, or Camp Davis. Beast Barracks was abolished and plebes spent their first summer receiving the same training a draftee got at an Infantry Replacement Training Center, although the plebes did it in five or six weeks instead of thirteen.

Faculty problems were enormous because Congress both increased the Corps to 2,496 and cut the course from four years to three. The faculty added more members, many of them civilians, shortened furlough time from 105 days to 31, dropped one

[16] Maxwell Van Zandt Woodhull, *West Point in our Next War* (New York, 1915), 71.
[17] Forman, *West Point*, 204.

year of English literature, and reduced the time allotted to the department of economics, history, and government.[18]

World War II was the great test of the ability of American society to organize its resources, both human and material. West Point's contribution to the successful meeting of that test was crucial. The Founding Fathers had wanted a military academy in order to avoid the expense and danger of a standing army. In World War II Academy graduates fulfilled their hopes, as the West Pointers led the way in showing that it was possible to avoid a standing army and still field the greatest army in the nation's history.

The first post-war Superintendent was Maxwell D. Taylor. Like the first Superintendent after World War I, Taylor was a brilliant young officer (he had graduated fourth in the class of 1922) with a dazzling record. He had served on the War Plans Division of the War Department General Staff, as the commanding general of the 82d Airborne's artillery, and as the commanding general of the 101st Airborne. He held the latter command during the last stages of the Bastogne battle. His combat experience was matched by his activities in the field of diplomacy. On the eve of the public announcement of the armistice with Italy he made a secret trip into Rome to make arrangements to drop the 82d Airborne on the city and secure it from the Germans but had to call off the operation at the last possible minute when the Italians got cold feet. Later, when the Allies were trying to get the Italians to declare war on Germany, Taylor was Eisenhower's representative with the Italian government and a key figure in getting the King and Marshal Badoglio to co-operate.

Taylor's tour as Superintendent was highly successful. He had one great advantage over MacArthur; he could build on the past instead of fighting it. The Chief of Staff, Dwight D. Eisenhower, was both his friend and supporter, and so was a majority of the

---

[18] *Assembly*, II (October, 1943), 3–7, has a good account of activities during the war; see also Baumer, *West Point*, 161–63.

Academic Board. Members of the Board who had been at the Academy through the war and were, like Beukema, ardent advocates of the MacArthur program had their position strengthened by the addition of a number of new permanent professors, as nine departments increased in size and added a second full professor. General George A. Lincoln was one of the new faculty members; he joined Beukema in the department of social sciences (in 1947 Beukema got the name changed from the department of economics, government, and history). A 1929 graduate, Lincoln had been a Rhodes Scholar and held an M.A. from Oxford. During the war he served on the Operations Division of the War Department General Staff and as a member of the Joint Planners Committee of the Combined Chiefs of Staff. Vincent J. Esposito, who became professor of military art and engineering, was a 1925 graduate who had served with Lincoln on the Operations Division. Esposito had also been a War Department representative at the Quebec, Malta, Yalta, and Potsdam Conferences. When he discussed strategy with the cadets, he did so with authority. William W. Bessell, Jr., a 1920 graduate, was another of the new professors who had served directly under Marshall on the War Department General Staff. All these officers, and most of the remainder of the faculty, had been cadets either while MacArthur was Superintendent or later, when his system was again in effect, and in addition had wide experience in war. Like Superintendent Taylor and Chief of Staff Eisenhower, they were all dedicated to carrying on MacArthur's work, to providing a broad education for the cadets while maintaining an emphasis on character building.

The Superintendent and the Board combined to make a number of changes in the curriculum. They dropped fencing and horsemanship, and the tactical department used the time gained to add amphibious training in close liaison with the Naval Academy. In foreign languages the old emphasis on reading and grammar gave way to concentration on speaking ability and aural comprehension. Three new languages, German, Portuguese, and Russian were added to the offerings. Nuclear physics, electronics, and communications were included in the curriculum. All cadets received a general course in aviation; those who wanted to join the Air Force had to wait until after their graduation for specialized training. The department of military art and engineering cut down the time devoted to engineering and began to emphasize the history of the military art. Advanced courses in the history of Russia, the diplomatic history of the United States, and in international economics were added.[19]

The most important addition to the curriculum, one that in a sense was the culmination of the MacArthur program, was a course in applied psychology. General Eisenhower first suggested the course. His experiences during the war had taught him that young officers tended to use empirical and ritualistic methods in handling their enlisted men, and he thought that theoretical and practical instruction in psychology would awaken cadets to the necessity of dealing with the human problems of leadership on a human basis. Taylor and the Board agreed, and in 1946 they dropped some time previously allotted to the department of tactics and added a First Class course in psychology with a civilian instructor. It concentrated on the individual psychology of the normal American citizen-soldier, military aspects of collective behavior, and the techniques of effective leadership.[20]

Vitality was everywhere evident in the post-war Academy. In social sciences top-ranking First Class cadets participated in a seminar in which they prepared policy papers on the problems of American foreign policy. In 1949 the department, in conjunction with the Cadet Forum, began an Annual Student Conference on United States Affairs (SCUSA). Students from ninety or so American and Canadian universities came to West Point for a four-day conference. Under the direction of some thirty-five senior men from college faculties, business, and government, the cadets and students met in small seminars to discuss major aspects of national security policy and to formulate policy recommendations. Guest speakers have included Nelson A. Rockefeller, Dean Rusk, John J. McCloy, Dean Acheson, Allen W. Dulles, and W. Averell Harriman.[21]

[19] *Assembly,* V (October, 1946), 1–4; *Report to Superintendent,* 109–11; *Post-War Curriculum at the USMA* ([pamphlet] West Point, 1945), 1–4.

[20] Taylor, *West Point,* 5–7; *Assembly,* V (October, 1946), 1–4.

[21] Masland and Radway, *Soldiers and Scholars,* 218; *1964–65 Catalogue, United States Military Academy,* 93–95.

The extent of the change at the Academy is best revealed in the lecture program. Before World War I hardly any speakers appeared at West Point, while in a single year after World War II, 1948–49, over forty came to give lectures. General Alfred M. Gruenther discussed "The National Military Establishment"; R. L. Eichelberger, "Post War Japan and Korea"; J. Lawton Collins, "A Concept of Future Warfare"; A. C. McAuliffe, "Army Research and Development"; L. L. Lemnitzer, "Military Cooperation and Western Europe"; and others examined various technical military subjects. Lecturers on general subjects included the professor of international relations at Oxford, E. L. Woodward, who discussed "The Meaning of the Western Tradition"; Miss Maria Tolstoy, "Leo Tolstoy—Early Years"; George Kennan, "Current Problems in International Relations"; John J. McCloy, "The World Bank"; Estes Kefauver, "Organization of the House and Senate"; and Douglas Southall Freeman, "Leadership." A series of lectures on finance included programs on investment analysis, banking in the United States, and the war economy of the Soviet Union. There were discussions of the National Guard, the Organized Reserves, and the Selective Service system. The department of military hygiene sponsored programs on anatomy and physiology, an introduction to military medicine, the strategic and tactical influence of disease in modern war, the military responsibility in civil public health, psychiatry, neuropsychiatric problems of modern war, and alcohol and drugs.[22] In short, the Academy offered the cadets a variety of outside speakers that could match that presented by most civilian institutions, while it met its responsibility to the army through both narrow and broad professional programs.

In the post-war world General Taylor, the Board, and senior army officers generally were aware that the old martial virtues were not enough any more, that army officers would be called upon to be diplomats or politicians at least as often as they would be called on to lead men in combat. They knew that the new officer had to possess intellectual sophistication and cultural maturity

[22] *Report to Superintendent,* 139–43.

and be able to cope with political and military ambiguities. Thus the emphasis on general lectures and on liberal arts courses (which by 1948 consumed 40 per cent of the curriculum) resulted.

The results were encouraging. In 1948 the First Class was tested against a control group of 1,174 senior men from forty-one liberal arts colleges. The examination was the General Education Test of the Graduate Record Exam. The average cadet general educational index was 589, while that of the liberal arts seniors was 523. Cadets did better on the average than 72 per cent of the control group; in general mathematics, cadets scored better than 93 per cent of the male seniors; in physical sciences, higher than 78 per cent; in social studies, higher than 65 per cent; in literature, higher than 67 per cent; in effectiveness of expression, higher than 77 per cent. Only in fine arts and biological science did the cadets fall below the general average, and neither subject was taught at the Academy.[23]

To meet the increasing excellence of the cadets, the faculty improved itself. Beukema's practice of seeing to it that his instructors had a year or two of graduate work in a civilian university before taking up their duties at the Academy was generally adopted, and most instructors held M.S. or M.A. degrees. As many as half were working towards the Ph.D. degree. Most departments held orientation programs or refresher courses during the summer for those instructors who were not enrolled in summer school at nearby institutions like Columbia University. The department of social sciences periodically sends an instructor to the University of Beirut to equip him to teach the history of the Near East or to Southeast Asia to prepare him to teach the history of the Far East.[24]

The upper ranks of the faculty revived the pre-Civil War tradition of creative scholarship. In the later fifties Professor Esposito published *The West Point Atlas of American Wars*, a two-volume work based on instructional maps used in the department of military art and engineering. A truly original work which includes textual matter that constitutes the best history of American wars

[23] *Ibid.*, 46–49; *Assembly*, VII (October, 1948), 2–4.
[24] Masland and Radway, *Soldiers and Scholars*, 183.

available, *The West Point Atlas* received critical praise and constituted a real contribution to scholarship. In the early sixties Esposito and his research assistant, John Elting, published a similar atlas for the Napoleonic Wars. Professor Lincoln, with the help of his staff, published an outstanding textbook that was widely adopted, *Economics of National Security*.

As Lincoln's work indicates, West Point had fully implemented MacArthur's program. Its curriculum, its faculty, and its contacts with the civilian world all matched his standards. The internal reforms that MacArthur began had now been completed, and the Academy could look to the future with confidence.[25]

---

[25] At the conclusion of World War II, West Point fought off a proposal, supported by President Truman and other high officials, to create a third academy which all cadets and midshipmen would attend for their first two years. Instead, when in 1954 a third academy was established, it was the Air Force Academy. The story of this struggle is admirably told in *ibid.*, 105–29.

Chapter XV

Football

In the fall of 1864, when the news of the capture of Atlanta reached West Point, Superintendent Zealous B. Tower allowed the cadets to fire a salute in honor of the victory, then returned them to their regular duties. One hundred years later, on November 28, 1964, Army beat Navy in a football game, 11 to 8. It was Army's first victory over Navy in six years. Superintendent James Lampert immediately announced that he was canceling all punishment tours, erasing all demerits, and giving the cadets three and a half days of extra Christmas leave.[1]

In the early 1870's Harvard, Yale, and other eastern schools began playing a game adapted from the English game of rugby. Unlike soccer's kicking style of play, a principal characteristic of the new game was running with the ball. The game, which Americans called football, caught on with remarkable rapidity, extending to all parts of the nation. By the turn of the century there was hardly a college in the land that did not have a football team to do battle for the honor of the school and the delight of the alumni. It was so widely adopted that for the first time in American history the colleges began to recognize each other's

[1] *Baltimore Sun,* November 29, 1964.

existence, and schools that had never deigned to consult each other on matters of curriculum or standards began to band together to regulate football. They were especially concerned with eligibility; so intent were some of the schools on winning that faculty members, professionals, and even college presidents were representing the college on the football field. Regulation began when midwestern colleges agreed in the early nineties to employ no more than two professionals per game.[2]

Intercollegiate football came late to West Point, although the cadets had played soccer as early as 1825.[3] Cadet James Longstreet enjoyed an occasional soccer game, and Philip Sheridan received demerits for kicking a "football" in the vicinity of barracks. In 1850 Jerome Napoleon Bonaparte, Jr., nephew of the great Napoleon, wrote his father, "The officers have presented a football to the Corps and you may depend the cadets take exercise enough now. It is amusing to hear them complaining at drill of being almost tired to death, and then as soon as drill is dismissed their fatigue passes off and they all turn out and kick football until parade. As soon, however, as they put on their belts for parade, they suddenly become tired again which lasts until after supper when they rest themselves by kicking the ball as hard as they can until call to quarters."[4] But thus far American football was practically unknown at the Academy, despite its great popularity among the colleges. In 1890 only two cadets had ever played the game. One of them was Professor Michie's son, Dennis Mahan Michie.

Young Michie, who had been born at West Point and spent his childhood there, had played football at prep school before entering the Academy. He was on familiar terms with the officers; a classmate related the story of walking across the Plain one day with Michie when they met Lieutenant Daniel Tate of the tacti-

[2] Rudolph, *American College,* 373–75. One of West Point's greatest players, Charles Daly, had been on the varsity at Harvard for three years before he went to the Academy in 1901. He played for three years at West Point and made Walter Camp's All-American team from both schools.

[3] Heintzelman Diary, October 5, 1825.

[4] Tim Cohane, *Gridiron Grenadiers: The Story of West Point Football* (New York, 1948), 6–7.

cal department. After the exchange of salutes, Tate said, "Hello, Denny." Michie answered, "Good morning, Danny," while his classmate gaped. Michie's father, a conservative old man resistant to innovation, headed the Academic Board and was the most powerful man on the post. He doted on his son and was likely to grant his every request. Young Michie arranged for some midshipmen friends to send a challenge to West Point for a football match; when it arrived, in the fall of 1890, Michie took it to his father and, arguing that a challenge from the Navy could not be ignored, persuaded the professor to agree to the game. It was scheduled for November 29.

Navy had been playing football for a number of years; at West Point, besides Michie, only Cadet Leonard M. Prince had ever played before. Michie undertook to coach the team, but Superintendent John M. Wilson only allowed the cadets to practice on rainy Saturday afternoons when no parades could be held. On the Saturday of the game the midshipmen appeared on the field, which was the southeast corner of the Parade Ground, and to the astonishment of their opponents began a series of organized calisthenics. The cadets were further surprised during the game when Navy called out its plays in nautical commands: "Clear decks for action," "Helm's a lee," "Reef top sails." The cadets soon picked the method up, and captain-coach Michie would call out, "In Battery, Heave," "Left Wheel," "Forward Guide Center." In the middle of the game there was a great cry of indignation from the officers and professors standing on the sidelines when a Navy man, back to punt, instead ran with the ball for a touchdown. The Army rooters contended that as an officer and a gentleman he should have kept his promise to punt, and they demanded, to no avail, that the officials recall the play. In the end the Navy wedge proved too much for the inexperienced cadets, and Navy won, 24 to 0.

The result of the game was widely reported, and at West Point and at army posts throughout the country the demand for a rematch, to avenge the defeat, was overwhelming. Every regiment in the army sent in a contribution to buy uniforms, hire a coach (Harry L. Williams, former Yale star), and pay the team's way to

Annapolis. In 1891 Army had a full schedule of six home games, of which it won four, but already only the Navy game really counted. Superintendent Wilson agreed to allow the team to go to Annapolis on Friday night, although he almost canceled the game when Michie informed him that substitutes were needed and that seventeen, not eleven, cadets would make the trip. When army officers heard that the game was to be played in Annapolis, some of the older ones had second thoughts. Seventeen men would miss an afternoon of recitation, an evening study hour, a morning inspection, a dress parade, and chapel. "The nation will pay for such idle indulgence on some future battlefield," one roared. Former Cadet James McNeill Whistler was disgusted at the whole idea of the Academy's fielding a football team. "They should hold themselves apart and not allow the other colleges and universities to dispute with them for a ball kicked round the field," he said. "It is beneath the dignity of officers of the United States."

Young Michie's influence with his father was sufficient, however, and the seventeen made the trip. One of the substitutes was detailed to send a telegram back to West Point after each score, but in the second half he got too excited and forgot, leaving the cadets still on the post in suspense. They finally got the result from a New York newspaper—Army 32, Navy 16.[5]

In 1892 the game was played at West Point, and in 1893 at Annapolis, Navy winning both games. After the 1893 game the new Superintendent, Oswald H. Ernst, made a detailed study of football and its place at the Academy. West Point graduates, he noted, were taking an intense interest in the fortunes of the "army" team.[6] Scores and play-by-play accounts of the games were printed in the *Army and Navy Journal,* and at officers' clubs around the nation the Army-Navy game was for months the only topic of conversation. It was considered a disgrace to be able to talk the day after a game; it was an honor to be so hoarse that one could not speak for a week.

[5] John M. Palmer, "Football at West Point," *Assembly,* I (January, 1943), 2–4; Baumer, *West Point,* 196–200; Wilson to Schofield, November 25, 1891, SLB.

[6] Ernst to Adjutant General, December 12, 1893, SLB.

What Ernst did not say was that in all this West Point graduates and cadets were not in any way atypical. All through the United States, alumni, whose tradition of collegiate rivalry had been rooted in a denominational fervor that had long ago waned, found their substitute in football. As a Bowdoin alumnus put it in 1903, when confronted with a 16 to 0 defeat by the University of Maine: "In my day the University of Maine was a standing joke. . . . We got licked to-day because we hadn't the stock—the stock, sir. . . . Old Bowdoin must fling wide open her gates and get some—some stock, sir." [7]

Ernst continued his review by noting that when he came to West Point, in the spring of 1893, plans for the coming season, including the scheduling of games and the employment of civilian coaches, had already been made. He learned nothing about the plans until September, and then in a casual way—no one ever thought to consult the Superintendent, whose sole authority over football consisted of approving the biennial trip to Annapolis. [8] Football at the Academy was controlled by the Army Officers' Athletic Association (changed in 1910 to the Army Athletic Association), a voluntary, self-supporting alumni group. The Association financed all intercollegiate competition, including a guarantee to visiting teams (except for the Navy game, West Point's games were at home), arranged schedules, purchased equipment, hired and paid coaches, and constructed athletic fields. The same thing had happened everywhere else; throughout the United States, alumni groups controlled football because neither the faculty nor the administration would have anything to do with it.

Ernst, a graduate of 1864 and a Civil War veteran, was shocked to find that there was anything going on at West Point, much less something of the magnitude of football, that the Superintendent not only did not control but did not even know about. After reflection, however, he allowed the games to be played, more or less as an experiment. At the end of the season he found that football had no discernible effect upon scholarship; as to dis-

---

[7] Rudolph, *American College*, 383.
[8] Ernst to Adjutant General, December 12, 1893, SLB.

cipline, "The surplus animal spirits of the young men finding a vent in foot-ball are much less likely to find it in mischievous pranks. Upon the whole I conclude that the game is an aid to discipline." The game, although rough, was not brutal and posed no danger to life and limb, so Ernst favored its continuation.

The Navy game was a different matter. He found that it "has undoubtedly for some days a bad influence. The excitement attending it exceeds all reasonable limit." He feared the excitement would continue to grow, that the game would be marked by increasing bitterness and would hurt relations between the two services. He recommended, therefore, that while football continue, the game with Navy be discontinued.[9]

The Secretary of War was favorably disposed towards Ernst's recommendation. He had just learned of a brigadier general and a rear admiral who got into such a heated argument at the Army-Navy Club in New York about the 1893 game that they almost arranged a duel. He also knew, as did the Secretary of the Navy, that acrimonious disputes about the game were not uncommon, so the two Secretaries decided to cancel it by the simple expedient of ruling that neither team could leave its grounds for a game. Thus the academies could continue to play football but not each other.[10]

Despite the loss of the Navy game, Army football prospered during the nineties. The giants of the East, Harvard, Yale, and Princeton, came up the Hudson to play, while Union, Brown, and Amherst helped complete the full schedule. Ernst managed to get the Secretary of War to detail recent graduates who had played football to the Academy, where they helped coach the team.[11] He allowed a New York newspaper to install a special telegraph line so that the results of the game could be wired immediately to New York. From there they were sent to the various army posts. Already the Academy officials were discovering the public relations possibilities inherent in football; never before had West

[9] *Ibid.*
[10] Cohane, *Gridiron Grenadiers*, 26–27.
[11] Ernst to Adjutant General, July 15, 1896, SLB.

Point been so widely noticed.[12] By 1897 Army was the fourth best team in the nation, which prompted a number of magazine articles on the Academy and countless newspaper columns.

The hired coaches, alumni control, and general enthusiasm for football at West Point all placed it in the mainstream of the sport's development in the United States. In a number of ways, however, the Academy stood apart. At most of the colleges the coaches set no limits of principle in their efforts to win, while the presidents, trustees, and faculty members looked the other way. At West Point, Superintendent Ernst and the other officials kept a tight control over the players. The Army Officers Athletic Association had to pay all the bills, as Ernst refused to put up stands or charge admission to the games—spectators stood along the sidelines.[13] Ernst would not allow a cadet who was deficient in any section to participate, and no one even dared raise the question with him of special inducements to persuade outstanding athletes to come to West Point. The only privileges the players received were some time off for practice—four Saturday afternoons in September and an hour before supper on Wednesday—and a modest training table supported by the Army Officers Athletic Association. The players supplemented their practice session by running around the post each morning before reveille, and each day after dinner the center practiced snapping the ball to the quarterback for twenty minutes. All this, however, had to be done in full cadet uniform. By contrast, the colleges were doing everything possible to attract athletes, giving the players numerous special privileges, and practicing for more than two hours every day. Despite the differences, in 1897 Army beat Trinity, Wesleyan, Tufts, Lehigh, Stevens, and Brown, tied Yale, and lost only to Harvard. In the last game of the season Army beat Brown, 42 to 0, and, although it had had a total of only ten practice sessions all year, did not fumble once.[14]

In 1897 the Republicans moved into the White House, and the new Secretary of War, Russell A. Alger, wanted to restore the

[12] Cohane, *Gridiron Grenadiers,* 26–27.
[13] Ernst to Miss Mason, November 1, 1896, SLB.
[14] "Football at West Point," *Harpers Weekly,* XLII (January 1, 1898), 22.

Army-Navy game. Superintendent Ernst was adamant. "The excitement of that match is unhealthy," he said. "It passes all reasonable limit." Ernst felt "we are getting all the good there is in foot-ball, with none of the evils of which so much is heard elsewhere. . . ."[15] The game was not resumed until Ernst left West Point. His successor in 1898, Colonel Albert L. Mills, finding the pressure for the game overwhelming, agreed with Alger, and the next year a game was arranged.[16]

In the 1899 renewal the game began to take on what have become its traditional trappings. Instead of being played at one or the other academy, it was held at Franklin Field, Philadelphia. Tickets were sold through the Army Officers Athletic Association. Superintendent Mills gave twenty tickets to the President of the Pennsylvania Railroad, who in return offered free transportation to the game to the entire Corps of Cadets. "The proposed outing," Mills told his superiors in the army in asking permission to make the trip, "will be a pleasant and beneficial one for the cadets who elect to go. . . ."[17] As it turned out, they all went, to see Army defeat Navy, 17 to 5.

By 1901 the 25,000 seats in Franklin Field did not accommodate all those who wanted to see the game, and ticket speculators were selling seats for as much as $40.00 each. The Secretary of War felt it necessary to send a telegram to the Army players, calling on them to exercise "only the most gentlemanly conduct." The Secretary of the Navy sent a similar telegram to the midshipmen.[18] Government officials, army and navy officers, and representatives of Philadelphia and Washington society were there, as was President Theodore Roosevelt. He sat on the Navy side of the field for the first half, then walked across the field to the Army side for the second half. The Army star that day was one of its great players, and later coach, Charles Daly. Among his other heroics, he ran a kick-off back one hundred yards for an 11 to 5 Army victory. Roosevelt went to Superintendent Mills after the

[15] Ernst to Secretary of War, August 23, 1897, SLB.
[16] Mills to Secretary of War, February 9 and May 19, 1899, SLB.
[17] Mills to Adjutant General, November 2, 1899, SLB.
[18] Treat to team, November 19, 1901, SLB.

game and boomed, "Extend my congratulations to your boys, and particularly to Daly. And tell Daly I said this was a great day for the Irish."[19]

Roosevelt's interest in football was keen. In 1908, when Harvard was having a poor season, the coach decided that he could use the help of Lieutenant Ernest Graves, a former Army lineman stationed at Washington barracks, as an assistant. The Army refused to detail him to Harvard, so the coach sent some Harvard alumni to visit the White House. They told Roosevelt, "Mr. President, if the colossus of Yale football is to be leveled, an imperative condition is the presence of Lieutenant of Engineers Graves to coach the Harvard Linesmen this fall, at least for a few weeks." Roosevelt gave them a note to take to Secretary of War William Howard Taft. "Dear Mr. Secretary," it said, "I was a Harvard man before I was a politician. Please do what these gentlemen want." Roosevelt took particular pleasure in detailing Graves because Secretary Taft was a Yale man. Harvard beat Yale that year, 4 to 0.[20]

Roosevelt liked football for the same reasons that most of the rest of the nation did; it was strenuous and exciting but restricted by rules that made sure it was marked by fair play and allowed the best team to win. It seemed the perfect game for Progressive America. These sentiments were challenged in 1905, however, when eighteen boys died playing the game. Roosevelt thundered that if the colleges did not clean up football he would abolish it by executive order. "Brutality and foul play should receive the same summary punishment given to a man who cheats at cards." He ordered the coaches of Harvard, Yale, and Princeton to the White House, which put them in the same category as the presidents of the Philadelphia and Reading Railroad and the United Mine Workers, and told them to make sure the game was "played on a thoroughly clean basis." The Presidential voice, however, proved larger than the Presidential stick. Nothing effective was done, and more deaths occurred.[21]

[19] Cohane, *Gridiron Grenadiers,* 43–46.
[20] *Ibid.,* 70.
[21] Rudolph, *American College,* 375–76.

There was talk of abandoning the sport, but football had too much to offer to be abandoned. America's first popular contact sport, it delighted a nation worried about softness owing to material plenty. A blend of teamwork and individual initiative, the game itself seemed to symbolize the competitive struggle out of which progress came. It turned boys into men; as Roosevelt put it in a 1907 speech to a Harvard audience, "As I emphatically disbelieve in seeing Harvard, or any other college, turn out mollycoddles instead of vigorous men I may add I do not in the least object to a sport because it is rough."[22] The paraphernalia that surrounded the game added to its appeal—pretty girls, fall color, marching bands, the opportunities it offered alumni to get together with classmates, the joy of victory. One West Pointer remarked in 1901, "When a cadet of today graduates, he does not carry with him a feeling of bitterness toward the Academy, as in the pre-athletic period. In his mind he bears memories of recreations and athletic triumphs which softened the asperities of his student life."[23]

But if Roosevelt and the rest of the Progressives, indeed the rest of the nation, did not object to roughness, they did to foul play, which had increasingly become football's chief characteristic. In 1909, during the Army-Harvard game, Cadet Eugene Byrne died of a broken neck. His death was the fifteenth of the season, which was barely half over. Army canceled the remainder of its games and it seemed for a time would never play football again. But that winter significant rules changes were introduced. Interlocking interference, which had been the cause of Byrne's broken neck, was prohibited, as was assisting the runner by pushing or pulling him. Seven men were required on the line of scrimmage, which eliminated the V, crawling was prohibited, and more leeway was afforded the forward pass. The playing time was divided into four fifteen-minute quarters, and freer substitution was allowed. Previously when a player left a game he had to stay out, so coaches kept their regulars in all the time. Under the new

[22] *Ibid.,* 376.
[23] Cohane, *Gridiron Grenadiers,* 45.

rules, which made possible a faster and less dangerous game, West Point decided to continue the sport.[24]

In the meantime it had been adding others. Cadets had been playing baseball since Abner Doubleday's era, and in the eighties class teams were formed. In 1890 these teams banded together to play three games, against the Merriams of Philadelphia, the Sylvans of New York, and the Atlantics of Governor's Island. In 1891 the inevitable challenge from Navy came, and with Superintendent Ernst's blessing the game was played and the series begun. Army won the game, 4 to 3, when its left fielder, Douglas MacArthur, walked, stole second, went to third on a wild throw from the catcher, and scored on a bad throw from center to third. The next year the baseball team had a full intercollegiate schedule.[25] Another innovation of 1902 was a track and field day, with teams from each class competing. Within a few years Army was holding meets with other schools. In 1903 Master of the Sword Koehler bought some hoops and a ball and formed an Army basketball team. In its first game, against the Yonkers Y.M.C.A., Army won, 54 to 10. The star of the team, who was also its manager, was Joseph W. Stilwell. In 1906 Stilwell returned to West Point as an instructor and assumed the duties of coaching the basketball team. The Army-Navy basketball series began in 1920.[26]

MacArthur and Stilwell were not the only Army athletes to go on to fame. Before he hurt his knee in the middle of the 1912 season, Dwight David Eisenhower was a regular halfback on the football team; he later became a cheerleader. Omar Bradley, a member of Eisenhower's 1915 class, was reputed to have the finest throwing arm of any outfielder in Army baseball history. George S. Patton, Jr., of the class of 1909, set a record in the 220-yard low hurdles and was a football player until he broke both arms as a Yearling. Malin Craig (1898), the Chief of Staff of the Army from 1935 to 1939, was a football halfback noted for his ability to make drop-kicks on the dead run. William D. Connor, Superintendent

[24] *Ibid.*, 62–63.

[25] Mills to Adjutant General, April 24, 1901, SLB; MacArthur, *Reminiscences*, 26.

[26] *Assembly*, III (April, 1944), 4–5.

of the Academy from 1932 to 1938, played halfback beside Craig. When he returned to West Point, Connor wore a little gold football on the blouse of his uniform to show how much he loved the game.[27]

Eventually West Point added nearly the entire repertoire of intercollegiate sports, some fourteen in all, but football always remained pre-eminent. A filler in *The Pointer* showed how much the cadets were imitating the college students. It said, "Talk Football! Think Football! Dream Football!" The sport received a boost when MacArthur became Superintendent. In 1918, because of the war, no games were played; in 1919 MacArthur revived the full schedule. He was a great enthusiast for the game and attended every practice session, jauntily striding up and down the practice field, waving his riding crop vigorously. As a part of his program to broaden the cadets' outlook by bringing them into closer contact with civilians, MacArthur arranged games away from West Point, with the entire Corps attending. Previously football trips had been limited to the Navy game, played either in Philadelphia or New York; under MacArthur the Corps traveled to games at Yale, Harvard, and Notre Dame.

Through its rise into the ranks of the major teams, West Point managed to avoid most of the evils that surrounded the sport elsewhere. The players ate at a special table, where they received special food, but in most ways they could not be distinguished from other cadets. At many of the colleges and universities the best of the backs were driving convertibles and taking physical education programs set up especially for them. At West Point the backs were walking punishment tours for hours on end and taking the same classes everyone else took. Other institutions went beyond all bounds to attract outstanding athletes, bidding for them on the marketplace as for beef on the hoof and lowering or abolishing standards to get them into school. West Point, especially during MacArthur's Superintendency, did try to persuade congressmen to appoint athletes, but they were offered no extra inducements to come to the Academy and had to pass the same

[27] Maher, *Bringing Up the Brass,* 158, 170, 121–22.

entrance examination everyone else did. At the colleges the players were segregated in special dormitories, and their class-mates seldom if ever saw the players who represented their school on Saturdays. At West Point the athletes lived in the barracks with the rest of the Corps.

In another way the Academy departed from the norm. The twenties was the Golden Age of Sport in the United States; to meet the insatiable appetite of the public, universities in Wiscon-sin, Michigan, Illinois and elsewhere built huge stadiums, capable of seating the student body, every living graduate, and the entire population of towns like Madison, Ann Arbor, or Urbana. Super-intendent MacArthur wanted to do the same thing at West Point and made plans for a stadium seating one hundred thousand. Nothing came of it, however, and when the stadium was finally built, in 1924, it blended with the Point landscape and made no concessions to size. Named Michie Stadium, after the first Army football captain, who had been killed in the Spanish-American War, its seating capacity was only sixteen thousand. Its beauty, however, exceeded that of any of the others. Situated just south of old Fort Putnam, in a natural amphitheater near Lusk Reser-voir, its shape was that of a square-cut letter C. The field ran north and south; the main stands were along the west side, which allowed the spectators to look out and down, to the reservoir, the knoll, the brick quarters, the Cadet Chapel, and the hills and mountains on the opposite bank of the Hudson. No more beauti-ful spot from which to watch a football game could be imagined.[28]

Army did well in its new stadium. Through the twenties and the thirties it won many more games than it lost; in 1933 an otherwise perfect season was spoiled only by Notre Dame in the last game, with a loss of 13 to 12.[29] The early forties were not so happy; in 1940 Army failed to win a single game. Then, in 1944, Colonel Earl Blaik, the head coach, assembled what was perhaps the finest college football team in history. Over the next three years Army went undefeated; during that period it accumulated a

[28] *Assembly,* XXIII (January, 1964), 9.
[29] James S. Edson, *The Black Knights of West Point* (New York, 1954), gives the year-by-year record of Army football.

total of ten All-American selections—Felix Blanchard (B), Glenn Davis (B), Joe Stanowicz (G), John Green (G), Doug Kenna (B), Barney Poole (E), De Witt Coulter (T), Henry Foldberg (E), Albert Nemetz (T), and Arnold Tucker (B). Using the modern "T" formation copied from the Chicago Bears and first used in college play by Notre Dame in 1942, Army rolled over opponents like Pittsburgh (69 to 7), Pennsylvania (62 to 7 and 61 to 0), Villanova (83 to 0 and 54 to 0), and Duke (27 to 7 and 48 to 13). In 1944 it defeated Notre Dame for the first time since 1931 by a score of 59 to 0 and Navy for the first time since 1938 by 23 to 7. After the Navy game the team received a wire from the Pacific: "THE GREATEST OF ALL ARMY TEAMS STOP WE HAVE STOPPED THE WAR TO CELEBRATE YOUR MAGNIFICENT SUCCESS. MACARTHUR."[30]

Blanchard and Davis became the two most celebrated young men in the country; when they graduated Hollywood made a movie about them. Blanchard was a big, fast fullback, and probably the better football player of the two; Davis was the better athlete. One spring Saturday in 1947 Davis, the captain of the Army baseball team, in a game against Navy, singled, stole two bases, scored a run, and played an outstanding game in the field. After the game he went over to the track to enter the meet against Navy; for the first time in college he ran the 100-yard dash, winning it in 9.7 seconds. After a short rest he entered the 220-yard dash, again for the first time, and won it while setting a new Academy record of 20.9 seconds.[31]

The climax for the great Army team came in the 1946 game against Notre Dame. Army had won the games of 1944 and 1945 by lopsided scores, but Notre Dame followers insisted that was only because their best players were in the service. In 1946 they were all back, ready to end Army's three-year winning streak. The build-up for the game was enormous. Thousands and thousands of words were written about it, for weeks in advance. One million requests for seats were turned back; end-zone seats in New York's Yankee Stadium were sold for $300. Army was ranked first among the nation's college football teams, Notre Dame second. Army

[30] Cohane, *Gridiron Grenadiers*, 263.
[31] Maher, *Bringing up the Brass*, 166.

had lost some of its '44 and '45 players, but Davis and Blanchard and Tucker were still there; Notre Dame had, among others, Jim Martin, George Connor, Terry Brennan, and John Lujack, all All-Americans. Billed as the Game of the Century, it was technically a well-played game. But it was not very satisfying to anyone, because the final score was 0 to 0.[32]

Immediately after the game the Academy and Notre Dame jointly announced that, after 1947, the series would be discontinued. It was really an Army decision. Superintendent Maxwell Taylor felt the game was not adding to the purpose of intercollegiate football at West Point, which was to provide recreation for the Corps and to enhance the position of the Academy in the eyes of the nation. From his point of view, there was scarcely anything acceptable about the Notre Dame game. Because of Notre Dame's position as the outstanding college team in the country, Army players and their followers were more interested in the Notre Dame game than they were in the one with Navy. Army could never hope to play Notre Dame consistently on even terms; of the thirty-four games played, Army won only seven. Huge amounts of money were being bet on the game, and it was proving to be especially attractive to ticket speculators. Most important, the game was taking on the overtones of being a match between the Catholic Church and the United States Army. So the series was ended.[33]

In 1947 Columbia broke Army's win streak at thirty-two, and Notre Dame also beat Army that year. The team won the last two games of the season and went undefeated for the next two years. By the time of the Navy game in 1950, Army had won twenty-eight in a row; Navy stopped the streak with a 14 to 2 upset. In all, from 1944 through 1950, Army had won seventy and lost three. By all indications it would be even better in 1951.

Then, in the late spring of 1951, Superintendent Frederick A. Irving discovered that mass violations of the honor code were

[32] Jim Beach and Daniel Moore, *Army Vs. Notre Dame* (New York, 1948), 271–79.
[33] Cohane, *Gridiron Grenadiers*, 307–8. The series was resumed on a home and home basis in 1965.

occurring in the Corps, principally among the football players and cadets who were assisting them. A special board was appointed to investigate the situation. Its chairman was Judge Learned Hand; the members were General Troy Middleton, president of Louisiana State University, and General Robert M. Danford, the former Commandant of Cadets. The Board found that cadets were violating the honor system by passing on questions asked in examinations to football players who would be taking the tests later. Feeling that the moral confidence of the country would be endangered if there were any compromise of the honor of men who led others in battle, the Board unanimously recommended that the Academy discharge some ninety cadets, including a large number of football players. Hand called it the most painful decision of his life.[34] In early August, Irving announced that the ninety cadets were being discharged (eventually they were allowed to resign).

The scandal touched off a nationwide discussion on honesty in American life. The profiteering of the Korean War, bribery in college basketball, the fur coats and deep-freezes of the Truman administration had shaken the nation, but they all paled beside the cheating at the Military Academy. Nothing ever illustrated quite so clearly how high was the pedestal on which the public had placed West Point as the reaction to the scandal. Shock was followed by disbelief, which was followed by anger. Senator William J. Fulbright proposed that intercollegiate football be abolished at West Point and Annapolis.[35] A young congressman from Massachusetts, John F. Kennedy, demanded an entirely new method of appointment of cadets.[36] There was talk of abolishing the Academy. West Point graduates were furious. The post was overrun with newspaper and magazine reporters, who quickly telegraphed back to New York City anything any cadet said, no matter how banal.

Cadet Harold J. Loehlein, the captain-elect of the football team and president of the First Class, did not help matters when, as one

[34] *New York Times,* August 4, 1951; *Time,* August 31, 1951.
[35] *Life,* August 13, 1951.
[36] *New York Times Magazine,* August 19, 1951.

of the discharged cadets, he tried to justify what he and the others had done. He said there would not be many football players or even students in the state universities if everyone who cheated were dismissed. "Everyone should realize that what we have done takes place in many universities and colleges," he said, and he added that the practices had been going on for years at West Point.[37] The point Loehlein missed was that the Academy claimed to be different.

As the situation became clearer and the discussion more detached, sympathy for the discharged cadets and an understanding of what had happened replaced the anger. Colonel Blaik led the way in a newspaper interview in New York City. Blaik, whose son was a star football player and one of the discharged cadets, pointed out that the players were "unbelievably fatigued" after their hours of practice but still had to face the iron scholastic schedule non-players did. The pressure on them to win, especially from old graduates, and the high morale of the team caused some of them to put winning above the reputation of the Corps as a whole.[38] There was, graduates and commentators recognized, much truth in what Blaik said. All across the nation alumni, with their unrestrained interest in football and their demands for more and more victories, were putting pressures on the coaches and administrations that could not be resisted. It was no different at West Point, and the players knew it. The cadets who cribbed were not the only guilty ones.

Criticism soon shifted away from the discharged cadets and onto the Academy itself, its system, its graduates, and its friends. *Time* magazine pointed out that for years "civilian alumni" had payed the salaries of instructors in a cram school operated during the late spring on Academy grounds. A dozen or so high-school football players were among those selected to attend the school, which helped them pass the West Point entrance examinations. Army officers were wrangling appointments from congressmen for boys chosen as good football material, all for the "honor" of the

[37] *New York Times,* August 6, 1951.
[38] *Time,* August 20, 1951.

Academy. The honor system itself was attacked as being too tempting. At Annapolis, *Time* pointed out, the honor system was tempered by providing proctors at examinations and by giving different examinations to midshipmen in the same class but in different sections.[39]

The Academy was inept in its handling of the case, and a number of legal problems were involved. The discharged cadets, who technically had resigned (they claimed their resignations were forced), had not been represented by counsel, did not know what they were accused of, and did not have a chance to explain themselves before the Honor Committee. Although their names were not made public, because many of them were football players it was obvious who they were. They were thus branded as cheats without having their day in court. They claimed the practice of passing on examination questions had been going on for years, which if true meant that a number of army officers then fighting in Korea were just as guilty as they. Cadet Harrison Travis told one reporter, "A lot of men who come in as plebes learn about the honor code violations and just think it is natural and fall into it." They also maintained that over two hundred cadets then at the Academy were guilty but that those who had lied to the Board were let off.[40]

The whole thing was, in truth, a mess. It was impossible to assign blame adequately or fairly. In the confusion, surrounded by many conflicting opinions and contradictory advice, the Corps of Cadets itself made the one clear statement. All of the explanations, which were in many ways valid, all of the sympathy for the discharged cadets, which was mostly justified, could not hide the fact that West Point's most prized possession had been soiled. In the final analysis, no one forced any cadet to cheat. Speaking for the Corps, in the alumni magazine *Assembly,* Cadet David C. Ahearn said, "There is no sympathy for the guilty cadets to be

[39] *Ibid.*

[40] *U.S. News and World Report,* August 17, 1951; *New York Times,* August 5, 1951; *Life,* August 13, 1951; *Time,* August 13, 1951. Obviously in any practical sense the cadets knew what they were charged with.

found in the ranks of the men who lived, worked, slept, and ate with them."[41]

Only the football season remained. In 1951 Army lost seven games, managing to beat only Columbia and the Citadel. Thereafter, along with the rest of the East Coast colleges and universities, West Point gradually de-emphasized football. With the Notre Dame game gone, only the annual contest with Navy attracted national attention. Football, and especially the Navy game, were still important at West Point, but the scandal and the reaction to it made it clear that other things counted more.

[41] David C. Ahearn, "A Statement from the Corps of Cadets," *Assembly*, X (January, 1952), 6.

Chapter XVI

The Modern Academy*

In 1962 David Boroff, associate professor of English at New York University, came to the Academy, studied it, and concluded, "West Point is a second-class college for first-class students." Boroff maintained that "the faculty isn't good enough. The students are over-loaded and have little or no time for the kind of contemplative activity that can alone make an educated man. The program, by virtue of its military coloration, tends to reward precision far more than critical ability. It is awkward to encourage the habit of unquestioned obedience on the one hand and intellectual freedom on the other. And one may well quarrel with the puerile emphasis on Big Football and the time-consuming rituals of the Plebe System." [1]

In 1957 two Dartmouth political scientists, John W. Masland and Laurence I. Radway, also examined the Academy. They were sympathetic with its aims and goals and generally favorable to what West Point was trying to do. They were most interested in the social sciences program, not only because it was the field they

---

* Author's Note: Shortly after this chapter was written, the Academy began an expansion program.

[1] David Boroff, "West Point: Good Enough?" *Harper's Magazine*, CCXXV (December, 1962), 59. In vol. CCXXVI of *Harper's* Boroff examines the modern Naval Academy and the Air Force Academy.

knew best but also because West Point's work in social sciences indicated the school's "sensitivity to the challenge posed by the growing employment of officers in policy level positions within the government." They concluded, "To those civilian social scientists who are skeptical of all military education we can say with conviction that the substantive content of the academies' work in the social sciences is as rich as the content of their own courses."[2]

It is difficult to make a balanced and fair judgment of the modern Academy. It resents being compared to civilian institutions because unlike them it has a specific mission; nevertheless, it is in the business of educating youth. It no longer influences the curriculum and program of civilian schools but rather is influenced by them. Still, it retains its uniqueness. There is a dedication to the student at West Point largely absent from the civilian institutions. Everything the faculty and the administration do, from the most advanced course in calculus to the first lesson in intramural golf, is done with a single end in view—graduating a cadet prepared to take his place in the army. All the instructors at West Point devote their working hours to teaching, while the professors concentrate on making the instructors better teachers. While the universities busy themselves collecting knowledge, storing knowledge, advancing knowledge, and publishing the results and tend to ignore the undergraduates, West Point concentrates on its cadets with an almost religious devotion. The Academy is a much different institution from the one Sylvanus Thayer created, but many things, and not just superficial ones, remain the same.

As Thayer intended, the West Point system consists of an almost completely prescribed course of study, small sections, objective and frequent grading, and the presentation and required assimilation of a great quantity of material. The Academy has refused to make any concessions to the elective system. In the fifties the Board of Visitors asked the Academic Board to study the feasi-

[2] Masland and Radway, *Soldiers and Scholars*, 219.

bility of introducing two or more majors at the end of the first or second year, perhaps granting a B.S. degree to students specializing in science and engineering and an A.B. to those specializing in humanities and social sciences. The Board made the study and rejected the suggestion. It cited both practical and theoretical reasons. Electives could be added only by dropping old courses, each of which had its staunch defender. Introducing an elective program for the last two years would call into question the program of the first two years—why should a cadet who is going to major in social sciences take all that mathematics? Some electives would probably prove to be easier than others, which would destroy the uniformity of the grading and ranking system. Finally, an elective system would introduce a divisive influence into the Corps of Cadets.

The last point is important. The army, America's largest single organization, has little enough holding it together as it is. Its operations are so far flung, its functions so diversified, that the only thing many officers have in common is their uniform—and West Point. It took a long and bitter struggle to change the army from a collection of separate branches with separate career systems—headed by bureau chiefs who emphasized their independence by looking to the Secretary of War and Congress rather than to the General in Chief for their direction and support—into a single, united force composed of branches which were responsible to the Chief of Staff. Few officers want to go back to the old days, and most regard anything that tends to separate them from their fellows with distaste.[3] Universities preparing students for a broad range of civilian activities can afford electives; West Point feels it cannot.

Thanks to the system of placing cadets in sections according to ability, however, the absence of electives does not mean that all cadets receive the same instruction. Today, as in the past, those in the higher sections progress further in their studies than the others, as the 1964–65 catalogue listing of courses indicates.

[3] There is an excellent discussion of this point in *ibid.,* 223–25.

The Modern Academy

	COURSES IN THE STANDARD ACADEMIC PROGRAM	COURSES IN THE ADVANCED ACADEMIC PROGRAM
Fourth Class (Freshman)	Engineering Fundamentals .	Advanced Engineering Fundamentals
	English Composition . . .	Evolution of American Ideals
	Environment	———
	Foreign Languages	Advanced French, German, or Spanish
	Mathematics	Advanced Mathematics
Third Class (Sophomore)	Chemistry	Inorganic Chemistry Organic Chemistry
	Comparative Literature . .	———
	Foreign Languages	Advanced French, German, or Spanish
	History of Europe and America: 1500–1870 . . .	Middle Eastern Studies
	History of Europe and America since 1870 . . .	History of Russia Latin American Studies History of U.S. Foreign Relations
	Mathematics	Advanced Mathematics
	Physics	Advanced Physics
	Psychology	———
Second Class (Junior)	Atomic and Nuclear Physics	———
	Economics	Comparative Economic Systems
	Electrical Science	Advanced Circuits Electromagnetic Fields Energy Conversion
	Law	———
	Mechanics of Fluids	Advanced Fluid Mechanics
	Mechanics of Solids	Advanced Engineering Mechanics I and II
	Thermodynamics	Accelerated Thermodynamics Classical Thermodynamics
	U.S. Government	Political Philosophy
First Class (Senior)	Civil Engineering	Honors Course in Civil Engineering Introduction to Nuclear Engineering

[325]

Contemporary Foreign Governments	———
Electives (2)	Additional Electives
History of Military Art . .	———
History of Modern Asia . .	———
International Relations . .	National Security Problems Problems of Developing Nations
Literature and Advanced Exposition	———
Military Leadership	———
Ordnance Engineering . .	Honors Course in Ordnance Engineering

If prescription was the first feature of Thayer's system, close supervision of the cadets' work was the second, and it too is intact. As of old, the cadets have little free time. They attend approximately twenty-one hours of class each week, in addition to required athletics and two hours of military training. Discipline is stiff. Rooms, clothes, hair, everything must be in order. In the words of one faculty member, "They live under the gun."[4]

Supervision reaches its apogee in the classroom. West Point has never employed the lecture method of imparting knowledge; sections number from twelve to sixteen students and are devoted to discussions. The old days of rigid questions and answers are gone, and the interchange between instructor and cadet is generally free and easy. "The cadet is expected to participate—please don't use the word recite—in every class," Superintendent William C. Westmoreland told Boroff.[5] But whether he "recites" or "participates," the point remains that the cadet must be prepared each day for each class. Quizzes are more frequent than in civilian colleges.

Much more than classroom performance is taken into account in the final class rankings, but academic achievement is still the most important factor. The faculty, conscious of the emphasis on scholarship, does all it can to make sure the grading is objective. Class standing is as important as it ever was; the top-ranked cadets can select not only the combat arm of their choice but their first

[4] Quoted in Boroff, "West Point," 54.
[5] *Ibid.*

station within that arm. The "goats" accept what is left. A uniform curriculum and the frequent quizzes assure a fair ranking of the cadets. So does the system of shifting instructors from section to section every two months or so, as it protects (or prevents) the cadet's grade from being influenced by personality. In many departments pre- and post-section conferences between the instructors and professors lead to a uniform presentation of the material to all cadets. It should be noted that this practice also obstructs the interchange of ideas and the pursuance of a line of thought by student and teacher that the small section could make possible. By contrast the department of military art and engineering encourages wide variation in teaching methods and in the material presented, insists on classroom discussion, and actively seeks air force and navy officers as instructors in order to make certain the cadets receive a variety of views. In nearly all departments the old true-false, multiple choice, and other forms of objective examination have given way, for the most part, to the essay form, but every precaution is taken to insure uniform grading.

The faculty is still inbred and by civilian standards is woefully lacking in credentials. During the academic year of 1964–65 West Point had a teaching faculty, excluding members of the physical education staff, of 388 officers. Some 310 of these were Academy graduates. About the same number, 316, held the M.A. degree, while only 35, or less than 10 per cent, held the Ph.D. And of the 35 Ph.D.'s, 11 were in the department of social sciences.[6] Most faculty members are chosen, as of old, by the professor when they are cadets. Three or four years (more in some departments) after they graduate, a professor asks his outstanding students to return to West Point for duty as instructors. Their tour remains short—four years usually—and the same criticisms are still heard. As soon as an officer becomes a qualified teacher, he leaves. However, the short tour has its defenders, who point out that the instructors come to the Academy of their own choice, are usually highly motivated, and retain their enthusiasm throughout their brief

[6] These figures are taken from the 1964–65 catalogue of the Academy.

teaching careers. "The students at West Point have a light in their eyes," one visiting professor observed. "They haven't been taught by disillusioned professors." [7] Most instructors have done some teaching in the army, where they often dealt with men of limited intelligence or men who would rather be somewhere other than in a stuffy room hearing about the character of the Chinese people or the workings of a rifle. One result is a heavy emphasis on the techniques and tricks of teaching, designed to capture and hold attention. This emphasis also exists at West Point, which has more audio-visual material available for its instructors than any other school in the country. As noted above, the instructors concentrate on teaching. They have no "publish or perish" worries; since all are army officers, all already have tenure. They do not need to shop around for new positions at conventions or indulge in the other rituals of academic life. Most are good teachers, some excellent ones.

The cadets are probably better today than they ever have been and compare favorably with the students at America's best schools. Nearly 80 per cent of the class of 1968 were in the top quintile of their high school classes, and 14 per cent were presidents of their student bodies or of their classes. [8] Only three institutions in the country have done better in receiving Rhodes Scholarships than West Point, and on College Boards and other examinations cadets score higher in the verbal sections than the students at the best engineering schools and higher in mathematics than those from the top-ranked liberal arts colleges.

Most of the cadets, some 86 per cent of them, are nominated by congressmen, who can either appoint a principal and an alternate or make six nominees and allow the Academy to choose from among them. Obviously, West Point prefers the latter method. The remaining 14 per cent come from competitive examinations among enlisted men in the Regular and Reserve Army, sons of deceased veterans, and Presidential nominees. There seems to be no uniform system of selection among the congressmen, but most

---

[7] Quoted in Boroff, "West Point," 55.
[8] *Ibid.,* 53.

use or at least refer to the results of a special Academy-oriented Civil Service examination.[9] The Academy admits the nominees on the basis of their academic achievement (weighted 60 per cent), physical aptitude (10 per cent), and leadership potential (30 per cent). "We're after a man," one official told Boroff, "who is not all egghead and not all football player. But we try to avoid the well-rounded man who is all radius."[10]

Cadets are fairly representative of their society, although a greater proportion are drawn from families whose origins are in the British Isles and northern Europe than the proportion of such families to the population at large. The percentages of Catholic and Jewish cadets is about the same as it is nationally; Negroes are under-represented, probably because they are under-represented in Congress. Because of the nomination system it is still difficult for a graduate to get his son into the Academy. West Point has fewer second and third generation students than almost any other college in the land. Only 6 per cent of the class of 1966 are sons of alumni.[11]

West Point gives the cadets their common bond. In the classroom, on the parade ground or intramural field, in the barracks, at the hops, indeed everywhere that it touches them, the Academy instills into its cadets the ancient virtues of the soldier. It is all done consciously. "The students should enter the Service Academies about the time they reach military age," a faculty group declared in 1949, "while they are still young enough to be susceptible to those features of education and training which are directed primarily toward mental and spiritual discipline and to accept without cynicism the idea of a lifetime of loyalty and service to the Nation."[12]

---

[9] The author sent a questionnaire to some forty congressmen, and this statement is based on their answers. Those answers are now in the USMA Library.

[10] Boroff, "West Point," 53.

[11] *Ibid.*

[12] *Report to Superintendent*, 3. In 1946 General Taylor told a congressional committee, "We must have these young men in their formative years if we are to implant the principles in them which we try to implant." Quoted in Masland and Radway, *Soldiers and Scholars*, 108.

The first principle the Academy teaches the cadets is, "Take responsibility for your actions regardless of their outcome." The course in the history of the military art places emphasis on the Great Captains and their personal attributes. West Point carefully draws for the cadets the image of the ideal military leader, and it expects the cadets to adopt his characteristics as their own. The soldier, cadets learn, is highly motivated, ready to dedicate his life to his country. He is able to examine a situation, come to a quick decision, and stick by it. He is a well dressed, well behaved gentleman. He enthusiastically performs the duties required of him and regards lethargy or indifference as a sign of weakness or worse. He is an unselfish team player. His sense of honor impels him to strive for truthfulness, sincerity, and straightforwardness in all things. He abhors deceit, quibbling, or evasiveness. Both physically and morally he is courageous. He respects the privileges and responsibilities of rank and takes pride in his profession. In short, he develops character.[13]

Shortly after World War II Superintendent Taylor laid a basis for making a final judgment about the Academy. "West Point is essentially a school for leaders," he said. "What it teaches its graduates from books is important, but is not everything. There is no academic department at West Point which is not excelled in size or scope by some other civilian school. Other colleges offer more advanced scientific and liberal courses to special students. We err if we measure West Point only by the yardstick of curriculum. West Point succeeds or fails in the future to the degree in which it continues to produce broad men of character, capable of leading other men to victory in battle."[14]

As Taylor admitted, and as everyone who takes even a casual interest in the education of the nation's soldiers has long since recognized, West Point can never hope to become the great national scientific university Jefferson had envisaged. Taylor cited the other motive behind the founding of the Academy, the desire

[13] Masland and Radway, *Soldiers and Scholars,* 199–202, has the most complete discussion of the duties of the modern officer.
[14] Maxwell D. Taylor, *West Point Looks Ahead* (West Point, 1946), 6–7.

for an officer corps that could lead citizen-soldiers in war, as a continued justification for West Point's existence and a criterion by which to judge the institution. In the nuclear age, however, it seems unlikely that West Pointers will ever again be called upon to lead huge masses of citizen-soldiers into combat. Korea, coming at the dawn of the nuclear era, may represent the last time the United States uses units as large as corps on the battlefield.

But all this only says what the Academy is not or cannot be. Its official mission is to provide qualified officers for the army, which in a sense continues to beg the question. The real problem is, what are army officers supposed to do in the nuclear age or, in other words, for what is West Point preparing its cadets?

The first requirement of the modern soldier, as in any profession, is technical proficiency. The army officer must know the army's organization, weapons, methods of fighting, and doctrine. But he must also know more. The modern officer is called upon to consult and work with foreign affairs experts, industrial managers, scientists, labor leaders, and educators. He helps prepare legislation, the national budget, and the American position on foreign policy issues. He must be able to understand and communicate with politicians and civilian specialists, both at home and in friendly foreign nations. He has to be able to evaluate the capabilities and probable reactions of potential enemies. Above all, in the words of Masland and Radway, "the new role of military leaders requires of them a heightened awareness of the principles of our democratic society."[15]

To meet the requirements the nation places upon it, the army maintains an extensive school system that leads upward from the narrowest technical institutions to the National War College. Undergirding the whole structure is West Point, which remains vocational in the sense that it prepares its cadets for only one profession but is broad and liberal in the sense that it gives its graduates the necessary base upon which they may build as they move through the army's schools into positions of tremendous responsibility.

[15] Masland and Radway, *Soldiers and Scholars*, vii.

Most of what West Point does could be done better, as Superintendent Taylor indicated, by civilian colleges. One thing, however, the civilians cannot do. In 1953 John A. Hannah, on leave
from the presidency of Michigan State University to serve as
Assistant Secretary of Defense for Manpower and Personnel, undertook a study of the service academies. At first he was hostile to
West Point and Annapolis; he felt the officers corps of both
services could receive "a desirable variety of background, training
and experience" only in the civilian colleges, which could also
give them "a high degree of specialization." But after intensive
study he changed his mind. In 1954 he explained his position to a
congressional committee. "Before I came to this post I weighed
West Point and Annapolis solely on the basis of educational
grounds," Hannah declared, a perspective he now felt was in
error. For "while there are some things they may not do as well
as our good civilian institutions . . . they do one thing much
better and that is they do instill in their students . . . a loyalty to
the service, a loyalty to the government, an appreciation for
ethics and integrity to a degree beyond what we do at our civilian
institutions." [16]

As Hannah indicated, there is more to soldiering than wearing
the uniform, firing the gun, or leading the men. These things are
necessary, indeed indispensable, but there are other essential
attributes any professional soldier, with his monopoly on violence,
must have at all times and in all places. The old military dictum
that tactics change but strategy remains the same applies here.
Army officers are engaged in the business of serving the public.
So are postmasters or file clerks, but there is a qualitative difference. The soldier puts his life on the line, or is always ready to
do so. That may also be true for all male civilians subject to the
draft or ready to enlist in an emergency, but the professional
soldier must go first. Today's West Point cadet can look forward
to years of small wars and crises, just as his counterpart a century
ago expected to take his chances in the constant Indian campaigns.
Even more important, the professional soldier works from day to

[16] Quoted in *ibid.*, 124–25.

day with weapons systems of awesome destructive power, capable of putting an end to civilization. He is also intimately involved in establishing and carrying out the nation's policies. Before 1945 a large authority was entrusted to the officer's care in time of war; now it is a crucial one. What the modern officer needs, aside from all technical abilities, is character, or so at least West Point believes, and that is what it gives its cadets.

Afterword

Beyond the years covered by Stephen Ambrose's history, written in the mid-1960s, West Point has had its full share of times both turbulent and tranquil. Challenge, response, and change have made their marks, reaching to every corner of the Academy's activity, even while the institution maintained a steady concentration on the basic work entrusted to it: preparing leaders of character and competence for their service as officers in the nation's military forces. All this has served to define a distinctive new era, the principal events of which add a new chapter to the institution's long and proud record of service. We do well to reflect on how the fundamentals that have shaped West Point over the years have stood the test of time, as well as how the institution has adhered to these fundamentals. How, we may ask, has West Point positioned itself, its cadets, and its graduates to deal with the daunting uncertainties the coming century surely holds in store?

Eventful Changes: 1966–1976

The years 1966 to 1976 brought a stream of changes and innovations that put stress on the fabric of the Academy. Some were internally motivated, bringing significant change to the life of the cadet. But the Academy felt many external influences at just the same time, with the result that the internal stresses sharply intensified. They came as the country at large, and its military forces in particular, were beset by unprecedented forces of division and alienation—and by an unprecedented breakdown of behavioral standards.

The Academy, and in particular its Corps of Cadets, was not spared the impact of this penetrating national trauma. Interviews conducted with cadets and others at the Academy during that decade revealed attitudes—far removed from the clear dedication to duty, honor, and country that had been the traditional hallmark of the Academy—among many cadets, and even within the faculty, which were of grave concern. These unhealthy trends and troubling tendencies were fed in part by America's experience in Vietnam. Disrespect toward our country and contempt for its armed forces became commonplace. These trends infected the youth of America, and were felt by the young men at West Point, who often found it best on home leave and elsewhere not to identify themselves as cadets of the Military Academy. Within the Corps, the effects, while varying widely by individual, were nevertheless pervasive. Widely publicized distrust of the nation's leaders undercut the very sinews of military discipline. The My Lai massacre of Vietnamese civilians, including women and children, scandalized all who took pride in the uniform they wore. The subsequent legal action against responsible former commanders, which ultimately led to the removal of the then-serving West Point Superintendent, added to the erosion of the cadet's respect for authority and military order, which lie at the core of the West Point experience.

These events deeply affected cadets' attitudes, especially their attitudes *in practice* toward duty, personal honor, and service to country, operationally defined—that is, to the actual ethos and culture of the cadets of the Corps. Some ripple effects of this national turmoil, demonstrated in cadets' day-to-day activities, cannot be clearly described even today.

The first of the major internal changes of the period was the near doubling of the size of the Corps, from 2,400 to 4,400 cadets. The expansion owed itself to a question attributed to President Kennedy at the Army-Navy football game in 1961, during the first year of his presidency. "Where is the rest of the Corps of Cadets?" The Brigade of Midshipmen at Philadelphia's Municipal Stadium, numbering some four thousand, had nearly filled the field during their march-on; the Corps of Cadets came to little more than half that number.

Some of the effects of the doubling proved to be adverse, particularly when added to other influences, resulting in a Corps less close-knit than before, with a lessening of common adherence to a common culture. Company-by-company differences became more noticeable, in some cases with unfavorable undertones. Such differences, well recognized, had long existed—between battalions and between companies within battalions, for example. This friction was especially evident when the Corps was still sized by height, that is, before cadets were "scrambled" in the late 1950s. But with the rapid increase in size, the differences within the Corps became sharper, and some dysfunctional elements became matters of pride and issues of particular concern when women were admitted into the Corps. Another adverse effect was the pressure on the admissions process to fill out the Corps, accompanied, in the views of some, by a decline in cadet commitment to military service and military responsibility which reflected, to a degree, attitudes and influences from the society at large. Many of these attitudes were of course part of the U.S. ideological and generational turmoil of the 1960s—to assess them here would take us far beyond this commentary and this book—but they were factors not to be overlooked in understanding the troubles that later arose.

The new barracks needed to accommodate the increased size of the Corps went up rapidly. Externals were thoughtfully designed and constructed, preserving appearances on the south and west sides of the Plain in a way that did credit to those responsible. Internally, the barracks were a departure from West Point tradition and from cadet culture. Built on a horizontal plan with long open hallways, the new barracks brought a style of cadet living quite different from that of the vertically organized sixteen-room "divisions" common in the past. In combination with other changes, the resulting greater openness brought less rigorous control. This was especially apparent during study hours when compounded by greater freedom to roam to the gymnasium and elsewhere, freedom to study together, an end of "call to quarters" and taps, and a rise in administrative activities unrelated to studies, which increasingly seemed to fill the hallways with a great deal of cadet movement back and forth.

By 1960, Army Chief of Staff Lyman Lemnitzer, USMA '20, formally approved a proposal to offer electives to cadets. (When proposed in the 1950s, this measure had been rejected as having a divisive influence within the Corps.) To undertake this innovation, cadets pursued a modified curriculum comprising both standard and advanced studies. Although the standard academic program adhered to the prescribed curriculum and the minimum courses required for graduation, cadets for the first time, on the basis of prior educational experience or demonstrated merit, could take advanced courses in mathematics, English, and foreign languages. It was recognized that the addition of electives was needed to take advantage of the different natural learning abilities of individual cadets, and that cadets might have successfully completed comparable courses elsewhere. Also, the revised curriculum would enable cadets to better keep up with the explosion of information. It was nevertheless one more element of division, and although the extent cannot be calculated with precision, it left the Corps with less in common, and with less cohesion.

In 1973 the Cadet Honor Committee took action to end one of the long-established practices of the Corps of Cadets—that of ostracizing, or "silencing," any cadet who was returned to the Corps by higher authority after being found by cadet peers to have violated the honor code. The committee considered the practice to have lost the support of large numbers of Corps members, the Academy, its graduates, and the general public. There was some thought that to keep it might risk an overturning of the honor code itself and a shift of its administration to an outside or higher authority.

In the same year, federal courts ended mandatory chapel for cadets. The decision invoked the First Amendment to the Constitution, separating church and state by prohibiting an establishment of religion. The decision preserved the principles of the Constitution, but its effect on the Corps of Cadets was to reduce the mandatory exposure of cadets to issues of ethics and moral standards. Voluntary chapel attendance continued, but there can be little doubt (at least in the minds of many old graduates) that the change had a weakening effect in the moral-ethical sector of cadet life, with nothing of equivalent strength provided to take its place.

Finally, among the major changes the social revolution of the 1960s inspired, Congress mandated the entry of women into the Corps of Cadets in 1976, to graduate with the class of 1980. For this transformation, the Academy carried out a thoughtful, comprehensive, timely effort of study, preparation, and indoctrination. The excellence of this work, carried out under the close attention of Superintendent Lt. Gen. Sidney Berry, was well demonstrated in the small number of significant changes that were later required in the conduct of the "coeducational" cadet experience. There were, however, significant negative strains, many of which were sub-surface. Although dealt with responsibly and forcefully by Academy authorities, problems were by no means completely eradicated. Especially during the first year, but continuing at a somewhat lesser level for years thereafter, harassment and abuse, sometimes including obscenity, were directed against the women, fueled by an undercurrent of resentment and opposition among male cadets and officers at West Point. The same attitude prevailed among a great many West Point graduates, including a sizable number on active duty. This problem remained a source of concern and added to the disruptive, divisive, and unresponsive tendencies among cadets and the whole West Point community.

Over the years there had been a rising emphasis on interpersonal competition as a motivator for cadets within the Corps. There was some indication that this competition was having some undesirable effects, encouraging a climate marked by self serving rather than the devotion to learning, duty, and responsibility that had traditionally characterized West Point graduates' governing and motivating goals. When coupled with the tenets of the "me generation" and the attitude of many cadets to "just get by, however you can," interpersonal competition placed added emphasis on grades over education and added strain on the cadet commitment not to lie, cheat, or steal or tolerate those who do.

These problems were compounded by the external effects of a society riven by Vietnam, marked by negative attitudes toward all authority, and suffering from the moral and ethical erosion of the 1960s and early 1970s. The cumulative effects took their toll on the overall state of health of the Academy, becoming widespread, though largely contained below the surface.

Scandal, Review, and Reform: 1976–1981

The basic facts regarding the cadet cheating on the Electrical Engineering examination in 1976 were widely reported. These violations occurred when an Electrical Engineering take-home examination was given to cadets in the spring of that year. When these papers were graded, many showed unmistakable signs of collusion. Investigation made clear that some two-hundred cadets had cheated, and the full number was thought by many to be possibly twice or even four times as great. Especially disquieting were statements by cadets themselves that they believed cheating and other honor violations had become widespread throughout the Corps, and that respect for the honor code had badly eroded.

At West Point and in society at large, dispute and acrimony quickly arose over the causes of what had occurred, where to place the responsibility, what action should be taken and by whom. A commission under Academy graduate and astronaut Frank Borman was appointed, made its review of honor at West Point, and submitted its report, including recommendations, in December 1976.

At this point Army Chief of Staff Gen. Bernard Rogers (USMA Jan. '43), with the assistance of Vice Chief of Staff W. T. (Dutch) Kerwin (USMA '39), took steps to bring about action that they intended to be both thoughtful and decisive. They set up the West Point Study Group, headed by three Brigadier Generals—Hillman Dickinson (USMA '49), Jack Mackmull (USMA '50), and Jack Merritt (OCS '53)—to examine and evaluate every aspect of Academy activity and submit a report with recommendations identifying needed improvements. They also initiated my own return to active duty to serve as Superintendent. After an exchange of letters between the Secretary of the Army and myself, affirming the authority I would exercise, and a personal meeting between us, I took the post in mid-June 1977. In the months just preceding I had had the opportunity to meet with the West Point Study Group and to review with them the excellent, searching work they were doing.

The first need as I saw it, against the background of the Study Group's work, was to provide a clearer, more focused statement of the purpose of West Point's efforts, couched in operational terms. "West Point," I wrote, "exists to provide to the cadets of the Corps an intellectual, military, physical, and moral-ethical experience of such high quality that it can serve as the bedrock on which they, as future military leaders, will develop the capability, in due time, to take responsibility for the security and well-being of our country."

An early step was to initiate the preparation of "concept papers" spelling out in explicit terms how we were to achieve cadet development in academic, military, physical-athletic, and moral-ethical sectors. This work involved the participation of all the constituent elements of the Academy including academic faculty, the tactical department, physical education instructors and athletic coaches, chaplains, honor representatives and other cadets, and supporting staff, in each one of the four sectors.

The Study Group Report, when complete, went to the Army Chief of Staff, who sent it on to me "for such action as you deem appropriate." In response to this tasking I established more than a dozen Academy committees, again with institution-wide participation. Against the backdrop of the work we had done on the concept papers, the committees made an item-by-item evaluation of each of the Study Group's nearly 250 recommendations. We concurred in and adopted the vast majority of the recommendations, some with modifications or other adaptations. For others, we pursued an alternative way of achieving the same end. A few were postponed for further study, and a handful were rejected. All in all, the Study Group's report served its purpose extremely well. It provided a basis for reform and gave reason for great confidence.

We also carried out some restructuring for purposes of governance. A Deputy Superintendent was appointed and charged with reviewing every activity at West Point to assure adherence to policy requirements and avoidance of improprieties. He relieved the Superintendent of an awesome administrative burden, thus permitting him to devote more of his attention directly to the intellectual, physical, moral-ethical, and professional development of the Corps of Cadets.

The role of the Academic Board was carefully reviewed. Over the years, it had acquired an accretion of functions. Many believed that the Board itself had not acted in a resilient and timely way during the period just before the honor violations, when there was a widening sense that all was not well within the Corps' honor environment. The academic board focused more tightly on the academic life of the Academy, with the Superintendent setting its agenda with the advice of the Academic Dean. The Superintendent established a policy board with representation from each of the Academy's four principal activities: academic, military, physical-athletic, and moral-ethical. The board considered, in particular, just how to integrate these sometimes mutually reinforcing, sometimes competing areas of effort as well as possible into the balanced whole of cadet development.

Steps were taken, for instance, to reduce the emphasis on interpersonal competition and focus instead on the cadet developmental experience at West Point. One objective was that cadet grades, ranks, and similar recognitions would become more a reflection of substantive achievement and less an end in themselves, sometimes acquired by cadets skirting the behavioral norms appropriate to the Academy's declared purposes.

A major achievement on the academic side was the adoption

of a new forty-course curriculum, with a thirty-course core and ten electives, in addition to six military science courses. The new curriculum featured uniform sixty-minute periods. Displacing the traditional eighty-minute periods for certain courses achieved a much greater overall flexibility. And the practice, previously observed by a few departments, of inviting a distinguished, civilian visiting professor for a year of service at the Academy, was extended to all departments, with excellent results. The faculty remained almost entirely military, composed, under mature leadership, of carefully selected young officers prepared for their task with up-to-date master's or doctoral degrees from the country's top universities.

Within the Academy's military program, emphasis centered on "positive leadership," an intensification of many previous efforts throughout the century. It highlighted a rigorous pursuit of demanding performance standards appropriate to the Academy's goals and an accompanying sharp departure from practices involving harassment and adversarial conduct. Such activities, in the hands of adolescents of limited experience, had often been counterproductive and dysfunctional and were, in any case, quite contrary to training practices within the army, which the cadets would shortly be joining. Conditions in the mess hall showed marked improvement as part of these efforts.

The integration of women was a matter of continuing command attention and emphasis, extending from the very top echelon through every level of authority and responsibility. Some islands of resistance and unsupportive attitudes still persisted, as did some abusive and harassing language. These lessened, however, as women became upper-class cadets. The women's incorporation into the Corps and throughout the institution moved steadily in the right direction.

Study conditions in the barracks also improved markedly. The cadet chain of command was called upon to shoulder responsibility for implementing changes in this regard, and it did so. Especially important was the reduction in any and all forms of activity that interfered with plebe study hours.

Meanwhile, a program we called "Project Teamwork"—comprising teams under the Superintendent, Deputy Superintendent, Dean, and Commandant, with participation from all constituent elements of the Academy (senior faculty, junior faculty, tactical officers and military instructors, cadets from each class, coaches and captains of sports and club teams, chaplains and others)—was developed to review Academy activity and cadet life. The project sought to eliminate practices that were purposeless and burdensome to cadets, introduce improved methods and practices, and, in general, seek positive movement and improvement in Academy activities. Once it became clear that the Superintendent would take such findings and recommendations seriously and act upon them, there was a palpable sense that the people participating or represented were "buying in" to what the Academy was doing. The "counterculture" that had been much in evidence and influence when reforms began had diminished as time went on and was no longer a significant problem.

An "honor concept" was developed, one that went beyond the traditional prohibitions of "lying, cheating, stealing, or tolerating those who do" to positive precepts: making good on promises, knowing what you stand for, standing up for what is right. Increased time and effort went into honor education, beginning at the very start of plebe year.

A "duty concept" was also developed, following cadet observations that whereas the honor system and honor concept had been well articulated and well taught, nothing so explicit existed in the area of duty. The concept focused on a progression from *obedience* (and response) for plebes, to *self-discipline* for yearlings, to *sense of responsibility* for Second Class cadets, and to *concept of service* for First Class cadets. This whole exercise made clear not only why cadets were at West Point and what was expected of them but also what role the staff and faculty of the institution were expected to perform.

Finally, at cadet initiative, Project Teamwork produced a "concept for the social development of cadets." A large part of its value lay in bringing out into the open questions regarding limits of behavior—constraints and standards—and goals appropriate (and inappropriate) to the role of a U.S. Army officer. The protocol also addressed cadet behavior involved in personal relaxation and "pursuit of happiness."

What West Point meant to the nation was shown in a striking way in late January of 1981, just as President Ronald Reagan took office. One of his first opportunities as President was to welcome U.S. hostages back to the United States after their release from Iran, where they had been imprisoned for over a year. He chose West Point to receive them. At Stewart Air Force Base, welcoming the hostages back on American soil, my brief remarks to them were first that they were now delivered from evil, then that they were home in America, and finally that they would have a few days with their families at West Point, free from outside cares, and could now give their thoughts to the new life that lay ahead for them. We at the Academy felt privileged to have them with us and to see their spirits rise. We took pride in honoring them, notably when four thousand cadets greeted them with overwhelming enthusiasm and exuberance in the cadet mess hall, and again when the entire Corps lined the roads to cheer them on as they left West Point for their future destinations.

In a symbolic way the selection of West Point to greet them, and the event itself, seemed to tell us that the damages of the honor scandal were now behind us and that West Point stood once more in its high traditional place in our country's confidence.

Much, in fact, had been accomplished. The core principles of the Academy—duty, honor, country—had been validated and reaffirmed. The commitment of all concerned, declared and practiced, had been strengthened. The alignment of activities for the academic, military, physical, and moral-ethical development of cadets had been reviewed and renewed. A similar step toward social development had been taken. The sense was strong that things were on the right track and that everyone at the Academy had reaffirmed its goals. Morale, it was fair to say, had been greatly enhanced, as well as pride in being a cadet and the earned pride of personal accomplishment on the part of the individual cadet.

Even so, there remained problems that could cause future trouble. One was cadet squeamishness over fulfilling the "non-toleration" obligation of the honor code in practice, which meant bringing honor charges against a fellow cadet when necessary. Another was the continuing, though much reduced and suppressed, antipathy toward having women in the Corps. On the personal level, the use and sometimes abuse of alcohol was damaging to the standards of appropriate cadet behavior, although New York's later raising of the minimum drinking age to twenty-one eased this problem, especially for plebe and yearling men and women. Study conditions in the barracks, although much improved, still warranted attention.

Moving On: 1981–1999

With the appointment in mid-1981 of a new Superintendent, Lt. Gen. Willard Scott, the Academy entered into an enduring period of stability and continued to fine-tune its constituent programs. Beginning with the class of 1985, the Academy adopted a program of sixteen optional academic majors, eight of which focused on the mathematics-science-engineering disciplines, and eight on the humanities-public affairs disciplines. This change was part of the evaluation dating back to the early 1960s, when electives were introduced along with accelerated courses for advanced cadets. The purpose in introducing majors was to provide a measure of academic specialization while maintaining the Academy's traditionally strong commitment to the solid, broad core of fundamental knowledge essential for a modern army officer. Beginning with the class of 1990, all cadets, staff, and faculty had access to personal computers, and the Academy soon took steps to network them and establish a "computer thread," integrating their use across the entire curriculum. Additional academic space in the cadet area became available when the Academy acquired the former Ladycliff College, which adjoined the grounds to the south. Its twenty-eight acres ultimately became Pershing Center, which accommodates many activities not central to cadet functions.

The tenure of General Scott, in his own words, emphasized the assimilation of women in the Corps of Cadets, varsity sports, and honor. A formal honor education program went forward during his superintendency, and a new multipurpose sports and athletic facility (the Holleder Center) was built. West Point's records in intercollegiate sports improved, and the participation of women in the Corps became an established, positively valued component of cadet life. The spirits and enthusiasm of the whole institution were visibly enhanced, quite notably by the infectious good nature of General Scott himself.

Under his successor, Lt. Gen. Dave Palmer, a wide range of individual refinements, improvements, and experiments ensued, reflecting his "Project 2002," which took note of the Academy's forthcoming 200th anniversary. General Palmer's program actions extended from a revised statement of mission to a decision for cadet "lights-out" at 2400 hours. It also included the experiment of separate barracks for cadets of the First Class (the seniors)—an idea later dropped. In 1990 the Cadet Leader Development System replaced the traditional Fourth Class System, marking another, and quite historic, step in the maturing of the superior-subordinate relationships. A new graduate program at the master's-degree level prepared incoming tactical officers for their duties and paralleled the master's or doctoral training at civilian institutions for officer-instructors in the academic disciplines. This program stressed the unique leadership responsibilities and opportunities at West Point.

An outside commission headed by Wesley Posvar (USMA '46), a Rhodes Scholar and later Chancellor of the University of Pittsburgh (1967–1991), reviewed the West Point honor code and pronounced it to be "an example for all public service"; he believed it "should be extended through the army, the government, and American society as a whole."

In 1986, reflecting years of devoted work, a beautiful Jewish chapel was dedicated at West Point. In a concrete way, it carried forward a Jewish experience at West Point that dated back to 1802, with the graduation of a Jewish cadet, one of only two graduates of that first class.

Illustrative of the quality of the highly diversified Corps of Cadets, Kristin Baker became the first woman selected as Brigade Commander (First Captain) of the 1990 class. This was but ten years after the first women had graduated from West Point. The first Hispanic American First Captain was Jose Morales of the class of 1976, Vincent Brooks became the first African American First Captain in 1980, and John Tien Jr., the first Asian American First Captain in 1987. In 1991 the Academy graduated its thousandth African American and its thousandth woman. The Academy—cadets, faculty, and staff—could take pride in this evidence of distance traveled along America's highway.

Dozens of studies and policy decisions during these years aimed at specific improvements in Academy activities had left a lasting imprint on cadet performance. While most were readily recognized as positive in their effect, a periodic concern reasserted itself as to whether the Academy was placing undue emphasis on academic over military objectives in cadet life, and on leadership in our society at large over military—and specifically army—service. Successive Superintendents, as well as Commandants and Deans, were attentive to the multiple dimensions of cadet experience in relation to these issues.

Meanwhile great changes were taking place in the geostrategic environment, in which West Point graduates would serve. These were first highlighted by the fall of the Berlin Wall in 1989, the subsequent collapse of the Soviet Union in 1991, and then by the emergence of new security concerns and new forms of military commitment in places like the Persian Gulf and Bosnia. With the end of the Soviet Union's strategic threat, the authorized strength of the army by the mid-1990s fell from just below 800,000 to just below 500,000, and the Corps of Cadets from 4,400 to 4,000. While at first some may have thought otherwise, it soon became clear that the responsibilities of the army would shift but by no means diminish, especially when measured in the demands of "Optempo"—the tempo (frequency and number) of operations in which soldiers and officers would participate, repeatedly away from home stations. Cadets could see that although the activities in which they would be involved as officers would inevitably be changing, the requirement for professional skill, leadership, and commitment surely would continue. Lt. Gen. Howard Graves, on assuming the superintendency in 1991, stated his intention to "continue to implement these plans, maintaining their relevance to a rapidly changing world."

Graves's years were marked by continuity of purpose, institutional progress, and stability in support of the enduring values of West Point. The strategic guidance was carefully coordinated between the Academy and the army, thus providing a sound and authoritative foundation for Academy operations. The Academy remained devoted to producing leaders of character for the army and the nation.

Under General Graves's leadership, the Academy reformulated its statement of vision as a set of "bedrock values" by which cadets would learn, inculcate, and put into practice such essential leadership responsibilities as establishing a healthy command climate, maintaining an honorable lifestyle, and understanding the importance of values as they influence command decisions. Honor was the first bedrock value. The second, termed "consideration of others," focused on an essential element of mutual trust and respect, of being supportive of and fair to others. An incident that took place in the fall of 1994 put this sense of responsibility to the test. During a football pep rally a few football players "groped" women cadets. The cadet chain of command and senior officers took prompt, decisive action. The incident, in fact, turned into a positive teaching and training lesson. A *New York Times* editorial on the episode and its outcome bore the title "Wisdom at West Point."

The Academy took many other significant steps to build on previous efforts, among them in the area of "outreach." The range and number of cadet, faculty, and staff contacts with external associations and organizations were increased, as was an array of government agencies that offered cadet summer internships.

Within its vision for the future, the Academy embarked on a massive, much-needed revitalization of key "quality-of-life" facilities: cadet barracks, the cadet mess and gymnasium, family housing for faculty and staff, and academic buildings. At the same time, responding to lowered funding levels as post-Cold War defense budgets were cut back, the Superintendent directed an intensive round of reviews aimed at economies and efficiencies to be achieved by the Academy while adhering to the strategies and priorities of its long-range vision. Augmenting governmental funding, the Academy increased its reliance on gifts and donor funds (expanded through the efforts of the West Point Association of Graduates) to sustain the "margin of excellence" in all aspects of the cadet developmental experience.

Some changes originated with higher authority. Congress in 1992 directed an increase of civilian faculty members from less than 10 percent of the Academy's total staff to more than 20 percent by the year 2002, further diversifying cadet educational opportunities and experiences. At the same time the overwhelming majority of academic instructors continue to be young, energetic military officers who, as role models, historically provide an important part of cadet experience and development—as cadets who studied under Omar Bradley and Maxwell Taylor, to name a few, will readily attest. Concern remains, however, speaking for myself and others, as to whether these and other changes will erode the distinctive role and achievements of West Point as a unique American institution.

Another legislative provision, which came into full effect with the class of 1998, denies cadets a regular army commission at graduation. Speaking again for myself (and numerous fellow graduates, including many who have borne senior command responsibilities), this measure seems a damaging and dangerous dilution to the idea of commitment to an honored profession in a lifetime of service to country—a bedrock idea that the

Academy and the army, we believe, should constantly strive to foster. It is, indeed, a primary reason for having a West Point.

In mid-1977, five former Superintendents (I among them) visited the Academy at the invitation of Lt. Gen. Dan Christman, who became Superintendent in 1996. We were to receive briefings on the state of the Academy and observe summer military training of cadets, which highlighted operations in the field. The visit coincided with questions that many Academy graduates were voicing over Academy priorities (military leadership development in particular) and related concerns about whether its "leader" orientation was focused on the army or was spreading to leadership in civilian pursuits. The results were reassuring. Military training, notably military leadership training, impressed us. It has probably never been stronger. On the basis of what we saw and heard, the controversy over statements of mission seemed more semantic than substantive. The new statement aimed at producing "leaders of character for a lifetime· of army service" goes far toward satisfying the concerns.

To enable the Academy to maintain its steady course, while continuing to strengthen and improve its programs, General Christman has moved toward a new model of financing aimed at providing more consistent and predictable levels of funding. With defense budgets already more tightly limited to the Academy's "core" developmental programs and activities, he has given added emphasis to the "margin of excellence" activities for which the institution looks to the private sector for funding. The Academy's bicentennial celebration in 2002 is considered as offering a special opportunity for this initiative, the primary stated motivation of which is to continue to attract the highest quality candidates to West Point and to a career in military service. It of course carries with it possible policy implications for the future nature of the Academy's priorities, the responsibilities of the government, and particularly any outside influences that may come to bear on the Academy's central purposes. Undoubtedly, it will be a matter deserving careful and continuing review.

In reflecting on the years covered here, it seems clear that the

Academy, despite the various misgivings that have been voiced, has come through the difficulties and demands of the post-1960s era still capable of contributing to our nation's well-being and security. Its renewed dedication to the demands of duty, honor, country; its restated mission to produce leaders of character for a lifetime of army service, and its clearly focused attention to the academic, military, physical, and moral-ethical development of cadets all give promise that it will continue to do so in the future. Challenges from within and without will of course continue. No institution grounded in discipline that brings together four thousand young Americans, male and female, in closely integrated living, study, and training arrangements, will be free of problems, some of which will prove to be complex and highly newsworthy. The impact of external decisions, often reflecting agendas within the government other than the Academy's health and well-being, will provide added difficulties. The task of melding the fourfold academic, military, physical, and moral-ethical responsibilities of the Academy into a working unity, in a dynamic society with a highly dynamic technological base, is bound to require the energies and continued vigilance of all, and will be taxing to all—on occasion severely taxing.

Yet the years have shown that the Academy has strengths equal to challenge. Through turbulence and tranquillity the Academy has held steadfastly to the main directions developed over the years, well illuminated in Professor Ambrose's account. These have included, in particular, the foundations of the academic program and standards of cadetship established by Sylvanus Thayer; the evolution of the Academy through the century that followed; the reshaping, broadening, and introduction of measures to make the Academy more relevant to the nation's military needs by Douglas MacArthur after World War I; and the intensified efforts regarding character, honor, and leadership carried out by Maxwell Taylor on the urging of Army Chief of Staff Dwight D. Eisenhower after World War II. To these were added, in my time, a renewed focus, strengthened commitment, and an explicit definition of Academy purpose stated in operational, cadet-developmental terms. The Academy's leaders must continue to receive the authority, support, and latitude they need and must continue to exercise firm leadership in order to ensure that the institution is responsive to the needs of the army and nation.

The institution is strong and resilient. Its principles have been well tested and well proven. They have been forged in two centuries of demanding experience. The interests of our country and our people will best be served by lending West Point our steadfast, continuing support.

I want to offer a special word of thanks regarding this afterword to Dr. Stephen Grove, U.S. Military Academy Historian, for the information and the comments shared with me throughout its preparation. His assistance is deeply appreciated. I should add, of course, that responsibility for the afterword's content rests with me.

Gen. Andrew J. Goodpaster, United States Army (Ret.)
Fifty-first Superintendent of the United States Military Academy

Bibliography

MANUSCRIPTS

Jacob Whitman Bailey Papers, Library, United States Military Academy.

William Whitman Bailey, "Recollections of West Point," Misc. Mss., Library, United States Military Academy.

———, "The Centennial at West Point," Archives, United States Military Academy.

Bryant Family Papers, New York Public Library.

George Washington Cullum Papers, Library, United States Military Academy.

George William Cushing Papers, Library, United States Military Academy.

Henry Dearborn Papers, Library, United States Military Academy.

Henry A. du Pont Papers, Winterthur Mss., Eleutherian Mills Historical Library (Wilmington, Del.).

Samuel Wragg Ferguson Papers, Archives, Louisiana State University.

David W. Gray, "The Architectural Development of West Point," Misc. Mss., Library, United States Military Academy.

Henry Wager Halleck Papers, Library, United States Military Academy.

William H. Harris Papers, New York Public Library.

Edward L. Hartz Papers, Library of Congress.

Samuel Peter Heintzelman Diary, Library of Congress.

Ethan Allen Hitchcock Papers, Library of Congress.

Edward S. Holden Collection, Archives, United States Military Academy (A collection of War Department letters relating to the Academy, covering 1801–38.)

O. O. Howard Papers, Bowdoin College Library.

Joseph K. Hyer Papers, Library, United States Military Academy.

Moses St. John Liddell Papers, Library, Louisiana State University.

John A. Logan Papers, Library of Congress.

George B. McClellan Papers, Library of Congress.

Dennis Hart Mahan Papers, Library, United States Military Academy.

Miscellaneous Papers, Library, United States Military Academy.

Alden Partridge Papers, Library, United States Military Academy.

George D. Ramsay, "Recollections of the U.S. Military Academy at West Point, New York, 1814–1820," typed copy in Library, United States Military Academy. Parts of this document are reprinted in Cullum, *Biographical Register*, III, 612–32, but Cullum omits paragraphs praising Partridge.

Records of the War Department: Office of the Judge Advocate General. GCM K-3. Case of Captain Alden Partridge, February, 1816, National Archives.

Records of the War Department: Office of the Judge Advocate General. GCM S-50. Case of Captain Alden Partridge, October, 1817, National Archives.

Charles D. Rhodes Papers, Archives, United States Military Academy.

John M. Schofield Papers, Library of Congress.

James Wall Schureman Letters, Library of Congress.

William T. Sherman Papers, Library of Congress.

William P. Smith Diary, Archives, Louisiana State University.

Superintendent's Letter Books, Archives, United States Military Academy.

Joseph G. Swift Papers, Library, United States Military Academy.

West Point Letters (the Sylvanus Thayer collection), Library, United States Military Academy.

PRINTED SOURCES

ADAMS, CHARLES F. (ed.). *Johns Adams' Works*. 10 vols. Boston, 1856.

ALEXANDER, SIR J. E. "United States Military Academy, West Point," *Colburn's United Service Magazine*, III (March, 1854).

ALLEN, HERVEY. *Israfel: The Life and Times of Edgar Allan Poe*. New York, 1934.

AMBROSE, STEPHEN E. *Halleck: Lincoln's Chief of Staff*. Baton Rouge, 1962.

———. *Upton and the Army*. Baton Rouge, 1964.

American State Papers: Military Affairs. 5 vols. Washington, 1832.

ANDREWS, GEORGE L. "The Military Academy and its Requirements," *Journal of the Military Service Institution*, IV (August, 1883).

———. "West Point and the Colored Cadets," *International Review*, IX (November, 1880).

Assembly (a quarterly published by West Point Alumni Foundation).

BARNARD, HENRY. *Military Schools and Courses of Instruction in the Science and Art of War, in France, Prussia, Austria, Russia, Sweden, Switzerland, Sardinia, England, and the United States*. New York, 1872.

BASSETT, JOHN S. (ed.). *Correspondence of Andrew Jackson*. 7 vols. Washington, 1926–35.

BATES, RALPH S. *Scientific Societies in the United States*. Boston, 1945.

BAUMER, WILLIAM H. *West Point: Moulder of Men*. New York, 1942.

Bibliography

BEDINGER, MARGERY. "Goose Step at West Point," *The New Republic*, LXIV (September, 1930).

BERARD, AUGUSTA. *Reminiscences of West Point in the Olden Time*. East Saginaw, Mich., 1886.

BERGH, ELBERT E. (ed.). *The Writings of Thomas Jefferson*. 20 vols. Washington, 1907.

BERKEY, CHARLES B., and RICE, MARION. "Geology of the West Point Quadrangle," *New York State Museum Bulletin,* Nos. 225, 226 (October, 1919).

BEUKEMA, HERMAN. *The United States Military Academy and Its Foreign Contemporaries*. West Point, 1939.

BINGHAM, ROBERT. "Sectional Misunderstandings," *North American Review,* CLXXIX (September, 1904).

BOROFF, DAVID. "West Point, Good Enough?" *Harper's Magazine,* CCXXV (December, 1962).

BOYNTON, EDWARD C. *History of West Point, and Its Military Importance During the American Revolution*. New York, 1863.

CAJORI, FLORIAN. *The Teaching and History of Mathematics in the United States*. Washington, 1890.

CALHOUN, DANIEL H. *The American Civil Engineer: Origins and Conflict*. Cambridge, Mass., 1960.

CARTER, ROBERT GOLDTHWAITE. *The Art and Science of War Versus the Art of Fighting*. Washington, 1922.

The Centennial of the United States Military Academy at West Point, New York. 2 vols. Washington, 1904.

CHURCH, ALBERT E. *Personal Reminiscences of the United States Military Academy*. West Point, 1879.

COHANE, TIM. *Gridiron Grenadiers: The Story of West Point Football*. New York, 1948.

"Comment and Criticism" [on Hubbard's "The Military Academy"], *Journal of the Military Service Institution,* XVI (March, 1895).

COUPER, WILLIAM. *One Hundred Years at V.M.I.* 3 vols. Richmond, 1939.

CRAIG, GORDON A. *The Politics of the Prussian Army, 1640–1945*. New York, 1956.

CROFFUT, W. A. (ed.). *Fifty Years in Camp and Field: The Diary of Major-General Ethan Allen Hitchcock*. New York, 1909.

CULLUM, GEORGE WASHINGTON. *Biographical Register of the Officers and Graduates of the United States Military Academy*. 3 vols. with additions. New York, 1863.

CURTI, MERLE, and CARSTENSEN, VERNON. *The University of Wisconsin*. 2 vols. Madison, 1949.

Debates and Proceedings in the Congress of the United States. Washington, 1853.

DENTON, EDGAR. "The Formative Years of the United States Military Academy, 1775–1833." Unpublished Ph.D. dissertation, Syracuse University, 1964.

DICKENS, CHARLES. *American Notes and Pictures from Italy*. London, 1867.

DOWNEY, FAIRFAX. *Sound of the Guns: The Story of American Artillery*. New York, 1955.

DUDLEY, COL. EDGAR S. "Was Secession Taught at West Point?" *Century Magazine*, LXXVIII (July, 1909).

DUPUY, R. ERNEST. *The Compact History of the United States Army*. New York, 1961.

———. *Where They Have Trod: The West Point Tradition in American Life*. New York, 1940.

Exposé of Facts, Concerning Recent Transactions, Relating to the Corps of Cadets of the United States Military Academy, at West Point, New York. Newburgh, 1819.

FARLEY, JOSEPH PEARSON. *West Point in the Early Sixties: With Incidents of the War*. Troy, N.Y., 1902.

FISH, WILLISTON. *Memories of West Point 1877–1881*. 3 vols. Batavia, N.Y., 1957.

FITZPATRICK, JOHN C. (ed.). *The Writings of George Washington from the Original Manuscript Sources, 1745–1799*. 39 vols. Washington, 1940.

FLEXNER, JAMES THOMAS. *The Traitor and the Spy: Benedict Arnold and John André*. New York, 1953.

FLIPPER, HENRY O. *The Colored Cadet at West Point*. New York, 1878.

"Football at West Point," *Harpers Weekly*, XLII (January, 1898).

FORCE, PETER (ed.). *American Archives*. 9 vols. Washington, 1837–53.

FORMAN, SIDNEY. "The First School of Engineering," *The Military Engineer*, I March–April, 1952).

———. "The United States Military Philosophical Society, 1802–1813," *William and Mary Quarterly*, II (July, 1945).

———. *West Point: A History of the United States Military Academy*. New York, 1950.

———. "West Point and the American Association for the Advancement of Science." *Science*, CIV (July, 1946).

FREEMAN, DOUGLAS SOUTHALL. *R. E. Lee: A Biography*. 4 vols. New York, 1936.

GANOE, WILLIAM A. *MacArthur Close-Up*. New York, 1962.

GODSON, WILLIAM F. H. *The History of West Point, 1852–1902*. Philadelphia, 1934.

GUTTMANN, ALLEN. "Political Ideals and the Military Ethic," *The American Scholar*, XXXIV (Spring, 1965).

HALL, ROBERT H. "Early Discipline at the United States Military Academy," *Journal of the Military Service Institution*, II (November, 1882).

HANCOCK, IRVING H. *Life at West Point*. New York, 1906.

Bibliography

HANSEN, ALLEN OSCAR. *Liberalism and American Education in the Eighteenth Century.* New York, 1926.

Hazing at the Military Academy. House Document No. 2768. Fifty-sixth Congress, Second Session. Washington, 1901.

HEMPHILL, W. EDWIN. *The Papers of John C. Calhoun.* 2 vols. Columbia, S.C., 1963.

HOLDEN, EDWARD S. *Biographical Memoir of William H. C. Bartlett.* Washington, 1911.

————. "The United States Military Academy at West Point," *Report of the Commissioner of Education for 1891–92.* 2 vols. Washington, 1894.

HOLLAND, LYNWOOD M. *Pierce M. B. Young: The Warwick of the South.* Athens, Ga., 1964.

HOWARD, OLIVER O. *Autobiography.* 2 vols. New York, 1908.

HUBBARD, ELMER W. "The Military Academy and the Education of Officers," *Journal of the Military Service Institution,* XVI (January, 1895).

HUGHES, NATHANIEL C., JR. *General William J. Hardee: Old Reliable.* Baton Rouge, 1965.

JACOBS, JAMES RIPLEY. *The Beginning of the United States Army, 1783–1812.* Princeton, 1947.

JAMES, JOSEPH B. "Life at West Point 100 Years Ago," *Mississippi Valley Historical Review,* XXXI (June, 1944).

JANOWITZ, MORRIS. *The Professional Soldier: A Social and Political Portrait.* Glencoe, Ill., 1960.

KEYES, E. D. *Fifty Years' Observation of Men and Events.* New York, 1884.

KIRBY, RICHARD SHELTON, and LAURSON, PHILLIP GUSTAVE. *The Early Years of Modern Civil Engineering.* New Haven, 1932.

LATROBE, JOHN H. B. "West Point Reminiscences," in *Eighteenth Annual Reunion of the Association of Graduates.* East Saginaw, Mich., 1887.

LENNEY, JOHN J. *Caste System in the American Army: A Study of the Corps of Engineers and their West Point System.* New York, 1949.

LEWIS, LLOYD. *Captain Sam Grant,* Boston, 1950.

LODGE, HENRY CABOT (ed.). *The Works of Alexander Hamilton.* 10 vols. New York, 1904.

MACARTHUR, DOUGLAS. *Reminiscences.* New York, 1964.

MAHER, MARTY. *Bringing up the Brass: My 55 Years at West Point.* New York, 1951.

MANN, CHARLES R. *A Study of Engineering Education.* New York, 1911.

MANSFIELD, E. D. *Personal Memories.* Cincinnati, 1879.

MASLAND, JOHN W., and RADWAY, LAURENCE I. *Soldiers and Scholars: Military Education and National Policy.* Princeton, 1957.

MAURY, DABNEY H. *Recollections of a Virginian in the Mexican, Indian, and Civil Wars.* New York, 1894.

MICHIE, P. S. "Education in its Relation to the Military Profession," *Journal of the Military Service Institution,* I (June, 1880).

————. *The Life and Letters of Emory Upton.* New York, 1885.

MILLER, WILLIAM J. "The Geological History of New York State," *New York State Museum Bulletin,* No. 255 (September, 1924).

MORISON, SAMUEL ELIOT. *Three Centuries of Harvard: 1636–1936.* Cambridge, Mass., 1936.

MOTT, T. BENTLEY. "West Point, a Criticism," *Harper's Magazine,* CLXVIII (March, 1934).

MULLETT, CHARLES F. "Classical Influences in the American Revolution," *The Classical Journal,* XXV (October, 1939).

NEVINS, ALLAN. *The State Universities and Democracy.* Urbana, 1962.

NYE, RUSSELL B. *The Cultural Life of the New Nation.* New York, 1960.

PARTRIDGE, ALDEN. *Capt. Partridge's Lecture on National Defence,* n.p., n.d.

————. *The Military Academy, at West Point, Unmasked: or, Corruption and Military Despotism Exposed.* Washington, 1830.

PENNELL, E. R. and J. *The Life of James McNeill Whistler.* 2 vols. London, 1908.

POGUE, FORREST C. *George C. Marshall: Education of a General.* New York, 1963.

Post-War Curriculum at the United States Military Academy. West Point, 1945.

PRESTON, RICHARD A., WISE, SYDNEY F., and WERNER, HERMAN O. *Men in Arms.* New York, 1956.

PULESTON, W. D. *Mahan: The Life and Work of Captain Alfred Thayer Mahan.* New Haven, 1939.

RAWLE, WILLIAM. *A View of the Constitution of the United States.* Philadelphia, 1825.

REED, HUGH T. *Cadet Life at West Point.* Chicago, 1896.

REEVES, IRA L. *Military Education in the United States.* Burlington, Vt., 1914.

Report of the Commission, Senate Document No. 3, Thirty-sixth Congress, Second Session. Washington, 1860.

Report on the Military Academy, House Document No. 476, Twenty-eighth Congress, First Session. Washington, 1844.

Report to the Superintendent by the United States Military Academy Committee on Service Academies. West Point, 1949.

RICHARDS, SAMUEL. "Personal Narrative of an Officer in the Revolutionary War," *United Service Magazine,* IV (August, 1887).

RICHARDSON, ROBERT C. *West Point: An Intimate Picture of the National Military Academy and of the Life of the Cadet.* New York, 1917.

Bibliography

RIEDLER, A. "American Technological Schools." House Executive Document. Fifty-third Congress, Second Session. Washington, 1895.

ROPP, THEODORE. *War in the Modern World*. New York, 1962.

ROWLAND, THOMAS (ed.). "Letters of a Virginia Cadet at West Point, 1859–1861," *South Atlantic Quarterly*, XIV–XV (1915–1916).

RUDOLPH, FREDERICK. *The American College and University*. New York, 1962.

———. *Mark Hopkins and the Log*. New Haven, 1956.

SCHAFF, MORRIS. *The Spirit of Old West Point*. Boston, 1907.

SCHMIDT, GEORGE P. *The Old Time College President*. New York, 1930.

SMITH, DAVID E., and GINSBERG, J. *A History of Mathematics in America Before 1900*. Chicago, 1934.

SMITH, FRANCIS H. *West Point Fifty Years Ago*. New York, 1879.

SMYTH, SIR JOHN. *Sandhurst*. London, 1961.

SULLIVAN, FRANCIS (ed.). "Letters of a West Pointer, 1860–1861," *American Historical Review*, XXXIII (April, 1928).

SWIFT, JOSEPH GARDNER. *Memoirs*. Privately printed, 1890.

TAYLOR, MAXWELL D. *West Point Looks Ahead*. West Point, 1946.

THOMAS, HUGH. *The Story of Sandhurst*. London, 1961.

TICKNOR, GEORGE. *Life, Letters and Journals*. 2 vols. Boston, 1877.

TILLMAN, SAMUEL. "Is There Necessity for a Second West Point?" *Journal of the Military Service Institution*, XXXV (December, 1904).

UPTON, EMORY. *The Military Policy of the United States*. Washington, 1902.

VAGTS, ALFRED. *A History of Militarism: Civilian and Military*. New York, 1959.

WATSON, RICHARD L. "Congressional Attitudes Toward Military Preparedness, 1829–1835," *Mississippi Valley Historical Review*, XXXIV (March, 1948).

WAUGH, E. D. J. *West Point*. New York, 1944.

WEBB, LESTER A. *Captain Alden Partridge and the United States Military Academy*. Northport, Ala., 1965.

WHEELER, JOSEPH. "West Point Fifty Years Ago," *The Golden Age*, XII (February, 1906).

WHITE, LEONARD D. *The Jacksonians*. New York, 1954.

———. *The Jeffersonians: A Study in Administrative History*. New York, 1951.

WILKINSON, NORMAN B. "The Forgotten 'Founder' of West Point," *Military Affairs*, XXIV (March, 1960).

WILLCOX, C. DEW. "The Preliminary Examination: West Point," *Journal of the Military Service Institution*, XVI (March, 1895).

WILLIAMS, T. HARRY. "The Attack Upon West Point During the Civil War," *Mississippi Valley Historical Review*, XXV (March, 1939).

WILSON, JAMES HARRISON. *Under the Old Flag*. 2 vols. New York, 1912.

Wood, C. Henry. "The General Education Movement and the West Point Curriculum" Unpublished D.Ed. dissertation, Teachers College, Columbia University, 1951.

Wood, Oliver E. *The West Point Scrap Book: A Collection of Stories, Songs, and Legends of the United States Military Academy.* New York, 1871.

Wood, Robert J. "Early Days of Benny Havens," *The Pointer,* February 26, 1937.

Index

A

Abbott, Jacob, 88
Abert, John J., 124
Academia Secretorum Naturae, 29
Academic Board: composition of, 39; and curriculum, 247, 323–24; and entrance requirements, 129, 244; establishment of, 39; and hazing, 223; influence of, on curriculum, 211; and MacArthur, 262, 265, 266–70, 282, 286–87; and Maxwell Taylor, 298; and modern Academy, 292, 299, 300; and Negro cadets, 234; and non-military faculty, 248–49; and Partridge, 50, 54, 57–58; proposes additional academies, 46; relationship to Board of Visitors, 56; role of, 202, 206, 265–66; and World War II, 289
Academies, in Europe, 3–5
Academy, the. *See* United States Military Academy
Acheson, Dean, 299
Adams, John: and Corps of Artillerists and Engineers, 12, 13; and education in U.S., 17; and need for an academy, 6–7, 8–9, 11, 18, 19; and plan for an academy, 14–15; and role of Academy, 112; and scientific societies, 29
Adams, John C.: on faculty, 248, 249, 251
Adams, John Quincy, 25, 31
Administration Building, 242
AEF (American Expeditionary Force), 254

Aguinaldo, Emilio, 239
Ahearn, Cadet David C., 320–21
Air Cadets, 296
Air Corps: officers at Academy, 296
Air Corps Activities Project, 296
Alexander, E. Porter, 189
Alger, Russell A., 309–10
All-American football teams, 304n, 316, 317
Allen, Ethan, 8
Alumni Association, 189
American Academy of Arts and Sciences, 29–30
American Association for the Advancement of Science, 95, 141
American Association for the Promotion of Science, Literature, and the Arts, 94–95
American Literary, Scientific and Military Academy, 113
American Philosophical Society, 17, 22, 29, 30
American Revolution: influence on European training, 6; and need for an academy, 7
American Society of Civil Engineers: influence of Academy on, 124
Ames, Cadet Adelbert, 143, 144, 153
Amherst College, 88, 308
Amosophic Society, 137–38
Anderson, Robert, 141, 167
André, John, 20
Andrews, George: and criticism of curriculum, 214; on faculty, 204, 206, 292

Index

aftermath at Academy, 188–90; effect of, on cadets, 171–72, 178, 179–80, 181, 254; effect of, on U.S. college curriculums, 192; effect of Academy graduates on, 183–87; effect of issues on pre-war Academy, 160, 161, 168–71; influence on development of postgraduate schools, 145; Mahan's influence on, 101, 102; ranks and commissions in, 173–75; use of cadets in, 178, 179

Clark, Mark, 274, 295

Class rush, 220–21

Clausewitz, Karl von, 101

Clay, Lucius, 295

Clemenceau, Georges, 293

Clemens, Samuel: at Academy, 219–20

Clinton, De Witt, 31, 80

Cochrane, John, 141

Cold Spring Foundry, 178

College Boards, 328

Collège Militaire of Brienne, 4

Colleges and universities, foreign: compared with American, 65–67; interchange with Academy, 299

Colleges and universities, U.S.: compared with Academy, 39, 125, 131, 132, 147–48, 151, 152, 159, 166, 182, 192, 269, 280, 281, 291, 301, 304, 307, 323, 330; influence of Academy on, 91, 123–24, 323; interchange with cadets, 299; Jacksonian views on, 107; in late 18th century, 15–18; mid-19th century, 62–66, 87–91; post-Civil War, 191–92; techniques of, studied, 289; as training for Academy, 216–17

Columbia College, 93, 123–24, 301, 317, 321

Command and General Staff School, 286, 287

Commandants of Cadets: Bliss, 77–79, 108; Danford, 265, 275, 277–78; and discipline, 77–79, 108–9, 110, 165, 227, 277–78, 279; Garnett, 136; Hardee, 136–37; Hein, 244–45, 251; Hitchcock, 108–9, 110; Reynolds, 136, 165; role of, 134–35, 136–37, 244–45, 251; Sibley, 227; Smith, 136; Stewart, 284; Thomas, 136; Upton, 279; Walker, 136

Commissions. *See* Ranks and commissions

Confederate States of America: and Academy, 167, 169–72, 175, 180, 181–

82; compared with the Union army, 186

Congress, U.S.: and appointment of cadets, 128–29, 142; and appropriations for Academy, 127; attempts to abolish Academy, 84–85; attitude toward Academy, 34–35, 36, 38–39, 43, 45, 111–12, 115–19; and B.S. degree, 290; and building program, 241; and Corps of Artillerists and Engineers, 11, 12; and entrance requirements, 179, 193–94, 244; and establishment of academies, 15; and football at Academy, 314–15; and founding of Academy, 8–9, 14, 15, 18, 22; and founding of Naval Academy, 127; influence on administration of Academy, 72, 194–95; and length of army service of graduates, 117; and length of course, 141, 262–63; and MacArthur, 275–76; and purchase of West Point, 10 and *n;* recommends changes in curriculum, 118; role of, at Academy, 179; and standing armies, 9–10; and size of Cadet Corps, 35, 39, 183, 185, 296

Connor, George, 317

Connor, William: as cadet, 313–14; as Superintendent, 284, 285, 290, 314

Corps of Artillerists and Engineers, 11, 12, 15, 19–22

Corps of Cadets: appointments to, 50, 83, 128–29, 142, 207, 239–40, 318, 319, 328–29; and Civil War, 167–77; competition in, 131; cost per cadet in 1844, 119; criticism of Academy, 149; on curriculum, 132–33, 142–44, 211–12; duels, 160–61; early functions of, 25; entrance requirements, 25, 32, 35, 39, 40, 49, 83–84, 128–29, 177, 179, 193–94, 196, 207, 244, 247, 263, 323–24; family circumstances of, 119, 129–30; life at Academy, 25, 39, 46–48, 147–66, 154–55, 165–66, 219–31, 241, 271–72, 290, 326; and MacArthur, 262, 267, 271–73, 277; pay of, 25, 70, 149, 179, 272; and post-Civil War changes at Academy, 219–21; and public, 81–82; regional sources of, 129–30; and selection of corps, 144–45; size of, 35, 39, 183, 185, 193, 239–40, 241, 275–76, 290, 296; and uniforms, 153–54; use political pressure, 108–10; used as instructors, 50. *See also* Discipline

Index

Corps of Engineers: as academy at West Point, 22; establishment of, 22–23; relationship to Academy, 26, 27–28, 36, 43–44, 127; responsibilities of, 33, 39; and School for Engineers, 210; size of, 25; and Superintendents, 126–27, 193

Corps of Invalids, 8–9

Coulter, Cadet De Witt, 316

Courtenay, Edward H.: on faculty, 95

Courts-martial, 42, 60, 78–79, 108, 164

Courts of inquiry, 54–55, 59, 78

Cozzens, Mr., 154

Cozzens' Hotel, 165

Craig, Malin: as cadet, 313, 314

Cram, Goodhue and Ferguson, architectural firm, 241, 290

Crawford, William H., 55–56, 79

Cret, Paul Philippe, 290

Crockett, David, 112

Crow's Nest, 26

Crozet, Claude: on faculty, 97–99, 100, 102–3

Cullum, George Washington: as cadet, 113–14, 151; as Superintendent, 188, 198; will of, 188–89

Cullum Memorial Hall, 188–89, 241, 242

Curriculum: applied psychology, 299; aviation, 296, 298–99; chemistry, 90, 91, 94–95, 197, 205, 270; by class, 55–56, 90, 325–26; criticism of, 118, 142–45, 187, 207–9, 211–18, 247, 263, 292–94, 322; difficulty of, 131–34, 142; drawing, 27, 39, 90, 94, 203, 270; early 19th century, 25–29, 39–42, 49, 51, 55; effect of, on Civil War, 181; effect of Civil War on, 176–77; effect of Philippine Insurrection on, 239; effect of Spanish-American War on, 238–39; effect of World War I on, 251–57; effect of World War II on, 289, 296–97; and elective system, 208, 323–24; encampment, 51, 55, 71, 72, 134, 147, 158, 159, 225, 228, 271, 282–83; engineering, 25, 39, 40, 41–42, 89–90, 91, 97–100, 123, 136–37, 177, 185, 197, 204, 205, 245, 296, 298, 299; English, 55, 89, 248, 249, 251, 270, 283, 286, 297; ethics, 90; examinations, 26–27, 39, 50, 55, 67–68, 72–73, 80–81, 133–34; first requirements for graduation, 49; and foreign academies, 143–44; French, 27, 28, 39, 55, 71, 90, 91–92, 94n, 97, 143, 204–5, 251; geography, 89; German,

196, 197, 298; history, 247, 248, 251, 270, 330; history, government, and economics, 269, 286–87, 297, 298, 299; length of course, 141, 262–63, 296; and MacArthur, 268, 269–70; mathematics, 28, 31, 39, 40, 41, 55–56, 90, 91, 92–94, 97, 99, 132, 185, 204, 205, 207, 213, 291, 323; modern languages, 204, 213, 247, 270; moral philosophy, 96; natural philosophy, 25, 39, 40, 41, 89, 90, 95–96, 132, 205, 270; and Naval Academy curriculum, 288–89; physics, 91, 291, 298; Portuguese, 298; post-Civil War, 192–209; post-World War II, 297–301; rhetoric, 89; Russian, 298; services of supply, 287; social sciences, 252, 322–23; Spanish, 143, 197, 204, 213, 251; tactics and strategy, 100–2, 134, 136–37, 244–45, 251, 253, 270, 298; textbooks, 26, 27, 31, 41, 42, 48–49, 91, 92, 93, 96, 98–99, 100, 101, 123, 137, 187, 193, 194–95, 203, 204, 206, 248, 301; and Thayer, 63, 67–80; 20th century, 244–45, 247–50, 268, 269–70, 323–33. *See also* Athletics; Extracurricular activities; Football

Cushing, Cadet George, 132–33, 150, 161–62, 163

Custer, George Armstrong: as cadet, 206

D

Daly, Charles, 304n, 310, 311

Danford, Robert M.: as Commandant of Cadets, 265, 275, 277–78; and honor system, 318

Darlan, Jean L. X. F., 274

Dartmouth College, 62, 64, 323

David, Jacques Louis, 4

Davies, Charles: on faculty, 92, 93, 94, 102, 110–11

Davis, Benjamin O., Jr., 237

Davis, Cadet Glenn, 316, 317

Davis, Henry Winter, 141

Davis, Jefferson: as cadet, 164; and curriculum, 136; president of CSA, 182; as Secretary of War, 136, 141; as senator, 141

Davis Commission, 141, 143, 144–46, 153

Dearborn, Henry, 19–21, 32–33, 34

De Gaulle, Charles. *See* Gaulle, Charles de

Delafield, Mrs. 153
Delafield, Richard: as Superintendent, 125, 126, 137, 138, 142, 153–54, 168, 170–71
Department of West Point, 233, 237
DeRussy, Rene E.: as Superintendent, 110
Detached service law, 240
Devore, Cadet Chauncey C., 226–27
Dewey, John, 269, 275
Dialectic Society, 137–38, 168, 219, 222, 290
Dickinson College, 92
Discipline: 51–52, 55, 69, 70, 74, 76, 77–79, 108–10, 136, 142, 150–51, 159–64, 194, 199, 220, 221–22, 225n, 226, 227, 234
Doak, Samuel, 62–63
Donelson, Andrew Jackson, 108
Doubleday, Abner, 179, 313
Douglas, Stephen A., 169
Douglass, David B.: on faculty, 92, 99, 100, 102–3
Drawing. *See* Curriculum
Driggs, Representative Edmund H., 230–31
Duke University, 316
Dulles, Allen W., 299
Du Pont, Henry A.: as cadet, 132, 138, 149, 174n, 181; as senator, 227
Dutton, Cadet William, 147

E

East Academic Building, 242, 291
Eaton, John H.: as Secretary of War, 115, 167–68
École de Mars, 4
École Militaire, 3–4
École Polytechnique, 4, 12, 66, 97, 144
Edward, Prince of Wales, 140
Eichelberger, Robert L., 300
Eisenhower, Dwight D.: as cadet, 313; as Chief of Staff, 297, 298; and curriculum, 299; and "honor," 274; and honor system, 207, 279; and Stewart, 285; as Supreme Allied Commander, 294–95, 297; in World War I, 258
Eliot, Charles W., 192, 263–64, 268
Elliott, Andrew: on faculty, 40, 41, 92
Elting, John, 302
Emergency officers, World War I, 253–54, 258

Encampment. *See* Curriculum
Engineering. *See* Civil engineering; Curriculum
Engineering and Ordnance Laboratory, 291
English. *See* Curriculum
Enlightment, the, 2–4
Entrance requirements. *See* Corps of Cadets
Ernst, Oswald: as Superintendent, 224–25, 239, 276, 306, 307–9, 310, 313
Esposito, Vincent J.: as author, 301–2; on faculty, 298
European military training, 1–6, 9
Eustis, William, 35–37, 39
Everett, Edward, 66, 81
Ewell, Cadet Richard S., 132
Ewing, Cadet James J., 133
Extracurricular activities, 137–39, 148, 150, 158–59, 219–22, 285, 290. *See also* Athletics; Football

F

Faculty: Adams, 248, 249, 251; Andrews, 204, 206, 292; attitude of, 202, 204, 211, 214; Bailey, 166; Barron, 25, 27, 28, 30, 32; Bartlett, 95, 96, 99, 102–3, 119, 203, 204; Bass, 203, 205, 206, 292; Berard, 91–92, 102–3; Bessell, 298; Beukema, 252, 287–89, 298, 301; Blaik, 315, 319; Church, 93, 94, 102–3, 132, 193, 203, 204, 205; Courtenay, 95; Crozet, 97–99, 100, 102–3; Davies, 92, 93, 94, 102–3, 110; Douglass, 92, 99, 100, 102; Elliott, 40, 41, 92; Esposito, 298; first permanent, 39; Forsyth, 205, 206; French, 165–66, 172; Gimbrede, 94; Hassler, 31; Holden, 249–50; Holt, 249, 251, 286–87; housing for, 291; Howard, 152; influence of, on Civil War, 197–98; influence of, on U.S. education, 91, 97; and instructors, 104, 240, 248; Kendrick, 165, 203, 205; Koehler, 246, 251, 313; Larned, 203, 214; Latrobe, 92–93; Lincoln, 298, 302; Mahan, 99–103, 110, 113, 115, 119, 123, 124, 136, 171–72, 181, 183, 185, 196, 203, 204, 213; Mansfield, 25–26, 27, 28, 32, 40, 41, 45–46, 71–72, 95; Masson, 27, 28, 31; Mather, 94–95; Michie, 203, 205–6, 211n, 292; Partridge, 31, 40, 41–42; pay of, in 1843, 119; Picton, 96;

Index

Index

Index